the
Quotable
Hitchens

ALSO BY CHRISTOPHER HITCHENS

Books

Hostage to History: Cyprus from the Ottomans to Kissinger
Blood, Class and Nostalgia: Anglo-American Ironies
Imperial Spoils: The Curious Case of the Elgin Marbles
Why Orwell Matters
No One Left to Lie To: The Triangulations of William Jefferson Clinton
Letters to a Young Contrarian
The Trial of Henry Kissinger
Thomas Jefferson: Author of America
Thomas Paine's "Rights of Man": A Biography
God Is Not Great: How Religion Poisons Everything
Hitch-22: A Memoir

Pamphlets

Karl Marx and the Paris Commune
The Monarchy: A Critique of Britain's Favorite Fetish
The Missionary Position: Mother Teresa in Theory and Practice
A Long Short War: The Postponed Liberation of Iraq

Collected Essays

Prepared for the Worst: Essays and Minority Reports
For the Sake of Argument
Unacknowledged Legislation: Writers in the Public Sphere
Love, Poverty and War: Journeys and Essays

Collaborations

James Callaghan: The Road to Number Ten (with Peter Kellner)
Blaming the Victims (edited with Edward Said)
When the Borders Bleed: The Struggle of the Kurds (photographs by Ed Kashi)
International Territory: The United Nations (photographs by Adam Bartos)
Vanity Fair's Hollywood (with Graydon Carter and David Friend)

Editor

The Portable Atheist: Essential Readings for the Non-Believer

the Quotable Hitchens

from **ALCOHOL** *to* **ZIONISM**

The VERY BEST *of*
CHRISTOPHER HITCHENS

Edited by WINDSOR MANN
Foreword by MARTIN AMIS

DA CAPO PRESS
A Member of the Perseus Books Group

Editorial production by Lori Hobkirk at the Book Factory
Set in 10-point Legacy Serif by Cynthia Young at Sagecraft

Library of Congress Cataloging-in-Publication Data

Hitchens, Christopher.
  [Selections. 2011]
  The quotable Hitchens : from alcohol to Zionism / by Christopher Hitchens ;
    and Windsor Mann, editor. — 1st Da Capo Press ed.
      p. cm.
  Includes bibliographical references and index.
  ISBN 978-0-306-81958-2 (alk. paper)
    1. Hitchens, Christopher—Quotations.   2. Quotations, American.   I. Mann,
  Windsor.   II. Title.
  CT275.H62575A25 2011
  081—dc22

                                                              2011003093

Published by Da Capo Press
A Member of the Perseus Books Group
www.dacapopress.com

Da Capo Press books are available at special discounts for bulk purchases in the U.S. by corporations, institutions, and other organizations. For more information, please contact the Special Markets Department at the Perseus Books Group, 2300 Chestnut Street, Suite 200, Philadelphia, PA 19103, or call (800) 810-4145, ext. 5000, or e-mail special.markets@perseusbooks.com.

10 9 8 7 6 5 4 3 2 1

For Professor Hitchens

Foreword
by MARTIN AMIS

"Spontaneous eloquence seems to me a miracle," confessed Vladimir Nabokov in 1962. He took up the point more personally in his foreword to *Strong Opinions* (1973):

> . . . I have never delivered to my audience one scrap of information not pre-pared in typescript beforehand. . . . My hemmings and hawings on the tele-phone cause long-distance callers to switch from their native English to pathetic French.
>
> At parties, if I attempt to entertain people with a good story, I have to go back to every other sentence for oral erasures and inserts. . . . [N]obody should ask me to submit to an interview. . . . It has been tried at least twice in the old days, and once a recording machine was present, and when the tape was rerun and I had finished laughing, I knew that never in my life would I repeat that sort of performance.

We sympathize. And most literary types, probably, would hope for inclusion somewhere or other on Nabokov's sliding scale: "I think like a genius, I write like a distinguished author, and I speak like a child."

Mr. Hitchens isn't like that. *Christopher and His Kind* runs the title of one of Ish-erwood's famous memoirs. And yet *this* Christopher doesn't have a kind. Everyone is unique—but Christopher is preternatural. And it may even be that he exactly in-verts the Nabokovian paradigm. He thinks like a child (that is to say, his judg-ments are far more instinctive and moral-visceral than they seem, and are animated by a child's eager apprehension of what feels just and true); he writes like a distinguished author; and he speaks like a genius.

As a result, Christopher is one of the most terrifying rhetoricians that the world has yet seen. Lenin used to boast that his objective, in debate, was not rebuttal and then refutation: it was the "destruction" of his interlocutor. This isn't Christo-pher's policy—but it is his practice. Toward the very end of the last century, all our greatest chess players, including Gary Kasparov, began to succumb to a computer (named Deep Blue); I had the opportunity to ask two grandmasters to describe the Deep Blue experience, and they both said, "It's like a wall coming at you." In argu-ment, Christopher is that wall. The prototype of Deep Blue was known as Deep Thought. And there's a case for calling Christopher Deep Speech. With his vast ar-ray of geohistorical references and precedents, he is almost googlelike; but google (with, say, its ten million "results" in 0.7 seconds) is something of an idiot savant, and Christopher's search engine is much more finely tuned. In debate, no matter what the motion, I would back him against Cicero, against Demosthenes.

Whereas mere Earthlings get by with a mess of expletives, subordinate clauses, and finely turned tautologies, Christopher talks not only in complete sentences but also in complete paragraphs. Similarly, although he mentions the phenomenon in these pages, he is an utter stranger to what Diderot called *l'esprit de l'escalier*: the spirit of the staircase. This phrase is sometimes translated as "staircase wit"— far too limitingly, in my view, because *l'esprit de l'escalier* describes an entire stratum of one's intellectual and emotional being. The door to the debating hall, or to the contentious drinks party, or indeed to the little flat containing the focus of amatory desire, has just been firmly closed; and now the belated eureka shapes itself on your lips. These lost chances, these unexercised potencies of persuasion, can haunt you for a lifetime—particularly, of course, when the staircase was the one that might have led to the bedroom.

As a young man, Christopher was conspicuously unpredatory in the sexual sphere (while also being conspicuously pan-affectionate: "I'll just make a brief pass at everyone," he would typically and truthfully promise a mixed gathering of fourteen or fifteen people, "and then I'll be on my way"). I can't say how it went, earlier on, with the boys; with the girls, though, Christopher was the one who needed to be persuaded. And I do know that in this area, if in absolutely no other, he was sometimes inveigled into submission.

The habit of saying the right thing at the right time tends to get relegated to the category of the pert riposte. But the put-down, the swift comeback, when quoted, gives a false sense of finality. *So-and-so, as quick as a flash, said so-and-so*—and that seems to be the end of it. Christopher's most memorable rejoinders, I have found, linger, and reverberate, and eventually combine, as chess moves combine. . . . One evening, close to forty years ago, I said, "I know you despise all sports—but how about a game of chess?" Looking mildly puzzled and amused, he joined me over the sixty-four squares. Two things soon emerged. First, he showed no combative will, he offered no resistance (because this was *play*, you see, and *earnest* is all that really matters). Second, he showed an endearing disregard for common sense. This prompts a paradoxical thought.

There are many excellent commentators, in the United States and the United Kingdom, who deploy far more rudimentary gumption than Christopher ever bothers with (we have a deservedly knighted columnist in London whom I always think of, with admiration, as Sir Common Sense). But it is hard to love common sense. And the salient fact about Christopher is that he is loved. What we love is fertile instability; what we love is the agitation of the unexpected. And Christopher always comes, as they say, from left field. He is not a plain speaker. He is not, I repeat, a plain man.

Over the years Christopher has spontaneously delivered many dozens of unforgettable lines. Here are four of them.

1. He was on TV for the second or third time in his life (if we exclude *University Challenge*), which takes us back to the mid-1970s and to Christopher's mid-twenties.

He and I were already close friends (and colleagues at the *New Statesman*); but I remember thinking that nobody so matinee-telegenic had the right to be so exceptionally quick-tongued on the screen. At a certain point in the exchange, Christopher came out with one of his political poeticisms, an ornate but intelligible definition of (I think) national sovereignty. His host—a fair old bruiser in his own right—paused, frowned, and said with skepticism and with helpless sincerity,

"I can't understand a word you're saying."

"I'm not in the least surprised," said Christopher, and moved on.

The talk ran its course. But if this had been a frontier western, and not a chat show, the wounded man would have spent the rest of the segment leerily snapping the arrow in half and pushing its pointed end through his chest and out the other side.

2. Every novelist of his acquaintance is riveted by Christopher, not just *qua* friend but also *qua* novelist. I considered the retort I am about to quote (all four words of it) so epiphanically devastating that I put it in a novel—indeed, I put Christopher in a novel. *Mutatis mutandis* (and it is the novel itself that dictates the changes), Christopher "is" Nicholas Shackleton in *The Pregnant Widow*—though it really does matter, in this case, what the meaning of "is" is. . . . The year was 1981. We were in a tiny Italian restaurant in West London, where we would soon be joined by our future first wives. Two elegant young men in waisted suits were unignorably and interminably fussing with the staff about rearranging the tables, to accommodate the large party they expected. It was an intensely class-conscious era (because the class system was dying); Christopher and I were candidly lower-middle bohemian, and the two young men were raffishly minor-gentry (they had the air of those who await, with epic stoicism, the deaths of elderly relatives). At length, one of them approached our table, and sank smoothly to his haunches, seeming to pout out through the fine strands of his fringe. The crouch, the fringe, the pout: these had clearly enjoyed many successes in the matter of bending others to his will. After a flirtatious pause he said,

"You're going to hate us for this."

And Christopher said, "We hate you already."

3. In the summer of 1986, in Cape Cod, and during subsequent summers, I used to play a set of tennis every other day with the historian Robert Jay Lifton. I was reading, and then rereading, his latest and most celebrated book, *The Nazi Doctors*; so, on Monday, during changeovers, we would talk about "Sterilization and the Nazi Medical Vision"; on Wednesday, " Wild Euthanasia': The Doctors Take Over"; on Friday, "The Auschwitz Institution"; on Sunday, "Killing with Syringes: Phenol Injections"; and so on. One afternoon, Christopher, whose family was staying with mine on Horseleech Pond, was due to show up at the court, after a heavy lunch in nearby Wellfleet, to be introduced to Bob (and to be driven back to the pond-front house). He arrived, much gratified by having come so far on foot: three or four miles—one of the greatest physical feats of his adult life. It was set point. Bob served, approached the net, and wrongfootingly dispatched my attempted pass. Now Bob was and is twenty-three years my senior; and the score was 6-0. I could, I suppose, plead preoccupation: that summer I was wondering (with eerie detachment) whether I had it in me to write a novel that dealt

with the Holocaust. Christopher knew about this, and he knew about my qualms.

Elatedly toweling himself down, Bob said, "You know, there are so few areas of transcendence left to us. Sports. Sex. Art. . . "

"Don't forget the miseries of others," said Christopher. "Don't forget the languid contemplation of the miseries of others."

I did write that novel. And I still wonder whether Christopher's black, three-ply irony somehow emboldened me to attempt it. What remains true, to this day, to this hour, is that of all subjects (including sex and art), the one we most obsessively return to is the Shoa, and its victims—those whom the wind of death has scattered.

4. In conclusion we move on to 1999, and by now Christopher and I have acquired new wives, and gained three additional children (making eight in all). It was mid-afternoon, in Long Island, and he and I hoped to indulge a dependable pleasure: we were in search of the most violent available film. In the end we approached a multiplex in Southampton (having been pitiably reduced to Wesley Snipes). I said,

"No one's recognized the Hitch for at least ten minutes."

"Ten? Twenty minutes. Twenty-five. And the longer it goes on, the more pissed off I get. I keep thinking: What's the matter with them? What can they feel, what can they care, what can they know, if they fail to recognize the Hitch?"

An elderly American was sitting opposite the doors to the cinema, dressed in candy colors and awkwardly perched on a hydrant. With his trembling hands raised in an Italianate gesture, he said weakly,

"Do you love us? Or do you hate us?"

This old party was not referring to humanity, or to the West. He meant America and Americans. Christopher said,

"I beg your pardon?"

"Do you love us, or do you hate us?"

As Christopher pushed on through to the foyer, he said, not warmly, not coldly, but with perfect evenness,

"It depends on how you behave."

Does it depend on how others behave? Or does it depend, at least in part, on the loves and hates of the Hitch?

Christopher is bored by the epithet *contrarian*, which has been trailing him around for a quarter of a century. What he is, in any case, is an autocontrarian: he seeks, not only the most difficult position, but the most difficult position for Christopher Hitchens. Hardly anyone agrees with him on Iraq (yet hardly anyone is keen to debate him on it). We think also of his support for Ralph Nader, his collusion with the impeachment process of the loathed Bill Clinton (who, in *The Quotable Hitchens*, occupies more space than any other subject), and his support for Bush-Cheney in 2004. Christopher often suffers for his isolations; this is widely sensed, and strongly contributes to his magnetism. He is in his own person the drama, as we watch the lithe contortions of a self-shackling Houdini. Could this be the crux of his charisma—that Christopher, ultimately, is locked in argument with the Hitch? Still, "contrarian" is looking shopworn. And if there must be an epithet, or what the press likes to call a (single-word) "narrative," then I can suggest a refinement: Christopher is one of nature's *rebels*. By which I mean that he has no automatic respect for anybody or anything.

The rebel is in fact a very rare type. In my whole life I have known only two others, both of them novelists (my father, up until the age of about forty-five; and my friend Will Self). This is the way to spot a rebel: they give no deference or even civility to their supposed superiors (that goes without saying); they also give no deference or even civility to their demonstrable inferiors. Thus Christopher, if need be, will be merciless to the prince, the president, and the pontiff; and, if need be, he will be merciless to the cabdriver ("Oh, you're not going our way. Well turn your light off, all right? Because it's fucking *sickening* the way you guys ply for trade"), to the publican ("You don't give change for the phone? Okay. I'm going to report you to the Camden *Consumer Council*"), and to the waiter ("Service is included, I see. But you're saying it's optional. Which?. . . What? Listen. If you're so smart, why are you dealing them off the arm in a dump like this?"). Christopher's everyday manners are beautiful (and wholly democratic); of course they are—because he knows that in manners begins morality. But each case is dealt with *exclusively on its merits*. This is the rebel's way.

It is for the most part an invigorating and even a beguiling disposition, and makes Mr. Average, or even Mr. Above Average (whom we had better start calling Joe Laptop), seem under-evolved. Most of us shakily preside over a chaos of vestigial prejudices and pieties, of semi-subliminal inhibitions, taboos, and herd instincts, some of them ancient, some of them spryly contemporary (like moral relativism and the ardent xenophilia, which, in Europe at least, always excludes Israelis). To speak and write without fear or favor (to hear no internal drumbeat): such voices are invaluable. On the other hand, as the rebel is well aware, compulsive insubordination risks the punishment of self-inflicted wounds.

Let us take an example from Christopher's essays on literature (which are underrepresented here, and impressive enough to deserve an appreciation of their own). In the last decade Christopher has written three raucously hostile reviews—of Saul Bellow's *Ravelstein* (2000), John Updike's *Terrorist* (2006), and Philip Roth's *Exit, Ghost* (2007). When I read them, I found myself muttering the piece of schoolmarm advice I have given Christopher in person, more than once: *Don't cheek your elders*. The point being that, in these cases, respect is mandatory, because it has been earned, over many books and many years. Does anyone think that Saul Bellow, then aged eighty-five, needed Christopher's half-dozen insistences that the Bellovian powers were on the wane (and in fact, read with respect, *Ravelstein* is an exquisite swansong, full of integrity, beauty, and dignity)? If you are a writer, then all the writers who have given you joy—as Christopher was given joy by *Augie March* and *Humboldt's Gift*, for example, and by *The Coup*, and by *Portnoy's Complaint*—are among your honorary parents; and Christopher's attacks were coldly unfilial. Here, disrespect becomes the vice that so insistently exercised Shakespeare: that of ingratitude. And all novelists know, with King Lear (who was thinking of his daughters), how sharper than a serpent's tooth it is to have a thankless reader.

Art is freedom; and in art, as in life, there is no freedom without law. The foundational literary principle is *decorum*, which means something like the opposite of its dictionary definition: "behavior in keeping with good taste and propriety" (that is, submission to an ovine consensus). In literature, decorum means the concurrence of style and content—together with a third element that I can only vaguely express as *earning the right weight*. It doesn't matter what the style is, and it doesn't matter what the content is; but the two must concur. If the essay is something of a literary art, which it clearly is, then the same law obtains.

Here are some indecorous quotes from the *The Quotable Hitchens*. "Ronald Reagan is doing to the country what he can no longer do to his wife." On the Chaucerian summoner-pardoner Jerry Falwell: "If you gave Falwell an enema, he'd be buried in a matchbox." On the political entrepreneur George Galloway: "Unkind nature, which could have made a perfectly good butt out of his face, has spoiled the whole effect by taking an asshole and studding it with ill-brushed fangs." The critic D. W. Harding wrote a famous essay called "Regulated Hatred." It was a study of Jane Austen. We grant that hatred is a stimulant; but it should not become an intoxicant.

The difficulty is seen at its starkest in Christopher's baffling weakness for puns. This doesn't much matter when the context is less than consequential (it merely grinds the reader to a temporary halt). But a pun can have no business in a serious proposition. Consider the following, from 2007: "In the very recent past, we have seen the Church of Rome befouled by its complicity with the unpardonable sin of child rape, or, as it might be phrased in Latin form, 'no child's behind left.'" Thus the ending of the sentence visits a riotous indecorum on its beginning. The great grammarian and usage-watcher Henry Fowler attacked the "assumption that puns are *per se* contemptible. . . . Puns are good, bad, or indifferent. . . . " Actually, Fowler was wrong. "Puns are the lowest form of verbal facility," Christopher elsewhere concedes. But puns are the result of an anti-facility: they offer disrespect to language, and all they manage to do is make words look stupid.

Now compare the above to the below—to the truly quotable Christopher. In his speech, it is the terse witticism that we remember; in his prose, what we thrill to is his magisterial expansiveness (the ideal anthology would run for several thousand pages, and would include whole chapters of his recent memoir, *Hitch-22*). The extracts that follow aren't jokes or jibes. They are more like crystallizations—insights that lead the reader to a recurring question: If this is so obviously true, and it is, why did we have to wait for Christopher to point it out to us?

"There is, especially in the American media, a deep belief that insincerity is better than no sincerity at all."

"One reason to be a decided antiracist is the plain fact that 'race' is a construct with no scientific validity. DNA can tell you who you are, but not what you are."

"A melancholy lesson of advancing years is the realization that you can't make old friends."

On gay marriage: "This is an argument about the socialization of homosexuality, not the homosexualization of society. It demonstrates the spread of conservatism, not radicalism, among gays."

On Philip Larkin: "The stubborn persistence of chauvinism in our life and letters is or ought to be the proper subject for critical study, not the occasion for displays of shock."

"[I]n America, your internationalism can and should be your patriotism."

"It is only those who hope to *transform* human beings who end up by burning them, like the waste product of a failed experiment.'

"This has always been the central absurdity of 'moral,' as opposed to 'political' censorship: If the stuff does indeed have a tendency to deprave and corrupt, why then the most depraved and corrupt person must be the censor who keeps a vigilant eye on it."

And one could go on. Christopher's dictum—"What can be asserted without evidence can be dismissed without evidence"—has already entered the language. And so, I predict, will this (coined too recently for inclusion here): "A Holocaust denier is a Holocaust affirmer." What justice, what finality. Like all Christopher's best things, it has the simultaneous force of a proof and a law.

"Is nothing sacred?" he asks. "*Of course not.*" And no Westerner, as Ronald Dworkin pointed out, "has the right not to be offended." We accept Christopher's errancies, his recklessnesses, because they are inseparable from his courage; and true valor, axiomatically, fails to recognize discretion. As the world knows, Christopher has recently made the passage from the land of the well to the land of the ill. One can say that he has done so without a visible flinch; and he has written about the process with unparalleled honesty and eloquence, and with the highest decorum. His many friends, and his innumerable admirers, have come to dread the tone of the "living obituary." But if the story has to end too early, then its coda will contain a triumph.

Christopher's personal devil is God, or rather organized religion, or rather the human "desire to worship and obey." He comprehensively understands that the desire to worship, and all the rest of it, is a direct reaction to the unmanageability of the idea of death. "Religion," wrote Larkin:

That vast moth-eaten musical brocade
Created to pretend we never die. . .

And there are other, unaffiliated intimations that the secular mind has now outgrown. "Life is a great surprise," observed Nabokov (b. 1899). "I don't see why death should not be an even greater one." Or Bellow (b. 1915), in the words of Artur Sammler:

Is God only the gossip of the living? Then we watch these living speed like birds over the surface of a water, and one will dive or plunge but not come up again and never be seen any more. . . . But then we have no proof that there is no depth under the surface. We cannot even say that our knowledge of death is shallow. There is no knowledge.

Such thoughts still haunt us; but they no longer have the power to dilute the black ink of oblivion.

My dear Hitch: there has been much wild talk, among the believers, about your impending embrace of the sacred and the supernatural. This is, of course, insane. But I still hope to convert you, by sheer force of zealotry, to my own persuasion: agnosticism. In your seminal book, *God Is Not Great*, you put very little distance between the agnostic and the atheist; and what divides you and me (to quote Nabokov yet again) is a rut that any frog could straddle. "The measure of an education," you write elsewhere, "is that you acquire some idea of the extent of your ignorance." And that's all that "agnosticism" really means: it is an acknowledgment of ignorance. Such a fractional shift (and I know you won't make it) would seem to me consonant with your character—with your acceptance of inconsistencies and contradictions, with your intellectual romanticism, and with your love of life, which I have come to regard as superior to my own.

The atheistic position merits an adjective that no one would dream of applying to you: it is Lenten. And agnosticism, I respectfully suggest, is a slightly more logical and decorous response to our situation—to the indecipherable grandeur of what is now being (hesitantly) called the multiverse. The science of cosmology is an awesome construct, while remaining embarrassingly incomplete and approximate; and over the last thirty years it has garnered little but a series of humiliations. So when I hear a man declare himself to be an atheist, I sometimes think of the enterprising termite who, while continuing to go about his tasks, declares himself to be an individualist. It cannot be altogether frivolous or wishful to talk of a "higher intelligence"—because the cosmos is itself a higher intelligence, in the simple sense that we do not and cannot understand it.

Anyway, we do know what is going to happen to you, and to everyone else who will ever live on this planet. Your corporeal existence, O Hitch, derives from the elements released by supernovae, by exploding stars. Stellar fire was your womb, and stellar fire will be your grave: a just course for one who has always blazed so very brightly. The parent star, that steady-state H-bomb we call the sun, will eventually turn from yellow dwarf to red giant, and will swell out to consume what is left of us, about six billion years from now.

Introduction
by WINDSOR MANN

Reflecting on his own career, H. L. Mencken said it was "the business of a journalist, as I conceived it, to stand in a permanent Opposition." Christopher Hitchens takes a similar approach, one based on "the presumption of guilt" for those in power.

Oppositionism—which combines skepticism with a compulsion to argue—is not contrarianism, which is a style more than a discipline. Its style is the anti-style, its principles are situational and transitory, and its adherents are as boring and imitative as any herd of dependent minds. The lingua franca of nonconformity, like the obsessively ironic costumes of Brooklyn hipsters, gets stale very quickly and, in the end, if not sooner, it is self-negating.

The contrarian dogma is simple and easy to understand: "Whatever is popular is wrong," as Oscar Wilde proclaimed at London's Royal Academy of Arts. As a conclusion, this statement is questionable. As a mindset, it's not bad.

"Think different," as Apple Inc. ungrammatically put it. It's a popular concept—in which hardly anyone actually believes. Much like daily flossing, it is easy to recommend but arduous to do. Different thinking, in any case, is not always independent thinking; sometimes it is a reflex, other times a pose, a means of getting attention by being "shocking."

Christopher Hitchens does not live for unpredictability, though he is capable of saying unsayable things. For example:

- He defended "teenage drinking and teenage smoking" in an appearance on C-SPAN.
- As the father of three still-young children, he denounced virginity.
- He defended the lyrics of the rap group 2 Live Crew—whose songs included "Me So Horny," "Dick Almighty," "Get the Fuck Out of My House," and "Balls"—defended the lyrics themselves, mind you, not merely the right to say them.
- On national television, he told his friend and fellow writer Andrew Sullivan, "Don't be such a lesbian."
- Also on national television, he pointed out that Jerry Falwell could be buried in a matchbox—if you gave him an enema first.
- He called the Dixie Chicks "fat sluts."

What the above examples reveal is not a man prone to the *faux pas*, but a gentleman—strictly defined, by Hitchens, as "someone who is never rude except on purpose."

A spectacular instance of his gentlemanliness occurred during an appearance on HBO's *Real Time with Bill Maher*. Unlike most guests, Hitchens did not try to flatter or pacify the audience. Instead, after being booed and jeered for pointing out the horrors of a nuclear Iran, he raised his middle finger and pointed it at them, while intoning, "Fuck you! Fuck you!" What this little episode demonstrated was not only his indifference to crowd opinion—impressive in itself—but also his binary nature: He has a large mind and a big mouth—neither of which ever seems to be closed.

Whereas many comedians are bitterly unfunny off the stage and countless actors unbearably dull off the screen, Hitchens manages to captivate on the page *and* off. Simply put, he is a writer who can talk and a speaker who can write. Indeed, he often emphasizes the connection between the two, insisting that good writing is impossible without good speaking.* He has based his career on this essential premise, to wit, that language must be mastered before it can be effectively deployed.

Irving Kristol defined an intellectual as "a man who speaks with general authority about a subject on which he has no particular competence." It is true that Hitchens has no particular competence, the key word being "particular." He is not a specialist. He has no advanced degrees and no formal training in any academic discipline—a brain without a chair, to borrow Nathan Glazer's phrase.

Of course, a chair can be confining just as it can be prestigious. Precisely *because* he lacks a chair and is free of its constraints and limitations, Hitchens boasts a stunning breadth of knowledge and learning on almost every conceivable subject—history, literature, politics, philosophy, science, art, theology, culture, and much else besides. Sports are perhaps the only subject about which he knows little and wishes he knew less. Given his erudition, talking to him is always enlightening—and sometimes embarrassing.

A few years ago, in an effort to be more productive by being somewhere else, I asked Hitchens if I could come over to his apartment to do some work. He said to stop by the next day at 10:30, and so I did—at 10:30 p.m. After I arrived at the door, I knocked on it—and knocked and knocked on it. I knocked for long enough that eventually Hitchens and his wife determined that this could be no burglar or door-to-door salesman. When they finally opened the door, I realized

---

*In one of the first emails he ever wrote to me, Hitchens elaborated on this point:

> You must get control of your speech if you wish to write. . . . It's ABSOLUTELY ESSENTIAL AND INDISPENSABLE that you begin the work of forming correct sentences in your head. Try writing things, even short things, and reading them aloud. Try reading aloud from any work that you admire. Make a resolution that you will not use obvious or easy words and phrases. . . . If you want to be any good at all as a writer you simply MUST throw aside the crap idioms that pass for speech these days. Purify the well of your English: there is no other way.

that I was late by twelve hours. I realized something else: Even when the subject is not Victorian literature or the history of Cyprus, Christopher Hitchens can make you—me—feel stupid.

The man is freakishly intelligent and unfailingly interesting, has been writing for nearly four decades and speaking for even longer, has defended *personae non gratae*, attacks the philistine masses as well as the *haut monde*, and is innovative both in his ideas and in how he communicates them. He is, in other words, highly quotable.

That no one had yet put together a book of his quotations was—to me—strange and very fortunate. I have been fixated with quotations for fourteen years and have known Hitchens for six years. The prospect of merging my fixation with his oeuvre was too good to be untrue and too enticing to delay. In early 2010, I approached Hitchens about the idea, and he put me in touch with his agent, who quickly became my agent. Almost overnight, it seemed, we had a book deal.

I mention this background simply to point out that this book came about with Hitchens's approval but without his orchestration. It's not as if he were vainly demanding that his best lines be commemorated. His involvement with the book ended almost as soon as it began, as he deliberately did not interfere in matters of its content. He created the quotations, but I selected them (I'll leave it to you to decide which is more impressive).

There were no formal criteria in the selection process. It was very simple: I picked the quotations I liked. Of course they needed to be relatively pithy,* and I wanted them, in the aggregate, to be as comprehensive as possible. In the end, they just had to be good, and it's possible that my viscera and intellect had equal parts in the decision-making.

While personal taste obviously was a factor in choosing which quotations to include, my politics and biases and so forth were irrelevant. This may sound hard to believe, but ideology has little to do with spotting quality sentences. Those who care should keep this in mind. For instance, as Martin Amis notes in his foreword, there are a lot of quotations about Bill Clinton. The reason for this is that Hitchens happened to say and write a lot of quotable things about Clinton—not because I have a deep personal interest in the former president (for what it's worth, I don't).

An inevitable problem with doing a book like this is that everyone will have complaints—about omissions, in particular. This or that remark wasn't included. Certain topics *aren't even addressed*. To this, all I can say is: Sorry. I apologize sincerely. There are several topics whose absence bothers me mightily. I had to cut more than sixty thousand words from the original manuscript just to get this book—the one you are reading—into production. A book of five hundred pages would have been nice, but it was not possible.

Winston Churchill said books of quotations were "a good thing for an uneducated man to read." Surely any book is a good thing for any man or woman, educated or not, to read. Quotations are, as Hitchens has said himself, by definition

---

*Much was left out simply because it could not be condensed easily. It somewhat defeats the point of a book of quotations to have quotations a full page or two long.

out of context. They are a preview; they are not a substitute for the real thing. But even as snippets, they can be useful, not only as entertainment and handy references but also as enticements to the reader to locate the original source and delve more deeply into its themes and ideas. In this way, reading quotations can lead to further reading, learning, and thinking. It is more like a vitamin than a narcotic, though the effects can be mind-altering in either case. Let's hope they are here.

Windsor Mann
February 2011

Acknowledgments

As obvious and trite as this is to say, I must say it: This book would not have been possible without Christopher Hitchens. For one thing, there would be no quotations. Less obvious are the things that he and his wife, Carol Blue, do behind the scenes and to no acclaim. Much like Winston Churchill's relationship with alcohol, I have gotten more out of them than they have gotten out of me. I consider both of them friends as well as mentors, and I will forever remain indebted to them for their inexplicable generosity toward me.

I should thank my parents, John Kimbrell Mann and Ruthie Windsor-Mann, for inventing me and for doing a remarkable job of it. Thanks also to Kathleen Carlson, who opened a few gates, so to speak, on the information superhighway.

Steve Wasserman, my agent, has made my life much easier and is fabulous at his job. The same goes for Ben Schafer of Da Capo Press, who has been a delight to work with and who has excellent taste in music. Lori Hobkirk proved to be of immense help in the final stages of the editing process. I hope to work with all three individuals in the future.

Of course, it would be nice to cross paths again with Martin Amis, who was gracious enough to contribute a foreword to this book. Amis is one of the great writers of our time, and to read his thoughts is a pleasure that never wanes.

Honor compels me to acknowledge my good friend Joseph Bernabucci. His service, though fairly minimal in regard to this book, was significant enough a few years ago, in various matters of writing and editing, for me to promise him that, if ever I were to produce a book, he would get his own paragraph in the acknowledgments section. As a man of my word, I am fulfilling that promise. Thanks, Heinrich—and you're welcome.

Thanks to my other friends for remaining more or less friendly, even as I, on occasion, did not. You know who you are.

—*Windsor Mann*

Abortion

"I have always been convinced that the term 'unborn child' is a genuine description of material reality. Obviously, the fetus is alive, so that disputation about whether or not it counts as 'a life' is casuistry. The same applies, from a materialist point of view, to the question of whether or not this 'life' is 'human.' What other kind could it be? As for 'dependent,' this has never struck me as a very radical criticism of any agglomeration of human cells in whatever state. Children are 'dependent' too." ["Minority Report," *Nation*, 4/24/89]

" . . . Anyone who has ever seen a sonogram or has spent even an hour with a textbook on embryology knows that the emotions are not the deciding factor. In order to terminate a pregnancy, you have to still a heartbeat, switch off a developing brain, and, whatever the method, break some bones and rupture some organs." ["Minority Report," *Nation*, 4/24/89]

"I can't think of a single circumstance in which I'd favor emptying a woman's uterus." [Quoted in Don Kowet, "Christopher Hitchens, Drawing Room Marxist," *Washington Times*, 1/02/90]

"Just as no human being of average moral capacity could be indifferent to the sight of a woman being kicked in the stomach, so nobody could fail to be far more outraged if the woman in question were pregnant. Embryology confirms morality." [*God Is Not Great* (New York: Twelve, 2007), 221]

"There may be many circumstances in which it is not desirable to carry a fetus to full term. Either nature or god appears to appreciate this, since a very large number of pregnancies are 'aborted,' so to speak, because of malformations, and are

1

politely known as 'miscarriages.' Sad though this is, it is probably less miserable an outcome than the vast number of deformed or idiot children who would otherwise have been born, or stillborn, or whose brief lives would have been a torment to themselves and others." [*God Is Not Great* (New York: Twelve, 2007), 221]

"The only proposition that is completely useless, either morally or practically, is the wild statement that sperms and eggs are all potential lives that must not be prevented from fusing and that, when united however briefly, have souls and must be protected by law." [*God Is Not Great* (New York: Twelve, 2007), 222]

"The whole case for extending protection to the unborn, and to expressing a bias in favor of life, has been wrecked by those who use unborn children, as well as born ones, as mere manipulable objects of their doctrine." [*God Is Not Great* (New York: Twelve, 2007), 223]

Abu Ghraib

"The superficially clever thing to say today is that Lynddie England represents all of us, or at any rate all her superiors, and that the liberation of Iraq is thereby discredited. One odd effect of this smug view is to find her and her scummy friends—the actual inflicters of pain and humiliation—somehow innocent, while those senior officers who arrested them and put them on trial are somehow guilty. There is something faintly masochistic and indecent about that conclusion." ["Abu Ghraib Isn't Guernica," *Slate*, 5/09/05]

Abu-Jamal, Mumia

"On the record, as it stands, there is no case for keeping Mumia Abu-Jamal in prison, let alone for keeping him guessing every day about the hour of his death." ["Death and the Maidens," *Nation*, 4/14/97]

Academia

"In the 1950s, the stereotypical academic looked a bit like Nabokov's Pnin: unworldly, innocuous, absorbed in the arcane. Today, the role model more nearly resembles a character in Don DeLillo's *White Noise*: wised-up, ambitious, more interested in deals and endowments, and the invention of lucrative new subdisciplines." ["American Notes," *Times Literary Supplement*, 9/25/87–10/01/87]

" . . . No one should take core-list revisions so seriously, because no one should take a core list seriously. The whole 'core' idea is phony, if somewhat quaint, like a wealthy man's bookshelf of leather-bound, unopened classics." ["The Toy Canon," *Harper's*, June 1988]

"If anything matches the incompetence and unworldliness of the West Coast liberal academic, it is his timorousness in the face of regulations on campus." ["Freelance," *Times Literary Supplement*, 4/07/89–4/13/89]

"What temptation should one avoid above all, if one is a former professor of English at Cambridge? The temptation to be matey, or hip, or cool—especially if one is essaying the medium of popular music." ["America's Poet?," *Weekly Standard*, 7/05/04–7/12/04]

Accents

"There are some things a British accent can't get away with." ["Downstairs Upstairs," *New York Times Magazine*, 6/01/75]

"In my native British Islands, homeland of this great universal language, there dwells a population that is famously 'branded on the tongue.' I can 'place' anyone as soon as he or she begins to utter. . . . Margaret Thatcher had to take several courses in elocution to rid herself of bumpkin and awkward tones and to become the queenly figure that I left England to get away from. (To get away from whom, I mean to say, I left England.)" ["Hooked on Ebonics," *Vanity Fair*, March 1997]

Accidents

"Yes, you can be compressed into a cube by accident if you are desperate enough to sleep in a trash compactor." ["America's Inescapable Crisis—the Homeless," *Newsday*, 2/24/88]

"It is human and natural to attempt to invest accidents with meaning, but the urge to do so is not always controlled by the rational faculty." ["Mother Teresa or Mrs. Simpson: Which Was the Real Diana?," *Los Angeles Times*, 9/01/97]

Accuracy

" . . . Not all arguments about accuracy are arguments about veracity." ["American Notes," *Times Literary Supplement*, 7/06/84]

Acting

"Anyone who has been on a set and watched repeated stagings of the same microscene will tell you the experience is one of thunderous tedium." ["Vintage Vanessa," *Vanity Fair*, December 1994]

Actors and Actresses

"Actresses with causes can be a real pain in the neck (everyone knows who I mean). You visualize them embracing some far-off movement, or signing some glamorous petition, in between being photographed in fashionable restaurants or having their names coupled with some current star. The stench of publicity-seeking is always there—often to the detriment of the cause." ["Into the Nuclear Battle with Julie Christie," *Daily Express*, 6/27/77]

"I'm sure there must be bombshells and starlets who hate animals, despise the poor, look down on the Third World, and prefer their aerosols to the ozone layer. But, somehow, their agents keep them *quiet*." ["Vintage Vanessa," *Vanity Fair*, December 1994]

Advice

"Beware the irrational, however seductive. Shun the 'transcendent' and all who invite you to subordinate or annihilate yourself. Distrust compassion; prefer dignity for yourself and others. Don't be afraid to be thought arrogant or selfish. Picture all experts as if they were mammals. Never be a spectator of unfairness or stupidity. Seek out argument and disputation for their own sake; the grave will supply plenty of time for silence. Suspect your own motives, and all excuses. Do not live for others any more than you would expect others to live for you." [*Letters to a Young Contrarian* (New York: Basic Books, 2001), 140]

"When I worked at the old *New Statesman* magazine in London, we had an annual competition for advice to tourists visiting the city for the first time. 'Try the famous echo in the British Museum Reading Room' was, I remember, one of the winners. We also advised people that prostitutes could be easily recognized by their habit of rattling collection tins, that it was considered ill-mannered not to shake hands with all other passengers before taking your seat on the London subway, and that readers doing the *Times* crossword on trains were always glad if you offered to help." ["I Fought the Law," *Vanity Fair*, February 2004]

" . . . Not everybody can take their own advice, or not forever. . . ." [Introduction to *Everyday Drinking: The Distilled Kingsley Amis*, by Kingsley Amis (New York: Bloomsbury USA, 2008), xi]

Afghanistan
"'Bombing Afghanistan back into the Stone Age' was quite a favorite headline for some wobbly liberals. . . . But an instant's thought shows that Afghanistan is being, if anything, bombed *out* of the Stone Age." ["Christopher Hitchens on Why Peace-Lovers Must Welcome This War," *Mirror*, 11/15/01]

"No possible future government in Kabul can be worse than the Taliban, and no thinkable future government would allow the level of al-Qaeda gangsterism to recur. So the outcome is proportionate and congruent with international principles of self-defense." ["The Ends of War," *Nation*, 12/21/01]

Africa
"Africa as a continent has been cut adrift. The great powers have no further use for it. It can be left to rot and crash." ["Africa Adrift," *Nation*, 5/27/96]

Aging
"As I look back on my long and arduous struggle to make myself over, and on my dismaying recent glimpses of lost babyhood, I am more than ever sure that it's enough to be born once, and to take one's chances, and to grow old disgracefully." ["On the Limits of Self-Improvement, Part II," *Vanity Fair*, December 2007]

" . . . The awful thing about growing older is that you begin to notice how every day consists of more and more subtracted from less and less." ["On the Limits of Self-Improvement, Part III," *Vanity Fair*, September 2008]

"Hardest of all, as one becomes older, is to accept that sapient remarks can be drawn from the most unwelcome or seemingly improbable sources, and that the apparently more trustworthy sources can lead one astray." [*Hitch-22* (New York: Twelve, 2010), 343]

"I sometimes feel that I should carry around some sort of rectal thermometer with which to test the rate at which I am becoming an old fart." [*Hitch-22* (New York: Twelve, 2010), 410]

" . . . I find that it is the fucking *old* fools who get me down the worst, and the attainment of that level of idiocy can often require a lifetime." [*Hitch-22* (New York: Twelve, 2010), 410]

Agnosticism
"In just the same way that any democracy is better than any dictatorship, so even the compromise of agnosticism is better than faith. It minimizes the totalitarian temptation, the witless worship of the absolute, and the surrender of reason, that may have led to saintliness but can hardly repay for the harm it has done." ["The Lord and the Intellectuals," *Harper's*, July 1982]

"It is sometimes used as a halfway house by those who cannot make a profession of faith but are unwilling to repudiate either religion or god absolutely. . . . An agnostic does not believe in god, or disbelieve in him. Nonbelief is not quite unbelief. . . . " [Introduction to *The Portable Atheist* (New York: Da Capo Press, 2007), xxiii–xxiv]

Air America
"There, one could hear the reassuring noise of collapsing scenery and tripped-over wires and be reminded once again that correct politics and smooth media presentation are not even distant cousins." ["Unfairenheit 9/11," *Slate*, 6/21/04]

Air Travel
"The great American airport has a distinction shared by no other national institution. When lined up at the New York Bank for Waiting, for example, you can laugh all you like about making an 'unauthorized withdrawal' at pistol-point. While detained by the pitiless warders of the Department of Motor Vehicles, you are allowed to joke about the relative merits of the Albanian Ministry of Tourism. But while passing through the sausage machine of aviation 'security,' it is a federal requirement that you keep a poker face. Jokes are not just frowned upon. They are unlawful." ["Airport Insecurity," *Vanity Fair*, June 1997]

"Flying is already funny enough. There are the bargain supersaver fares. ('Some restrictions apply.') There is the food. There is the numbing crush around the capsule-size bathrooms at the rear, where you run the risk of pulling down someone else's zipper, or indeed pulling up someone else's pants. There is the get-to-know-your-neighbor seating plan. ('My God! My leg! It's lost all feeling!' 'That's my leg, Big Boy.') And then, of course, there are the planes themselves. ('Some assembly required.')" ["Airport Insecurity," *Vanity Fair*, June 1997]

"'I need to see at least one form of government-issued photo ID.' Whew—thank heaven they remembered that. The terrorist isn't born who can get hold of a New Jersey driver's license." ["Airport Insecurity," *Vanity Fair*, June 1997]

"Those ridiculous beeping scanners, which pick up the change in your pocket and the tinfoil on your Rolaids, are not equipped to detect plastic explosives of the kind that brought down Pan Am 103. They are there not to protect you but to give employment to the semi-employable and to give you the illusion of protection." ["Airport Insecurity," *Vanity Fair*, June 1997]

"'Did you pack your own bags?' Well, I'd sure crack if I were a bomber and I heard *that* tough question." ["Airport Insecurity," *Vanity Fair*, June 1997]

"The penalty for getting mugged in an American city and losing your ID is that you can't fly home." [Quoted in Peter Carlson, "The Journalist's Sharpened Pen," *Washington Post*, 2/12/99]

" . . . Law-abiding passengers are treated like criminals as well as fools, and deprived of their in-flight cutlery and their nail-scissors. (The FAA has made sure of one thing. The next suicide-murderer who manages to get on a plane will find that his victims have been thoroughly and efficiently disarmed. . . .)" ["Knowledge (and Power)," *Nation*, 6/10/02]

"And airport security is still a silly farce that subjects the law-abiding to collective punishment while presenting almost no deterrent to a determined suicide-killer. . . . Every day, people are relieved of private property in broad daylight, with the sole net result that they wouldn't have even a nail file with which to protect themselves if (or rather when) the next hijacking occurs." ["Terminal Futility," *Slate*, 6/06/05]

"Routines and 'zero tolerance' exercises will never thwart determined jihadists who are inventive and who are willing to sacrifice their lives. That requires inventiveness and initiative. But airport officials are not allowed to use their initiative. People who have had their names confused with wanted or suspect people, and who have spent hours proving that they are who they say they are, are nonetheless compelled to go through the whole process every time, often with officials who have seen them before and cleared them before, because the system that never seems to catch anyone can never seem to let go of anyone, either." ["Terminal Futility," *Slate*, 6/06/05]

"Why do we fail to detect or defeat the guilty, and why do we do so well at collective punishment of the innocent? The answer to the first question is: Because we can't—or won't. The answer to the second question is: Because we can." ["Flying High," *Slate*, 12/28/09]

Al-Qaeda
" . . . The objective of al-Qaeda is not the emancipation of the Palestinians but the establishment of tyranny in the Muslim world by means of indiscriminate violence in the non-Muslim world, and those who confuse the two issues are idiots who don't always have the excuse of stupidity." ["Saving Islam from bin Laden," *Age*, 9/05/02]

Al-Qaeda in Mesopotamia
" . . . If there is any distinction to be made between the apple and the tree, it would involve saying that AQM is, if anything, even more virulent and sadistic and nihilistic than its parent body." ["Fighting the 'Real' Fight," *Slate*, 8/13/07]

Alcohol
"The most lethal and fascistic of our current enemies—the purist murderers of the Islamic jihad—despise our society for, among other things, its tolerance of

alcohol. We should perhaps do more to earn this hatred and contempt, and less to emulate it." ["Living Proof," *Vanity Fair*, March 2003]

" . . . An opened flask of alcohol is a mouth that can lead to hell as well as heaven." [Introduction to *Everyday Drinking: The Distilled Kingsley Amis*, by Kingsley Amis (New York: Bloomsbury USA, 2008), ix]

"The plain fact is that it makes other people, and indeed life itself, a good deal less boring." [Introduction to *Everyday Drinking: The Distilled Kingsley Amis*, by Kingsley Amis (New York: Bloomsbury USA, 2008), x]

"Having long been annoyed by people who called knowingly for, say, 'a Dewar's and water' instead of a scotch and water, I decided to ask a trusted barman what I got if I didn't specify a brand or label. The answer was a confidential jerk of the thumb in the direction of a villainous-looking, tartan-shaded jug under the bar. The situation was even grimmer with gin and vodka and became abysmal with 'white wine,' a thing I still can't bear to hear being ordered. If you don't state a clear preference, then your drink is like a bad game of poker or a hasty drug transaction: It is whatever the dealer says it is. Please do try to bear this in mind." [Introduction to *Everyday Drinking: The Distilled Kingsley Amis*, by Kingsley Amis (New York: Bloomsbury USA, 2008), x–xi]

"Alcohol is a good friend but a bad master." [Quoted in Christopher Garland, "Incendiary Author Spares No Targets," *New Zealand Herald*, 5/24/08]

"Alcohol makes other people less tedious, and food less bland, and can help provide what the Greeks called *entheos*, or the slight buzz of inspiration when reading or writing." [*Hitch-22* (New York: Twelve, 2010), 351]

"Cheap booze is a false economy." [*Hitch-22* (New York: Twelve, 2010), 352]

Alcoholism
" . . . It's a sign of alcoholism to make rules about how much you drink." ["Booze and Fags," *London Review of Books*, 3/12/92]

Alger, Horatio
"Everything one discovers about Horatio Alger is somehow apt." ["American Notes," *Times Literary Supplement*, 4/04/86]

Aliens
"If the huge number of 'contacts' and abductees are telling even a particle of truth, then it follows that their alien friends are not attempting to keep their own existence a secret. Well, in that case, why do they never stay still for anything more than a single-shot photo?" [*God Is Not Great* (New York: Twelve, 2007), 144]

Allegations
"Start by calling something alleged, and you end by denying it altogether." ["Minority Report," *Nation*, 4/13/85]

"Nothing is more helpful, to a person with a record of economizing with the truth, than a false and malicious and disprovable allegation." [*No One Left to Lie To* (New York: Verso, 2000), 4]

Allegiance

"Very often the test of one's allegiance to a cause or to a people is precisely the willingness to stay the course when things are boring, to run the risk of repeating an old argument just one more time, or of going one more round with a hostile or (much worse) indifferent audience." [*Hitch-22* (New York: Twelve, 2010), 337]

Allies

"It would be nice to think that we could choose our allies or proxies on the basis of their similarity to our 'own' ideals. But we would first have to be sure that these were, in fact, our ideals. And we would in any case have to make a prudent guess as to how long it might take for us to be vindicated in that choice." ["Forcing Freedom," *Reason* magazine, August 2003]

Allred, Gloria

"If you absolutely have to have a 'palimony' tussle, a vulgar brawl over paternity, or an airing of dirty linen about breach of promise, the best advice a Californian can give you, especially if you are a man, is to hope that Gloria Allred stays out of it. But the chances of her doing so are never very great, at least if the profile is high and the implications are feminist." ["Get Me Gloria," *Evening Standard*, 8/14/97]

Altruism

" . . . One may choose to be altruistic, whatever that may mean, but by definition one may not be *compelled* into altruism." [*God Is Not Great* (New York: Twelve, 2007), 214]

America

" . . . If rags to riches is what the country is all about, why so much surprise when it actually happens to someone?" ["American Notes," *Times Literary Supplement*, 6/10/83]

"Myself, I love America as only an immigrant can and am grateful to be spared the paradoxes and antinomies of its native intelligentsia." ["American Notes," *Times Literary Supplement*, 9/23/83]

"There is more to the country than its coasts, delightful and absorbing as both of them (or all of them) may be." ["American Notes," *Times Literary Supplement*, 9/23/83]

"The contemporary United States expresses the greatest of all paradoxes. It is at one and the same time a democracy—at any rate a pluralist open society—and an empire. No other country has ever been, or had, both things at once. Or not for long." ["The Chorus and Cassandra," *Grand Street*, Autumn 1985]

"In contrast with what some Europeans affect to believe, America is a country remarkably free from taboo. There is practically no received or general opinion that is not subject to continual 'revisionist' criticism, and very little 'revisionist' work goes unchallenged itself." ["American Notes," *Times Literary Supplement*, 5/30/86]

"In America, something deemed unsayable is, sooner or later, bound to be *said*. And it may be said rather more heatedly as a result of its having been a taboo." ["American Notes," *Times Literary Supplement*, 5/30/86]

"The United States is a country obsessed by credentials. It contains almost a million people who are entitled to call themselves 'professor,' and even those who must be content with 'doctor' are often inclined to insist upon it." ["American Notes," *Times Literary Supplement*, 9/25/87–10/01/87]

"Any Patagonian, Canadian, or Mexican is an 'American' by right of being in the Americas; the appropriation of a bicontinental title by the United States is much resented. As for 'New World' and 'discovery,' one can almost hear the spirits asking: 'New to whom, paleface?'" ["Hello, Columbus, What Took You So Long?," *Independent*, 2/03/91]

"What a country, and what a culture, when the liberals cry before they are hurt, and the reactionaries pose as the brave nonconformists, while the radicals make a fetish of their own jokey irrelevance." ["Minority Report," *Nation*, 10/21/91]

"Today, the United States is simultaneously swamped in mass popular culture and uncomfortably stuck with a 'toney' and plutocratic art establishment. It actually needs someone from a younger and more egalitarian society, both to challenge its vulgarity *and* to mock its elitist pretensions." ["Angel in the Outback," *Vanity Fair*, May 1997]

"America does not just pledge to its true believers a better future. If they really play their hand well, it can promise them a better past. Its narrative, read aright, was not progress from an age of innocence to a time of bitterness and bigotry and ethnic cleansing, but *through* a time of bigotry and bitterness and ethnic cleansing toward a time of relative innocence." ["Ireland," *Critical Quarterly*, Spring 1998]

" . . . It's the only place in history where patriotism can be divorced from its evil twins of chauvinism and xenophobia." ["For Patriotic Dreams," *Vanity Fair*, December 2001]

" . . . In America your internationalism can and should be your patriotism." ["On Becoming American," *Atlantic Monthly*, May 2005]

"The truth is that America has committed gross wrongs and crimes, as well as upheld great values and principles. It is a society chiefly urban and capitalist, but significantly rural or—as some prefer to say—pastoral. It has an imperial record as well as an isolationist one. It has a secular constitution but a heavily religious and pietistic nature." [*Thomas Jefferson: Author of America* (New York: HarperCollins, 2005), 186–187]

" . . . The United States is simultaneously the most conservative and the most radicalizing force on the planet." ["What's Left?," *Atlantic Monthly*, March 2006]

"Here was a country that could engage in a frightening and debilitating and unjust war, and undergo a simultaneous convulsion of its cities on the question of justice for its oldest and largest minority, *and* start a national conversation on the rights of women, *and* turn its most respectable campuses into agitated seminars on right and wrong, *and* have a show trial of confessed saboteurs in Chicago where the incredibly guilty defendants actually got off, *and* put quite a lot of this onto its television and movie screens in real time. This seemed like a state of affairs worth fighting for, or at least fighting over." [*Hitch-22* (New York: Twelve, 2010), 215–216]

American Empire

" . . . The displacement of Britain by America as a world gendarme and guarantor was a chaotic, brutal, and dishonest process. On the British side there were residual commitments to a continued imperial role, and on the American side a repressed reluctance to actually *seem* to be seeking one." [*Blood, Class and Empire* (New York: Nation Books, 2004), 252]

"American empire, indeed, tends to define itself in terms of strategic jargon rather than grand design and noble mission." [*Blood, Class and Empire* (New York: Nation Books, 2004), 290]

American Revolution

"If the American Revolution, with its secularism, its separation of powers, its Bill of Rights, and its gradual enfranchisement of those excluded or worse at its founding, has often betrayed itself at home and abroad, it nevertheless remains the only revolution that still retains any power to inspire." [*Thomas Jefferson: Author of America* (New York: HarperCollins, 2005), 187–188]

"No nation had managed to evolve a system of government that did not depend on some form of autocracy. This whole case was now altered by the American Revolution, which had bound itself and its heirs, in the name of the people, to certain inscribed rules and laws that no successor regime was allowed to break." [*Thomas Paine's Rights of Man: A Biography* (New York: Atlantic Monthly Press, 2006), 112–113]

Americans

"By and large, Americans refuse to believe that humanity or society can be ameliorated by collective or political action. But they cannot do without the belief in amelioration, which is accordingly manifested in so many versions of 'personal growth' and 'individual fulfillment.' This supplies the energy and daring of the Utopian enterprise, and also commonly condemns it to defeat or disappointment." ["Tottering Utopias," *Times Literary Supplement*, 9/18/87]

"Many Americans, schooled in the national dream of promise and abundance and opportunity, are condemned to experience life as a disappointment and to wonder if the fault is in themselves or in their stars that they are perpetual underlings. If this were not so, Ann Landers would be out of a job in the same way that so many of her readers are." [*The Missionary Position* (New York: Verso, 1995), 96]

" . . . There is no such thing as an 'English-American' let alone a 'British-American,' and one can only boggle at the idea of what, if we did exist, our national day parade on Fifth Avenue might look like." [*Hitch-22* (New York: Twelve, 2010), 227]

"Hyphenation—if one may be blunt—is for latecomers." [*Hitch-22* (New York: Twelve, 2010), 228]

Americans and Monarchy

"Given that the Americans were the first English-speaking subjects to expel the Hanoverian monarchy from their territory and their constitution, it's amazing they now allow it so much space on their supermarket check-out racks and in their hearts." ["No Wonder America Is Baffled," *Evening Standard*, 6/26/92]

Amis, Martin

"So far from being some jaded Casanova, Martin possesses the rare gift—enviable if potentially time consuming—of being able to find something attractive in almost any woman. If this be misogyny, then give us increase of it." [*Hitch-22* (New York: Twelve, 2010), 159]

Anarchism

"Just as you may—must—believe in the power of love but not know quite how to *institutionalize* it, so you may say with the anarchist that 'No one is good enough to be another's master' while believing or suspecting that this is a vital but impossible precept." ["Loss Leaders," *Grand Street*, Spring 1989]

"There is a reason for the affected profession of 'anarchist sympathies' among Tories and grandees, and of 'libertarian principles' by Hobbesian yahoos of the Right. Among the former, one sees the upholding of the view that a gentleman's business and property are his own, and none of the government's. Among the latter, a distaste for democracy, for taxation, and for the need to consult others about the planet. The unmolested gent and the selfish *commerçant* are not the models of autonomy that anarchists are supposed to have in mind. . . ." ["Loss Leaders," *Grand Street*, Spring 1989]

"Yet precisely because they deal in 'eternal verities,' purist anarchists must operate independently of history and politics. There is, for them, no important distinction between sufficient and necessary conditions; no need to study the evolution of society or production. Their often religious and millennial attitude to the future derives in part from a religious attitude toward the past; toward some primordial and timeless hellhole of ignorance, innocence, and simplicity such as Eden is reported to have been." ["Loss Leaders," *Grand Street*, Spring 1989]

" . . . For the anarchist the democratic notion of 'the consent of the governed'—actually a rather highly-evolved concept—is only another form of acquiescence." ["Loss Leaders," *Grand Street*, Spring 1989]

"It's easy now to forget that the figure of 'the anarchist'—the swarthy, sullen bomb-thrower—once haunted the official imagination even more than the word 'Bolshevik' or 'terrorist.' (I have always thought myself that its resemblance in print to the word 'antichrist' may have had a subliminal effect on the untutored eye.)" ["Sacco and Vanzetti: Proletarian Outlaws," *Newsday*, 3/06/91]

Andress, Ursula
"Fleming gave stupid mock monikers to many of his cock-fodder heroines, from Pussy Galore to Kissy Suzuki, but Ursula Andress is a natural porn name if ever I've struck one." ["Bottoms Up," *Atlantic Monthly*, April 2006]

Angels
"Angels, whether or not crammed with yeast, are notorious for their lack of sexual organs." [Introduction to *The Mating Season*, by P. G. Wodehouse (New York: Penguin Books, 1999), vi]

Anglophilia
" . . . The reverence and affection for things English has increased in direct proportion to the overshadowing and relegation of real British power." [*Blood, Class and Empire* (New York: Nation Books, 2004), 251]

Animals
"Those who worry about the treatment of animals are often accused of sentimentality or of putting the plight of beasts before the immense problems of humanity. But it is quite rare to find a humanitarian who is indifferent to animals and surprisingly common to find that those who belittle animal rights are the same ones who find the pain of humans easy to bear." ["Minority Report," *Nation*, 2/02/85]

"Our own fate is closely bound up with that of other species, and the loss of them would mean more than the loss of our pleasure in their company. Knowledge, science, medicine, and nutrition are all enhanced for humans by other creatures." ["Minority Report," *Nation*, 2/02/85]

"Those who campaign for 'animal liberation' have confused the issue unnecessarily by borrowing human terminology. While the proletarian condition can be abolished and women can cease to be chattels and whole races can throw off slavery, there is no means of freeing animals from the condition of being beasts. For all I know, that is just as well." ["Minority Report," *Nation*, 2/02/85]

" . . . Concern with the suffering and exploitation of animals can be expected to arise only in a fairly advanced and complex society where human beings are thoroughly in charge, and where they no longer need fear daily challenges from other species." ["Political Animals," *Atlantic Monthly*, November 2002]

"There are sound reasons for concluding that all life is ultimately random. But there is no way of living and acting as if this is true; and if it is true, human beings cannot very well be condemned for making the best of things by taking advantage of other animals." ["Political Animals," *Atlantic Monthly*, November 2002]

" . . . One of the most idiotic jeers against animal lovers is the one about their preferring critters to people. As a matter of observation, it will be found that people who 'care'—about rain forests or animals, miscarriages of justice or dictatorships—

are, though frequently irritating, very often the same people. Whereas those who love hamburgers and riskless hunting and mink coats are not in the front ranks of Amnesty International." ["Political Animals," *Atlantic Monthly*, November 2002]

"Rights have to be asserted. Animals cannot make such assertions. We have to make representations to ourselves on their behalf. To the extent that we see our own interest in doing so, we unpick both the tautology that hobbles the utilitarian and the idealist delusion that surrounds the religious, and may simply become more 'humane'—a word that seems to require its final vowel as never before." ["Political Animals," *Atlantic Monthly*, November 2002]

Anti-Americanism

"Criticism of the United States from the international left is usually of a rather naïve, unoriginal kind, tending to stress the gulf between the ideals of the Founding Fathers and the practice of the new imperium." ["Minority Report," *Nation*, 3/08/86]

"Suspicion and alarm about American foreign policy go hand in hand, on the European left, with admiration for American constitutional procedures. The harshest critic of SDI, cruise missiles, or the contras can be heard to say that he envies the First Amendment. This is an apparent paradox, for which those who go on about 'anti-Americanism' never allow." ["Beware of Allies Bearing Advice," *Washington Post*, 12/28/86]

"More is going on, when the American flag is being burned, than a protest against a superpower. Quite often, especially in some European tones of voice, one can detect a petty resentment of America for being in the right." ["Anti-Americanism," in *A Long Short War: The Postponed Liberation of Iraq* (New York: Plume Books, 2003), 29]

Anti-Communism

"They [anticommunists] regard themselves as lonely, reviled, and embattled when, in point of fact, their opinions are often officially sanctioned and lavishly sponsored. When discussing the cultural ruthlessness of the totalitarian enemy, the Zhdanov mentality that interprets all dissent as a symptom of rot and decay, they occasionally betray a very slight tinge of repressed vicarious approval." ["American Notes," *Times Literary Supplement*, 5/11/84]

Antidepressants

"There may be successful methods for overcoming the blues, but for me they cannot include a capsule that says: 'Fool yourself into happiness, while pretending not to do so.' I should actually *want* my mind to be strong enough to circumvent such a trick." [*Hitch-22* (New York: Twelve, 2010), 342]

Anti-Semitism

" . . . There is no necessary, no logical, identity between anti-Israeli (or anti-Begin) views and anti-Jewish ones. Anti-Semites are people who dislike Jews *because they are Jews*. Moreover, they dislike them for reasons not merely of complexion or physique or supposed inferiority but for reasons having to do with religion, history, secrecy, mysticism, blood, soil, and gold. Given the 'right' circumstances, such a prejudice can and does become murderous and unappeasable. To be accused of harboring it, therefore, is no joke." ["On Anti-Semitism," *Nation*, 10/09/82]

"No honest person would be the loser if the morally blackmailing argument of 'anti-Semitism' were dropped from the discourse." ["On Anti-Semitism," *Nation*, 10/09/82]

"It would be a pity if a term like 'anti-Semite,' which ought to be a very grave and solemn charge, were cheapened by propagandistic over-use." ["American Notes," *Times Literary Supplement*, 5/30/86]

"Anti-Semitism is a *theory* as well as a prejudice. It can be, and is, held by people who have never seen a Jew. . . . It may have special attractions for those who are themselves victimized by their own kind. And typically the anti-Semite has an interest, however sublimated, in a Final Solution. Nothing else will do. The usual outward sign of this is an inability to stay off the subject." ["The Charmer," *Grand Street*, Winter 1986]

" . . . Black demagogy turns on the Jews not in spite of the fact that they are more liberal and more sensitive to the persecuted, but *because* of it." ["The Charmer," *Grand Street*, Winter 1986]

"It must count as a gain for civilization that in today's America you are finished if you flirt with anti-Semitism. But it can be irritating to see with how uneven a hand this standard is applied." ["Minority Report," *Nation*, 6/13/94]

"It's impossible not to notice that anti-Jewish propaganda . . . is a virtual synonym for paranoia." ["Scars and Bars," *Nation*, 2/21/00]

"The idea that a group of people—whether defined as a nation or as a religion—could be condemned for all time and without the possibility of an appeal was (and is) essentially a totalitarian one." [*God Is Not Great* (New York: Twelve, 2007), 250]

"Anti-Semitism is an elusive and protean phenomenon, but it certainly involves the paradox whereby great power is attributed to the powerless. In the mind of the anti-Jewish paranoid, some shabby-bearded figure in a distant shtetl is a putative member of a secret world government: hence the enduring fascination of *The Protocols of the Learned Elders of Zion*." ["The 2,000-Year-Old Panic," *Atlantic Monthly*, March 2008]

" . . . The sickness is somehow ineradicable and not even subject to rational analysis, let alone to rationalization. Anti-Semitism has flourished without banking or capitalism (for which Jews were at one time blamed) and without Communism (for which they were also blamed). It has existed without Zionism (of which leading Jews were at one time the only critics) and without the state of Israel. There has even been anti-Semitism without Jews, in states like Malaysia whose political leaders are paranoid demagogues looking for a scapegoat. This is enough to demonstrate that anti-Semitism is not a mere prejudice like any other: Sinhalese who don't like Tamils, or Hutu who regard Tutsi as 'cockroaches,' do not accuse their despised neighbors of harboring a plan—or of possessing the ability—to bring off a secret world government based on the occult control of finance." ["Chosen," *Atlantic Monthly*, September 2010]

"What strikes the eye about anti-Semitism is the godfather role it plays as the organizing principle of other bigotries." ["Chosen," *Atlantic Monthly*, September 2010]

" . . . Anti-Semitism is protean and contradictory, but then, so are Judaism and Zionism." ["Chosen," *Atlantic Monthly*, September 2010]

"The chief impetus of anti-Semitism remains theocratic, and in our epoch anti-Semitism has shifted from Christian to Muslim: a more searching inquiry into its origins and nature might begin by asking if faith is not the problem to begin with." ["Chosen," *Atlantic Monthly*, September 2010]

Anti-Theism

"I myself have tried to formulate a position I call 'anti-theist.' There are, after all, atheists who say that they wish the fable were true but are unable to suspend the requisite disbelief, or have relinquished belief only with regret. To this I reply: who wishes that there was a permanent, unalterable celestial despotism that subjected us to continual surveillance and could convict us of thought-crime, and who regarded us as its private property even after we died? How happy we ought to be, at the reflection that there exists not a shred of respectable evidence to support such a horrible hypothesis." [Introduction to *The Portable Atheist* (New York: Da Capo Press, 2007), xxii]

"I am not so much an atheist as an *anti*-theist. I am, in other words, not one of those unbelievers who wishes that they had faith, or that they could believe. I am, rather, someone who is delighted that there is absolutely no persuasive evidence for the existence of any of mankind's many thousands of past and present deities." [*Is Christianity Good for the World?* (Moscow, ID: Canon Press, 2008), 12]

Antiwar Movement

" . . . All the learned and conscientious objections [to war], as well as all the silly or sinister ones, boil down to this: Nothing will make us fight against an evil if that fight forces us to go to the same corner as our own government. (The words 'our own' should of course be appropriately ironized, with the necessary quotation marks.) To do so would be a betrayal of the Cherokees." ["Stranger in a Strange Land," *Atlantic Monthly*, December 2001]

"The friends of Galtieri, Saddam Hussein, Mullah Omar, and Milosevic make unconvincing defenders of humanitarian values, and it can be seen that their inept and sometimes inane arguments lack either the principles or the seriousness that are required in such debates." [Letter, *Nation* (online), 1/10/02]

" . . . It's obvious to me that the 'antiwar' side would not be convinced, even if all the allegations made against Saddam Hussein were proven, and even if the true views of the Iraqi people could be expressed." ["Taking Sides," *Nation*, 10/14/02]

"Not only does the 'peace' movement ignore the anti-Saddam civilian opposition, it sends missions to console the Ba'athists in their isolation. . . ." ["So Long, Fellow Travelers," *Washington Post*, 10/20/02]

"The Left has employed arguments as contemptible as those on whose behalf they have been trotted out. . . . [T]he element of bad faith in the argument is far worse than the feeble-minded hysteria of its logic. . . . Now, however, the same people are all frenzied about an American-led 'attack on the Muslim world.' Are the Kurds not Muslims? Is the new Afghan government not Muslim? Will not the next Iraqi government be Muslim also? This meaningless demagogy among the peaceniks can only be explained by a masochistic refusal to admit that our own civil society has any merit, or by a nostalgia for Stalinism that I can sometimes actually taste as well as smell." ["So Long, Fellow Travelers," *Washington Post*, 10/20/02]

"There is, of course, a soggier periphery of more generally pacifist types, whose preferred method of argument about regime change is subject change." ["So Long, Fellow Travelers," *Washington Post*, 10/20/02]

"A year or so ago, the 'peace movement' was saying that Afghanistan could not even be approached without risking the undying enmity of the Muslim world; that the Taliban could not be bombed during Ramadan; that a humanitarian disaster would occur if the Islamic ultra-fanatics were confronted in their own lairs. Now we have an imperfect but recovering Afghanistan, with its population increased by almost two million returned refugees. Have you ever seen or heard any of those smart-ass critics and cynics make a self-criticism? Or recant?" ["Chew on This," *Stranger*, 1/16/03–1/22/03]

"If the counsel of the peaceniks had been followed, Kuwait would today be the nineteenth province of Iraq (and based on his own recently produced evidence, Saddam Hussein would have acquired nuclear weapons). Moreover, Bosnia would be a trampled and cleansed province of Greater Serbia, Kosovo would have been emptied of most of its inhabitants, and the Taliban would still be in power in Afghanistan. Yet nothing seems to disturb the contented air of moral superiority that surrounds those who intone the 'peace movement.'" ["Chew on This," *Stranger*, 1/16/03–1/22/03]

"It would be just as accurate to say, 'No quarrel with Saddam Hussein,' as it would be to say, 'No war on Iraq.'" ["Inspecting 'Inspections,'" *Slate*, 2/13/03]

"There's no real way of being 'antiwar,' but there are several means of evading the dilemma." ["Preview of Coming Attractions: Sontag Looks at Images of War," *New York Observer*, 3/17/03]

"The deformities of the anti-war faction are nonetheless threefold: they underestimate and understate the radical evil of Nazism and fascism, they forget that many 'peace-loving' forces did the same at the time, and they are absolutist in their ahistoricism. A war is a war is a war, in their moral universe, and anyone engaging in one is as bad as anyone else." ["Just Give Peace a Chance?," *New Statesman*, 5/19/08]

Apartheid

"It is, together with saving the whales and defending the Constitution, one of the few things about which people with advanced opinions appear to agree. It came almost as a relief to me, then, to find that the leaders of Margaret Thatcher's Student Federation had passed a resolution calling for Nelson Mandela to be hanged. Here, I thought, are neoconservatives who are not afraid to stand up and be counted. Let's have no hypocrisy." ["Minority Report," *Nation*, 8/31/85]

"Apartheid cannot, by definition, be reformed or modified." ["Minority Report," *Nation*, 8/31/85]

Apocalypse

"The Christian fundamentalist view of Doomsday may be unpolished, but it is unfalsifiable, just like the opposing view that God does *not* want our extinction." ["The Lord and the Intellectuals," *Harper's*, July 1982]

"With a necessary part of its collective mind, religion looks forward to the destruction of the world. . . . Perhaps half aware that its unsupported arguments are not entirely persuasive, and perhaps uneasy about its own greedy accumulation of temporal power and wealth, religion has never ceased to proclaim the Apocalypse and the day of judgment." [*God Is Not Great* (New York: Twelve, 2007), 56]

"One of the very many connections between religious belief and the sinister, spoiled, selfish childhood of our species is the repressed desire to see everything smashed up and ruined and brought to naught. This tantrum-need is coupled with two other sorts of 'guilty joy,' or, as the Germans say, *schadenfreude*. First, one's own death is canceled—or perhaps repaid or compensated—by the obliteration of all others. Second, it can always be egotistically hoped that one will be personally spared, gathered contentedly to the bosom of the mass exterminator, and from a safe place observe the sufferings of those less fortunate." [*God Is Not Great* (New York: Twelve, 2007), 57]

Apologetics

"While some religious apology is magnificent in its limited way—one might cite Pascal—and some of it is dreary and absurd—here one cannot avoid naming C. S. Lewis—both styles have something in common, namely the appalling load of strain that they have to bear. How much effort it takes to affirm the incredible!" [*God Is Not Great* (New York: Twelve, 2007), 7]

Apology

"If you don't want to sound like the Pope, who apologizes for everything and for nothing, then your apology should cost you something." ["Who's Sorry Now?," *Nation*, 5/29/00]

"It is often in the excuses and in the apologies that one finds the real offense." ["Tea'd Off," *Vanity Fair*, January 2011]

Apparatchik

"There's no real trick to thinking like an apparatchik. You just keep two sets of ethical books." ["Thinking Like an Apparatchik," *Atlantic Monthly*, July/August 2003]

Appearance

"I also take the view that it's a mistake to try to look younger than one is, and that the face in particular ought to be the register of a properly lived life. I don't want to look as if I have been piloting the Concorde without a windshield, and I can't imagine whom I would be fooling if I did." ["On the Limits of Self-Improvement, Part I," *Vanity Fair*, October 2007]

"In the continuing effort to gain some idea of how one appears to other people, nothing is more useful than exposing oneself to an audience of strangers in a bookstore or a lecture hall." [*Hitch-22* (New York: Twelve, 2010), 350]

Appeasement

"Of course, since 'appeasement' is the standard metaphor whenever a test of American resolve is in prospect, the figure of Hitler is as difficult to exclude as the head of King Charles. The drawback in the analogy is that, from a Hitler, it is impossible to demand much less than his complete destruction or unconditional surrender." ["Diary," *London Review of Books*, 9/13/90]

" . . . The term 'appease' has become worn out by repetition." [*Letters to a Young Contrarian* (New York: Basic Books, 2001), 134]

"It was the vague term chosen by the Tories themselves to mask a collaboration with fascism and also their candid hope that the ambitions of Hitler could be directed eastward against Stalin. . . . It wasn't at all that the British rightists were vacillating and pacifistic—an absurd notion to begin with. It was that they thought they could save their empire by a tactical alliance with Berlin. . . . Quite obviously, these people thought they saw in fascism a future ally and not a future rival." ["The Medals of His Defeats," *Atlantic Monthly*, April 2002]

Approval Ratings

"It now doesn't seem ridiculous to have 'approval ratings' that fluctuate week by week, because these are based upon the all-important 'perception' factor, which has in turn quite lost its own relationship to the word 'perceptive.'" ["Credibility Brown," *London Review of Books*, 8/31/89]

Arab Street

" . . . Those who once annexed the term have been forced to drop it, and for a good reason. The struggle for public opinion in the region is a continuing one and cannot be determined in advance, least of all by pseudo-populists who grant the violent Islamists their first premise." ["The Arab Street," *Slate*, 2/28/05]

Arendt, Hannah

" . . . She was the arriving, irrupting, avenging conscience of outraged exile Europe and the one who rendered isolationist positions no longer tenable by the 'herd of independent minds' (expression of Mr. Harold Rosenberg)." ["Performing Seals," *London Review of Books*, 8/10/00]

Argument

"An argument that can be used to prove anything is open to the objection that it proves nothing." ["Minority Report," *Nation*, 1/01/90]

" . . . I try to argue as if I think I am right, not as if I know I am right." ["We Know Best," *Vanity Fair*, May 2001]

"It's often a bad sign when people defend themselves against charges that haven't been made." ["A Rejoinder to Noam Chomsky," *Nation* (online), 10/15/01]

"The test of a well-conducted argument is not its ability to convert or to persuade. It lies in its capacity to refine or to redefine the positions of the other side." [Introduction to *Left Hooks, Right Crosses: A Decade of Political Writing*, ed. Christopher Caldwell and Christopher Hitchens (New York: Nation Books, 2002), 211]

"The first requirement of anyone engaging in an intellectual or academic debate is that he or she be able to give a proper account of the opposing position(s). . . ." ["The End of Fukuyama," *Slate*, 3/01/06]

Argument from Authority

"The 'Argument from Authority' is the weakest of all arguments. It is weak when it is asserted at second or third hand ('the Good Book says'), and it is even weaker when asserted at first hand, as every child knows who has heard a parent say 'because I say so' (and as every parent knows who has heard himself reduced to uttering words he once found so unconvincing)." [*God Is Not Great* (New York: Twelve, 2007), 150]

Armageddon

"Those who brood on the imminence of Armageddon, with its visions of dreadful woman-beasts, or who employ it to frighten others, are prey to awful fears themselves." ["Umberto Umberto," *In These Times*, 1/30/85–2/05/85]

Armchair General

"The concept embodied in the contemptuous usage is this: someone who wants intervention in, say, Iraq ought to be prepared to go and fight there. An occasional corollary is that those who have actually seen war are not so keen to urge it. . . . It is said, for example, that someone like former Nebraska Senator Bob Kerrey has more right to pronounce on a war than someone who avoided service in Vietnam. Well, last year Kerrey was compelled to admit that he had led a calamitous expedition into a Vietnamese village and had been responsible for the slaughter of several children and elderly people. . . . Do I turn to such a man for advice on how to deal with Saddam Hussein? The connection is not self-evident, more especially since, as far as I am aware, Kerrey knows no more about Iraq than I know about how to construct a chess-playing computer." ["'Armchair General,'" *Slate*, 11/11/02]

" . . . If the 'armchair' arguers got their way and asked only war veterans what to do about Saddam Hussein, there would have been a rather abrupt 'regime change' in Iraq long before now." ["'Armchair General,'" *Slate*, 11/11/02]

Arms Race

" . . . It is flatly untrue to say that anybody has ever been democratically consulted about the arms race." ["Minority Report," *Nation*, 9/18/82]

"The arms race was a *ding an sich*, to borrow a phrase from Hegel: a thing-in-itself that might, even by accident, terminate in the closure of civilized life, or indeed any life, on earth. Such an eventuality seemed to me not just infinitely worse than any imaginable dictatorship, but also considerably more probable." ["How I Became a Neoconservative," *La Règle du Jeu*, 9/15/05]

Arms Race vs. Cold War
"Although the arms race and the cold war started at about the same time, they have never run in sync. The United States has generally been the initiator in the arms race, while the Soviet Union, through the original sin of the Stalinization of Eastern Europe, was the gravest offender in beginning the Cold War." ["Minority Report," *Nation*, 1/01/90]

Ashcroft, John
"Senator Ashcroft was defeated last November by a dead man: Governor Mel Carnahan of Missouri, whose name stayed on the ballot after his demise (and whose widow has been nominated to fill his seat). In these circumstances, Ashcroft's 'pro-life' position must be considered as rather a sporting one." ["Bush: The First 100 Hours," *Evening Standard*, 1/25/01]

" . . . John Ashcroft, a 'born-again' type whose ability to find his way around town unaided is a marvel to all who know him." ["Hey, I'm Doing My Best," *Observer*, 1/20/02]

" . . . A tuneless, clueless, evangelical Confederate dunce." ["The God Squad," *Nation*, 4/15/02]

"Bush once appointed an attorney general, John Ashcroft, who knew so little about the United States Constitution that he announced that, in America, 'we have no king but Jesus.' That moronic statement was exactly two words too long." ["Power Suits," *Vanity Fair*, April 2006]

Association of Christian Broadcasters
"President Reagan's first campaign speech was to the Association of Christian Broadcasters, a rather bovine and literal-minded group of evangelists who not only think that you can live twice, but believe that they themselves are already doing so." ["Perceptions and Signals," *Spectator*, 2/18/84]

Astrology
"The pseudoscience of astrology has survived many refutations. . . . But this month, I think, stargazing has been dealt a crippling empirical blow. Who will bother to consult the zodiac now that we know that the Reagan family used it to make their decisions?" ["Muddy Insights from an Ex-Grand Vizier," *Newsday*, 5/25/88]

" . . . Happening to glance at the projected situation for Aries one morning, as I once did to be told that 'a member of the opposite sex is interested and will show it,' I found it hard to suppress a tiny surge of idiotic excitement, which in my memory has outlived the later disappointment." [*God Is Not Great* (New York: Twelve, 2007), 74]

Atheism

"Intellectuals have lost the courage of their nonbelief." ["The Lord and the Intellectuals," *Harper's*, July 1982]

"Atheism, and the related conviction that we have just one life to live, is the only sure way to regard all our fellow creatures as brothers and sisters. The alleged 'fatherhood' of God does not, as liberation theology has it, make this axiomatic. All it has meant, throughout history, is a foul squabble for primacy in Daddy's affections." ["The Lord and the Intellectuals," *Harper's*, July 1982]

"There are, as it happens, many people who regard the origin of the universe as, according to excellent evidence and disinterested inquiry, a black hole. They (we) do not choose to make a black hole an object of worship. They (we) worry about those who do; most especially about those who defend *their* black hole interpretation with thermonuclear devices. . . . There is only one humanity, but an infinite number of gods." ["Siding with Rushdie," *London Review of Books*, 10/26/89]

"In the ordinary way, nothing fuels the secular impulse more than a public competition of religions. Such a competition usually shows people that since not all religions can possibly be right, and since it is improbable that only one of them is right, one is justified in suspecting that all of them may be equally wrong." ["City of Cults," *Guardian*, 8/19/93]

"The intellectual advantage [of atheism] hardly needs elaboration: we do not normally accept unprovable assertions at face value, however devoutly they are maintained, and we possess increasingly convincing explanations of matters that once lay within the province of the supernatural." ["The Future of an Illusion," *Daedalus*, Summer 2003]

" . . . The atheist can expect to be free of the pervasive solipsism that disfigures religious thought. If an earthquake should occur, or a comet fill the sky, he can be sure that this development is not all, indeed not at all, about his own brief existence and vain human aspirations." ["The Future of an Illusion," *Daedalus*, Summer 2003]

"Atheism can defend itself intellectually against any majority of the credulous and usually has to do so." ["Public Solidarity Does Not Help Humanism," *Free Inquiry*, Summer 2003]

"Atheist humanism has no resemblance to a faith, let alone a church. Any thinking person can accept its conclusions independently, without any catechism, and these reasoned conclusions do not require the incessant rituals of reinforcement that are necessitated by a belief in the incredible or the impossible. Our state of mind needs no priesthood, no congregation, no reassurance that we are all of one mind or one body. Leave that to the weak-minded and the insecure." ["Public Solidarity Does Not Help Humanism," *Free Inquiry*, Summer 2003]

"Our belief is not a belief. Our principles are not a faith. We do not rely solely upon science and reason, because these are necessary rather than sufficient factors, but we distrust anything that contradicts science or outrages reason. We may differ on many things, but what we respect is free inquiry, open mindedness, and the pursuit of ideas for their own sake." [*God Is Not Great* (New York: Twelve, 2007), 5]

"One day a decent candidate for high office will say that he is not a person of faith, and the sky will not fall." ["God Bless Me, It's a Best-Seller!," *Vanity Fair*, September 2007]

" . . . Atheists have always argued that this world is all that we have, and that our duty is to one another to make the very most and best of it. Theism cannot coexist with this unexceptional conclusion." [Introduction to *The Portable Atheist* (New York: Da Capo Press, 2007), xvi]

"The rejection of the man-made concept of god is not a sufficient condition for intellectual or moral emancipation. Atheists have no right to go around looking superior. They have only fulfilled the *necessary* condition by throwing off the infancy of the species and disclaiming a special place in the natural scheme. They are now free, if they so choose, to become nihilists or sadists or solipsists on their own account." [Introduction to *The Portable Atheist* (New York: Da Capo Press, 2007), xxi]

"The atheist does not say and cannot prove that there is no deity. He or she says that no persuasive evidence or argument has ever been adduced for the notion. Surely this should place the burden on the faithful, who do after all make very large claims for themselves and their religions." ["What We Were Reading: 2006," *Guardian*, 12/05/09]

"What we [atheists] don't know, we don't claim to know." [Debate with Dinesh D'Souza ("Is Religion the Problem?"), Notre Dame University, Notre Dame, IN, 4/07/10]

Atonement
"Previous sacrifices of humans, such as the Aztec and other ceremonies from which we recoil, were common in the ancient world and took the form of propitiatory murder. An offering of a virgin or an infant or a prisoner was assumed to appease the gods: once again, not a very good advertisement for the moral properties of religion." [*God Is Not Great* (New York: Twelve, 2007), 208]

Authenticity
" . . . The desire for authenticity—for the genuine and unfeigned—can at least sometimes be the equal of the lust for modernity, for prosperity, for unbearable lightness and emancipation from guilt." ["Ireland," *Critical Quarterly*, Spring 1998]

Authority
" . . . There are always secular authorities, masquerading as divine, who already know that they are right and who are deaf to the necessity of skepticism." ["Now, Who Will Speak for Rushdie?," *New York Times*, 2/17/89]

"Mere fear of unseen authority is not a sound basis for ethics." ["The New Commandments," *Vanity Fair*, April 2010]

Autobiography

"When I first formed the idea of writing some memoirs, I had the customary reservations about the whole conception being perhaps 'too soon.' Nothing dissolves this fusion of false modesty and natural reticence more swiftly than the blunt realization that the project could become, at any moment, ruled out of the question as having been undertaken too 'late.'" [*Hitch-22* (New York: Twelve, 2010), 3]

" . . . One's memoirs must always strive to avoid too much retrospective lens adjustment. . . ." [*Hitch-22* (New York: Twelve, 2010), 232]

BRIAN LAMB: I have your memoir in my hands . . .
CHRISTOPHER HITCHENS: So should everybody. ["Q&A with Christopher Hitchens," C-SPAN, 1/14/11 (first aired: 1/23/11)]

Awards and Prizes

"The unstoppably inflating awards business exists to reward sponsors, to pacify egos, to generate sales, and to puff reputations. This doesn't matter so much in the world of ads and artifacts, any more than it does in the world where you see the 'hotel employee of the month' scowling at you from a reusable plastic frame as you drum your gnawed fingers at an abandoned ('Thank you for giving us the opportunity to serve you better') reception desk. It does make a difference, though, in the world of letters." ["These Glittering Prizes," *Vanity Fair*, January 1993]

"Writing is meant to be a solitary and egotistical business, and heaven knows what minor or mediocre writers did in the days before half the dust jackets carried the words 'award-winning' (or the even more pathetic, catch-penny appeal 'nominated for the X award'). Nowadays, though, the thirst for trophies is putting writers through hoops that ought to embarrass even a hardened Oscar seeker." ["These Glittering Prizes," *Vanity Fair*, January 1993]

"As with the Peace Prize, the award of the laureateship for literature has come to approximate the value of a resolution of the U.N. Special Committee on Human Rights." ["The Sinister Mediocrity of Harold Pinter," *Wall Street Journal*, 10/17/05]

Baby Boomers

"Every generation, of course, thinks of its predecessor as hopelessly hidebound and its successor as absurdly spoiled and selfish and disorderly. But the boomers are in the awkward and compromised position of the mule, which can claim neither pride in ancestry nor hope of posterity." ["The Baby-Boomer Wasteland," *Vanity Fair*, January 1996]

"For all the glib talk about social 'concern,' boomers have become more swiftly hardened to stepping over bums in the street, or stepping around panhandlers, than their parents ever did during a time of mass unemployment and destitution. A certain kind of cognitive dissonance seems to be at work. Let's deplore waste and ostentation while getting a new model of car every three or four years. . . . In the therapy generation, which scripts even its own lenient satires, you are by all means allowed, if not encouraged, to feel guilty. Just as long as you don't feel *responsible*." ["The Baby-Boomer Wasteland," *Vanity Fair*, January 1996]

Bacteria

" . . . If you could never get your mind off bacteria, you might never risk anything (this is, I hope, the most unromantic sentence I will ever write). . . ." ["Why Men Love Toe Cleavage," *Evening Standard*, 8/28/02]

Baldwin, James

"James Baldwin always described himself as a cat—sometimes but not always as a black cat—and the loveliness of the term falls happily on the inner ear. . . . The word happened to fit Baldwin like a skin: silky, jumpy, contemptuously independent, poised for flight or fight, sensual, and vain." ["A Cat's Life," *Times Literary Supplement*, 6/08/90–6/14/90]

Barry, Marion

" . . . Marion Barry, who has led the capital city into beggary and corruption, and who covers his nakedness by calling for mandatory prayer in schools." [*The Missionary Position* (New York: Verso, 1995), 8]

"Only Marion Barry, reborn in prison and re-elected as a demagogue, has really mastered the uses of redemption." [*The Missionary Position* (New York: Verso, 1995), 11]

"Barry, if you remember, cashed in on public dislike for the sting operation, went through an elaborate and emotional public theater of repentance and redemption, haunted prayer meetings and shout 'n' holler revivals, and eventually became the 'comeback kid' of Washington, DC—to the deep detriment of every citizen of the town. Beware of those who just won't go away because they have nowhere to go." ["It's Not the Sin. It's the Cynicism," *Vanity Fair*, December 1998]

Bauer, Gary

"Mr. Bauer may or may not have been born again, but he does an almost faultless impersonation of a fetus." ["It's Not the Sin. It's the Cynicism," *Vanity Fair*, December 1998]

Bay of Pigs Invasion

"In the Third World, the Bay of Pigs is a synonym for aggression. In the United States, it is a synonym for fiasco and embarrassment. When North American liberals warn against 'another Bay of Pigs,' what do they mean? No more aggressions, or no more botched ones?" ["The Peril of Success in Nicaragua," *New York Times*, 7/27/83]

"Washington was very fortunate in the incompetence of its covert action specialists and the brutal stupidity of its Cuban mercenaries. If they had won, captured Havana, and perhaps killed Fidel Castro and Che Guevara, they would have been faced with the awesome task of governing a resentful and defiant Cuba." ["The Peril of Success in Nicaragua," *New York Times*, 7/27/83]

Beauty

" . . . There are some places so humblingly beautiful that it is possible to imagine dying for them oneself." ["Hobbes in the Himalayas," *Atlantic Monthly*, September 2005]

Beck, Glenn

" . . . A tear-stained, semi-literate shock jock. . . ." ["Tea'd Off," *Vanity Fair*, January 2011]

Beer

" . . . The Coors family's Colorado beer, which, besides financing the fascist fringe, tastes like a cross between sheep-dip and shark repellent and is thus quite easily avoided. . . ." ["Minority Report," *Nation*, 5/10/93]

Belgium

"I pause to ask myself what it's like to be a Belgian, if there is such a thing. Too proud? Too masochistic? Difficult to decide. Like the mule, it seems to be a country without pride in paternity or hope of posterity." ["Not So Hidden Influences," *Slate*, 10/04/10]

Belief and Believers

" . . . If you believe in religion as a reinforcement for other people's *morality*, then why not Mormonism? Or snake-handling? Or Mithras or Dagon or Zeus, or any of the thousands of defunct deities added up by H. L. Mencken? True believers always balk at this point, murmuring feebly on occasion that one has to believe in *something*. Satanism does very well by this argument." ["The Lord and the Intellectuals," *Harper's*, July 1982]

"Even the men who made it [religion] cannot agree on what their prophets or redeemers or gurus actually said or did. . . . And yet—the believers still claim to know! Not just to know, but to know *everything*." [*God Is Not Great* (New York: Twelve, 2007), 10]

"The true believer cannot rest until the whole world bows the knee." [*God Is Not Great* (New York: Twelve, 2007), 31]

"If one must have faith in order to believe something, or believe *in* something, then the likelihood of that something having any truth or value is considerably diminished." [*God Is Not Great* (New York: Twelve, 2007), 71]

" . . . To believe in a god is in one way to express a *willingness* to believe in anything. Whereas to reject the belief is by no means to profess belief in nothing." [*God Is Not Great* (New York: Twelve, 2007), 185]

Bellow, Saul

"When I think of Bellow, I think not just of a man whose genius for the vernacular could seem to restate Athenian philosophy as if run through a Damon Runyon synthesizer, but of the author who came up with such graphic expressions for vulgarity and thuggery and stupidity—the debased currency of those too brutalized to have retained the capacity for wonder." ["The Great Assimilator," *Atlantic Monthly*, November 2007]

Benedict XVI

"Ratzinger himself may be banal, but his whole career has the stench of evil—a clinging and systematic evil that is beyond the power of exorcism to dispel." ["The Great Catholic Cover-Up," *Slate*, 3/15/10]

"Mentally remove his papal vestments and imagine him in a suit, and Joseph Ratzinger becomes just a Bavarian bureaucrat who has failed in the only task he was ever set—that of damage control." ["Bring the Pope to Justice," *Newsweek*, 5/03/10]

Bennett, William

"Bennett's style illustrates admirably the connection between laissez-faire and authoritarian beliefs. There should be, in other words, a 'do-nothing' regime, which limits itself to inculcating the catechism and creationism." ["Minority Report," *Nation*, 6/08/85]

Berlin, Isaiah

"It was Berlin, whenever faced with a conflict of rights, who sought to emulsify it. In other words, his emphasis on complexity had a strong element of . . . simplification." ["Moderation or Death," *London Review of Books*, 11/26/98]

"In every instance . . . from the Cold War through Algeria to Suez to Vietnam, Berlin strove to find a high 'liberal' justification either for the status quo or for the immediate needs of the conservative authorities." ["Moderation or Death," *London Review of Books*, 11/26/98]

" . . . He never broke any really original ground in the field of ideas. He was a skilled ventriloquist for other thinkers." ["Moderation or Death," *London Review of Books*, 11/26/98]

Bevin, Ernest

"He was almost incapable of sounding an 'h' at the beginning of a word. He looked and dressed like a burst horse-hair sofa. . . . Joseph Stalin thought Bevin 'no gentleman.'" ["Ernest Bevin: A Class Act," *Washington Post*, 4/22/84]

Bhutto, Benazir

"Beautiful but not sexy." [Quoted in Sonia Verma, "'My Life Is My Writing . . . My Children Come Later,'" *Globe and Mail*, 10/22/10]

The Bible

"The apologetic 'modern Christian' who argues faintly that of course the Bible isn't meant to be taken literally is saying that it isn't the word of God. He is, thereby, revising his faith out of existence." [*In These Times*, 11/16/83–11/22/83]

"The Revised Standard Version is a dull and worthy authority, which might be described as King James with the sonority and grandeur flattened out." ["American Notes," *Times Literary Supplement*, 3/08/85]

"The King James Bible . . . is the product of one of the most intense committee meetings of all time." ["Blessed Are the Phrasemakers," *New York Times*, 5/18/03]

" . . . It was exceedingly dangerous to try to translate the Good Book into a language that the people could understand. Like the secret work of Emmanuel Goldstein in 'Nineteen Eighty-Four,' the Bible was the possession of an inner-party elite, and its arcane were part of the stage management of priestcraft." ["Blessed Are the Phrasemakers," *New York Times*, 5/18/03]

"The Old Testament is bad enough: The commandments forbid us even to envy or covet our neighbor's goods, and thus condemn the very spirit of emulation and ambition that makes enterprise possible. But the New Testament is worse: It tells us to forget thrift and saving, to take no thought for the morrow, and to throw away our hard-earned wealth on the shiftless and the losers." [" . . . And Why I'm Most Certainly Not!," *Wall Street Journal*, 5/05/05]

"The Bible may, indeed does, contain a warrant for trafficking in humans, for ethnic cleansing, for slavery, for bride-price, and for indiscriminate massacre, but we are not bound by any of it because it was put together by crude, uncultured human mammals." [*God Is Not Great* (New York: Twelve, 2007), 102]

The Bible: New Testament
"The gospels do not agree on the life of the man Jesus, and they make assertions—such as his ability to cast demonic spells on pigs—that seem to reflect little credit upon him." [Letter, *New York Review of Books*, 12/19/96]

" . . . Just like the Old Testament, the 'New' one is also a work of crude carpentry, hammered together long after its purported events, and full of improvised attempts to make things come out right." [*God Is Not Great* (New York: Twelve, 2007), 110]

"The book on which all four [Gospels] may possibly have been based, known speculatively to scholars as 'Q,' has been lost forever, which seems distinctly careless on the part of the god who is claimed to have 'inspired' it." [*God Is Not Great* (New York: Twelve, 2007), 112]

"The Gospels are useful . . . in re-demonstrating the same point as their predecessor volumes, which is that religion is man-made." [*God Is Not Great* (New York: Twelve, 2007), 115]

"Either the Gospels are in some sense literal truth, or the whole thing is essentially a fraud and perhaps an immoral one at that." [*God Is Not Great* (New York: Twelve, 2007), 120]

The Bible: Old Testament
"Here again one sees the gigantic man-made fallacy that informs our 'Genesis' story. How can it be proven in one paragraph that this book was written by ignorant men and not by any god? Because man is given 'dominion' over all

beasts, fowl, and fish. But no dinosaurs or plesiosaurs or pterodactyls are specified, because the authors did not know of their existence, let alone of their supposedly special and immediate creation." [*God Is Not Great* (New York: Twelve,
2007), 90]

"Who—except for an ancient priest seeking to exert power by the tried and tested
means of fear—could possibly *wish* that this hopelessly knotted skein of fable had
any veracity?" [*God Is Not Great* (New York: Twelve, 2007), 103]

"People attain impossible ages and yet conceive children. Mediocre individuals engage in single combat or one-on-one argument with god or his emissaries, raising
afresh the whole question of divine omnipotence or even divine common sense,
and the ground is forever soaked with the blood of the innocent. Moreover, the
context is oppressively confined and *local*. None of these provincials, or their deity,
seems to have any idea of a world beyond the desert, the flocks and herds, and the
imperatives of nomadic subsistence. This is forgivable on the part of the provincial yokels, obviously, but then what of their supreme guide and wrathful tyrant?
Perhaps he was made in their image, even if not graven?" [*God Is Not Great* (New
York: Twelve, 2007), 107]

Big Bang
"The forces set off by the big bang—the great redshifts and waves of radiation that
send the galaxies and nebulas speeding apart from one another—are morally neutral. These forces do not know or care whether you are a Baptist, a snake handler,
a Druze, or a Hindu." ["Mr. Universe," *Vanity Fair*, December 1992]

Bigotry
"In some ways I feel sorry for racists and for religious fanatics, because they so
much miss the point of being human and deserve a sort of pity. But then I harden
my heart and decide to hate them all the more, because of the misery they inflict
and because of the contemptible excuses they advance for doing so." [*Letters to a
Young Contrarian* (New York: Basic Books, 2001), 109]

"All bigots and frauds are brothers under the skin." ["Faith-Based Fraud," *Slate*,
5/16/07]

"Where is hatred and tribalism and ignorance most commonly incubated, and
from which platform is it most commonly yelled? If you answered 'the churches'
and 'the pulpits,' you got both answers right." ["Blind Faith," *Slate*, 3/24/08]

" . . . Bigotry of all sorts is freely available, and openly inculcated into children, by
any otherwise unemployable dirtbag who can perform the easy feat of putting
Reverend in front of his name." ["Blind Faith," *Slate*, 3/24/08]

Biogenetics
"One need not be Utopian about biogenetics, which like any other breakthrough
can be exploited by the unscrupulous." ["Forging the Magic Bullet," *Vanity Fair*,
November 1993]

Biography

"*Jesus* [by A. N. Wilson] is a biography, which is not so much a profane undertaking as it is, in the absence of any reliable evidence, a near-impossible one." ["Mr. Universe," *Vanity Fair*, December 1992]

"The great thing about biographies, and about great troves of personal papers, is that they remind us how few years, in a real human life, are well spent." ["Critic of the Booboisie," *Dissent*, Summer 1994]

"To entitle a biography 'the life' rather than 'a life' might seem boastful, even if the intention was to distinguish the study of 'the life' from 'the work.'" ["Dragon Slayer," *Washington Post*, 9/28/03]

Bipartisanship

" . . . 'Bipartisanship,' by which is meant backroom decision-making, mutual soft-peddling and covering-up, and all other manner of governing most accurately captured by the word 'complicity.'" ["The Loyally Complicit," *Harper's*, July 1991]

"The truth is . . . that the *bi*-represents the fusion of two parties into one: the highest good of the consensus." ["Party of One," *Nation*, 2/15/99]

"A proposal is partisan if made by one party, but becomes 'bipartisan' (while remaining exactly the same as a proposal) if it is endorsed by enough members of the other party. There's no trick to it really. It's all a matter of wooing rather than principle." ["Multilateralism and Unilateralism," *Slate*, 12/18/02]

Blair, Tony

" . . . Tony Blair, at once the most radical and the most conservative of politicians." ["Eric the Red," *New York Times*, 8/24/03]

"Measured by the base standard of his immediate predecessors as Labor prime minister, James Callaghan and Harold Wilson, Tony Blair was a man of almost inordinate attachment to principle. When compared to those who led the party to repeated defeat at the hands of Margaret Thatcher—the old-style leftists Michael Foot and Neil Kinnock—he was a man who crossed the road only to get to the middle of it." ["Almost Noble," *Atlantic Monthly*, October 2010]

" . . . Blair became the first Labor politician ever to influence the British monarchy rather than be overawed by it. In doing so, he also very probably did the monarchy an enormous favor. By effectively telling the Queen what to do, he almost accidentally put an end to centuries of deference and . . . moved Britain toward a more presidential style of government." ["Almost Noble," *Atlantic Monthly*, October 2010]

"He now operates under the somehow touching name of the Tony Blair Faith Foundation, which can sound rather like a body set up to express faith in Tony Blair. His principal day job is to serve as mediator for the 'Quartet' of powers that supervise the Israeli-Palestinian 'peace process.' This means regular efforts to reconcile Muslims, Jews, and Christians in the Holy Land. Cheer up, I want to tell him. At least it's a job for life." ["The Blair-Hitch Project," *Vanity Fair*, February 2011]

Blame America First

"In Washington these days, a person who asks the question 'How does this policy look from the perspective of country X?' is instantly bullied into silence and accused of 'blaming America first.' The exercise of sympathetic imagination is regarded as a sign of weakness rather than intelligence or curiosity. A hectic philistine mood prevails, whereby the United States of America in some special sense *owns* the world, and watch what you say, buster, or we'll start asking whose side you're on." ["Minority Report," *Nation*, 5/25/85]

Blasphemy

" . . . Nobody should shrink from the accusation of blasphemy. It is a term of moral blackmail, used by the dogmatic to put an end to discussion." ["Minority Report," *Nation*, 3/13/89]

"Almost every historic battle for free expression, from Socrates to Galileo, has begun as a struggle over what is and is not 'blasphemy.'" ["Assassins of the Mind," *Vanity Fair*, February 2009]

Bloomberg, Michael

"But in the New York of Mayor Bloomberg, there are laws that are not possible to obey, and that nobody can respect, and that are enforced by arbitrary power. . . . Tyranny can be petty. And 'petty' is not just Bloomberg's middle name. It is his name." ["I Fought the Law," *Vanity Fair*, February 2004]

"May he one day be cornered in the schoolyard at recess, and without his team of hired toadies and informers, and taught the lesson of a lifetime." ["I Fought the Law," *Vanity Fair*, February 2004]

Blumenthal, Sidney

"If I hadn't had some relish for the ironic contrast between the sublime and the ridiculous, I would never have become a friend of Sidney Blumenthal's in the first place, and would never have been pushed to the length that this friendship eventually required of me: a decision to testify that a president who was certifiably filthy in small things might deserve to be arraigned on larger matters also." ["Thinking Like an Apparatchik," *Atlantic Monthly*, July/August 2003]

"And one could not avoid sometimes hearing Blumenthal, in his hard-boiled mode, speaking rather alarmingly of Chicago relatives who knew what was what and how to fix things, even people. I admit that I thought of this as a bit of a pose, because his general appeal depended so much on his almost foppish manner and tenue and also on his happy resemblance to the young Christopher Reeve." ["Thinking Like an Apparatchik," *Atlantic Monthly*, July/August 2003]

Bohemia

"The life of bohemia, of the small café and the little bar that never quite closes, is essential to cultural production. It may seem like a small thing. It doesn't add very much to the GNP. But if you take it away, you may not know what you've lost until it's too late." ["Tobacco, Smoking, and Insider Trading," *Cato Policy Report*, March/April 2005]

Bohemian Lifestyle

"I always knew that there's a risk in the bohemian lifestyle, and I decided to take it because, whether it's an illusion or not—I don't think it is—it helped my concentration, it stopped me [from] being bored, [and] stopped other people [from] being boring, to some extent. It would keep me awake. It would make me want the evening to go on longer, to prolong the conversation, to enhance the moment. If I was asked, would I do it again, the answer is probably yes. I'd have quit earlier, possibly, hoping to get away with the whole thing. Easy for me to say, of course, [but] not very nice for my children to hear." ["Q&A with Christopher Hitchens," C-SPAN, 1/14/11 (first aired: 1/23/11)]

Bojaxhiu, Agnes [See: Mother Teresa]

Bolton, John

"The nice thing about Bolton, you have to say, is that he's been described by the North Koreans as a beast in human shape." [*Hardball with Chris Matthews*, MSNBC, 4/26/05]

Bond, James

" . . . The central paradox of the classic Bond stories is that, although superficially devoted to the Anglo-American war against communism, they are full of contempt and resentment for America and Americans. And not just political contempt, or the penis envy of a declining power for a burgeoning one, but cultural contempt as well. And not just with cultural contempt in general, but more specifically disgust about America's plebeian interest in sex and consumerism, the two Bond staples." ["Bottoms Up," *Atlantic Monthly*, April 2006]

"Fleming once confessed that he hoped to 'take the story along so fast that nobody would notice the idiosyncrasies.' Fat chance. His 'idiosyncrasies' jut out like Tatiana Romanova's ass." ["Bottoms Up," *Atlantic Monthly*, April 2006]

Books

"In this Lilliputian world, which is chiefly written about by correspondents and practitioners who have every interest in keeping the clichés alive, it is only exceptionally that a genuine political book is written, or indeed read." ["Choosing Between Clichés," *Times Literary Supplement*, 6/25/82]

"The need for the programmatic book is still felt most keenly on the left of centre." ["Choosing Between Clichés," *Times Literary Supplement*, 6/25/82]

"I rate this book [*The Politics of Change*, by William Rodgers] as the least amusing of the many SDP [Social Democratic Party] volumes; less weighty even than David Owen's and much less hilarious than Shirley Williams's. In terms of pith, it ranks with Jaroslav Hasek's famous manifesto for 'The Party of Moderate Progress Within the Bounds of the Law.'" ["Choosing Between Clichés," *Times Literary Supplement*, 6/25/82]

"An unread book is an unendorsed one. . . ." ["The Chorus and Cassandra," *Grand Street*, Autumn 1985]

"No reviewer, however desperate, should ever say of a book that it cannot be put down. It is such a cliché, and it puts too much of a strain on the credulity of a reader." ["Collected Thoughts on the Evolution of War," *Newsday*, 3/30/88]

" . . . The notion of Great Books, when 'cored,' gets reduced to Great Names." ["The Toy Canon," *Harper's*, June 1988]

"But America is haunted by the search for the Great American Novel, or GAM, and remains haunted by it, even if Michael Herr does say so." ["Excuse Me But I Think You Just Dropped This Name," *Evening Standard*, 12/11/97]

"Take the thirst of the blue-chip critics for a new subject or a new author, add the quest for the GAM [Great American Novel] and stir in the nervous appetites of publishers, and you can have a ready-made best-seller." ["Excuse Me But I Think You Just Dropped This Name," *Evening Standard*, 12/11/97]

" . . . The fact that a book has won every garland before the actual customers have even got hold of it is not on its own a proof or a sign that the novel itself is no good." ["Excuse Me But I Think You Just Dropped This Name," *Evening Standard*, 12/11/97]

"The great thing about writing a book is that it brings you into contact with people whose opinions you should have canvassed before you ever pressed pen to paper. They write to you. They telephone you. They come to your bookstore events and give you things to read that you should have read already. It's this dialectical process that makes me glad I chose the profession I did: a free education that goes on for a lifetime." ["Finding Morals Under Empty Heavens," *Science & Spirit*, July/August 2007]

Borat
"Among the 'cultural learnings of America for make benefit glorious nation of Kazakhstan' is the discovery that Americans are almost pedantic in their hospitality and politesse. . . . The only people who are flat-out rude and patronizing to our curious foreigner are the stone-faced liberal Amazons of the Veteran Feminists of America." ["Kazakh Like Me," *Slate*, 11/13/06]

Boredom and Bores
"Properly deployed, the fear of boredom can keep a man going for a lifetime making him a useful danger to all those who surround him." [Introduction to *Money for Old Rope*, by Charles Glass (New York: Picador Books, 1992), ix]

" . . . If you really care about a serious cause or a deep subject, you may have to be prepared to be boring about it." [*Letters to a Young Contrarian* (New York: Basic Books, 2001), 122]

" . . . Barricades and Bastilles are not everyday occurrences. It's important to be able to recognise and seize crux moments when they do appear, but much of the time one is faced with quotidian tasks and routines. There's an art and a science to these things; the art consists in trying to improvise more inventive means of breaking a silence and the science consists in trying to make the periods of silence bearable." [*Letters to a Young Contrarian* (New York: Basic Books, 2001), 125]

Bork, Robert
"Whatever the Framers may have intended, it doesn't seem that they can have wanted a morally deaf and self-centered dreamer placed on the Supreme Court as the prime Constitutional legacy of those great jurists Ronald Reagan and Ed Meese." ["Reflections on the Bork Nomination," *Newsday*, 11/08/89]

Born Again
"If a guy believes he has been born again, it's reasonable to assume that he will believe anything." ["The Lord and the Intellectuals," *Harper's*, July 1982]

Bosnia
"If America's answer to the Bosnians is 'No, we can't see a reason to discourage the destruction of Sarajevo or Dubrovnik,' then the antiwar movement is entitled to call for America's complete and unilateral disarmament." ["Minority Report," *Nation*, 9/21/92]

" . . . The indifference to Bosnia must have to do with the fact that the victims are part Muslim, part secular, part cosmopolitan but above all powerless. Which is precisely why anyone with the least self-respect as an internationalist must be on their side." ["Minority Report," *Nation*, 5/24/93]

" . . . When did anyone in the administration even attempt to educate or motivate Americans about the Bosnian cause? All we got was the usual reflexive drumroll about possible military commitment in a nightmarish-sounding place that might as well have been 'Brosnia.'" ["Betrayal Becomes Farce," *Washington Post*, 8/15/93]

"The Bosnians asked for the right to defend themselves, and were denied even that. So the pragmatic arguments should be tempered with humility, as we come to the realization that the Bosnians would have been better off with no American pledges at all. They, too, are learning that Bill Clinton's indecision is final." ["Betrayal Becomes Farce," *Washington Post*, 8/15/93]

"When will our anti-interventionists protest the use of force to mutilate Bosnia rather than preserve it?" ["Minority Report," *Nation*, 3/07/94]

"Bosnia has been, and is, a moral and political crisis. An element of shame is involved in merely *watching* such things happen." ["The Death of a Nation," *Washington Post*, 3/20/94]

"If by now you don't think the attempted genocide in Bosnia in the early nineties was a moral crisis, you never will." ["Signature Sontag," *Vanity Fair*, March 2000]

"I was secretly relieved that none of the Kissingerites was signing pro-Bosnian statements, though even if they had I would still have signed them myself." ["How I Became a Neoconservative," *La Règle du Jeu*, 9/15/05]

"In Bosnia . . . I was brought to the abrupt admission that, if the majority of my former friends got their way about non-intervention, there would be another genocide on European soil." [*Hitch-22* (New York: Twelve, 2010), 415]

"In order to be clear: to say that the United States was bombing 'Yugoslavia' seemed to me false. To say that a dictatorial and expansionist Serbia had been bombing the rest of Yugoslavia seemed to be true." [*Hitch-22* (New York: Twelve, 2010), 416]

Bradley, Bill

"Bill Bradley—boring and pompous and tenth-rate but used to play basketball and take showers with African Americans." ["Diary," *London Review of Books*, 1/06/00]

Brave New World

"He [George Orwell] didn't get around to reviewing *Brave New World* until July 1940, when Britain seemed to have more urgent problems than the supposed nightmare of too much free sex and narcosis." [Foreword to *Brave New World*, by Aldous Huxley (New York: HarperCollins, 2004), ix]

Bribery

"When estimating the propensity of anyone to take money or gifts, one must also balance the propensity of a regime to offer them." ["Unmitigated Galloway," *Weekly Standard*, 5/30/05]

Brideshead Revisited

"*Brideshead Revisited* is not a comedy of social manners, or a tract. It is not the intellectual's *Upstairs, Downstairs*. It is not a bland celebration of the English country house. It is an imperfect, often awkward, but finally haunting rendition of a national myth." ["Total Waugh," *Nation*, 1/23/82]

Britain

"The British seem to need saving from their own mistakes about every ten years or so." ["The Way to Rescue Britain," *New York Times*, 7/04/79]

"The idea of Britain as a family with the queen at its head and various colonies as its junior relatives has never looked all that convincing. It tended to feature more as propaganda than reality even in the good old days. Now it's a joke in bad taste." ["This Thatchered Land, This England," *Nation*, 7/19/80–7/26/80]

" . . . There is a general feeling that Britain has been denied her special and proper standing in the world over the last twenty years. But until Thatcher, most politicians were too embarrassed to make any capital out of the Union Jack. There are no reliable reports on whether or not this enhanced national pride has made the unemployed feel any better." ["This Thatchered Land, This England," *Nation*, 7/19/80–7/26/80]

"It has been Britain's role to provide, between George Smiley and James Bond, the only element of romance in the generally tawdry and brutish business of the Cold War." ["Minority Report," *Nation*, 9/12/87]

"Neither the English/British nor their foreign admirers and rivals know quite what the country is called." [*The Monarchy: A Critique of Britain's Favorite Fetish* (London: Chatto & Windus Ltd, 1990), 4]

"Too many crucial things about this country turn out to be highly recommended because they are 'invisible.' There is the 'hidden hand' of the free market, the 'unwritten' Constitution, the 'invisible earnings' of the financial service sector, the 'magic' of monarchy, and the 'mystery' of the Church and its claim to the interpretation of revealed truth. When we do get as far as the visible or the palpable, too much of it is deemed secret." [*The Monarchy: A Critique of Britain's Favorite Fetish* (London: Chatto & Windus Ltd, 1990), 40]

"It is time that the country grew up and got itself a name, instead of titling itself after a ramshackle political compromise ('UK' has come to have all the resonance of 'United Arab Emirates')." [Quoted in "Should We Scrap Our Royals?," *Daily Express*, 3/12/96]

British Empire
"In point of fact, the United States went to some trouble to acquire the British Empire. . . . Perhaps it was inevitable that America would hanker after the outward pomp, form, show, and style as well." ["Minority Report," *Nation*, 11/23/85]

"I don't care about the loss of the British Empire and feel that the United States did Britain—but not itself—a large favor by helping to dispossess the British of their colonies." ["The Medals of His Defeats," *Atlantic Monthly*, April 2002]

"It can be said for 'receivership' that, painful though it was, it spared Britain the protracted misery endured by Belgium, Holland, France, and Portugal during the course of decolonization. Suez was a textbook case of shambles and humiliation, but at least it was brief and decisive. There was no bloody, drawn-out torture of the Algerian or Angolan variety. This was not just because, as many British commentators believe, the Empire was wound up with relative humanity and dispatch. It was because Britain, unlike her European imperial rivals, had the option of a partial merger with another empire, linked through kinship and alliance in war." [*Blood, Class and Empire* (New York: Nation Books, 2004), 261]

"The empire on which the sun never set was also the empire on which the gore never dried." ["Scoundrel Time," *Vanity Fair*, March 2006]

Broaddrick, Juanita
"She did not want to be exposed, and she did not expect to be believed. Finally—and very importantly—she didn't 'go public.' She was made public." ["The Clinton Swamp," *Nation*, 3/29/99]

"If Juanita Broaddrick is not telling the truth, then she is either an especially cruel and malicious liar, who should at a minimum be sued for defamation, or a delusional woman who should be seeking professional help." [*No One Left to Lie To* (New York: Verso, 2000), 114]

Brock, David
" . . . He is incapable of recognizing the truth, let alone of telling it." ["The Real David Brock," *Nation*, 5/27/02]

" . . . David Brock: a young man who could not get himself believed even when he claimed to be a liar." [Introduction to *Left Hooks, Right Crosses: A Decade of Political Writing*, ed. Christopher Caldwell and Christopher Hitchens (New York: Nation Books, 2002), 208]

Buchanan, Patrick J.
"I do not think he is a Nazi. He is a solid, homegrown McCarthyite with proto-fascist tendencies. (He does not think that the Jews killed his Christ, but he has the stout patrolman's suspicion that they may not have told us everything they know.)" ["Minority Report," *Nation*, 10/15/90]

" . . . When he doesn't 'think with the blood,' he thinks with his sect." ["Buchanan's Twisted History," *Nation*, 11/01/99]

"Some things may be true even if Pat Buchanan says them. . . ." ["Our Rigged Elections," *Nation*, 11/15/99]

Buckley Jr., William F.
"The old defender of Joe McCarthy and Barry Goldwater has more common sense than Clinton and Gore combined." ["Minority Report," *Nation*, 11/14/94]

"The late William F. Buckley Jr. was a man of incessant labor and productivity, with a slight allowance made for that saving capacity for making it appear easy." ["A Man of Incessant Labor," *Weekly Standard*, 3/10/08]

"William F. Buckley Jr. was never solemn except or unless on purpose, and seldom if ever flippant where witty would do, and in saying this I hope I pay him the just tribute that is due to a serious man." ["A Man of Incessant Labor," *Weekly Standard*, 3/10/08]

Buddhism
"'Make me one with everything.' So goes the Buddhist's humble request to the hot-dog vendor." [*God Is Not Great* (New York: Twelve, 2007), 198]

Bureaucracy
"Kicking the old bureaucrat . . . everybody should be in favor of that, especially intelligence bureaucrats." [*Hardball with Chris Matthews*, MSNBC, 4/26/05]

Burke, Edmund
" . . . The man often misrepresented as the father of modern conservatism. . . ." ["The Limits of Democracy," *Vanity Fair*, September 2001]

"Whatever view one takes of Burke's deepening pessimism and dogmatic adherence to the virtues of Church and King, whether in Britain or France, the fact is that after the summer of 1791 the Jacobins did their best to prove him right." [*Thomas Jefferson: Author of America* (New York: HarperCollins, 2005), 85]

Burr, Aaron

"He was well able to make friends, and enemies, for life." [*Thomas Jefferson: Author of America* (New York: HarperCollins, 2005), 121]

Bush, George H. W.

"He's got a very irritating name, and he's a very irritating guy." ["Persian Gulf War," C-SPAN, 2/04/91]

"I believe that President Bush will do many stupid things in order to avoid looking stupid." [*Crossfire*, CNN, 2/21/91]

"I don't trust the record of a proven hostage trader and arms dealer like George Bush. . . . I don't trust him either as the future arbiter of all border disputes in the Middle East and the controller of the government of Iraq—a role to which he has no right." [*McLaughlin's One on One*, 2/22/91]

"I certainly do think the guy from *Wayne's World* would be a better president than George Bush." ["Events in the News," C-SPAN, 3/23/92]

"George Bush . . . [has] nothing between his ears but perfectly fresh air." [CNN, 5/21/92]

Bush, George H. W. and the Gulf War

"And may George Bush someday understand that a president cannot confect a principled call to war—'hostages,' 'Hitler,' 'ruthless dictator,' 'naked aggression'—when matters of principle have never been the issue for him and his type." ["Why We Are Stuck in the Sand," *Harper's*, January 1991]

"[President Bush] has told the Soviet Union, very coldly, in effect, that their assistance is not welcome, is determined, in other words, to prove, though people are still amazingly reluctant to see it, that this is not about the emancipation of Kuwait—it's about the establishment of who's in charge over Iraq. And, therefore, there must be, at any cost, a final confrontation with Saddam Hussein." [*McLaughlin's One on One*, 2/22/91]

"Having called the nation to war in the name of the most exalted precepts, Bush only waited a matter of days to convert the result into a piece of transparent *realpolitik*." ["Washington Diary," *London Review of Books*, 8/20/92]

"With Bush, you could have both imperialism *and* fascism: American and Saudi power restored and the Kuwaiti monarchy returned to power, with a chastened Saddam Hussein allowed to keep his own throne and bluntly admonished to remember from now on who was the boss. This was the very worst of both worlds." [*Hitch-22* (New York: Twelve, 2010), 292]

Bush Administration (1989–1993)

"The first months of the Bush regime have sunk everybody into such a coma of boredom and disgust that even jokes about the 'thousand points of light' have become wearisome." ["Minority Report," *Nation*, 5/08/89]

"The Bush administration uses strong measures to ensure weak government abroad and has enfeebled democratic government at home. The reasoned objection must be that this is a dangerous and dishonest pursuit, in which the wealthy gamblers have become much too accustomed to paying their bad debts with the blood of others." ["Why We Are Stuck in the Sand," *Harper's*, January 1991]

Bush, George W.

"What did he do to be shorn at birth of his Herbert?" ["Bush's Death Watch," *Nation*, 8/23/99–8/30/99]

"Much nodding is required at his public events, as sympathetic but baffled audiences do their decent best to show that they know what he thinks he meant to say." ["In Dog We Trust," *Evening Standard*, 9/14/00]

"He's unusually incurious, abnormally unintelligent, amazingly inarticulate, fantastically uncultured, extraordinarily uneducated, and apparently quite proud of all these things." [*Hardball with Chris Matthews*, MSNBC, 10/30/00]

" . . . One of the most mediocre candidates in U.S. history." ["Dirty Rotten Scoundrels," *Observer*, 11/12/00]

" . . . He is the least smart guy ever to have sought the office; a dingbat and a stumbler and a dyslexic and a former piss-artist who has the same chance of finding his own rear end with both hands as he once had of parking his car without scraping a wall." ["Kelsey for President," *Evening Standard*, 1/23/01]

"George Bush chokes on a pretzel while gaping at the television screen, and comes away with a loud blush on his cheek. What a free gift that would once have been. I can do the routine in my sleep: since he utters chunks of twisted and convoluted matter, it's no wonder that he ingests the raw material before spewing it." ["Hey, I'm Doing My Best," *Observer*, 1/20/02]

"Only the other day, he assured an audience of rich people that 'not over my dead body will they raise your taxes.' This amazing mangling of an easy cliché could only invite the question: well, then, Mr. President, over whose cadaver will those taxes be increased?" ["Hey, I'm Doing My Best," *Observer*, 1/20/02]

"A year or so ago, George Walker Bush looked like a sorry second act to George Herbert Walker Bush (and I was the origin of the unkind remark about the cruel circumcision of his Herbert)." ["Hey, I'm Doing My Best," *Observer*, 1/20/02]

"To this president, it is an axiom that the rich are the means of elevating the poor, and that it is therefore the rich who need elevation." ["Hey, I'm Doing My Best," *Observer*, 1/20/02]

"His vices are . . . the vices of a provincial American conservative who preferred oil-men as friends, or even oilmen to friends." ["Hey, I'm Doing My Best," *Observer*, 1/20/02]

"I have never met anybody, even among the dimmest of my students, who wouldn't in some ways be better qualified to be president of the United States." ["My Dimmest Student Is Better Qualified to Be the President of the United States," *Mirror*, 9/11/02]

"I think his simple-mindedness is a virtue, in a sense. He's not going to have his mind changed by the last person he spoke to." [Quoted in "Christopher Hitchens: Off the Cuff, in His Own Words," *Georgetowner*, 5/27/04]

"President Bush is accused of taking too many lazy vacations. (What *is* that about, by the way? Isn't he supposed to be an unceasing planner for future aggressive wars?)" ["Unfairenheit 9/11," *Slate*, 6/21/04]

"It's [been] quite a few years now since George W. Bush took down the Democratic Party's then-favorite daughter, Ann Richards, as governor of Texas. Since then, he has regularly beaten every Democrat who has run against him. But this hasn't prevented many supposedly clever people from continually underestimating him. And now look what he's done: won the popular vote, cleaned up the electoral college vote, increased his party's hold on both Houses, while enabling a successful election in Afghanistan and fighting to hold one in Iraq. What an idiot!" ["Not So Dumb Then?," *Mirror*, 11/11/04]

"His eyes are so close together he could use a monocle." [*Real Time with Bill Maher*, HBO, 9/23/05]

"One recalls the governor of Texas who, asked if the Bible should also be taught in Spanish, replied that 'if English was good enough for Jesus, then it's good enough for me.' Rightly are the simple so called." [*God Is Not Great* (New York: Twelve, 2007), 110]

Bush, George W. and Alcohol

"Bush, if anything, follows the pattern of many Christian moralizers by overstating how bad he was, and how close to the Devil's claws. One DUI, one face-off with his father (the famous *mano a mano* episode), and a few confrontations with the lady of the house. You call that serious drinking?" ["The Teetotal Effect," *Vanity Fair*, August 2004]

"That Bush did not surrender to the need for a colossal bourbon on September 11 stands, I think, to his credit." ["The Teetotal Effect," *Vanity Fair*, August 2004]

Bush, George W. and Secularism

"George Bush may subjectively be a Christian, but he—and the U.S. armed forces—have objectively done more for secularism than the whole of the American agnostic community combined and doubled." ["Bush's Secularist Triumph," *Slate*, 11/09/04]

Bush, George W. and September 11, 2001

"In this society, anybody can be president. And this particular anybody has happened to match an hour in which it is precisely the ordinary people of the country who have behaved with distinction." ["Hey, I'm Doing My Best," *Observer*, 1/20/02]

"Apart from one foolish slip, where he used the crass word 'crusade,' he was, if anything, too immaculate in his deference to Muslim sensitivities at home and abroad." ["Hey, I'm Doing My Best," *Observer*, 1/20/02]

"The president was sitting awkwardly on an infant-classroom chair in Florida when he got the news from New York and Washington. He got it on camera. No chief executive has ever looked so small and shrunken in public. That image has become his and America's metaphor." ["My Dimmest Student Is Better Qualified to Be the President of the United States," *Mirror*, 9/11/02]

"He remembered to say, in the ghastly early days of the rubble and the stench, that America's enemies always made the mistake of confusing freedom with weakness. A noble thought, but his envoys abroad, and his cops at home, make that blunder all the time." ["My Dimmest Student Is Better Qualified to Be the President of the United States," *Mirror*, 9/11/02]

"His first post-attack speeches were almost herbivorous in their timidity. He didn't hit Afghanistan for almost a month. He found a voice only when talking to rescue workers in New York, and if you can't sound macho when denouncing al-Qaeda and the Taliban on a mass American grave, you ought not to be president at all." ["The Teetotal Effect," *Vanity Fair*, August 2004]

Bush Administration (2001–2009)

"Pound for pound of brainpower, Karl Rove and Paul Wolfowitz can blow most liberals straight out of the water. Fact." ["Not So Dumb Then?," *Mirror*, 11/11/04]

Byron, Lord

"He meant what he said and will be remembered as one of the very few Englishmen who thought to ask what Greek emotion might be. At a period when every other participant in the argument was disputing the interest rate on sculpture and asking after the well-being and security of Lord Elgin, Byron had a sense of the Parthenon. In this respect he was more modern, as well as more 'romantic,' than his contemporaries." [*The Parthenon Marbles: The Case for Reunification* (New York: Verso, 2008), 54]

California

"All right, you say, this is California; what can you expect? They think they'll be young and beautiful forever, even though most of them aren't even young and beautiful now." ["We Know Best," *Vanity Fair*, May 2001]

Camera

"The ambition of the camera, to approximate as nearly as possible to reality, has some distance to travel before it's vindicated. We're still being shielded more than we're being exposed. . . ." ["Preview of Coming Attractions: Sontag Looks at Images of War," *New York Observer*, 3/17/03]

Cameron, David

"He seems content-free to me. Never had a job, except in PR, and it shows. People ask, 'What do you think of him?' My answer is: he doesn't make me think." [Quoted in George Eaton, "Interview: Christopher Hitchens," *New Statesman*, 7/12/10]

Canada

"Everybody knows that there's lots of spare room in Canada, combined with a disagreeable tendency to whinge." ["Casting Bread on the Senators," *Spectator*, 5/31/86]

"Say 'Toronto' or 'Ontario' and the immediate thought associations are with a somewhat blander version of North America: a United States with a welfare regime and a more polite street etiquette, and the additionally reassuring visage of Queen Elizabeth on the currency." ["The Blair-Hitch Project," *Vanity Fair*, February 2011]

Cancer

"I have more than once in my time woken up feeling like death. But nothing prepared me for the early morning last June when I came to consciousness feeling as if I were actually shackled to my own corpse. . . . Any movement, however slight, required forethought and planning." ["Topic of Cancer," *Vanity Fair*, September 2010]

" . . . An official met for the first time may abruptly sink his fingers into your neck. That's how I discovered that my cancer had spread to my lymph nodes, and that one of these deformed beauties—located on my right clavicle, or collarbone—was big enough to be seen and felt. It's not at all good when your cancer is 'palpable' from the outside." ["Topic of Cancer," *Vanity Fair*, September 2010]

"In one way, I suppose, I have been 'in denial' for some time, knowingly burning the candle at both ends and finding that it often gives a lovely light. But for precisely that reason, I can't see myself smiting my brow with shock or hear myself whining about how it's all so unfair: I have been taunting the Reaper into taking a free scythe in my direction and have now succumbed to something so predictable and banal that it bores even me." ["Topic of Cancer," *Vanity Fair*, September 2010]

"Of course my book hit the best-seller list on the day that I received the grimmest of news bulletins, and for that matter the last flight I took as a healthy-feeling person (to a fine, big audience at the Chicago Book Fair) was the one that made me a million-miler on United Airlines, with a lifetime of free upgrades to look forward to. But irony is my business, and I just can't see any ironies here: would it be less poignant to get cancer on the day that my memoirs were remaindered as a box-office turkey, or that I was bounced from a coach-class flight and left on the tarmac?" ["Topic of Cancer," *Vanity Fair*, September 2010]

"To the dumb question 'Why me?' the cosmos barely bothers to return the reply: Why not?" ["Topic of Cancer," *Vanity Fair*, September 2010]

"You've heard it all right. People don't *have* cancer: they are reported to be battling cancer. No well-wisher omits the combative image: You can beat this. It's even in obituaries for cancer losers, as if one might reasonably say of someone that they died after a long and brave struggle with mortality." ["Topic of Cancer," *Vanity Fair*, September 2010]

"I sometimes wish I were suffering in a good cause, or risking my life for the good of others, instead of just being a gravely endangered patient. Allow me to inform you, though, that when you sit in a room with a set of other finalists, and kindly people bring a huge transparent bag of poison and plug it into your arm, and you either read or don't read a book while the venom sack gradually empties itself into your system, the image of the ardent soldier or revolutionary is the very last one that will occur to you. You feel swamped with passivity and impotence: dissolving in powerlessness like a sugar lump in water." ["Topic of Cancer," *Vanity Fair*, September 2010]

"These are my first raw reactions to being stricken. I am quietly resolved to resist bodily as best I can, even if only passively, and to seek the most advanced advice. My heart and blood pressure and many other registers are now strong again: indeed, it occurs to me that if I didn't have such a stout constitution I might have led a much healthier life thus far." ["Topic of Cancer," *Vanity Fair*, September 2010]

"If you maintain that god awards the appropriate cancers, you must also account for the numbers of infants who contract leukemia." ["Unanswerable Prayers," *Vanity Fair*, October 2010]

" . . . My so far uncancerous throat . . . is not *at all* the only organ with which I have blasphemed." ["Unanswerable Prayers," *Vanity Fair*, October 2010]

" . . . Why not cancer of the brain? As a terrified, half-aware imbecile, I might even scream for a priest at the close of business, though I hereby state while I am still lucid that the entity thus humiliating itself would not in fact be 'me.' (Bear this in mind, in case of any later rumors or fabrications.)" ["Unanswerable Prayers," *Vanity Fair*, October 2010]

"Of the astonishing and flattering number of people who wrote to me when I fell so ill, very few failed to say one of two things. Either they assured me that they wouldn't offend me by offering prayers, or they tenderly insisted that they would pray anyway. . . . [There] are some quite reputable Catholics, Jews, and Protestants who think that I might in some sense of the word be worth saving. The Muslim faction has been quieter." ["Unanswerable Prayers," *Vanity Fair*, October 2010]

" . . . What if I pulled through and the pious faction contentedly claimed that their prayers had been answered? That would somehow be irritating." ["Unanswerable Prayers," *Vanity Fair*, October 2010]

" . . . As often as I am encouraged to 'battle' my own tumor, I can't shake the feeling that it is the cancer that is making war on me." ["Tumortown," *Vanity Fair*, November 2010]

" . . . In Tumortown you sometimes feel that you may expire from sheer *advice*." ["Tumortown," *Vanity Fair*, November 2010]

"Cancer victimhood contains a permanent temptation to be self-centered and even solipsistic." ["Miss Manners and the Big C," *Vanity Fair*, December 2010]

Capital Punishment
" . . . Capital punishment strikes directly at democracy and due process. It can't be coincidence that it is used most frequently in countries that consider the citizen to be the property of the state." ["Minority Report," *Nation*, 8/29/87]

"Racist, brutalizing, antidemocratic, sadistic, and thoughtless—is it any wonder that this special symbol of primitivism is undergoing a recrudescence in the era of Edwin Meese?" ["Minority Report," *Nation*, 8/29/87]

"On January 5, a confessed sadist and child-slayer named Wesley Allan Dodd was placed on a trap door with a length of lubricated rope around his hooded neck and dropped into the air. This happened because *he* demanded death, and because *he* selected that very specialized means of exit. . . . In a really good rope-and-ladder session between consenting adults, the payoff is erection and ejaculation for both parties." ["Minority Report," *Nation*, 2/01/93]

"My case against capital punishment is simply this: The state does not have the right to decide life and death questions." [Quoted in Bill Steigerwald and Bob Hoover, "Objectivity and Other Lies," *Pittsburgh Post-Gazette*, 4/27/97]

"See how the cameras dwelt on those semi-hysterical Babbitts after the McVeigh sentence, as they clasped and simpered and in general groped for 'closure.' Can there be anything more contemptible than the idea of capital punishment as therapy?" ["Dirty Stories," *Nation*, 7/07/97]

"The McVeigh jurors have since made a parade of their emotions, for all the world as if the decision to kill him was theirs alone. As they all knew perfectly well, any failure to give him the ultimate penalty would have exposed them to charges of differential race, class, and regional justice. The more you 'do' executions, the more you have to do them." ["Dirty Stories," *Nation*, 7/07/97]

"Adults sentenced to death in this country are almost always vicious creeps, pitiable failures, or innocent losers." ["Old Enough to Die," *Vanity Fair*, June 1999]

" . . . It is the practice itself that is unjust, rather than merely its—pardon the expression—anomalous execution." ["Bush's Death Trip," *Nation*, 3/06/00]

"In the case of the United States, we await a writer who can summon every nerve to cleanse the country of the filthy stain of the death penalty. Other priorities might seem at first to make larger claims, but there is probably no single change that would cumulatively amount to more than this one. Abolition would repudiate the heritage of racial bigotry and mob justice while simultaneously limiting the over-mighty state." [Foreword to *Unacknowledged Legislation* (New York: Verso, 2000), xvii]

"Something that has become an international as well as a national disgrace. Something that shames and besmirches the entire United States, something that is performed by the professionalized elite in the name of an assumed public opinion. In other words, something that melds the worst of elitism and the absolute foulest of populism." [Quoted in "The Future of the Public Intellectual: A Forum," *Nation*, 2/12/01]

"If the Founders had wanted to forbid capital punishment . . . they would have done so in plain words." [*Hitch-22* (New York: Twelve, 2010), 253]

Capitalism

" . . . The thirst of capital for profit is not so much a matter of greed as one of survival. Without it, the motor power of the system is lost." ["Monkey's Paw," *New Statesman*, 8/18/72]

"'But what will you put in its place?' A familiar question to any socialist, and on the face of it a formidable poser as well. It is extremely hard in the first instance to think of replacements for unemployment, racialism, war, poverty, exploitation, and oligarchy. But we'll probably think of something." ["Last Swing of the Crane," *New Statesman*, 10/06/72]

"The genius of the capitalist system lies in its inventive and creative nature—in its scorn for tradition, custom, and fetish. The menace of that same system occurs when it erects, by apparently voluntary labor, a thing beyond the control of its creators." ["Minority Report," *Nation*, 4/02/83]

"As a system of innovation and productivity it has no rival. But it compels people to combine in complex ways, and then tries to regulate the combination in simple ones. In other words, what is made or manufactured socially is still appropriated privately. Those who have capital, few though they are, can outvote those who have none. Investment decisions that have life-and-death consequences for everyone can be taken at the prompting of individual and unaccountable gain." ["Taking Socialism Seriously with Michael Harrington," *Newsday*, 7/19/89]

"There is something about capitalism that abhors not a vacuum but any nonvacuous square foot of the planet that hasn't yet succumbed. 'Free to choose' was once the simplistic marketeer slogan, but now it's more accurate to say that one is compelled to choose." ["Cartier Latin," *Nation*, 7/08/96]

"Our own contemporary world suggests that the energy of capital is not easily compatible with stasis." [Foreword to *Brave New World*, by Aldous Huxley (New York: HarperCollins, 2004), xvi]

" . . . Those who do think they've got a critique of capitalism turn out to be reactionaries. They prefer feudalism or agrarianism; they're pre-capitalists." [Quoted in "Christopher Hitchens," *Prospect Magazine*, May 2008]

" . . . Global capitalism now seems to be the only thing that is revolutionary. That's my Marxist way of looking at it." [Quoted in "Christopher Hitchens," *Prospect Magazine*, May 2008]

"Whether one adopts a moralistic or an analytic approach, there is scant doubt that capitalism continues to outmaneuver all attempts by wage earners to shift the odds in favor of shorter hours and more pay. In the story of the class struggle, it's invariably a case of one step forward and two steps back." ["The Revenge of Karl Marx," *Atlantic Monthly*, April 2009]

Carter, Jimmy

"Jimmy Carter, obeying the law that says you should 'Hang a Lantern on your Problem,' made a virtue of his lack of intimacy with the Democratic Establishment and his ignorance of Washington life. Carter loses points here only for taking his pose too far and acting as if he really believed it." ["Political Curve Balls Thrown from the Hill," *Newsday*, 8/31/88]

"A series of White House evenings with the likes of [Christopher] Lasch led to a lugubrious Carter speech in July 1979, about limits and stress and about there being more important things than money and consumption. Only one word of this address survived, and that was 'malaise.' The politics of moaning. Thanks a lot. After that, intellectuals were told to ask not what the president could do for them, but *exactly* what they could do for the president." ["What's Love Got to Do with It?," *Vanity Fair*, September 1993]

" . . . A corny, Southern, conscience-monger." ["Unthreatening of Owl Creek," *Times Literary Supplement*, 2/16/01]

Carter Administration (1977–1981)

" . . . The Carter administration could not tell a friend from an enemy." ["Peanut Envy," *Slate*, 5/21/07]

Carville, James and Mary Matalin

" . . . The bizarre marriage of Mary Matalin and James Carville, who actually contrived to run opposing presidential campaigns in 1992 while still, at the end of the day, proving that the two parties were essentially in bed together." ["Thinking Like an Apparatchik," *Atlantic Monthly*, July/August 2003]

Castro, Fidel

"People call him 'Fidel,' but I find I can't, since I don't know the guy." ["Havana Can Wait," *Vanity Fair*, March 2000]

"Fidel Castro has at least made it into the twenty-first century, but at the price of becoming a bloated and theatrical caricature." ["The Old Man," *Atlantic Monthly*, July/August 2004]

Catholic Church

"On his death, Pope John Paul was praised among other things for the number of apologies he had made. . . . This seemed to say that the church had mainly been wrong and often criminal in the past, but was now purged of its sin by confession and quite ready to be infallible all over again." [*God Is Not Great* (New York: Twelve, 2007), 193]

"State or no state, the church is a highly disciplined multinational corporation that allows little or no autonomy to its branches and can no more be the judge in its own cause than British Petroleum." ["Is the Vatican a Sovereign State?," *Slate*, 5/31/10]

Catholic Church and Abortion

"Question: Would the Pope favor aborting a fetus with a gay gene?" ["Forging the Magic Bullet," *Vanity Fair*, November 1993]

Catholic Church and Fascism

"Fascism—the precursor and model of National Socialism—was a movement that believed in an organic and corporate society, presided over by a leader or guide. (The 'fasces'—symbol of the 'lictors' or enforcers of ancient Rome—were a bundle of rods, tied around an axe, that stood for unity and authority.) Arising out of the misery and humiliation of the First World War, fascist movements were in favor of the defense of traditional values against Bolshevism, and upheld nationalism and piety. It is probably not a coincidence that they arose first and most excitedly in Catholic countries, and it is certainly not a coincidence that the Catholic Church was generally sympathetic to fascism as an idea." [*God Is Not Great* (New York: Twelve, 2007), 235]

Catholic Church and Nazism

"The Church badly needs a Holocaust saint, because whenever and wherever it could it helped Nazis and Fascists into power." ["Holy Men," *Nation*, 1/15/83]

"Believers are supposed to hold that the pope is the vicar of Christ on earth, and the keeper of the keys of Saint Peter. They are of course free to believe this, and to believe that god decides when to end the tenure of one pope or (more important) to inaugurate the tenure of another. This would involve believing in the death of an anti-Nazi pope, and the accession of a pro-Nazi one, as a matter of divine will, a few months before Hitler's invasion of Poland and the opening of the Second World War." [*God Is Not Great* (New York: Twelve, 2007), 240]

"Studying that war, one can perhaps accept that 25 percent of the SS were practicing Catholics and that no Catholic was ever even threatened with excommunication for participating in war crimes. (Joseph Goebbels *was* excommunicated, but that was earlier on, and he had after all brought it on himself for the offense of marrying a Protestant.)" [*God Is Not Great* (New York: Twelve, 2007), 240]

"The connection of the church to fascism and Nazism actually outlasted the Third Reich itself." [*God Is Not Great* (New York: Twelve, 2007), 241]

Catholic Scandals

" . . . The existence of a vast pedophile ring in the United States in the twenty-first century is something more than an affront to 'family values.'" ["Pedophilia's Double Standard," *Free Inquiry*, Summer 2002]

"The Roman Catholic Church . . . has been behaving as if, without the opportunity for sex with the underage, its whole ministry would collapse." ["Pedophilia's Double Standard," *Free Inquiry*, Summer 2002]

"In the very recent past, we have seen the Church of Rome befouled by its complicity with the unpardonable sin of child rape, or, as it might be phrased in Latin form, 'no child's behind left.'" [*God Is Not Great* (New York: Twelve, 2007), 4]

"When priests go bad, they go very bad indeed, and commit crimes that would make the average sinner pale. One might prefer to attribute this to sexual repression than to the actual doctrines preached, but then one of the actual doctrines preached is sexual repression." [*God Is Not Great* (New York: Twelve, 2007), 186]

"'Child abuse' is really a silly and pathetic euphemism for what has been going on: we are talking about the systematic rape and torture of children, positively aided and abetted by a hierarchy which knowingly moved the grossest offenders to parishes where they would be safer. Given what has come to light in modern cities in recent times, one can only shudder to think what was happening in the centuries where the church was above all criticism." [*God Is Not Great* (New York: Twelve, 2007), 228]

"The scandal is not the presence of pedophiles in the church, but the institutionalization of child-rape by the knowing protection and even promotion (by non-pedophiles) of those who are guilty of it." ["My Response to Benedict" (On Faith), *Washington Post* (online), 4/16/08]

"The Catholic Church has to spend almost as much time in apologizing for its past crimes against humanity as it has to spend money on compensating the living victims of its rape-and-torture policy toward children." [*Is Christianity Good for the World?* (Moscow, ID: Canon Press, 2008), 14]

"Nobody has yet been excommunicated for the rape and torture of children, but exposing the offense could get you into serious trouble. And this is the church that warns us against moral relativism!" ["The Great Catholic Cover-Up," *Slate*, 3/15/10]

"All it is good at is forgiving the criminals and ignoring the pleas of the victims." [*Morning Joe*, MSNBC, 3/30/10]

Ceausescu, Nicolae
"He was the perfect postmodern despot—a market Stalinist." ["On the Road to Timisoara," *Granta*, Spring 1990]

"Caligula once said that he wished the Roman mob had only one head so that he might decapitate them all at one stroke. The Romanian crowd wished only that the Ceausescus had had a million lives so that everyone could have a turn at killing them." ["On the Road to Timisoara," *Granta*, Spring 1990]

Celebrity
"All I know is that I've danced with a girl who's danced with a chap who's danced with the Princess of Wales." ["American Notes," *Times Literary Supplement*, 8/21/87]

" . . . The police are in the ghastly position of seeming either to favor celebrities or to be too hard on them." ["Curse of the Kennedys Alights on the Smith Boy," *Independent*, 4/07/91]

"For some time now, there has been no infamy in America and no notoriety. There is only celebrity." ["This Forlorn Chase for the Wrong Role Model," *Evening Standard*, 6/20/94]

"I have learned not to point and squeak and say: 'Look, isn't that the girl from *Dirty Dancing*!'" ["National Treasure," *London Review of Books*, 11/14/96]

Censorship

"Censorship is instituted precisely to mask distinctions . . . and to make sure that bad news can come only from the same source as good news, which is from on high." ["Minority Report," *Nation*, 9/04/89–9/11/89]

"Living under censorship is like being permanently hectored by a parrot and occasionally savaged by it. Be ready to denounce tomorrow what we made you affirm yesterday." ["Minority Report," *Nation*, 9/04/89–9/11/89]

"This has always been the essential absurdity of 'moral,' as opposed to 'political,' censorship: If the stuff does indeed have a tendency to deprave and corrupt, why then the most depraved and corrupt person must be the censor who keeps a vigilant eye upon it." ["Minority Report," *Nation*, 7/30/90–8/06/90]

"The viability of censorship depends on whom you grant the authority to be the censor." [Quoted in "Forbidden Thoughts: A Roundtable on Taboo Research," *American Enterprise*, January/February 1995]

"Moral endangerment comes from people with dirty minds, which censors have a tendency to possess." ["Let's Be Adult About Sex in the Movies," *Evening Standard*, 2/01/00]

"Censorship in wartime . . . usually turns out to be even more stupid than censorship in peacetime." ["Forcing Freedom," *Reason* magazine, August 2003]

Central Intelligence Agency

"Every CIA station loathes the press because the last thing it wants is a reporter whacked out by a pro-Western goon squad." ["Minority Report," *Nation*, 2/16/85]

"The CIA can do one thing: military coups." [Quoted in "'Don't Cross Over if You Have Any Intention of Going Back,'" *Common Review*, Summer 2005]

"The CIA got *everything* wrong before 9/11, and thereafter. It was conditioned by its own culture to see no evil." ["Rove Rage," *Slate*, 7/18/05]

"It's better to have no intelligence service at all than one that actively works against you." ["In Depth with Christopher Hitchens," C-SPAN, 9/02/07]

"Despite a string of exposures going back all the way to the Church Commission, the CIA cannot rid itself of the impression that it has the right to subvert the democratic process both abroad and at home. Its criminality and arrogance could perhaps have been partially excused if it had ever got anything right, but, from predicting the indefinite survival of the Soviet Union to denying that Saddam Hussein was going to invade Kuwait, our spymasters have a Clouseau-like record." ["Abolish the CIA," *Slate*, 12/10/07]

"The system is worse than useless—it's a positive menace. We need to shut the whole thing down and start again." ["Abolish the CIA," *Slate*, 12/10/07]

Certainty
"The person who is certain, and who claims divine warrant for his certainty, belongs now to the infancy of our species." [*God Is Not Great* (New York: Twelve, 2007), 11]

"It is not that there are no certainties, it is that it is an absolute certainty that there are no certainties." [*Hitch-22* (New York: Twelve, 2010), 420]

Chamberlain, Neville
"To call Chamberlain an appeaser in 1938 was to flatter him by presuming that his objective was the avoidance of war." ["Chamberlain: Collusion, Not Appeasement," *Monthly Review*, January 1995]

Change
"The stages by which one mutates or pupates from one identity to another are not always evident while they are being undergone." [*Hitch-22* (New York: Twelve, 2010), 239]

Charity
"The rich world likes and wishes to believe that someone, somewhere, is doing something for the Third World. For this reason, it does not inquire too closely into the motives or practices of anyone who fulfills, however vicariously, this mandate." [*The Missionary Position* (New York: Verso, 1995), 49]

"As ever, the true address of the missionary is to the self-satisfaction of the sponsor and the donor, and not to the needs of the downtrodden. Helpless infants, abandoned derelicts, lepers and the terminally ill are the raw material for demonstrations of compassion." [*The Missionary Position* (New York: Verso, 1995), 50]

"Charity . . . is a form of condescension." [*Hugh Hewitt Show*, 12/05/07]

"I just won't give a donation to those who hand out religious propaganda to the powerless and try to convert them with bowls of soup. A waste of money is the least one can say about that." ["Who Says the Nonreligious Don't Give?," *Free Inquiry*, April/May 2010]

" . . . One can't indefinitely do for somebody what he is reluctant to do for himself." ["All the Views Fit to Print," *Slate*, 11/01/10]

Chauvinism
"The stubborn persistence of chauvinism in our life and letters is or ought to be the proper subject for critical study, not the occasion for displays of shock." ["Something about the Poems: Larkin and 'Sensitivity,'" *New Left Review*, July 1993]

Checks and Balances
"'Checks and balances' refers to the exchange of bribes and emoluments on the floor of committee rooms." ["Minority Report," *Nation*, 6/17/91]

"Rightly is it said that our system is one of checks—and balances, too." ["The In-corporated Debates," *Nation*, 10/21/96]

Chemotherapy
"Chemotherapy isn't good for you. So when you feel bad, as I am feeling now, you think, 'Well, that is a good thing because it's supposed to be poison. If it's making the tumor feel this queasy, then I'm OK with it.'" [Interview with Melissa Block, *All Things Considered*, National Public Radio, 10/29/10]

Chicken Hawk
"The louder a man shouts for bombing and strafing, the less likely he is to have felt the weight of a pack." ["The Hawks with White Feathers," *Spectator*, 8/10/85]

"Best of all, from the esthetic point of view, is Sylvester Stallone himself. He dodged the draft in the most agreeable possible way, hiding in Switzerland as coach to a pri-vate school for girls." ["The Hawks with White Feathers," *Spectator*, 8/10/85]

"Look into the past of any rabid patriot of the moment—and you will find that they wangled a job at the base. There never was such a collection of bad knees, weak lungs, urgent academic priorities, or, as in the case of [Sylvester] Stallone, sheer bloody gall." ["The Hawks with White Feathers," *Spectator*, 8/10/85]

"Someone ought to point out that the term 'chicken-hawk' originated as a partic-ularly nasty term for a pederast or child molester: It has evidently not quite lost its association with sissyhood. It's a smear, in other words, and it is a silly smear. . . ." ["'Armchair General,'" *Slate*, 11/11/02]

Children
"The zombie kids we complain about are the result of a collapse—from hippie to mall rat—that has taken one generation of mutation to bring about." ["The Baby-Boomer Wasteland," *Vanity Fair*, January 1996]

"Normally, anything done in the name of 'the kids' strikes me as either slightly sentimental or faintly sinister—that redolence of moral blackmail that adheres to certain charitable appeals and certain kinds of politician. (Not for nothing is baby-kissing the synonym for public insincerity.)" ["Child-Proof," *Nation*, 6/24/96]

"I decline to use the word 'illegitimate' as a description of a baby. . . ." [*No One Left to Lie To* (New York: Verso, 2000), 2]

"The law prosecutes those who violate children, and it does so partly on behalf of children who haven't been violated yet. We take an individual instance, whoever the individuals happen to be, and we use it for precedent. And we do not know how lucky we are to be able to do so." ["Save the Children," *Slate*, 10/05/09]

"A cruel or rude child is a ghastly thing, but a cruel or brutal parent can do infinitely more harm." ["The New Commandments," *Vanity Fair*, April 2010]

". . . Nothing reminds one of impending extinction more than the growth of one's children, for whom room must be made, and who are in fact one's only hint of even a tincture of a hope of immortality." [*Hitch-22* (New York: Twelve, 2010), 5]

Children's Books

"I went and stationed myself in the children's book section of Doubleday in New York, where I kept a loitering vigil until I attracted too many glances." ["The Grimmest Tales," *Vanity Fair*, January 1994]

"There is a reason Twain and Kipling and Saki go on succeeding generation after generation, even more than the ghastly Brothers Grimm, and it is the same reason that motivates the bores and schoolmarms to try to repress them. Much to the discombobulation of respectable and tedious parents, their children quite like the idea of a mysterious uncle, and, given the choice, they will always pick the wicked one." ["The Grimmest Tales," *Vanity Fair*, January 1994]

China

"The antiquity and complexity and density of China as a subject means and has meant that many people have studied 'Chinese studies' rather than China itself." ["China: Big and Deep and Old and More," *Newsday*, 7/22/92]

"China's tormented history has meant a long vacillation between xenophobia on the one hand and a hunger for modernization and innovation on the other. Even the ostensibly internationalist Communist cadres were determined both to expunge the influence of foreign powers and to emulate and surpass their technology." ["China: Big and Deep and Old and More," *Newsday*, 7/22/92]

" . . . The 'one child' policy now followed in Communist China, where to the extent that the program is successful we will not only see a formerly clannish society where everyone is an only child but a formerly Marxist one that has no real cognate word for 'brotherhood.'" [Foreword to *Brave New World*, by Aldous Huxley (New York: HarperCollins, 2004), vii–viii]

Chirac, Jacques

"Here is a man who had to run for reelection last year in order to preserve his immunity from prosecution, on charges of corruption that were grave. Here is a man who helped Saddam Hussein build a nuclear reactor and who knew very well what he wanted it for. Here is a man at the head of France who is, in effect, openly for sale. He puts me in mind of the banker in Flaubert's 'L'Education Sentimentale': a man so habituated to corruption that he would happily pay for the pleasure of selling himself." ["The Rat That Roared," *Wall Street Journal*, 2/06/03]

"You can often tell a principled policy by the fact that Jacques Chirac opposes it." ["Countdown to War: Two Mirror Writers with Opposing Views," *Mirror*, 3/18/03]

Chomsky, Noam

" . . . The more Chomsky was vindicated [in the 1960s], the less he seemed to command 'respect.'" ["The Chorus and Cassandra," *Grand Street*, Autumn 1985]

"As a philosophical anarchist, Chomsky might dislike to have it said that he had 'done the state some service,' but he is a useful citizen in ways that his detractors are emphatically not." ["The Chorus and Cassandra," *Grand Street*, Autumn 1985]

"People ask why you don't see Noam Chomsky on the tube. It's not just flat-out bias so much as the fact that his views are literally unutterable in the time and format available." ["Buckley's Cease-Fire Line," *Nation*, 12/27/99]

"Regarding almost everything since Columbus as having been one continuous succession of genocides and land-thefts, he did not really believe that the United States of America was a good idea to begin with." [*Hitch-22* (New York: Twelve, 2010), 244]

Christ, Jesus

"If Jesus could heal a blind person he happened to meet, then why not heal blindness?" [*God Is Not Great* (New York: Twelve, 2007), 3]

"There were many deranged prophets roaming Palestine at the time, but this one reportedly believed himself, at least some of the time, to be god or the son of god." [*God Is Not Great* (New York: Twelve, 2007), 118]

"I can't hate anyone whose existence I don't really believe." [*Red Eye*, Fox News Channel, 5/12/07]

"Again, then, suppose that I grant the virgin birth and the resurrection. . . . These events, even if confirmed, would not prove that Jesus was the son of god. Nor would they prove the truth or morality of his teachings. . . . His miracles, if verified, would likewise leave him one among many shamans and magicians, some of them mentioned in the Old Testament, who could apparently work wonders by sorcery." [Introduction to *The Portable Atheist* (New York: Da Capo Press, 2007), xix]

"If you have a virgin for a mother, it doesn't prove anything about your doctrines. You could be born of a virgin and be a satanic imp, easily." [Quoted in Gregg LaGambina, "Christmas with Christopher Hitchens," *A. V. Club*, 12/20/07]

Christian Coalition

"The Christian Coalition is one of the most overrated forces in America, its main role being to give Frank Rich something to write about and to supply a Medusa's head to keep liberals in line behind Clinton and Gore." ["Bush's Death Trip," *Nation*, 3/06/00]

Christianity

"Once you concede that humanity possessed numerous truths and values before the Bible, you may as well admit that Christianity is just another religion." ["Umberto Umberto," *In These Times*, 1/30/85–2/05/85]

"Even the Christian image of the shepherd, which reduces the believer to a member of a flock, conveys the idea of guarding a human-organized and quasi-domesticated system from animal predators. And that, in turn, reminds us that the shepherd protects the sheep and the lambs not for their own good but the better to fleece and then to slay them." ["Political Animals," *Atlantic Monthly*, November 2002]

"But Christianity as a religion of peace and tolerance and forgiveness is not, superficially at least, compatible with ringing phrases about judgment and the sword: In order to believe in the apparently kindly and reassuring verses about taking no thought for the morrow, one had better have a lively sense of the second coming." ["America's Poet?," *Weekly Standard*, 7/05/04–7/12/04]

"There would have been no established Byzantine or Roman Christianity if the faith had not been spread and maintained and enforced by every kind of violence and cruelty and coercion." ["Papal Bull," *Slate*, 9/18/06]

"Of the thousands of possible desert religions there were, as with the millions of potential species there were, one branch happened to take root and grow. Passing through its Jewish mutations to its Christian form, it was eventually adopted for political reasons by the Emperor Constantine, and made into an official faith with—eventually—a codified and enforceable form of its many chaotic and contradictory books." [*God Is Not Great* (New York: Twelve, 2007), 185]

"One recalls the question that was asked by the Chinese when the first Christian missionaries made their appearance. If god has revealed himself, how is it that he has allowed so many centuries to elapse before informing the Chinese?" [*God Is Not Great* (New York: Twelve, 2007), 262]

"Everything about Christianity is contained in the pathetic image of 'the flock.'" [*Hitch-22* (New York: Twelve, 2010), 10]

Christians

"Half the time when you meet people who say they are churchgoing Christians, they don't know what they're supposed to believe, they don't believe all of it, they have a lot of doubt, and they go to church largely for social reasons." [Quoted in Gregg LaGambina, "Christmas with Christopher Hitchens," *A. V. Club*, 12/20/07]

Christmas

"The problem is not the grinches who steal Christmas. It's the grinches who celebrate it." ["Mention Christmas and Get Yourself Sued," *Evening Standard*, 12/22/95]

"I absolutely abominate absolutely everything about this season of the year. . . . The schools teach even less than usual and begin to rehearse dismal chants under the guidance of wan instructors. Workplaces are given over to paroxysms of repetitive celebration. And it's not just that attendance and observance are compulsory and conscripted (though that would be bloody bad enough). It's that *enthusiasm is compulsory too*. You can't just conform and get by. You are always being urged to join in. Of what does this remind me? Of the Leader's Birthday in some godawful one-party banana republic or people's democracy, that's what." ["China Syndrome," *Nation*, 1/13/97–1/20/97]

"And don't get me wrong. I'm not one to spoil children's fun by brutish literal-mindedness. I dress up as Santa with the best of them ('Mummy, Father Christmas has fallen down again')." ["Fairy Tales Can Come True . . . ," *Vanity Fair*, October 1997]

"I say 'Merry Christmas' to people I don't know, or to people I know are Christians. I say 'Happy Hanukkah' to people I know to be or suspect to be Jewish. And I don't say 'Happy Kwanzaa,' because I think African Americans get enough insults all year round." [Quoted in Gregg LaGambina, "Christmas with Christopher Hitchens," *A. V. Club*, 12/20/07]

"Most objectionable of all, the fanatics force your children to observe the Dear Leader's birthday, and so (this being the especial hallmark of the totalitarian state) you cannot bar your own private door to the hectoring, incessant noise, but must have it literally brought home to you by your offspring. Time that is supposed to be devoted to education is devoted instead to the celebration of mythical events." ["'Tis the Season to Be Incredulous," *Slate*, 12/15/08]

"Originally Christian, this devotional set-aside can now be joined by any other sectarian group with a plausible claim—Hanukkah or Kwanzaa—to a holy day that occurs near enough to the pagan winter solstice." ["'Tis the Season to Be Incredulous," *Slate*, 12/15/08]

"I don't mind if Christians honor the moment by displaying, and singing about, reindeer (a hard species to find in the greater Jerusalem/Bethlehem area). Same for the pine and fir trees that also don't grow in Palestine." ["It's Not the White Christmas House" (On Faith), *Washington Post* (online), 12/10/09]

Church
"Once the Church loses its monopoly and becomes just another competitor in the battle of ideas, it loses everything else that makes for the domination of faith." [*In These Times*, 11/16/83–11/22/83]

"For some reason, which I believe I can guess, the churches want control of people when or while they are most vulnerable or suggestible. If they can't get them in school, then they can get them when they are hungry, or frightened, or ill, or homeless, or unemployed. Same difference. Here's your gruel, and here's a tract." ["Return of the Salvation Army," *Free Inquiry*, Winter 2000–2001]

"Many services, in all denominations and among almost all pagans, are exactly designed to evoke celebration and communal fiesta, which is precisely why I suspect them." [*God Is Not Great* (New York: Twelve, 2007), 16]

" . . . There aren't enough churches in the country to hold the hordes who boast of attending." ["God Bless Me, It's a Best-Seller!," *Vanity Fair*, September 2007]

Church and State

" . . . The American Founding Fathers decided on a 'wall of separation' between church and state, *whether the Bible was true or not*. In other words, religious and even Christian though many of them were, they wanted to insure against any future religious demagogy and opportunism, and *for that purpose* counted their own faith as one among many. This essential and unprecedented maturity is what marks them off from their forerunners and their successors." ["Siding with Rushdie," *London Review of Books*, 10/26/89]

Church of England

"The headship of the Church of England—a church founded on the family values of Henry VIII and more or less consecrated to divorce and caprice—would be a bit of a laugh even if it still were what it most conspicuously is not: a national church." ["Away with Them and Their Overweening Power," *Independent*, 6/02/93]

Churchill, Winston

"Savior of the country, rock of national unity, guardian of the pure fount of majestic English prose, sworn foe of despotism—who did this guy think he was, a member of the House of Windsor?" ["Bulldog Mythology," *Guardian*, 6/16/95]

"If he has a titanic place in history, it is largely because he was instrumental in engaging the United States in two world wars, and thus acted as (inadvertent) midwife to the successor role of America as an imperial power." ["The Medals of His Defeats," *Atlantic Monthly*, April 2002]

"He failed to preserve his own empire, but succeeded in aggrandizing two much larger ones. He seems to have used crisis after crisis as an excuse to extend his own power. His petulant refusal to relinquish the leadership was the despair of postwar British Conservatives; in my opinion this refusal had to do with his yearning to accomplish something that 'history' had so far denied him—the winning of a democratic election. His declining years in retirement were a protracted, distended humiliation of celebrity-seeking and gross overindulgence." ["The Medals of His Defeats," *Atlantic Monthly*, April 2002]

" . . . Alone among his contemporaries, Churchill did not denounce the Nazi empire merely as a threat, actual or potential, to the British one. Nor did he speak of it as a depraved but possibly useful ally. He excoriated it as a wicked and nihilistic thing. That appears facile now, but was exceedingly uncommon then." ["The Medals of His Defeats," *Atlantic Monthly*, April 2002]

Churchill, Winston and Joseph Stalin

"In many of his communications and confidences one gets the distinct sense that he admired the great despot not in spite of his cruelty and absolutism but because of it." ["The Medals of His Defeats," *Atlantic Monthly*, April 2002]

Churchill Cult

"The Churchill cult has lasted too long, and still lasts too long. But in order for it to be dethroned, we will need to face recent Anglo-American history without self-pity and without neo-colonial nostalgia." ["Bulldog Mythology," *Guardian*, 6/16/95]

"The Churchill cult in England . . . is mild and reflective in comparison with the Churchill cult in the United States. . . . [T]he rest of us might wish that if the United States is going to stand for something, it (or its overpaid speechwriting class) would try to come up with some mobilizing rhetoric of its own." ["The Medals of His Defeats," *Atlantic Monthly*, April 2002]

Churchill Rhetoric

"Invested with the awesome grandeur and integrity of the 1940 resistance to Hitler, and gifted as few before or since with the power to make historic phrases, Churchill is morally irrefragable in American discourse, and can be quoted even more safely than Lincoln in that he was never a member of any American faction." [*Blood, Class and Empire* (New York: Nation Books, 2004), 180]

"An easy resort to a Churchillism can be a safe indication that the speaker is in a tight corner. A politician detected in lying, bullying, or antisocial conduct is unusually apt to reach for his glossary of bulldoggery." [*Blood, Class and Empire* (New York: Nation Books, 2004), 182]

Cinema

" . . . Film directors may make use of cutout, disposable characters while fiction writers can't." ["A Postwar Period Pastiche," *Washington Post*, 3/31/89]

"Consider what the boomer generation has wrought with the great national art form of cinema. The predecessor group—Altman, Scorsese, Coppola—made some unforgettable stuff. But sometime after *Jaws* there was a steep decline into block-busterdom and the empty, formulaic, and mechanistic world of Sly Stallone, Joel Silver, and Larry Gordon. By their fruits shall ye know them, and their fruits are *Die Hard* and *Lethal Weapon*." ["The Baby-Boomer Wasteland," *Vanity Fair*, January 1996]

"I had been to the movies and had been annoyed, as one often is, by people chatting and commenting in the back row. This is the height of antisocial behavior, because it ruins the pleasure of others while bringing no benefit to the offender. I normally deal with it as I do when people in cinemas fail to turn off their cell phones. I turn round and tell them that I know where they live, and I know where their children go to school." ["I Fought the Law," *Vanity Fair*, February 2004]

Circumcision

"As to immoral practice, it is hard to imagine anything more grotesque than the mutilation of infant genitalia. Nor is it easy to imagine anything more incompatible with the argument from design." [*God Is Not Great* (New York: Twelve, 2007), 223]

"Full excision, originally ordered by god as the blood price for the promised future massacre of the Canaanites, is now exposed for what it is—a mutilation of a powerless infant with the aim of ruining its future sex life. . . . If religion and its arrogance were not involved, no healthy society would permit this primitive amputation, or allow any surgery to be practiced on the genitalia without the full and informed consent of the person concerned." [*God Is Not Great* (New York: Twelve, 2007), 226]

Civil Liberties

"The better the ostensible justification for an infringement upon domestic liberty, the more suspicious one ought to be of it." ["Statement: Christopher Hitchens, NSA Lawsuit Client," American Civil Liberties Union, 1/16/06]

" . . . A power or a right, once relinquished to one administration for one reason, will unfailingly be exploited by successor administrations, for quite other reasons." ["Statement: Christopher Hitchens, NSA Lawsuit Client," American Civil Liberties Union, 1/16/06]

"If you get yourself involved in a civil-liberty lawsuit, you will invariably find that you have teamed up with people you don't like." ["Power Suits," *Vanity Fair*, April 2006]

Civil Rights

" . . . Nobody would know from a detached study of U.S. foreign policy that the country had any black citizens at all. It is when we come to civil rights, in education in particular, that we find affirmative action being taken in support of discrimination and segregation." ["Minority Report," *Nation*, 10/16/82]

"If, like me, you come from a country that has no constitution and therefore no amendments, it is oddly impressive to see mountainous black policemen stolidly defending the civil rights of the Ku Klux Klan." ["Minority Report," *Nation*, 12/11/82]

Civil War (U.S.)

"It was not at all the tear-jerking sentiment of *Uncle Tom's Cabin* that catalyzed the War Between the States. It was, rather, the blood-spilling intransigence of John Brown, field-tested on the pitiless Kansas prairies and later deployed at Harpers Ferry." ["The Man Who Ended Slavery," *Atlantic Monthly*, May 2005]

"The motto of the Confederacy was *Deo Vindice*, or 'God on Our Side.' Atlanta was burned to ashes by people who thought that the deity took the other view." ["God Bless Me, It's a Best-Seller!," *Vanity Fair*, September 2007]

Civil War Reenactments

"Some of these [reenactors] are in need of a life; others are genuine history students; still others tend to regard the movie *Deliverance* as an invasion of their personal privacy." ["Rebel Ghosts," *Vanity Fair*, July 1999]

"About 55,000 men were blown to shreds or died of appalling wounds or expired from thirst and neglect on the Gettysburg field, and it seemed to me somewhat profane to be strolling this nearby turf and buying kitsch souvenirs, or pamphlets with titles such as *Freemasons at Gettysburg*, or T-shirts emblazoned with the legend

'It's a Southern Thing—You Wouldn't Understand.' (Why is it, when I see a Confederate battle flag flapping from the rear of a pickup truck, that I don't axiomatically make the association with courtesy, gentility, chivalry, and hospitality? Perhaps that's the bit I don't understand.)" ["Rebel Ghosts," *Vanity Fair*, July 1999]

" . . . Those who can't forgive the past are condemned, not without pathos, to reenact it." ["Rebel Ghosts," *Vanity Fair*, July 1999]

Civilization

"If civilization means the sum of human intellectual accomplishment, it needn't be qualified by an adjective." ["The Toy Canon," *Harper's*, June 1988]

"Every advance in human civilization, from the spread of science and literacy to the abolition of slavery, has had to meet the objection that it violated God-given laws." ["Minority Report," *Nation*, 3/13/89]

" . . . The word 'civilization' has no need of the prefix 'Western.'" ["Words Fail Us," *Independent*, 6/13/93]

"Civilization could never have arisen in any form if people had not been willing to subordinate their own ego to a general good, and it hardly matters if we decide that this concept of a general good is itself actuated partly by self-interest." [*Thomas Paine's Rights of Man: A Biography* (New York: Atlantic Monthly Press, 2006), 109]

Clancy, Tom

"With no official enemy on the radar screen (and even the foul Iranians better-armed thanks to North and Reagan), Clancy has become the junk supplier of surrogate testosterone. His books bear the same relationship to reality as Oliver North's lachrymose and bragging speeches do to patriotism, and his writing is to prose what military music is to music." ["Something for the Boys," *New York Review of Books*, 11/14/96]

Class

"A sort of moral blackmail is exerted from both poles. The underclass, one gathers, should be dulled with charity and welfare provision lest it turn nasty. The upper class must likewise be conciliated by vast handouts, lest it lose the 'incentive' to go on generating wealth. A rising tide, as we have recently learned, does not lift all boats, nor does a falling tide sink them all. If people were to recognize that they are all in the same boat, they would take better care of its furnishings, its comfort and its general décor." ["Minority Report," *Nation*, 2/20/88]

"An underclass is a handy thing. In fact, no ruling class should be without one. It scares the middle class, and it arouses the contempt of the working class. These are powerful emotions: in the former instance the fear of crime, and in the latter the traditional dislike for the indigent and the unskilled." ["Minority Report," *Nation*, 4/30/90]

"The division of the world economy into classes is a fact that is only ignored because it is so frighteningly obvious." ["In the Bright Autumn of My Senescence," *London Review of Books*, 1/06/94]

"Class is a topic that doesn't get very much ventilation in America and when it does come up it is usually accompanied by a certain amount of embarrassment. In fact, to be frank, it is often the last-resort plea of poor whites, especially since they were shorn of their status as society's last frontier against the black underclass." ["Fall of a Poor White Heroine," *Evening Standard*, 2/25/94]

Clergy

"I see that some cleric has attacked me for not having a towering intellect. Well, if Pastor Dave LeMoine is so smart, how come he can't hold down a real job?" ["Minority Report," *Nation*, 12/01/84]

" . . . There is no vileness that cannot be freely uttered by a man whose name is prefaced with the word *Reverend*. Try this: Call a TV station and tell them that you know the Antichrist is already on earth and is an adult Jewish male. See how far you get. Then try the same thing and add that you are the Rev. Jim-Bob Vermin. 'Why, Reverend, come right on the show!'" ["Faith-Based Fraud," *Slate*, 5/16/07]

Cliché

"If you want a cultural cliché to be born in your own name, it doesn't pay to be too subtle." ["A Wolfe in Chic Clothing," *Mother Jones*, January 1983]

" . . . Repetition can dull even the most piercing truth." ["Minority Report," *Nation*, 6/30/84]

"'Never forget'—I'll never forget that." ["Pre-Millennial Syndrome," *Salmagundi*, Summer 1996]

"High on the list of idiotic commonplace expressions is the old maxim that 'it is better to light a candle than to curse the darkness.' How do such fatuous pieces of folk wisdom ever get started on their careers of glib quotation? *Of course* it would be preferable to light a candle than to complain about the darkness. You would only be bitching about the darkness if you didn't *have* a candle to begin with." ["Bah, Hanukkah," *Slate*, 12/03/07]

"It is cliché, not plagiarism, that is the problem with our stilted, room-temperature political discourse. It used to be that thinking people would say, with at least a shred of pride, that their own convictions would not shrink to fit on a label or on a bumper sticker. But now it seems that the more vapid and vacuous the logo, the more charm (or should that be 'charisma'?) it exerts. Take 'Yes We Can,' for example. It's the sort of thing parents might chant encouragingly to a child slow on the potty-training uptake." ["Words Matter," *Slate*, 3/03/08]

Clinton, Bill

"If you want to put Clinton's principles to the test, make sure to be the last person to have spoken to him. The man is like a big, fat cushion. He bears the impression of whoever last sat upon him." ["Minority Report," *Nation*, 7/05/93]

"Every time Clinton betrays a friend, or abandons a cause, or rats on a principle, it's *him* we are supposed to feel sorry for." ["Minority Report," *Nation*, 7/05/93]

"Here, evidently, is a man who can be callous with subordinates while fawning on superiors. A greedy, vain, insecure man who needs approval from authority and who will seek it in the only way open to a 'New Democrat,' which is systematic betrayal of his base and his electorate." ["Minority Report," *Nation*, 7/05/93]

"Like a fleshy man caught in a fight outside a sordid bar, he sometimes bellows for aides to hold his coat and let him at them but often looks grateful for the arms that are restraining him from the fray." ["Betrayal Becomes Farce," *Washington Post*, 8/15/93]

" . . . Clinton seems to get teary whenever he speaks of anything but the deficit, so he's carrying either a large onion around with him or else a copy of *Tikkun*." ["What's Love Got to Do with It?," *Vanity Fair*, September 1993]

"When Clinton isn't redefining self-criticism as a form of narcissism, he is extremely hostile to any form of tough questioning. And he has an unpleasing tendency to hide behind his womenfolk." ["Minority Report," *Nation*, 2/21/94]

" . . . He seems to have a flaunting need for abasement, and an awful lust to earn the approval of those who sneer at him, even at his wife and his daughter." ["Minority Report," *Nation*, 2/27/95]

" . . . Nobody knows where shyness and decency ought to end and shame to begin. Example: Is it kosher to ask the president about his underwear on MTV? Yes, Virginia, it is kosher to ask this particular president, because he is bursting with desire to fill you in on his briefs." ["The Death of Shame," *Vanity Fair*, March 1996]

"When the president finally unearths his 'inner child,' I hope it throws up all over him." ["Child-Proof," *Nation*, 6/24/96]

"He still seems to feel no embarrassment at making his own 'pain' the center of attention. (There was a time when he at least affected to know that a president's job is to register the feelings of the voters, not to get them to register his.)" ["The Starr Report: That Cigar," *Guardian*, 9/12/98]

" . . . It is made clear by Clinton's own conduct and arguments that for him foreign policy and domestic policy do not exist in parallel universes, but are one and the same." ["Weapons of Mass Distraction," *Vanity Fair*, March 1999]

"It's one thing to say, with reasonable confidence, that the Oval Office is currently occupied by a war criminal, a rapist, and a pathological liar. It's another to ponder the full implications. If half of what one knows about Clinton's business deals and date-rapes is half-true, then he has been going through political life for years, aware or quasi-aware that any or every telephone call might be the one he has been dreading. That's more stress than most of us could take: Only a certain kind of personality could be expected to endure it. You can find this under the simpering liberal media description of 'Comeback Kid,' or you can check it in a taxonomy of an entirely different kind, where the key phrase is 'Threat to self and others.'" ["The Clinton Swamp," *Nation*, 3/29/99]

"I had become utterly convinced, as early as the 1992 campaign, that there was something in the Clinton makeup that was quite seriously nasty. The automatic lying, the glacial ruthlessness, the self-pity, the indifference to repeated exposure, the absence of any tincture of conscience or remorse, the awful piety—these were symptoms of a psychopath." ["I'll Never Eat Lunch in This Town Again," *Vanity Fair*, May 1999]

"The president always uses political correctness as the bodyguard of his incredibly corrupt policies." [*The Drudge Report*, Fox News Channel, 5/15/99]

"Here is a man immune to shame, dishonor, embarrassment, and disgrace. A man so wanting in pride and self-respect that, as president on a foreign trip (this was in Jerusalem on the eve of impeachment), he publicly recommended censure as the best punishment for himself. A man so proof against feeling that he put his own daughter out on the public stage, his own entwined with hers, as evidence first of his truth-telling (in January) and then as evidence of his contrition (in August)." ["'It's Our Turn,'" *American Enterprise*, May/June 1999]

"He will be remembered as the man who used the rhetoric of the New Democrat to undo the New Deal. He will also be remembered as a man who offered a groaning board of incentives for the rich and draconian admonitions to the poor." [*No One Left to Lie To* (New York: Verso, 2000), 59]

"And, even in a political system renowned worldwide for its venality, Bill Clinton seemed anxious to be bought, and willing if not indeed eager to advertise the fact in advance." [*No One Left to Lie To* (New York: Verso, 2000), 75]

"I have known a number of people who work for and with, or who worked for and with, this man. They act like cult members while they are still under the spell, and talk like ex-cult members as soon as they have broken away." [*No One Left to Lie To* (New York: Verso, 2000), 76]

" . . . It remains a fact that in all his decades of logorrhea Clinton has failed to make a single remark (absent some lame catch phrases like 'New Covenant' and of course the imperishable 'It all depends on what the meaning of "is" is') that could possibly adhere to the cortex of a thinking human being." [*No One Left to Lie To* (New York: Verso, 2000), 77]

"In power, he has completed the Reagan counter-revolution and made the state into a personal friend of those who are already rich and secure. He has used his armed forces in fits of pique, chiefly against the far-off and the unpopular, and on dates which suit his own court calendar. The draft-dodger has mutated into a pliant serf of the Pentagon, the pot smoker into the chief inquisitor in the 'war on drugs,' and the womanizer into a boss who uses subordinates as masturbatory dolls. But the liar and the sonofabitch remain, and who will say that these qualities played no part in the mutation?" [*No One Left to Lie To* (New York: Verso, 2000), 83–84]

"The tin pots and yahoos of Khartoum and Kabul and Baghdad are micro-megalomaniacs who think of their banana republics as potential superpowers. It

took this president to 'degrade' a superpower into a potential banana republic."
[*No One Left to Lie To* (New York: Verso, 2000), 101]

Clinton, Bill and the
Al-Shifa Pharmaceutical Factory (Khartoum, Sudan)

" . . . Clinton's rocketing of Khartoum—supported by most liberals—was a gross
war crime, which would certainly have entitled the Sudanese government to
mount reprisals under international law." ["Let's Not Get Too Liberal," *Guardian*,
9/21/01]

"The crime was directly and sordidly linked to the effort by a crooked president to
avoid impeachment (a conclusion sedulously avoided by the Chomskys and Hus-
seinis of the time)." ["Of Sin, the Left and Islamic Fascism," *Nation* (online),
10/08/01]

Clinton, Bill and Juanita Broaddrick

"It seems to me morally feeble, as well as intellectually slack, to split the difference
between Clinton and Broaddrick or to characterize her allegation as unprovable.
The feeblest summary of this compromise is contained in the lazy phrase 'he said,
she said.' In the case of the 'he,' we already know that he is a hysterical, habitual
liar. We also know that almost no allegation ever made by a woman and denied by
him has proven to be untrue. And we know that ex-girlfriends have been subjected
to extraordinary campaigns of defamation, amounting in some cases to intimidation, merely for speaking about 'consensual' sex. What allegation could be more
horrific than that of rape? And yet, 'he' hasn't said anything yet. If I were accused
of rape and the woman making the charge were a lady of obvious integrity, I
would want to do better than have a lawyer speak for me and make a routine disclaimer. . . ." ["The Clinton Swamp," *Nation*, 3/29/99]

"After reading the testimony of Juanita Broaddrick, I'll never be able to think of
his lip biting in the same way again." ["I'll Never Eat Lunch in This Town Again,"
Vanity Fair, May 1999]

" . . . The mute reception of Juanita Broaddrick's charges illuminates the expiring,
decadent phase of American liberalism." [*No One Left to Lie To* (New York: Verso,
2000), 117]

Clinton, Bill and Cigars

"Did he inhale this time?" ["The Starr Report: That Cigar," *Guardian*, 9/12/98]

Clinton, Bill and Hillary Rodham Clinton

"In a schizophrenic White House, the motto ought perhaps to be 'Let Clinton be
Clintons.'" ["What's Love Got to Do with It?," *Vanity Fair*, 1993]

"The whole problem with the Clintons is that they are moralists and traditionalists and churchgoers one week and beneficiaries of political correctness the
next." ["She Didn't Marry Him to Stay Among the Catfish," *Evening Standard*,
8/19/98]

Clinton, Bill and Gennifer Flowers

"I never met any reporter who believed the Clinton line on Flowers, but neither did I meet anyone who didn't know when the time had come to put the lie behind us and move on." ["'It's Our Turn,'" *American Enterprise*, May/June 1999]

"A gentleman, having once implied that Gennifer Flowers was a lying gold digger, does not make it up to her, or to those he misled, by agreeing in a surly manner years later that perhaps he did sleep with her 'once.' All other considerations to one side, doesn't he know that it's the height of bad manners to make love to somebody only once?" [*No One Left to Lie To* (New York: Verso, 2000), 80]

Clinton, Bill and Newt Gingrich

"These two bloated, Southern-strategizing, God-bothering, pot-smoking, self-pitying, draft-dodging, wife-cheating, unreadable-book-writing, money-scrounging bigmouths and pseudo-intellectuals lean on each other like Pat and Mike, in a shame-free double-act where all the moves and gags are plotted in advance. Indeed, the last election campaign was explicitly 'Clinton-Gingrich '96.'" ["Hail to the Chiefs," *Nation*, 2/03/97]

Clinton, Bill and Impeachment

"Clinton can go on saying that this is all a distraction from the nation's real business, but people may start to reply, well, whose fault is that?" ["Yes Mr. President, But the Usual Excuses Won't Work This Time," *Evening Standard*, 1/22/98]

"If Starr cracks this case he will have demonstrated that the most powerful man in the world is, in practice as well as theory, within reach of the law." ["Why Starr Is Determined to Nail Clinton," *Evening Standard*, 7/29/98]

Clinton, Bill and Iraq

"Is it possible that this president, seeing his options narrowing to nothing, suddenly found the nerve that had so often failed him, and decided that Saddam Hussein could only be punished on the day preceding a crucial vote [on impeachment] in the House of Representatives? It is not only possible. It is a moral certainty. . . . Since all the facts about Iraq have been 'in' for so long, there was also no reason for Clinton not to obey the law and to ask Congress, and the UN Security Council, for leave to proceed. This was no emergency except on the domestic front." ["Weapon of Mass Distraction," *Evening Standard*, 12/18/98]

"Policy toward Baghdad has been without pulse or direction or principle ever since Mr. Clinton took office. . . . The only moment when this president showed a glimmer of interest in the matter was when his own interests were involved as well." [*No One Left to Lie To* (New York: Verso, 2000), 95]

Clinton, Bill and Paula Jones

"It was, taken all in all, a big mistake for him to try and trash Paula as a no-account hick from Arkansas. It invited a certain inevitable response. To use class, you have to have class." ["Penthouse Sweetie," *Evening Standard*, 5/30/97]

Clinton, Bill and Osama bin Laden

"Clinton's only 'serious' move against Osama bin Laden came in 1998, with his wag-the-dog missile attacks on Sudan and Afghanistan." ["Knowledge (and Power)," *Nation*, 6/10/02]

Clinton, Bill and the Left

"He's imposed warrantless searches of public housing. He's throwing women off welfare because their moral standards don't meet what he says they ought to be. He's a zero-tolerance, law-and-order Democrat who now, suddenly, has turned into a civil libertarian, you'll notice. . . . He says that homosexuals do not have the right to wear the American uniform, unless they're prepared to lie about it—'don't ask, don't tell.' This is an extraordinary record of hypocrisy and very reactionary hypocrisy, too. And, it seems to me, the most startling thing in this whole business is the willingness of liberals to carry water for someone who does not give a damn for them and who's betrayed them at every turn." [*Meet the Press*, NBC, 11/29/98]

"What does make me gasp is the limitless gullibility of the liberals, as they tamely watch this man tossing all of their 'concerns' off the back of a fleeing sled that contains only his own incriminated self." ["Political Defense System," *Nation*, 2/01/99]

" . . . What impresses me about Clintonism is this: Lying and perjury and neat evasions and sordid double talk are not just excused but praised and justified by a strategic majority of liberals. The most serious problem of the Clinton administration arises not from the pathetic lying, but from the approbation which the falsehoods receive from wised-up ideological allies." ["'It's Our Turn,'" *American Enterprise*, May/June 1999]

"Nobody on the Left has noticed . . . that it is the Left that swallows the soft promises of Clinton and the Right that demands, and gets, hard guarantees." [*No One Left to Lie To* (New York: Verso, 2000), 24]

"He gutted welfare, bombed Sudan, and rented out the White House. If he were a Republican, liberals would have been appalled." ["Bill of Goods?," *Mother Jones*, September/October 2000]

" . . . I think history will record with some astonishment that this remorseless progress toward a corporate state was accompanied by a chorus of support from the politically correct. . . . A price has to be paid for all this, and the immediate as well as longer lasting cost is this: American Democratic liberalism has lost its honor and prestige and has proved itself as adept in making excuses for power as any Babbitt in the Nixon era." ["Bill of Goods?," *Mother Jones*, September/October 2000]

"The genius of Clinton lay in his ability to emasculate his party's Left, and to make that party a guarantor of Wall Street and NAFTA and NATO and the Federal Reserve, while managing to appeal incessantly and successfully to political correctness." ["Officer Material," *Times Literary Supplement*, 11/03/00]

"So one legacy of this person is our cultural resignation—perhaps better say surrender—to the triumph of reputation over performance. . . . Obviously, much of this irony—if we still have the right to that word—comes at the expense of the credulous liberals. The man who coldly executed Rickey Ray Rector is garlanded as an honorary black man by Toni Morrison, and the man who savaged Juanita Broaddrick and defamed several other truth-telling women is fawned upon by Betty Friedan and Gloria Steinem. Labor leaders embrace the favored son of Tyson Foods." ["The Clinton Legacy: The Peronista Presidency," *Wall Street Journal*, 1/16/01]

Clinton, Bill and Monica Lewinsky

" . . . I think the Monica Lewinski story has absolutely everything and is bloody good fun to boot. A president with too much time on his hands, a First Lady who publishes a book calling for sexual abstinence among American teenagers (nice try), a Democratic Party obsessed by everybody else's sexual harassment potential, tremendous official worrying about the divorce and adultery statistics, a White House campaign to install a special chip in family TVs so that the little ones don't see any accidental smut. And all the while it's: Come on darling, nobody's here, get 'em off and get over that desk." ["Whatever You Do, Don't Mention Sex in America," *Evening Standard*, 1/23/98]

"At least with the Clinton-Lewinsky imbroglio we knew from the start the identity of 'Deep Throat.'" ["Sorry, Mr. President," *Evening Standard*, 2/04/98]

"In their upwards of a dozen trysts, according to Ms. Lewinsky under oath, she would perform unconsummated oral sex on the leader of the Free World. She would then step back a few paces, disrobe, and perform a little dance while he completed matters on his own. . . . The president denies that this was a sexual relationship and, by my standards, he's correct in doing so. This is the CD-Rom version of romancing a copy of *Penthouse*." ["The Diary: What Clinton and Lewinsky Really Got Down To," *Independent*, 8/16/98]

Clinton, Bill and Lying

"Clinton cannot call anything a lie. He may, he thinks, have given 'a false impression.' He may even have 'misled' people, 'including even my wife.' Even?" ["Clinton— 'Like a Gorilla Playing a Violin,'" *Evening Standard*, 8/18/98]

"He lies even when it won't do him any good—a bad sign." ["It's Not the Sin. It's the Cynicism," *Vanity Fair*, December 1998]

"One reason a gentleman may be obliged to lie is to protect the reputation of the woman. Clinton has lied in order to trash them." ["The Clinton Swamp," *Nation*, 3/29/99]

"You could easily say, in fact, that the whole Clintonian project was a lie, or at least a series of consciously strategized half-truths that added up to less than one truth." ["'It's Our Turn,'" *American Enterprise*, May/June 1999]

Clinton, Bill and Marijuana

"I happen to know, by having been at the same university at the same time, that Clinton was telling the truth when he said he never inhaled. (He had no aversion to the brownies and cookies that were then a favorite method of marijuana main-line ingestion.) There was a clue, in this tiny but insanely elaborate deception, to the later presidential style." ["The Teetotal Effect," *Vanity Fair*, August 2004]

Clinton, Bill and the Media

"He may be no John Kennedy, but he already has a Camelot press." ["Flattery from a Fool," *Evening Standard*, 7/17/92]

"The White House is said to have hated the press since the Gennifer Flowers af-fair. If so, this must rank as one of the greatest instances of ingratitude on record." ["Minority Report," *Nation*, 7/05/93]

Clinton, Bill and the Presidency

"The Oval Office may have presented itself to him as a potentially therapeutic loca-tion, but once he arrived there he half realized that he had no big plans, no grand thoughts, no noble dreams." [*No One Left to Lie To* (New York: Verso, 2000), 77]

"The Clinton years were a degradation of the idea of a democratic republic. They showed us how far a president can go, in the Peronist direction, if he is lucky with the media and Wall Street and the treasury all at the same time." ["The Clinton Legacy: The Peronista Presidency," *Wall Street Journal*, 1/16/01]

Clinton, Bill and Rickey Ray Rector

" . . . He broke off from the New Hampshire primary in 1992 to supervise the ex-ecution of a brain-damaged black convict named Rickey Ray Rector. . . . If a con-servative politician had done such a thing, Rector would be as famous today as Willie Horton. But Rector was put to death in order that Clinton could not be 'Willie Hortoned' out of the nomination." ["Gore on the Hands," *Nation*, 6/26/00]

Clinton, Bill and Religion

"This concept of faith as therapy is now incarnate in the figure of Bill Clinton, who is never happier than when shutting his eyes tight at a prayer breakfast, and speaking huskily of the comfort he has recently found in the Book of Psalms. It's probably just as well that nobody asked the president which Psalm in particular." ["Pre-Millennial Syndrome," *Salmagundi*, Summer 1996]

Clinton, Bill and the Right

" . . . The Right hates Clinton because it fears him. And it obviously cannot fear him as a radical reformer. It *can* fear him, however, as a man who threatens to pur-loin conservative clothes." ["Minority Report," *Nation*, 11/14/94]

" . . . Everything from his oration at Nixon's graveside, to his policy toward Bosnia and Cuba and Iraq, to his attitude on welfare seems to have been conditioned by the question: 'What would George Bush have done?'" ["Minority Report," *Nation*, 11/14/94]

"By using 'government,' Clinton hopes to create a new center-right majority that would put a crimp in the GOP style." ["Minority Report," *Nation*, 11/14/94]

"But Bill Clinton, who has gone further than Reagan ever dared in repealing the New Deal and seconding the social Darwinist ethic at home and abroad, is nonetheless detested on the Right. The old slogan, 'draft-dodging, pot-smoking, lying, womanizing sonofabitch' still resonates. As why should it not, given that a person of such qualities has been able to annex and even anticipate the Republican platform, thereby demonstrating conclusively that there is no sufficient or necessary connection between the said platform and personal honor, or personal honesty?" [*No One Left to Lie To* (New York: Verso, 2000), 79]

"It was not only liberals who failed the test set by Clintonism: the world of the 'prayer breakfast' was his ally as surely as were the boardrooms and the Dow Jones." [*No One Left to Lie To* (New York: Verso, 2000), 150]

"In all essentials, the Clinton-Gore administration has been Republican, and not all that moderate." ["Bill of Goods?," *Mother Jones*, September/October 2000]

"The right detested Clinton because he had stolen and enacted their program and, with the help of Dick Morris, seduced many of their traditional big donors. And he had done all this while being a flagrant and shameless sleaze, thus proving that the right's agenda had nothing to do with 'values'! You'd be pissed off, too, if you were a Republican." ["Bill of Goods?," *Mother Jones*, September/October 2000]

Clinton, Bill and Franklin D. Roosevelt

"At least Clinton can claim something in common with the patrician of Hyde Park. Like him, the president is a traitor to his class." ["F.D.R.—the Good, the Bad and the Banal," *Nation*, 5/26/97]

Clinton, Bill and Sex

"So, at least metaphorically, there is a crossover between the sexual-spoils system and the financial one. (Gennifer Flowers and Paula Jones were on the payroll—it's almost as if Bill has no confidence in his ability to get laid on his own merits.)" ["It's a Scandal, But Nothing like the One about to Break," *Independent*, 9/13/98]

"'It's a private matter.' Well, then, who claims the Oval Office as private space? 'Why all this fuss about sex?' But the president says it wasn't sex. 'Let's get on with the agenda.' Excuse me—what fucking agenda?" ["It's Not the Sin. It's the Cynicism," *Vanity Fair*, December 1998]

"One feels almost laughably heavy-footed in pointing out that Mrs. Clinton's prim little book, *It Takes a Village*, proposes sexual abstinence for the young, and that the president was earnestly seconding this very proposal while using an impressionable intern as the physical rather than moral equivalent of a blow-up doll." [*No One Left to Lie To* (New York: Verso, 2000), 41–42]

"Those who claim to detect, in the widespread loathing of Clinton, an aggressive 'culture war' against the freedom-loving sixties should be forced to ask themselves if Clinton, with his almost sexless conquests and his eerie affectless claim that the female felt no pleasure, represents the erotic freedom that they had in mind." [*No One Left to Lie To* (New York: Verso, 2000), 80–81]

"The first president, or even human being, to say that he had a climax and she felt nothing, so it wasn't sex." ["The Clinton Legacy: The Peronista Presidency," *Wall Street Journal*, 1/16/01]

Clinton, Bill and Kathleen Willey
" . . . Kathleen Willey, the recently widowed employee who came to the Oval Office for advice and counsel in her distress, and was rewarded by an enveloping hug and the crushing of her hand against the distended presidential groin, may take offense at reading that Clinton ridiculed the very idea of his bothering with a woman who had such small tits. You know how 'judgmental' some women can be." ["It's a Scandal, But Nothing like the One about to Break," *Independent*, 9/13/98]

Clinton, Chelsea
" . . . Chelsea Clinton was barely into her teens when she was pressed into service as a protective shield for her father's mendacity, and hustled onto the White House lawn (with her mother's complicity) as a facile assurance of ongoing First Family values." ["'Clindit,'" *Wall Street Journal*, 9/07/01]

Clinton, Hillary Rodham
" . . . That heroic anti-smoker, low-cal-food campaigner, and spare-time patroness of good causes. . . ." ["Ring Around the Clintons," *Vanity Fair*, July 1994]

"It takes a child to believe in Hillary Clinton's village. In this beloved community, for one thing, you can never be sure whether the pressure is to grow up too fast, or to grow up too slowly." ["Child-Proof," *Nation*, 6/24/96]

"Her scornful and scrupulous denial that there is any such thing as 'a left in the White House' is one of the few completely verifiable statements that she has made on any subject." ["The Greater Evil," *Nation*, 11/18/96]

"She's a mediocre, self-pitying woman who's never held a proper job." [*Hardball with Chris Matthews*, MSNBC, 7/01/99]

"What has this woman ever done for the liberal cause but betray it?" [*Hardball with Chris Matthews*, MSNBC, 7/01/99]

"I haven't yet had it convincingly explained to me . . . why a nomination to the United States Senate is not just hers for the asking, but hers even *without* the asking." ["Home-Free Hillary," *Nation*, 7/26/99–8/02/99]

"Mrs. Clinton has the most unappetizing combination of qualities to be met in many days' march: she is a tyrant and a bully when she can dare to be, and an ingratiating populist when that will serve. She will sometimes appear in the guise of a 'strong woman' and sometimes in the softer garb of a winsome and vulnerable female. She is entirely un-self-critical and quite devoid of reflective capacity, and has never found that any of her numerous misfortunes or embarrassments are her own fault, because the fault invariably lies with others. And, speaking of where things lie, she can in a close contest keep up with her husband for mendacity. Like him, she is not just a liar but a lie; a phoney construct of shreds and patches and hysterical, self-pitying, demagogic improvisations." [*No One Left to Lie To* (New York: Verso, 2000), 123]

"The plain fact is the more people see of the senator from New York, the less they warm to her." ["And the Real Winner Could Be . . . ," *Mirror*, 1/05/08]

"For Senator Clinton, something is true if it validates the myth of her striving and her 'greatness' (her overweening ambition in other words) and only ceases to be true when it no longer serves that limitless purpose." ["The Case Against Hillary Clinton," *Slate*, 1/14/08]

"Those of us who follow politics seriously rather than view it as a game show do not look at Hillary Clinton and simply think 'first woman president.' We think—for example—'first ex-co-president' or 'first wife of a disbarred lawyer and impeached former incumbent' or 'first person to use her daughter as photo-op protection during her husband's perjury rap.'" ["The Peril of Identity Politics," *Wall Street Journal*, 1/18/08]

"She has no tears for anyone but herself." ["The Tall Tale of Tuzla," *Slate*, 3/31/08]

Clinton, Hillary Rodham and Rudy Giuliani
"They both ban smoking materials anywhere they can ban them (Mrs. Clinton having failed with the use of cigars in the White House)." ["Party of Two," *Vanity Fair*, December 1999]

Clinton Administration (1993–2001)
"These people are experts in not quite breaking the law." ["Bodies Everywhere, No 'Smoking Gun,'" *Nation*, 9/08/97–9/15/97]

"Mr. Nixon went down for actions committed by his ghastly aides. Mr. Clinton's aides are going down because of things done by their ghastly president." ["The Groveller with Nowhere Left to Hide," *Evening Standard*, 9/10/98]

" . . . The Clinton administration always had its banana republic side. For all the talk about historic presidential 'philandering,' it is hard to recall any other White House that has had to maintain a quasi-governmental or para-state division devoted exclusively to the bullying and defamation of women." [*No One Left to Lie To* (New York: Verso, 2000), 7]

"Two full terms of Clintonism and of 'triangulation,' and of loveless but dogged bipartisanship, reduced the American scene to the point where politicians had become to politics what lawyers had become to the law: professionalized parasites battening on an exhausted system that had lost any relationship to its original purpose (democracy or popular sovereignty in the first instance; justice or equity in the second)." [*No One Left to Lie To* (New York: Verso, 2000), 120]

Closure

"I can see why people in this country talk so much about closure, because they never get it." [Interview with Paul Kilduff, *Berkeley Monthly*, May 1998]

"There is no such thing . . . [and] it wouldn't be worth having if it were available because all it would mean is that some quite important part of you had gone numb." [*Anderson Cooper 360*, CNN, 8/05/10]

Cochran, Johnnie

" . . . By turning up at court with a Farrakhan-supplied bodyguard and by stressing 'blood' over blood, as well as by insinuating that there would be trouble in South Central should his client be found guilty, Johnnie Cochran showed that he was a racist in the trivial, unscientific sense if not in the political one." ["Minority Report," *Nation*, 10/23/95]

Cockburn, Alexander

"Alexander is a dashing and courageous foe of the diseased version of American anticommunism. Surveying the evidence of murder and depredation by empire and capital, he has refused the toadlike option of demonstrating anticommunist credentials before—or instead of—mounting a counterattack. This is not Stalinism on his part. . . ." ["Minority Report," *Nation*, 10/09/89]

Coincidence

" . . . Coincidence is no accident." ["Forging the Magic Bullet," *Vanity Fair*, November 1993]

Cold War

"If anything, the process of unfreezing Eastern Europe has been retarded by the sound and fury of American imperialism, just as it was retarded by Washington's earlier habit of bringing ex-Nazis into the CIA for the fantasy of 'rollback.'" ["Minority Report," *Nation*, 1/01/90]

"The Cold War . . . *can* continue to be fought by contractors and pseudo-scientists even if there is no longer a believable adversary." ["The Repackaging of Dan Quayle," *Harper's*, April 1990]

"To proclaim the end of the Cold War and to begin babbling about the peace dividend is to ignore the continued existence in our lives, and the lives of others, of Cold War institutions." ["Minority Report," *Nation*, 4/16/90]

"No country ever won a war as utterly and convincingly as the United States went on to win the Cold War." ["America Counts Its Cold War Casualties," *Newsday*, 6/18/92]

"In the depths of the Cold War it was a poor day that did not bring some invocation of 'Munich' or 'appeasement' from the tribunes of the powerful." ["Chamberlain: Collusion, Not Appeasement," *Monthly Review*, January 1995]

"And how often one was to notice, during the Cold War, a sort of Western penis-envy for the ruthlessness of Soviet methods, coupled with incantations about the relative 'decadence,' even tendency to suicide, displayed by the effete democracies." [*Why Orwell Matters* (New York: Basic Books, 2002), 95]

"Cold War 'moral equivalence' was morally null." ["Bang to Rights," *Times Literary Supplement*, 2/17/06]

"For the decades of the Cold War, the standard taunt against anybody even marginally to the left of the centre was that he or she might feel more comfortable back in the USSR. 'Love it or leave it,' said the red, white and blue bumper stickers to anyone who had the smallest reservations about the US of A. 'Moscow gold' was the supposedly hidden incentive for any disagreement, from the early civil rights movement to those who declined the opportunity to serve in Vietnam." ["My Week," *Observer*, 8/16/09]

Collectivism

"If we don't hang together, we *will* hang separately. The bell *does* toll for us all. . . . The values of solidarity, collectivism, and internationalism are not so much desirable as they are actually mandated by nature and reality itself." [*Observer*, 9/13/87]

"You do not solve the contradictions of a society by nationalizing them, as the Soviet Union long sought to do, and announcing that they have disappeared." ["Taking Socialism Seriously with Michael Harrington," *Newsday*, 7/19/89]

Comfort and Discomfort

"We can always be sure of one thing—that the messengers of discomfort and sacrifice will be stoned and pelted by those who wish to preserve at all costs their own contentment." [Foreword to *Brave New World*, by Aldous Huxley (New York: HarperCollins, 2004), xv]

Communism

"To have marched in the last legal Communist demonstration in Berlin in 1933 may have been an experience as delicious as protracted sexual intercourse (Hobsbawm's metaphor, not mine), but the experience of defending the indefensible and—more insulting—of being asked to believe the unbelievable was far less delightful and, equally to the point, very much more protracted." ["Eric the Red," *New York Times*, 8/24/03]

" . . . Communism proved itself able to adapt but not to reform. . . ." ["The Old Man," *Atlantic Monthly*, July/August 2004]

"Communist absolutists did not so much negate religion, in societies that they well understood were saturated with faith and superstition, as seek to *replace* it. The solemn elevation of infallible leaders who were a source of endless bounty and blessing; the permanent search for heretics and schismatics; the mummification of dead leaders as icons and relics; the lurid show trials that elicited incredible confessions by means of torture . . . none of this was very difficult to interpret in traditional terms." [*God Is Not Great* (New York: Twelve, 2007), 246]

" . . . By 1982 Communism had long passed the point where it needed anything more than the old equation of history with the garbage can." [*Hitch-22* (New York: Twelve, 2010), 418]

Compassion

"What those hypocrites mean when they intone the hack word 'compassion' is that we should not forget the needy and the desperate as we pursue our glorious path of self-advancement." ["Minority Report," *Nation*, 2/20/88]

"Like the quality of mercy, the prompting of compassion is not finite, and can be self-replenishing." ["Political Animals," *Atlantic Monthly*, November 2002]

"'Compassion fatigue' is a syndrome from which only others are alleged to suffer." ["Preview of Coming Attractions: Sontag Looks at Images of War," *New York Observer*, 3/17/03]

Compassionate Conservatism

"One of Bush's first presidential acts was to forbid federal funding for any group overseas that even gives advice on abortion. This is, by all reports, just the compassionate treatment that the African AIDS epidemic needs." ["God and Man in the White House," *Vanity Fair*, August 2003]

Concentration Camps

"It's also very instructive to read of American reporters being given conducted tours of 'concentration camps'—the term was the official one—in order to be reassured about the humane conditions prevailing there." ["Germany in the Year Hitler Came to Power," *Newsday*, 11/09/88]

Condescension

"What I do mind is the pitying glance, or the heavy sigh, that is deployed these days. I am not ready to be patronized, or condescended to, unless by someone of some eminence who has earned that right. And even then I regard it as a sign of weakness rather than strength." ["Not So Dumb Then?," *Mirror*, 11/11/04]

Condit, Gary

"Poor Mr. Condit. He has borrowed enough Clintonian tactics and rhetoric to make one sure that he wishes he had a particle of Clintonian Teflon. . . . Yet somehow, with far less on his court docket, he has generated far less sympathy. The lesson seems to be that the bigger the offense, and the more shameless the offender, the better the chance of exculpation." ["'Clindit,'" *Wall Street Journal*, 9/07/01]

Conflict of Interest

"'Conflict of interest' has become a smooth and well-worn term, used to describe trivial behavior by people like book reviewers and special prosecutors. Really serious interests—class interests, as I sometimes ruefully think of them—are now so concerted and so omnipresent that nothing so vulgar as a conflict can ever arise." ["The Incorporated Debates," *Nation*, 10/21/96]

Conformity

"If you really don't fit, or conform, you can be dumped even if you are in the majority." ["Voting in the Passive Voice," *Harper's*, April 1992]

Congregations

"What the 'congregations' have, by way of fatuous togetherness, is not worth envying." ["Public Solidarity Does Not Help Humanism," *Free Inquiry*, Summer 2003]

Conquest, Robert

"Robert Conquest was and still is the most distinguished and authoritative anti-Communist (and ex-Communist) writing in English. . . ." [*Hitch-22* (New York: Twelve, 2010), 170]

Conscience

"Ordinary conscience will do, without any heavenly wrath behind it." [*God Is Not Great* (New York: Twelve, 2007), 214]

"Those who believe that the existence of conscience is a proof of a godly design are advancing an argument that simply cannot be disproved because there is no evidence for or against it. The case of Socrates, however, demonstrates that men and women of real conscience will often have to assert it against faith." [*God Is Not Great* (New York: Twelve, 2007), 256–257]

Conscription

"The idea of a society in mobilization for war, by way of a standing army and a draft, is one of the medieval ideas that the United States was founded to escape. Having escaped it, and put the ocean between itself and the killing fields of the Old World, some time and effort was required to redress the balance. World War I had been, from the American point of view, too short and too easy to put the point to the proof." ["An Unlikely Military Tradition Comes of Age," *Newsday*, 12/24/91]

"One way you can liberate a lot of people from serfdom is to abolish conscription. You have to prove that you don't intend to rule the country in which you've intervened by means of proxy armed forces, which is the way the United States has always operated—in places like Indonesia, El Salvador, and Greece." [Quoted in "'Don't Cross Over if You Have Any Intention of Going Back,'" *Common Review*, Summer 2005]

"Today, almost the only people who call for the return of the system are collectivists and liberals." [*Hitch-22* (New York: Twelve, 2010), 106]

Consensus

"Don't take refuge in the false security of consensus." [Debate ("Be It Resolved: Freedom of Speech Includes the Freedom to Hate"), Hart House, University of Toronto, Toronto, Canada, 11/15/06]

"It's both amusing and educational to observe a consensus when it suddenly starts to give way at all points without yielding an inch." ["Multicultural Masochism," *Slate*, 11/23/09]

Consequences

"Unintended consequences aren't always disastrous." ["The Children of '68," *Vanity Fair*, June 1998]

Conservatism

"When viewed from any objective standpoint to its immediate Left, the American conservative movement manifests one distinct symptom of well-being. It is fairly conspicuously schismatic, and it possesses the confidence to rehearse its differences in public." ["American Conservatism: A View from the Left," *Wall Street Journal*, 1/13/03]

"Conservatism cannot and does not, despite itself, remain static. It mutates into something far more reactionary than anything from which the hippies were ever fleeing." ["Where Aquarius Went," *New York Times*, 12/19/04]

Conservatives

"As it is, all the mileage is going to the conservatives, who mean what they say and who are busy constructing a society where the state cares for you before you are born and after you are dead but doesn't give a shit for you in between." ["Minority Report," *Nation*, 9/22/84]

" . . . The young conservatives have almost cheered me up about growing old." ["Epitomizing the Eighties," *Newsday*, 12/30/90]

"The words 'young conservative' will always have, for me, a slightly doom-laden tone to them." ["Young Brit Defends American People, Politics and Policies," *Washington Examiner*, 8/30/06]

Conservatives and Religion

"The attitude of conservatives toward belief has always been a fairly cynical one; it reinforces tradition and continuity and (in some fortunate epochs) actual obedience." ["The Lord and the Intellectuals," *Harper's*, July 1982]

Consistency

" . . . There is nothing to prevent a man from changing his mind. Consistency is not a virtue in itself." ["Shotgun Wedding for a *Grande Dame*," *Los Angeles Times*, 2/01/81]

"Nobody human is ever consistent. . . ." [*Hitch-22* (New York: Twelve, 2010), 417]

Conspiracy

"Conspiracy is, more than any other human activity, subject to the law of unintended consequences (which is why it should always be conjoined to cock-up rather than counterposed to it)." ["On the Imagining of Conspiracy," *London Review of Books*, 11/07/91]

"In certain respects I've come to think that there really is a Vast Right-wing Conspiracy concerning the Clintons—and that it is helping keep Bill and Hillary in power, just as stupid conservatives helped the Roosevelts to four successive terms." ["Is Hillary Clinton Eleanor Roosevelt?," *American Enterprise*, July/August 2000]

Conspiracy Theory

"One has become used to this stolid, complacent return serve: so apparently grounded in reason and scepticism but so often naïve and one-dimensional. In one way, the so-called 'conspiracy theory' need be no more than the mind's needful search for an explanation, or for an alternative to credulity." ["On the Imagining of Conspiracy," *London Review of Books*, 11/07/91]

"Conspiracy theory thus becomes an ailment of democracy. It is the white noise that moves in to fill the vacuity of the official version. To blame the theorists is therefore to look at only half the story, and sometimes even less." ["On the Imagining of Conspiracy," *London Review of Books*, 11/07/91]

Constitution

" . . . The ground of political dispute in the United Staes is about the nature and extent of the Constitution, a carefully wrought form of words devised by Englishmen in revolt against the Crown and amended by their successor generations. The ideas contained within it can be reverenced and disputed at the same time." ["Away with Them and Their Overweening Power," *Independent*, 6/02/93]

"Because of the great roof of the Constitution, which stubbornly refuses to make any mention of any god of any kind whatsoever, and which was rightly denounced as 'godless' by its enemies and critics at the time of its promulgation, America is the most religious country in the world and the one that is furthest from any official denomination of national faith." ["Ireland," *Critical Quarterly*, Spring 1998]

Consumerism

" . . . Even the most sophisticated consumers do not have sovereignty over the most basic things. They certainly do not have sovereignty over commodities, like air and sunlight, that they are forced to consume." [*Observer*, 9/13/87]

Containment

"It was an axiom of 'containment' that no part of the known world could be considered neutral. 'Neutralism' was among the cold warriors' gravest curse words, applied with caustic hostility to India and even France. Those who were not with were against, subjected to intense economic and ideological and sometimes military pressure to fall into line." ["How Neoconservatives Perish," *Harper's*, July 1990]

Contract with America

" . . . The Contract was the most completely poll-driven manifesto in modern history." ["Newtopia," *London Review of Books*, 8/24/95]

Contradiction

"Some people say it's a sign of intelligence to be able to keep two contradictory ideas in your head at the same time, and it can be a sign of intelligence. It can also be a sign of stupidity, or of unwillingness to make up the mind." [*Hardball with Chris Matthews*, MSNBC, 10/30/00]

"No serious person is without contradictions. The test lies in the willingness or ability to recognize and confront them." ["A Hundred Years of Muggery," *Weekly Standard*, 5/05/03]

"It's a commonplace to propose that authors are haunted by paradox and contradiction, and quite another thing to make plain what those paradoxes and contradictions actually are." ["Dragon Slayer," *Washington Post*, 9/28/03]

"No position can be without contradiction. The only way to evaluate somebody is how they handle contradiction." [Quoted in "'Don't Cross Over if You Have Any Intention of Going Back,'" *Common Review*, Summer 2005]

Contrarianism
"I was contrarian enough to say that I thought contrarianism was a stupid title [of *Letters to a Young Contrarian*]." [Quoted in Boris Kachka, "Are You There, God? It's Me, Hitchens," *New York*, 5/07/07]

"Sit me down across a table with an ashtray and a bottle on it, and cue the other person to make an argument, and I am programmed by the practice of a lifetime to take a contrary position." ["On the Limits of Self-Improvement, Part II," *Vanity Fair*, December 2007]

"Right though I so very often am, it always makes me feel distinctly queasy to find myself in the majority." ["Don't Forget Why We're in Afghanistan and Iraq," *Slate*, 9/07/09]

Contras
"As long as they undertake to break relations with Cuba and the Soviet Union, they are deemed by Washington to have a fully rounded political program. How they propose to govern the Nicaraguan people, apart from by the gun, is not discussed." ["The Peril of Success in Nicaragua," *New York Times*, 7/27/83]

"The Reagan administration will obviously carry on arming and paying the Nicaraguan contras whatever Congress decides. We should dread the possibility of their 'success.' It would be in the best interests of the United States and of Nicaragua if these mercenaries were soundly and finally defeated." ["The Peril of Success in Nicaragua," *New York Times*, 7/27/83]

"These bandits and killers do their work in the name of the Virgin Mary, as did their Francoist and Phalangist forerunners. Poor Nicaragua, to be so loved by the Christians." ["Minority Report," *Nation*, 12/01/84]

" . . . It's asking a lot to expect us to regard the mercenaries, or their two-faced spokesmen, as brave democrats. The proper historical analogy for these people is not the Founding Fathers but Benedict Arnold." ["Minority Report," *Nation*, 4/27/85]

" . . . Nobody who has seen the *contras*' work can doubt that, if they came to power, they would emulate the ways of the military governments in Guatemala and El Salvador if they got the chance. And military regimes—especially in Latin America—are just as hard to remove as Stalinist ones." ["Nicaragua," *Granta*, Summer 1985]

Conversion

"In medieval Spain, where Jews and Muslims were compelled on pain of death and torture to convert to Christianity, the religious authorities quite rightly suspected that many of the conversions were not sincere." [*God Is Not Great* (New York: Twelve, 2007), 40]

"It seems to me a bit crass to be trying to talk to people about conversion when you know they're ill. The whole idea of hovering over a sick person who's worried and perhaps in discomfort and saying, 'Now's the time to reconsider,' strikes me as opportunist at the very best and has a very bad history in the past." [Interview with Tony Jones, *Lateline*, Australian Broadcasting Corporation, 11/17/10]

Corporal Punishment

"While it continues it will be hard to find a substitute, but in the meantime we might just stop hitting children." ["Last Swing of the Crane," *New Statesman*, 10/06/72]

Corruption

"The whole point about corruption in politics is that it can't be done, or done properly, without a bipartisan consensus." ["Bodies Everywhere, No 'Smoking Gun,'" *Nation*, 9/08/97–9/15/97]

Counterrevolution

"Counterrevolutions can also be betrayed." ["Minority Report," *Nation*, 4/27/85]

" . . . Many is the honorable radical and revolutionary who may be found in the camp of the apparent counterrevolution. And the radical conservative is not a contradiction in terms." [*Letters to a Young Contrarian* (New York: Basic Books, 2001), 100]

"Counterrevolutions devour their children, too." [*Why Orwell Matters* (New York: Basic Books, 2002), 188]

"You do not forget, even if you come from a free and humorous society, the first time that you are with unsmiling seriousness called a 'counterrevolutionary' to your face." [*Hitch-22* (New York: Twelve, 2010), 118]

Courage

" . . . There will always be rewards as well as punishments for people with the courage of their convictions." ["Thatcher: An 'Ism' in Her Own Time," *Newsday*, 10/12/89]

"There is also the down side to the courageous personality, which is that of the leader who cannot be convinced of a mistake." ["Thatcher: An 'Ism' in Her Own Time," *Newsday*, 10/12/89]

"Courage can be as infectious as cowardice. . . ." ["Signature Sontag," *Vanity Fair*, March 2000]

"Physical courage is in some part the outcome of sheer circumstance. You can't actually stay hidden forever on that corner at which the snipers are taking aim.

You will starve to death, for one thing. So make the dash that you were going to have to make anyway, and you will have crushed your own cowardice for a moment, which is a tremendous feeling." [*Hitch-22* (New York: Twelve, 2010), 413]

Courts
"There is a reason why the courtroom is America's chief cockpit of drama. Everything else in this country—the Congress, the media, the worlds of business and the academy—is devoted to achieving consensus, by means of 'management' and the pleasing of the largest possible number of consumers. Only in the courtroom is there confrontation. And only in the courtroom does the unpredictable hold sway." ["Hustler with a Cause," *Vanity Fair*, November 1996]

Cowardice
"Moral crisis is the vile residue of moral cowardice. . . ." ["Scorched Earth," *Weekly Standard*, 7/31/06]

Creation Evidence Museum
" . . . The Creation Evidence Museum: a pathetic freak show featuring organisms allegedly so complex that they must have been invented and let loose by the divine hand all in one day." ["My Red-State Odyssey," *Vanity Fair*, September 2005]

Creationism
"If you want a cheap or a hollow laugh, just study the faces of those who believe that their own presence among us is due to a sublime and brilliant plan. The pen of a Mencken would be required just to fill in the tiny expanse between their eyebrows and their hairlines." ["Pre-Millennial Syndrome," *Salmagundi*, Summer 1996]

"I have been called arrogant myself in my time, and hope to earn the title again, but to claim that I am privy to the secrets of the universe and its creator—that's beyond my conceit." [*Letters to a Young Contrarian* (New York: Basic Books, 2001), 57]

" . . . God does not explicitly seek the credit for rats, flies, cockroaches, and mosquitoes. Most important of all, there is no mention of the mind-warping variety and beauty and complexity of the micro-organisms. Again, either the scribes didn't know about viruses and bacteria, or the Creator didn't appreciate with how lavish a hand he had unleashed life on the only planet in his solar system that can manage to support it." ["Political Animals," *Atlantic Monthly*, November 2002]

"We notice that creationism often entails 'dispensationalism'—the demented belief that there is no point in preserving nature, because the Deity will soon replace it with a perfected form. This popular teleology does not just dispense with creatures and plants: it condemns human beings to an eternity of either torment or—what may well be worse—praise and jubilation." ["Political Animals," *Atlantic Monthly*, November 2002]

"How much vanity must be concealed—not too effectively at that—in order to pretend that one is the personal object of a divine plan?" [*God Is Not Great* (New York: Twelve, 2007), 7]

" . . . Creationism, or 'intelligent design' (its only cleverness being found in this underhanded rebranding of itself), is *not even a theory*. In all its well-financed propaganda, it has never even attempted to show how one single piece of the natural world is explained better by 'design' than by evolutionary competition." [*God Is Not Great* (New York: Twelve, 2007), 86]

" . . . What kind of designer or creator only chooses to 'reveal' himself to semi-stupefied peasants in desert regions?" [Introduction to *The Portable Atheist* (New York: Da Capo Press, 2007), xviii]

" . . . The fans of the designer must convict him either of a good deal of waste and fumbling or a great deal of cruelty and indifference, or both." [Debate with Kenneth R. Miller ("Does science make belief in God obsolete?"), A Templeton Conversation]

Credibility

"It is rather a pity, considered from the standpoint of the professional politician or opinion-taker, that nobody knows exactly what 'credibility' is, or how one acquires it. 'Credibility' doesn't stand for anything morally straightforward, like meaning what you say or saying what you mean. Nor does it signify anything remotely quantifiable—any correlation between evidence presented and case made." ["Credibility Brown," *London Review of Books*, 8/31/89]

Credulity

"Gullibility and credulity are considered undesirable qualities in every department of human life—except religion." ["The Lord and the Intellectuals," *Harper's*, July 1982]

"Credulity may be a form of innocence, and even innocuous in itself, but it provides a standing invitation for the wicked and the clever to exploit their brothers and sisters, and is thus one of humanity's great vulnerabilities." [*God Is Not Great* (New York: Twelve, 2007), 160–161]

"Credulity, in the sense of simple-mindedness, is often praised by those who claim to admire the 'simple faith' of the devout. But the problem with credulity is that it constitutes an open invitation to the unscrupulous, who will take advantage of those who are prepared to believe things without evidence. This is why, for so many of us, the notion of anything being 'faith-based' is a criticism rather than a recommendation." ["Astrology Not the Only Cosmic Hoax" (On Faith) *Washington Post* (online), 5/23/07]

Cricket

"It can be compared at once to a ballet, and to the Olympic ethic of Classical Greece. It is also, both as a game and as an entertainment, inherently democratic. And it teaches the values of equality and fairness." ["Mid Off, Not Right On," *Times Literary Supplement*, 1/18/02]

Crime and Punishment

" . . . If I was confined in a windowless cell shortly after my eighteenth birthday, and was kept waiting for eight years to know if I would live or go to the bottle, I would believe that I was in prison not *as* punishment but *for* punishment. That is torture." ["Minority Report," *Nation*, 8/29/87]

"Sinners may be washed as white as snow by unearthly power, but the British warder has no mandate for cleansing white trash." ["High Life, Low Life," *Washington Post*, 6/02/91]

"It is possible to learn real lessons in the joint, about character as well as race and class." ["High Life, Low Life," *Washington Post*, 6/02/91]

"The repeat offender, as we all know, is a threat to a civilized society. Sometimes, though, it is possible to take a lenient and nuanced view. Certain classes of offender simply cannot help themselves. Their pathological behavior reveals an unconscious wish to be apprehended; to make some kind of clean breast and to cease living a lie." ["Spectator Sport: Hit and Myth," *Observer*, 5/17/98]

"For many poor Americans of all colors, jail is the only place where doctors, lawyers, teachers, and chaplains are, however grudgingly, made available to them." [*No One Left to Lie To* (New York: Verso, 2000), 35]

" . . . As often as not you will find that—whatever the high-sounding pretext may be—the worst crimes are still committed in the name of the old traditional rubbish: of loyalty to nation or 'order' or leadership or tribe or faith." [*Letters to a Young Contrarian* (New York: Basic Books, 2001), 138]

Crimean War
" . . . A war that was launched over a stupid quarrel about great-power stewardship in Jerusalem, and thus a war that is still, in our own day, continuing to be fought." ["The Grub Street Years," *Guardian*, 6/16/07]

Criticism
"It may be too much to ask people to be self-critical all the time." ["Minority Report," *Nation*, 5/03/86]

"Plainspoken critics . . . often degenerate into snarling, reactionary bores, convinced that they are the last honest men and droning interminably about the slackness of modern mores." ["Grunt Criticism from a Foe of Mock Heroics," *Newsday*, 6/15/88]

MORT KONDRACKE: "You can pack more misinformation into one sentence than anybody I've ever encountered."
CHRISTOPHER HITCHENS: "That'll be on my next dust jacket." ["Persian Gulf War," C-SPAN, 2/04/91]

" . . . The right and warrant of an individual critic does not need to be demonstrated in the same way as that of a holder of power. It is in most ways its own justification." [*Letters to a Young Contrarian* (New York: Basic Books, 2001), 81]

"We seem to have a need, as a species, for something noble and lofty. The task of criticism could be defined as the civilizing of this need—the appreciation of true decency and heroism as against coercive race legends and blood myths." ["The Medals of His Defeats," *Atlantic Monthly*, April 2002]

"I think it is absolutely essential that no accusation of disloyalty be leveled against those who criticize the authorities in time of war: criticism at such a time being more of a civic duty than a right." ["Narcissist and Windbag," *Wall Street Journal*, 2/11/04]

"My critics increasingly use the ad hominem in replying to me, and I regard that as a small moral victory." [Quoted in "'Don't Cross Over if You Have Any Intention of Going Back,'" *Common Review*, Summer 2005]

" . . . The panel of my critics contains a Muslim woman scholar, a Buddhist nun, and a charismatic Catholic. What if all these people were to walk into a bar at the same time?" ["God Bless Me, It's a Best-Seller," *Vanity Fair*, September 2007]

Cromwell, Oliver
" . . . Without Oliver Cromwell there might well not have been a Parliament to which Our Sovereign Lady might make her gracious address." [*The Monarchy: A Critique of Britain's Favorite Fetish* (London: Chatto & Windus Ltd, 1990), 13]

Crossfire
"Way back in Reagan's first term, I was invited to CNN's *Crossfire* studio to debate something or other. The usual form was—and still is—that some right-wing bigmouth would be asked to say how bad Communism or terrorism or child abuse or drug addiction was, and some liberal or leftist would be given a few moments to say that they weren't so bad after all. Two conservative moderators, one extreme and one rabidly extreme, were on hand to see fair play." ["Newtopia," *London Review of Books*, 8/24/95]

Crowds
"Any fool can lampoon a king or a bishop or a billionaire. A trifle more grit is required to face down a mob, or even a studio audience, that has decided it knows what it wants and is entitled to get it." [*Letters to a Young Contrarian* (New York: Basic Books, 2001), 76–77]

" . . . I am bored by the idea of 'Million Man,' 'Million Mom,' or any other sort of manifestation—the 'Great Peace March' of the 1980s was an example—that asks to be taken at face value and demands to be called by a name that it can't live up to. This is self-sustaining but pointless publicity, and it evaporates in less than the time of an average news cycle. It is staged for no reason except the vain ambition of attracting media attention, and it also suggests the repulsive idea that there is safety in numbers. This might be true for some ephemeral causes, but it is emphatically not true of any important idea." ["Public Solidarity Does Not Help Humanism," *Free Inquiry*, Summer 2003]

Cuba

"Spare me the letters that remind us all that Cuba has a good health care system and has abolished illiteracy. A healthy, literate people do not need to be told what they can read—least of all by those who once obliged them to read and revere the very output that is now forbidden." ["Minority Report," *Nation*, 9/04/89–9/11/89]

"Cuba—an island, like Ireland, which refuses to accept its real size and weight in the world, and whose writers and poets and musicians populate our imagination." ["Havana Can Wait," *Vanity Fair*, March 2000]

"Old people sell lavatory paper, square by square, at the doors of public bathrooms. Avid vendors of everything jostle outside the hotels. Ungifted street musicians remove their fingers from their instruments as soon as they see a hand drift toward a pocket. Girls—and boys—strike up conversations, only to reveal that they don't just like you for your mind or even—this is especially hurtful—for your body. It seems a long, long time . . . since there was serious public discussion of the abolition of money. (This Utopian accomplishment has been at least partially realized, since the Cuban peso note would now be refused even by those whose job in life it is to sell lavatory paper by the sheet.)" ["Havana Can Wait," *Vanity Fair*, March 2000]

"Slowly emerging behind the Fidelist flourishes and slogans is a system not unlike that in China, where capitalism and profiteering are permitted but democracy and free expression are not. You might call that the worst of both worlds." ["Havana Can Wait," *Vanity Fair*, March 2000]

" . . . Cuban socialism was too much like a boarding school in one way and too much like a church in another." [*Hitch-22* (New York: Twelve, 2010), 114]

"One of the claims of the Cuban revolution was to have abolished prostitution and though I had never personally believed this to be feasible (the withering away of the state being one thing but the withering away of the penis quite another), the whore scene in Santa Clara was many times more lurid than anything to be imagined in a 'bourgeois' society." [*Hitch-22* (New York: Twelve, 2010), 115]

Cuba and the Soviet Union

"Actually, despite its sorry endorsement of the Brezhnev doctrine, Cuba very often did pursue a course independent of the Soviet Union. In the cases of Angola and Nicaragua it did so quite honorably, in my opinion, and in the case of Ethiopia very much less so." ["Minority Report," *Nation*, 9/04/89–9/11/89]

Culture Wars

"The culture wars consist of more and more noise about less and less." ["Angel in the Outback," *Vanity Fair*, May 1997]

Cynicism

"Surrounded as one is by babble and mendacity, it's nonetheless important to avoid cynicism." ["Minority Report," *Nation*, 5/11/85]

"In any case, isn't there a wholesome case for cynicism? Why should it be 'bad for democracy' that most people think of their politicians as clowns on the make? Better, surely, than those awful images of adoring crowds bleating 'Now More than Ever' or 'Four More Years' at some empty jackass. And what is true of public opinion ought to hold still more for 'intellectuals.' What business is it of theirs to sweeten the atmosphere of power?" ["What's Love Got to Do with It?," *Vanity Fair*, September 1993]

"Between those who are hardily cynical about human nature and those who profess a belief in original sin, there is no necessary agreement." ["Critic of the Booboisie," *Dissent*, Summer 1994]

"Cynicism, which is most often the affectation of conservatives, can also be part of the armor of those who are prepared to go through life as a minority of one." ["Critic of the Booboisie," *Dissent*, Summer 1994]

Cyprus

"The island of Cyprus may look small, but it remains oddly hard to ignore. Like a pebble hurled into a pool, it makes waves much larger than its own modest circumference." ["Reagan-Kyprianou Meeting Puts New Focus on Cyprus," *Los Angeles Times*, 12/03/81]

"No matter what claims the Turkish Cypriots may make as a minority, they cannot justify the military occupation of 40 percent of the territory (and the most prosperous and developed 40 percent at that)." ["Reagan-Kyprianou Meeting Puts New Focus on Cyprus," *Los Angeles Times*, 12/03/81]

Dahl, Roald

"Dahl, it appears, was mean to his wife. He was explicitly anti-Semitic. He's been accused of giving dope and booze to his own kids to keep them quiet. So, is it true? *Of course* it's bloody well true. How else could Dahl have kept children enthralled and agreeably disgusted and pleasurably afraid? By being Enid Blyton?" ["The Grimmest Tales," *Vanity Fair*, January 1994]

"And, just as you can't have the pathos of Smike without the cruelty of Wackford Squeers, so you can't appreciate Dahl unless you have a taste for the grotesque as well as the innocent." ["Welcome to the Dahl House," *Vanity Fair*, September 1997]

Dalai Lama

"The greatest triumph modern PR can offer is the transcendent success of having your words and actions judged by your reputation, rather than the other way about. The 'spiritual leader' of Tibet has enjoyed this unassailable status for some time now, becoming a byword and synonym for saintly and ethereal values. Why this doesn't put people on their guard, I'll never know." ["The Divine One," *Nation*, 7/27/98]

"While he denies being a Buddhist 'pope,' the Dalai Lama is never happier than when brooding in a celibate manner on the sex lives of people he has never met." ["The Divine One," *Nation*, 7/27/98]

"The Dalai Lama . . . is entirely and easily recognizable to a secularist. In exactly the same way as a medieval princeling, he makes the claim not just that Tibet should be independent of Chinese hegemony—a 'perfectly good' demand, if I may render it into everyday English—but that he himself is a hereditary king appointed by heaven itself. How convenient!" [*God Is Not Great* (New York: Twelve, 2007), 200]

Damascus

" . . . The whole point of the Damascus legend is that it refuses the very idea of the mind's evolution, replacing it with the deranged substitute of instant divine revelation." [*Hitch-22* (New York: Twelve, 2010), 406]

Darwin, Charles

"Like so many people however brilliant, he was prone to that solipsism that either makes or breaks faith, and which imagines that the universe is preoccupied with one's own fate. This, however, makes his scientific rigor the more praiseworthy, and fit to be ranked with Galileo, since it did not arise from any intention but that of finding out the truth." [*God Is Not Great* (New York: Twelve, 2007), 270]

Darwinism

"People used to think that accepting Darwinism would lead to 'social Darwinism,' but, in fact, the reduction of people to the status of animals or machines is as likely to be opposed by atheists and humanists as anyone else." ["Finding Morals Under Empty Heavens," *Science & Spirit*, July/August 2007]

Dean, Howard

"It's not just that Mr. Dean doesn't know anything at all about Iraq, it's that he doesn't care. His bored shrug at, first, the overthrow and, second, the capture of Saddam Hussein was a shrug of indifference as well as ignorance. And how can a man who flirts with moral equivalence between Washington and bin Laden expect to be listened to when he talks about a 'distraction' from the hunt for the latter? He clearly thinks that the main enemy is at home." ["Narcissist and Windbag," *Wall Street Journal*, 2/11/04]

" . . . An insecure narcissist and vain windbag. . . ." ["Narcissist and Windbag," *Wall Street Journal*, 2/11/04]

Death

"The desire—or the need—for the death of better men is probably the special property of two groups—the chronically inferior and the incurably insecure." ["Touch of Evil," *London Review of Books*, 10/22/92]

" . . . Some men, at any rate, love the thing that kills them." ["Lord Trouble," *New York Review of Books*, 9/21/00]

"To be resigned to death and extinction is not always a consolation, even to the Stoic—though it does have its satisfactions." ["The Future of an Illusion," *Daedalus*, Summer 2003]

"I'm not that keen on the idea of being unconscious. There's plenty of time to be unconscious coming up." [Quoted in Ian Parker, "He Knew He Was Right," *New Yorker*, 10/16/06]

"The death wish, or something not unlike it, may be secretly present in all of us." [*God Is Not Great* (New York: Twelve, 2007), 59]

"It was widely believed by the devout of those days [early nineteenth century] that unbelievers would scream for a priest when their own death-beds loomed. Why this was thought to be valuable propaganda it is impossible to say. Surely the sobbing of a human creature *in extremis* is testimony not worth having, as well as testimony extracted by the most contemptible means?" [*Thomas Paine's Rights of Man: A Biography* (New York: Atlantic Monthly Press, 2006), 139]

"People are not on their oath when speaking of the dead." ["A Death in the Family," *Vanity Fair*, November 2007]

"Indeed, if you make the right propitiations you may even find that death has no sting, and that an exception to the rules of physical annihilation may be made in your own case. It cannot be said often enough that this preachment is immoral as well as irrational." [Introduction to *The Portable Atheist* (New York: Da Capo Press, 2007), xvi]

"I'm not afraid of death myself, because I'm not going to know I'm dead. I'm awed a bit by the idea, but I'm perfectly reconciled to it. Certainly I am, as everyone is, reconciled to everyone else's death but their own. They think an exception can be made in their own case." [Quoted in Gregg LaGambina, "Christmas with Christopher Hitchens," *A. V. Club*, 12/20/07]

"I have often thought that when I do die it will be of sheer boredom. . . ." ["On the Limits of Self-Improvement, Part III," *Vanity Fair*, September 2008]

"Those who die young and whose brief lives are fretted with anxiety sometimes appear in retrospect to have invited their fate, and to be too much sunken in introspection and self-pity." ["An Introduction to the Poetry of Percy Bysshe Shelley," *Guardian*, 1/28/10]

"There's nothing quite like reading about your own death. . . . I recommend it. A constant reflection on demise is a good thing." ["Book and Author Luncheon," C-SPAN2, 5/27/10]

"I personally want to 'do' death in the active and not the passive, and to be there to look it in the eye and be doing something when it comes for me." [*Hitch-22* (New York: Twelve, 2010), 7]

"I do not especially *like* the idea that one day I shall be tapped on the shoulder and informed, not that the party is over but that it is most assuredly going on—only henceforth in my absence. . . . Much more horrible, though, would be the announcement that the party was continuing forever, and that I was forbidden to leave." [*Hitch-22* (New York: Twelve, 2010), 337]

"I have sometimes noticed in other people that a clear-eyed sense of impending extinction can have a paradoxically liberating effect, as in: at least I don't have to do
that anymore." [*Hitch-22* (New York: Twelve, 2010), 395]

"It's one thing one is certainly born to do." ["Q&A with Christopher Hitchens,"
C-SPAN, 1/14/11 (first aired: 1/23/11)]

Decadence
"As with theories of the collapse of Rome, you can tell a good deal about some-
body from the cause of decadence, and the date of same, in which he believes. . . ."
["Newtopia," *London Review of Books*, 8/24/95]

Decisions
"One always has the vague illusion of taking or making one's own decisions, the
illusion itself running in parallel with the awareness that most such calls are made
for you by other people, or by circumstances, or just made." [*Hitch-22* (New York:
Twelve, 2010), 220]

Declaration of Independence
"There is no other example in history, apart from the composition of the King
James version of the Bible, in which great words and concepts have been fused
into poetic prose by the banal processes of a committee." [*Thomas Jefferson: Author
of America* (New York: HarperCollins, 2005), 23]

" . . . 'The pursuit of happiness' belongs to that limited group of lapidary phrases
that has changed history, and it seems that the delegates realized this as soon as
they heard it." [*Thomas Jefferson: Author of America* (New York: HarperCollins,
2005), 26]

Defeat
"Glorious defeats often have a greater emotional effect than muddy victories."
["Rebel Ghosts," *Vanity Fair*, July 1999]

Defectors
" . . . Many things are forgiven those who see the error of their formerly radical
ways." ["The Chorus and Cassandra," *Grand Street*, Autumn 1985]

Deficit
"About this we are supposed to feel bad. We are supposed to feel bad, in particular, on behalf of our children." ["Minority Report," *Nation*, 11/03/84]

"The deficit, then, is not the difference between what America spends and what
America earns; it is, to a striking extent, the difference between what the rich owe
and what the rich pay." ["Minority Report," *Nation*, 11/03/84]

Definitions
"Definitions, like simplifications, are dangerous but necessary." [*Cyprus* (London:
Quartet Books, 1984), 51]

Deicide

"Remember that the Vatican did not assert that it was *some Jews* who had killed Christ. It asserted that it was *the Jews* who had ordered his death, and that the Jewish people as a whole were the bearers of a collective responsibility. It seems bizarre that the church could not bring itself to drop the charge of generalized Jewish 'deicide' until very recently. But the key to its reluctance is easy to find. If you once admit that the descendants of Jews are not implicated, it becomes very hard to argue that anyone else not there present was implicated, either. One rent in the fabric, as usual, threatens to tear the whole thing apart (or to make it into something simply man-made and woven, like the discredited Shroud of Turin). The collectivization of guilt, in short, is immoral in itself, as religion has been occasionally compelled to admit." [*God Is Not Great* (New York: Twelve, 2007), 210]

Demagogues

" . . . Here's the thing about self-righteous, born-again demagogues: Nothing they ever do, or did, can be attributed to anything but the very highest motives." ["Peanut Envy," *Slate*, 5/21/07]

Democratic Leadership Council

" . . . The DLC thinks the Democrats are 'perceived' not so much as pink as yellow." ["The Loyally Complicit," *Harper's*, July 1991]

"What we have from the DLC is an old gambit, one that continues to attract politicians despite the fact that it does not work. The thinking goes this way: One wins a presidential election only by adopting the slogans and strategy of the candidate who won last time. You don't so much try to accrue votes as to subtract them from the other guy—in this case, the Republican guy." ["The Loyally Complicit," *Harper's*, July 1991]

Democracy

"Democracy should not need to be imposed. There is a necessary contradiction there." [Quoted in "Promoting Democracy: A Panel Discussion," *Temple Law Quarterly*, Winter 1987]

"Japan had to be defeated in order for democracy to be empowered. Democracy was not imposed upon Japan; democracy was permitted." [Quoted in "Promoting Democracy: A Panel Discussion," *Temple Law Quarterly*, Winter 1987]

Democratic Party

"They apparently do not want war. But, equally important, they do not want to be accused of not wanting one." ["Minority Report," *Nation*, 6/22/85]

"The Democratic Party does not think, ergo it is not." ["The Loyally Complicit," *Harper's*, July 1991]

" . . . A sitting Democrat president who can't pitch to Irishness ought to be in another line of work." ["The Luck That Does No One Any Good but Clinton," *Evening Standard*, 8/10/98]

Democratic Party and Abortion

"Abortion is the only thing that keeps the Democratic Party together." [Quoted in Neil Munro, "Leaving the Left," *National Journal*, 4/05/03]

Denial

"It's never a good sign when someone denies something that hasn't been alleged." ["Saddam's 'Agent' Is New Danger to Him," *Mirror*, 10/26/05]

"There can be no serious ethical position based on denial or a refusal to look the facts squarely in the face." [Introduction to *The Portable Atheist* (New York: Da Capo Press, 2007), xxii]

" . . . Perhaps you notice how the denial is so often the preface to the justification. . . ." [*Hitch-22* (New York: Twelve, 2010), 202]

Department of Defense

"[Secretary of Defense Caspar] Weinberger may have had a point at Oxford, where he argued that the American people could stop a war they didn't like. But it is he and his bureaucrats who have the power to *start* one, and there is no consultation process for that." ["Minority Report," *Nation*, 7/21/84–7/28/84]

"I would change the name of the Defense Department back to the War Department right away." ["Theater of War," *Claremont Review of Books*, Winter 2006]

Department of State

"It is always encouraging when the department shakes off the dusty euphemisms that make up the small change of diplomatic habit." ["Powell Valediction," *Foreign Policy*, November/December 2004]

Despair

" . . . The moment of near despair is quite often the moment that precedes courage rather than resignation. In a sense, with the back to the wall and no exit but death or acceptance, the options narrow to one. There can even be something liberating in this realization." [*Letters to a Young Contrarian* (New York: Basic Books, 2001), 86–87]

Destiny

" . . . The right people do sometimes meet at the right time, and perhaps are meant to do so. . . ." ["Kings of Comedy," *Vanity Fair*, December 1995]

Deterrence

" . . . A *paradox* may mean something that is only apparently contradictory, or it may mean something that is actually self-contradictory. Considered as a strategy, deterrence has certainly toppled into the latter category. In order for, say, the Soviet Union to be deterred, the deterrent must be 'credible.' You must mean what you say, and you must be able to make good your threats. In practice, this means you must be prepared to strike first; it isn't deterrent if you can only strike second or not at all. Thus, capacity becomes strategy." ["Minority Report," *Nation*, 9/18/82]

Princess Diana

"She has done more, even if only by accident, to undermine the idea of 'the succession' than I could ever have done by trying. Indeed, by her devotion to her children, she has put the whole idea of 'the succession' into doubt." ["Tarnished Crown," *Vanity Fair*, September 1997]

" . . . It seemed that every person in Britain believed she cared for them individually and would be at her happiest when dining in a homeless shelter." ["Throne & Altar," *Nation*, 9/29/97]

"The quarrel between the Spencer girl and the Windsors was one in which no side needed to be taken. With any luck, I used to think, they would both lose." ["Four Poems and a Funeral," *Nation*, 9/29/97]

"Princess Diana made one trip to Angola in her jeans, which I think was one of the best things she did." [Interview with Paul Kilduff, *Berkeley Monthly*, May 1998]

" . . . It's only a step from nominating the 'people's princess' to developing the fatal illusion that you can cure scrofula by being the princely people's prime minister." ["End of the Line," *Guardian*, 12/06/00]

Princess Diana: Death

"To say that Diana, Princess of Wales, was killed by those seeking publicity is as absurd as it is to say that she was killed by seeking it herself. The speed limits are the same for everybody; there are some dangers from which a bodyguard cannot protect you; if you wish to dine incognito, then it is probably best to avoid the Paris Ritz. These are the few, paltry 'lessons' of her death." ["Mother Teresa or Mrs. Simpson: Which Was the Real Diana?," *Los Angeles Times*, 9/01/97]

"This was not, as some oafish spokesman from Buckingham Palace apparently told CNN, 'an accident waiting to happen.' It was just an accident, of the sort that happens to people whether they symbolize 'life in the fast lane' or otherwise." ["Mother Teresa or Mrs. Simpson: Which Was the Real Diana?," *Los Angeles Times*, 9/01/97]

Princess Diana and Prince Charles

"'Are you with Charles or Di?' Can't say I know them well enough to be sure. Have you conceivably confused me with someone else? Someone who cares?" ["Diary," *London Review of Books*, 12/14/95]

"In the pending case of Windsor v. Windsor, the only card the poor sap [Prince Charles] holds is seniority: the very reason the masses have apparently rallied to the side of his poor, lamblike, innocent airhead of a wife. . . . People feel that they know her. They don't feel they know him. The vicarious identification wins out every time." ["Diary," *London Review of Books*, 12/14/95]

"I went to see her at the British Embassy several years ago . . . and was quite shocked by how thin and miserable she seemed. She looked like a dog being washed." ["Diary," *London Review of Books*, 12/14/95]

Dickens, Charles
" . . . A man who really was much more conservative than he seemed. . . ." [*Why Orwell Matters* (New York: Basic Books, 2002), 101]

Dictatorship [See: Tyranny]

Diet Books
"The diet book is one of those fool-and-money separation devices that seems, like roulette or slot machines, never to lose its power." ["I Don't Do Diets," *Mirror*, 8/18/03]

Dignity
" . . . something that is by definition inefficient is fairly certain also to be undignified." ["End of the Line," *Guardian*, 12/06/00]

"There's an old argument about whether full bellies or empty bellies lead to contentment or revolt: it's an argument not worth having. The crucial organ is the mind, not the gut. People assert themselves out of an unquenchable sense of dignity." [*Letters to a Young Contrarian* (New York: Basic Books, 2001), 112]

Discontent
"Discontent is never wrong, after all. There's never been a summer of content that I can remember, or even a winter one." ["Events in the News," C-SPAN, 5/31/94]

Discrimination
"In the absence of any standard of discrimination, there are no standards of discrimination." ["American Notes," *Times Literary Supplement*, 6/27/86]

"Incidentally, by what awful ironic betrayal of our language do we find ourselves accusing bigots and tribalists of the sin of 'discrimination'? They are the ones who judge severely by category, and yet can't tell anyone apart. 'Discrimination' is only one of the moral and intellectual exercises that they are quite unable to perform." ["Ireland," *Critical Quarterly*, Spring 1998]

Disillusionment
"The long withdrawing roar of disillusionment is, of course, for all seasons. Alas, it's a twice-told tale. Stories of radical disappointment, unlike stories of unhappy families, are all the same." ["Novelists in Their Youth," *New York Times*, 4/19/92]

"Choked-up feelings of emotion at liberation are the surest sign that a moment of disillusion and disappointment is at hand." [Epilogue to *A Long Short War: The Postponed Liberation of Iraq* (New York: Plume Books, 2003), 90]

Dissent
" . . . One usually registers dissent not from what he says but from what he omits." ["History as Handbook: Europe Since the War," *Newsday*, 1/08/92]

"Many people who are prepared to be quite brave in defying an aroused public opinion, who in fact consider it almost their job to flout conventional views, will exhibit none of this intellectual courage when it comes to anything that seems to be within the family." [Quoted in "Forbidden Thoughts: A Roundtable on Taboo Research," *American Enterprise*, January/February 1995]

"Having a fight with your cohorts may greatly increase your marketability." [Quoted in "Forbidden Thoughts: A Roundtable on Taboo Research," *American Enterprise*, January/February 1995]

"The noble title of 'dissident' must be earned rather than claimed; it connotes sacrifice and risk rather than mere disagreement, and it has been consecrated by many exemplary and courageous men and women." [*Letters to a Young Contrarian* (New York: Basic Books, 2001), 1]

"For the dissenter, the skeptical mentality is at least as important as any armor of principle." [*Letters to a Young Contrarian* (New York: Basic Books, 2001), 33]

" . . . The role of dissident is not, and should not be, a claim of membership in a communion of saints. In other words, the more fallible the mammal, the truer the example." [*Letters to a Young Contrarian* (New York: Basic Books, 2001), 94]

"There will always be Trotskys and Goldsteins and even Winston Smiths, but it must be clearly understood that the odds are overwhelmingly against them, and that as with Camus's rebel, the crowd will yell with joy to see them dragged to the scaffold." [*Why Orwell Matters* (New York: Basic Books, 2002), 191]

Diversity
" . . . 'Diversity' . . . has lost its meaning by evolving into a candy-striped version of—guess what—uniformity." ["We Know Best," *Vanity Fair*, May 2001]

Dixie Chicks
"Yes I did refer to the so-called Dixie Chicks as 'fat sluts' (having not the least idea of what any of them looked like)." [Afterword to *Christopher Hitchens and His Critics: Terror, Iraq, and the Left*, ed. Simon Cottee and Thomas Cushman (New York: NYU Press, 2008), 332]

Dixiecrats
" . . . The Dixiecrats know exactly which antique Southern traditions they are calling upon, and they don't mean chivalric courtesy to women, or mansions with Attic porticoes." ["Waiving the Flag," *Nation*, 7/21/97]

Do-Gooders
"*Corruptio optimi pessima*: no greater cruelty will be devised than by those who are sure, or are assured, that they are doing good." ["Lightness at Midnight," *Atlantic Monthly*, September 2002]

Dole, Bob
"In the only political trope for which he will ever be remembered, Bob Dole described the Second World War as one of the 'Democrat wars.' (This was during his vice presidential debate in 1976, the moment at which he achieved the amazing distinction of being defeated by Walter Mondale.)" ["Child-Proof," *Nation*, 6/24/96]

Dole, Bob and Prince Charles

"I look at the face of Bob Dole, and I see the features of Prince Charles looking miserably back at me. Both do what they do because they have to, and because it is expected of them. Both of them have spent a lifetime preparing for a high office that will be dust and ashes when (and if) they succeed to it. Both know, at some profound level, that nobody really wants them. Both know that to admit this would be to admit that their lives so far, in the waiting rooms and antechambers of authority, had been so much wasted time." ["The Blind Leading the Dumb," *Nation*, 4/01/96]

Domino Theory

"The 'domino theory' was rivaled in our time only by the 'nuclear umbrella' as a stupid *Realpolitik* coinage that euphemized mass murder and debased statecraft." ["Goodbye to Berlin," *Nation*, 12/08/97]

Don't Ask, Don't Tell

"Ever since Clinton came up with his atrocious slogan 'Don't ask, don't tell' (and has there ever been a chief executive who stood to gain more by such an injunction?), the rule designed for the moral blackmail of homosexuals has become regnant in general. In the armed forces of this commander in chief, you can 'be all you can be' on condition that you are a committed and habitual liar. So, let's have homosexual men and women in the armed forces as long as they agree to practice full-time falsehood." ["Dirty Stories," *Nation*, 7/07/97]

Dowd, Maureen

"I don't find it hard to guess what her political prejudice is—democratic with a small *d*." ["Top Dowd," *Vanity Fair*, June 1995]

" . . . If Dowd says you have a knack for PR, you have acquired one even if you didn't have one before." ["Cindy Sheehan's Sinister Piffle," *Slate*, 8/15/05]

Dreams

"Good grief! Is there anything less funny than hearing a woman relate a dream she's just had?" ["Why Women Aren't Funny," *Vanity Fair*, January 2007]

Driberg, Tom

"Tom had, after all, been indubitably the most consecrated blow-job artist ever to take his seat in either House. . . . He would go anywhere and do anything for the chance to suck somebody off. . . . He didn't go in much for the anal end of the business. . . . He just liked to administer free blow-jobs to the masses. How many modern members of Parliament can claim as much?" ["Reader, He Married Her," *London Review of Books*, 5/10/90]

"If there had been scientific proof of vaginal fangs, he could hardly have been more cold on the idea." ["Reader, He Married Her," *London Review of Books*, 5/10/90]

"He was not so much a snob as an élitist, and helped me to realize that the two things are often wrongly confused. The path of the rebel, as followed by Tom, was a protest against boredom and the ordinary, conformist, utilitarian precept. It was a hopeless search for a good life where ugliness and need would not always be sovereign, and where there would be wit and booze and wickedness, and it ended in a taxi between Paddington Station and the Barbican." ["Reader, He Married Her," *London Review of Books*, 5/10/90]

Drinking

"Many people who might otherwise have died of boredom and irritation, or taken a running jump at themselves, have been kept going by a steady intake of toxins and by the low company this naturally forces them to keep." ["Why Genius Cries Out for a Drink," *Evening Standard*, 4/02/92]

"Not just the occasional drink—the daily drink. Not just red wine—any alcohol is better than none. An apple a day, they said in my boyhood, kept the doctor away. Yeah, that's right—just bathe your teeth in sugar water and acid and see what happens. Much better to hurl the heartburn-inducing fruit into the trash and reach firmly for the corkscrew, which was the strategy that I began to adopt when I was about fifteen." ["Living Proof," *Vanity Fair*, March 2003]

"Even if it makes you look like a brand snob, do specify a label when ordering spirits in particular. . . . Pick a decent product and stay with it. Upgrade yourself, for Chrissake. Do you think you are going to live forever?" ["Living Proof," *Vanity Fair*, March 2003]

"I noticed early in life that some colleagues drank because of the writer's life, and others had seemingly become scribblers because it gave them a high-toned excuse to drink. Some drank to meet a deadline, and some drank to give themselves an excuse to miss one. The latter crew had a tendency to clock out prematurely." ["Living Proof," *Vanity Fair*, March 2003]

"What the soothing people at Alcoholics Anonymous don't or won't understand is that suicide or self-destruction would probably have come much earlier to some people if they could not have had a drink." ["Living Proof," *Vanity Fair*, March 2003]

"In moderation, of course, yes, if you insist . . . but how was 'moderation' established except by transcending itself just a bit?" ["Living Proof," *Vanity Fair*, March 2003]

"Winston Churchill was half in the bag for the whole of the Finest Hour, if not longer. General Ulysses Grant managed to stay in the saddle only by means unknown. Richard Nixon, according to the latest release of Kissinger tapes, was too 'loaded' to talk to the British prime minister during the Yom Kippur War of 1973. Boris Yeltsin was too plastered to get off his plane during a stopover at Shannon Airport, with the Irish government waiting on the tarmac. Not all these examples are encouraging. But, then, neither is the idea of a man who doesn't trust himself, and isn't trusted by those who know him, to take even a sip. Nobody likes a quitter." ["The Teetotal Effect," *Vanity Fair*, August 2004]

"A glass of refreshment, in my view, never hurt anybody." ["On the Limits of Self-Improvement, Part I," *Vanity Fair*, October 2007]

"When all is said, isn't there something very slightly fussy about all this mixing and shaking and measuring: something, perhaps, fractionally light in the loafers?" ["At the Filling Station," *Weekly Standard*, 12/24/07]

"Don't drink if you have the blues: it's a junk cure. Drink when you are in a good mood." [*Hitch-22* (New York: Twelve, 2010), 352]

"It's not true that you shouldn't drink alone: these can be the happiest glasses you ever drain." [*Hitch-22* (New York: Twelve, 2010), 352]

"It's much worse to see a woman drunk than a man: I don't know quite why this is true, but it just is." [*Hitch-22* (New York: Twelve, 2010), 352]

Drudge, Matt
" . . . The salacious and unreliable Matt Drudge, sleaze king of the Internet." ["The Story America Almost Missed," *Evening Standard*, 1/28/98]

Drugs
"With 20,000 different chemicals being used in our food alone the threat is that, under pressure from drug companies, and from consumers who think that there must be a cure for everything, our society will poison itself in the search for a good and comfortable life." ["Does It Have to Be Drugs with Everything?," *Daily Express*, 6/28/77]

"Alcohol and nicotine are, by some part of their very nature, social. This is what distinguishes them from narcotic drugs that, while always hyped as allowing voyages of the imagination, never quite succeed in getting these voyages under way." ["Why Genius Cries Out for a Drink," *Evening Standard*, 4/02/92]

"I don't think that what you do or who you do it with or what you insert in any way into your own body is anyone's business but your own or can be." [Quoted in Bill Steigerwald and Bob Hoover, "Objectivity and Other Lies," *Pittsburgh Post-Gazette*, 4/27/97]

"Sex—yes. Rock 'n' roll—by all means. Drugs—no. Drugs rot the brain and give opportunities to the forces of law and order, and are self-indulgent." ["The Children of '68," *Vanity Fair*, June 1998]

"Avoid all narcotics: these make you more boring rather than less and are not designed—as are the grape and the grain—to enliven company." [*Hitch-22* (New York: Twelve, 2010), 352]

Dukakis, Michael
" . . . A personal coward and political dolt who had lost an easy argument about capital punishment in a public debate with George Bush, and who had also suffered from a sleazy 'subliminal' campaign about a dusky parole-breaking rapist named Willie Horton." [*No One Left to Lie To* (New York: Verso, 2000), 34]

Duke, David

"If you take all Duke's open and covert statements over his long career, it is clear that the black question basically bores him. Why stop at saying what Republicans can imply and Democrats can be shamefaced in not denying? The real energy of his theory and practice is provided by anti-Semitism." ["Minority Report," *Nation*, 12/16/91]

Dylan, Bob

"Of his ability as a poet . . . there can be no reasonable doubt." ["America's Poet?," *Weekly Standard*, 7/05/04–7/12/04]

Earth Tones

"Earth tones—shouldn't you already know when you're in the toilet?" ["Funniest Celebrity in Washington" Contest, Washington, DC, 11/03/99]

Ebonics

"Whether we agree to call it a slang, an idiom, a vernacular, or a debased survival, the fact is that Black English does exist and is spoken, and does define (and circumscribe) the world of many Americans. . . . Should it be taught? No—it's already been taught before the child gets to school." ["Hooked on Ebonics," *Vanity Fair*, March 1997]

"There is tragedy and history and emotion involved in the survival of a black speech in America, and giggling at its expense is not good manners. But the worst irony of all would be to congratulate, hypocritically, the 'richness' of something that threatens to imprison its speakers in the confines of a resentful, baffled, muttering serfdom." ["Hooked on Ebonics," *Vanity Fair*, March 1997]

Economics

"By a nice chance, cupidity and avarice are the spur to economic development." [*God Is Not Great* (New York: Twelve, 2007), 214]

Editing

"Every author has his or her favorite horror story, usually involving the insertion of mistakes and infelicities that were not in the original. In fact, editing here [in America] has become rewriting; and rewriting of a very low standard." ["American Notes," *Times Literary Supplement*, 5/10/85]

Education

"Those who rush to say that Oakland teachers are failing the kids had better acknowledge that they had been 'failed' well before now." ["Hooked on Ebonics," *Vanity Fair*, March 1997]

"The measure of an education is that you acquire some idea of the extent of your ignorance. And it seems at least thinkable that today's history students don't quite know what subject they are not being taught." ["Goodbye to All That," *Harper's*, November 1998]

"Let no one doubt the extent of the damage done by comfort teaching or thera-peutic education, which has reversed the idea that educators should be educated (a decent teacher will teach in order to learn) and which has made the relation-ship of instructor to student into an exercise in the mutual, restful softening of the cortex." ["Goodbye to All That," *Harper's*, November 1998]

"The presumed educator must be educated." [*Letters to a Young Contrarian* (New York: Basic Books, 2001), 30]

Edward VIII

" . . . The chief difficulty at every stage of Edward VIII's life lay in the finding and invention of things for him to do. The same principle—of pointless duties joy-lessly undertaken—underlay his very conception." ["How's the Vampire?," *London Review of Books*, 11/08/90]

"Further elements of stage-management were added as it became more necessary to shield the British people from the true character of their monarch-to-be. This awkward necessity was laid upon the Establishment not by Edward's politics but by his penis, which was errant and capricious and was the only part of him in-clined to disregard class distinctions. . . ." ["How's the Vampire?," *London Review of Books*, 11/08/90]

"Edward was the first of the modern monarchs; the magic of the throne is now in-extricable from Charles and the Annenbergs, Diana and Donald Trump—the ex-tension of Edward's international white-trash habit into modern showbiz and celeb culture." ["How's the Vampire?," *London Review of Books*, 11/08/90]

Edwards, John

"Some people do come into politics for serious and honorable reasons. He's the first for a long time." [Quoted in Neil Munro, "Leaving the Left," *National Journal*, 4/05/03]

"John Edwards is a good man who is in politics for good reasons, but there is something about his populism that doesn't quite—what's the word?—translate." ["Run, Al, Run," *Slate*, 9/24/07]

Einstein, Albert

"We have more reason to be grateful to him than to all the rabbis who have ever wailed, or who ever will." [*God Is Not Great* (New York: Twelve, 2007), 272]

El Salvador

"The FMLN [Faribundo Marti National Liberation Front] is the only reason why there's been any reform at all in El Salvador. But I ask myself everyday: If the FMLN won the war, would it commit the same mistakes as the old regime? The answer is yes." [Quoted in Don Kowet, "Christopher Hitchens, Drawing Room Marxist," *Washington Times*, 1/02/90]

Electability

"The road from 'credibility' to 'electability' lies through plausibility, and people don't like you if all you want of them is to be liked." ["Minority Report," *Nation*, 5/11/92]

"I like 'electable' as a term, don't you? It has that marvelous suggestion of being O.K., of being allowed." ["Minority Report," *Nation*, 10/31/94]

Elections

"An American election is something that is too precious to be other than utterly transparent." ["Diary," *London Review of Books*, 1/06/00]

"Every four years, we suddenly discover that the only people worth noticing or mentioning in the United States are those who are ill, or unemployed, or uninsured, or underpaid, or homeless, or some combination of the above." ["Let Them Count Houses," *Slate*, 9/01/08]

"Haven't we all heard some irritating person saying that if so-and-so is elected, then he/she is absolutely definitely leaving the country? There must be some reason why it is mainly liberals who tend to say this . . . but the chief thing to note about the promise is that it is usually an empty one." ["Suburbs of Our Discontent," *Atlantic Monthly*, December 2008]

Elections: 1796

"It is perhaps both heartening and sobering to reflect that, in the contest between Jefferson and Adams in 1796, the electors were offered a choice between the president of the American Philosophical Society and the founder of the American Academy of Arts and Sciences, and chose both of them." [*Thomas Jefferson: Author of America* (New York: HarperCollins, 2005), 107]

Elections: 1800

"This is the period at which Americans began to revere the notion of orderly transitions of power between opposing parties, a thing that was still unknown anywhere else in the world." [*Thomas Jefferson: Author of America* (New York: HarperCollins, 2005), 118]

Elections: 1988

"The 1988 campaign has shown that people know they are being got at, and don't like it, but simply have no say in the matter unless they are donors—and not always even then." ["The Merchandising of Our Candidates," *Newsday*, 11/02/88]

Elections: 1996

" . . . The whole of the 1996 presidential election was hijacked . . . by a money-driven, donor-dominated Dick Morris machine, in which there was simply no chance or need to engage the Republicans in a battle of ideas (unless this battle took the form of preempting Republican positions)." ["Conspiracies with Sidney," *Nation*, 3/30/98]

Elections: 2000

"Meantime, the normally pro-life Republicans are grimly intent on aborting all pregnant or even budding chads. . . . Well, when you have heard top-dollar attorneys and former secretaries of state solemnly disputing the degree of penetration to which a virgin chad may be subjected, and still be undefiled, you too will begin to see the Electoral College as a college of cardinals disputing the immaculacy of a presidency. And if Al Gore wins by these means, it is already clear that the entire Republican Party will consider his conception and birth to be utterly illegitimate." ["A Saga of Dimples and a Heartless Babe," *Evening Standard*, 11/22/00]

"A few liberal dolts have been going around saying in an ominous manner that they 'won't forget' what Nader did; well, guess what? Some of us won't be forgetting the Stalinist mentality of those same dolts, either." ["What Crisis?," *Nation*, 12/04/00]

Elections: 2004

" . . . Unless he conclusively repudiates the obvious defeatists in his own party (and maybe even his own family), we shall be able to say that John Kerry's campaign is a distraction from the fight against al-Qaeda." ["Flirting with Disaster," *Slate*, 9/27/04]

"It seems that anyone fool enough to favor the reelection of the president is by definition a God-bothering, pulpit-pounding, Armageddon-artist, enslaved by ancient texts and prophecies and committed to theocratic rule." ["Bush's Secularist Triumph," *Slate*, 11/09/04]

Electoral College

" . . . The Electoral College system must be reformed or abolished to give expression to the popular vote. This will also compel a reconsideration of the small state/swing state tyranny, whereby small and rural states outvote large, populous, urban, and multiethnic ones. That is several decades overdue." ["Dirty Rotten Scoundrels," *Observer*, 11/12/00]

Elitism

"It's often noticeable that the person who rails against 'elites' and the person who profits by oligarchy are the same person." ["Bourgeois Blues," *Vanity Fair*, November 1992]

"Actually, it is a real shame that America *doesn't* have a cultural elite. It could really use one, or make better use of what it has by way of one. . . . My point about the missing cultural elite is that—unlike the indiscriminate non-elites of the hereditary or the commercial or the Irish bootlegging or the show biz and celeb—*anyone* who really wants to can join." ["Bourgeois Blues," *Vanity Fair*, November 1992]

Elitism and Populism

"The palace and the mob may superficially make natural allies. Elitism and populism are not as antithetical as some people believe. (Both, for example, are hostile to democracy.)" ["Royal Flush," *Los Angeles Times*, 10/05/97]

"That elite is most successful which can claim the heartiest allegiance of the fickle crowd; can present itself as most 'in touch' with popular concerns; can anticipate the tides and pulses of opinion; can, in short, be the least apparently 'elitist.'" [*No One Left to Lie To* (New York: Verso, 2000), 18]

"Just as a populist may be a foe of democracy even if he commands a temporary majority, so a man taunted as 'elitist' can be a man of the people if he argues for popular and constitutional sovereignty." [Foreword to *1968: War & Democracy*, by Eugene J. McCarthy (Petersham, MA: Lone Oak Press, 2000), 8]

"*Elitism* and *populism* . . . are too often found in the same person." ["All the Views Fit to Print," *Slate*, 11/01/10]

Empire

"It is finer as well as safer to have a republic. It can be nasty as well as risky to have an empire. Empire leads to big government, vast military budgets, and intrusive state intervention in the private lives of citizens." ["Rumble on the Right," *Vanity Fair*, July 2004]

Enemies

" . . . Most of the time the enemy wears a banal face." [*Letters to a Young Contrarian* (New York: Basic Books, 2001), 123]

" . . . Perfectionism and messianism are the chief and most lethal of our foes." ["Lightness at Midnight," *Atlantic Monthly*, September 2002]

"Time spent in understanding and studying a foe is always time well spent, and absolutist categories may easily blunt this rigorous undertaking." ["'Evil,'" *Slate*, 12/31/02]

" . . . An *ad hominem* attack is almost by definition an admission that my enemies would rather not engage with my arguments." ["Open Letter to Readers and Letter Exchange with Victor Navasky," Christopher Hitchens Web, 2003]

England

" . . . The famously absolute refusal of the English to talk as if anything deserved to be taken seriously." ["A Postwar Period Pastiche," *Washington Post*, 3/31/89]

"The English have long been convinced that they are admired and envied by the rest of the world for their eccentricities alone. Many of these eccentricities—red telephone boxes with heavy doors, unarmed policemen, courtesy in sporting matters—are now more durable as touristic notions than as realities." [*The Monarchy: A Critique of Britain's Favorite Fetish* (London: Chatto & Windus Ltd, 1990), 3]

" . . . Given the ravenous appetite of the press and the public for royal trivia, England often seems like some princeling-infested Ruritanian theme park." ["Windsor Knot," *New York Times Magazine*, 5/12/91]

Enlightenment

"One should never miss an opportunity to celebrate the Enlightenment or to mock priestcraft and the worship of mediocre princes and tycoons." ["Minority Report," *Nation*, 6/19/89]

Enthusiasm

"It is, in a deep way, an *insult* to live under a regime that demands, not just acquiescence, but actual participating enthusiasm and applause." ["Still Red: The Last Bastions of Communism," *Washington Post*, 8/25/91]

Environment

" . . . The 'environment' is not the gift of entrepreneurs, risk takers, or investors. It is the common, inherited property of humanity." ["Minority Report," *Nation*, 4/02/83]

Environmentalism

" . . . The 'green' movement indicts both the state-accumulation socialisms of the East and the short-term opportunism of private enterprise in the West, not to mention the Bhopal and Brazil horrors of the Third World. Inscribed in the idea of a planetary and holistic concern is the mandate for a humane collectivism and solidarity. . . ." ["Credibility Brown," *London Review of Books*, 8/31/89]

Envy

" . . . The spirit of envy can lead to emulation and ambition and have positive consequences." [*God Is Not Great* (New York: Twelve, 2007), 100]

Espionage Act

"The point of using the Espionage Act against the press, and those who share information with the press, is this: we don't care whether the Russians know or not. It's the voters and taxpayers who mustn't know. For them, there can never be enough ignorance. In their minds, there must always be the suspicion that debate itself, let alone disclosure, is disloyalty. If that suspicion can be hardened into law, so much the better." ["Minority Report," *Nation*, 11/09/85]

Etiquette

" . . . It's often necessary to be rudest to the nicest people." ["The Lord and the Intellectuals," *Harper's*, July 1982]

Euphemism

"For the sake of argument, then, one must never let a euphemism or a false consolation pass uncontested." [Introduction to *For the Sake of Argument* (New York: Verso, 1993), 3]

"Let us by all means not 'sanitize' anything, let alone euphemize it." ["Theater of War," *Claremont Review of Books*, Winter 2006]

"Euphemisms about sin and repentance are useless." ["Bring the Pope to Justice," *Newsweek*, 5/03/10]

Europe

"There's no such thing as an average European, a fact for which there is good reason to be thankful. And there's no such thing as a representative European, either (though there may be European representatives). I'm not sure how thankful to be about that." ["Beware Allies Bearing Advice," *Washington Post*, 12/28/86]

"European prosperity and integration still provide a series of 'highs,' but European history never leaves us alone to enjoy them." ["Europe, Light and Dark," *Vanity Fair*, July 2002]

European Union

"I'd rather have 'Brussels' the concept than 'Brussels' the actuality anytime." ["Europe, Light and Dark," *Vanity Fair*, July 2002]

"It will be infinitely harder to create a more perfect union out of old states than of new ones." ["Europe, Light and Dark," *Vanity Fair*, July 2002]

Evidence

" . . . What can be asserted without proof can be dismissed without proof. . . ." ["Less than Miraculous," *Free Inquiry*, February/March 2004]

" . . . The most persuasive evidence is the evidence that looks us in the face." ["The Arab Street," *Slate*, 2/28/05]

" . . . Exceptional claims demand exceptional evidence." [*God Is Not Great* (New York: Twelve, 2007), 143]

"I tend to believe that the absence of evidence is the evidence of absence." ["Hitchens Takes on Mother Teresa," *Newsweek*, 8/29/07]

"I think we shall do better if we do not resist evidence that may at first sight appear unwelcome or unsettling, just as we shall do better if we refuse conclusions for which there is no evidence at all." [*Is Christianity Good for the World?* (Moscow, ID: Canon Press, 2008), 62]

Evil

"There is probably no easier way to beckon a smirk to the lips of a liberal intellectual than to mention President Bush's invocation of the notion of 'evil.'" ["Evil," *Slate*, 12/31/02]

" . . . If we think of the evils that afflict humanity today and that are man-made and not inflicted by nature, we would be morally numb if we did not feel strongly about genocide, slavery, rape, child abuse, sexual repression, white-collar crime, the wanton destruction of the natural world, and people who yak on cell phones in restaurants." ["The New Commandments," *Vanity Fair*, April 2010]

Evolution

" . . . Evolution does not have eyes, but it can create them." [*God Is Not Great* (New York: Twelve, 2007), 84]

" . . . Evolution is, as well as smarter than we are, infinitely more callous and cruel, and also capricious." [*God Is Not Great* (New York: Twelve, 2007), 87]

"It may be too soon to say that all the progress is positive or 'upward,' but human development is still under way. It shows in the manner in which we acquire immunities, and also in the way in which we do not. . . . No divine plan, let alone angelic intervention, is required." [*God Is Not Great* (New York: Twelve, 2007), 95]

Exercise

" . . . A high-anxiety lifestyle and a minimum of strenuous exercise means that I can still see my feet (on a clear day, that is, and if for any reason I should wish to see them)." ["I Don't Do Diets," *Mirror*, 8/18/03]

"And, just as a bank won't lend you money unless you are too rich to need it, exercise is a pastime only for those who are already slender and physically fit. It just isn't so much fun when you have a marked tendency to wheeze and throw up, and a cannonball of a belly sloshing around inside the baggy garments." ["On the Limits of Self-Improvement, Part I," *Vanity Fair*, October 2007]

"Finally to the most vexed question of all. Exercise. When you are still smoking, this doesn't really come up. A nice long walk? I'd rather have a cigarette. A visit to the gym? Some other time. What about a nice game of tennis? Are you by any chance *joking*? I have half a pack to get through. The only thing that could conceivably interest me would be a late-night snack, perhaps *avec* cocktails and wine, so as to give me a reason to open a fresh carton." ["On the Limits of Self-Improvement, Part III," *Vanity Fair*, September 2008]

"I started to hear about the ROM. This device—the initials stand for 'Range of Motion'—was the perfect 'no excuses' invention for slothful mammals. It promised to give you a workout in just four minutes. No: it was better than that. It insisted that you never give it *more* than four minutes. The catch was that it cost well over $14,000." ["On the Limits of Self-Improvement, Part III," *Vanity Fair*, September 2008]

Experts

"Yet we stumble on, consoling ourselves with the idea that the experts must know something we don't. In fact, they know a lot of things that ain't so." ["Collected Thoughts on the Evolution of War," *Newsday*, 3/30/88]

Exploitation

" . . . The term 'exploitation' need not mean starvation and misery—though in much of the capitalist world it still does. It signifies the extent to which the skills and abilities of those without capital are appropriated by those with it." ["Minority Report," *Nation*, 4/02/83]

"The term *exploitation* . . . should be not a moralizing one but a cold measure of the difference between use value and exchange value, or between the wages earned at the coal face and the real worth of that labor to the mine owner." ["The Revenge of Karl Marx," *Atlantic Monthly*, April 2009]

Extremists

"Since the political 'mainstream' is whatever it says it is, it follows that an 'extremist' is anybody defined by the mainstream as such." ["Extremists on Whose Side?," *Nation*, 3/18/96]

Ezekiel

"Every now and then you get a decent story out of the old bastard—the valley of dry bones is the best of these—but usually it's killing and laying waste on a psychotic scale." ["Another March, Another Prick in the Wall," *Nation*, 10/27/97]

Fahrenheit 9/11

"To describe this film as dishonest and demagogic would almost be to promote those terms to the level of respectability. . . . In fact, I don't think Al Jazeera would, on a bad day, have transmitted anything so utterly propagandistic." ["Unfairenheit 9/11," *Slate*, 6/21/04]

"*Fahrenheit 9/11* is a sinister exercise in moral frivolity, crudely disguised as an exercise in seriousness. It is also a spectacle of abject political cowardice masking itself as a demonstration of 'dissenting' bravery." ["Unfairenheit 9/11," *Slate*, 6/21/04]

" . . . Moore's film has the staunch courage to mock Bush for his verbal infelicity. Yet it's much, much braver than that. From *Fahrenheit 9/11* you can glean even more astounding and hidden disclosures, such as the capitalist nature of American society, the existence of Eisenhower's 'military-industrial complex,' and the use of 'spin' in the presentation of our politicians. It's high time someone had the nerve to point this out." ["Unfairenheit 9/11," *Slate*, 6/21/04]

Faith

"Real, old-fashioned visceral faith is now found only in those countries where it is persecuted." [*In These Times*, 11/16/83–11/22/83]

"Faith is one of the seven deadly virtues, and it is probably the most overrated of those deadly virtues, too." [*Hardball with Chris Matthews*, MSNBC, 4/26/05]

"The 'evidence' for faith, then, seems to leave faith looking even weaker than it would if it stood, alone and unsupported, all by itself." [*God Is Not Great* (New York: Twelve, 2007), 150]

" . . . Either faith is sufficient or else miracles are required to reassure those—including the preachers—whose faith would otherwise not be strong enough." [Introduction to *The Portable Atheist* (New York: Da Capo Press, 2007), xix]

" . . . 'Faith' is at its most toxic and dangerous point not when it is insincere and hypocritical and corrupt but when it is genuine." ["Belief in Belief," *Free Inquiry*, January 2008]

" . . . If I had faith I would not presume to act or think as if god owed me an explanation. Surely that is the point of faith to begin with: to fill the unbridgeable void between evidence and the entire lack of it." [Debate with Kenneth R. Miller ("Does science make belief in God obsolete?"), John Templeton Foundation, 2008]

Falklands War

"The Falklands/Malvinas episode dissolved into a clumsy argument about which ally to betray." ["Minority Report," *Nation*, 4/21/84]

" . . . The assurances given to Haig's equivalents in Buenos Aires had all been predicated on the assumption that the British would not fight for a stony archipelago at the wrong end of the world. I abruptly realized, for reasons that I believed had little if anything to do with my blood and heritage, and despite the impediment placed in the way of my becoming more American, that I would be unable to bear the shame if this assumption proved to be correct." [*Hitch-22* (New York: Twelve, 2010), 230–231]

"It really counts as an irony of history that it was Mrs. Thatcher's bellicosity that robbed the neo-cons of their favorite proxy. . . ." [*Hitch-22* (New York: Twelve, 2010), 231]

Falsehood

"Everyone is entitled to their own invented past. It's the invented present that bothers me." ["O'Rourke's Drift," *Mail on Sunday*, 12/10/95]

"All claims by public persons to be apolitical deserve critical scrutiny, and all claims made by those who affect a merely 'spiritual' influence deserve a doubly critical scrutiny. The naïve and simple are seldom as naïve and simple as they seem, and this suspicion is reinforced by those who proclaim their own naivety and simplicity. There is no conceit equal to false modesty, and there is no politics like antipolitics, just as there is no worldliness to compare with ostentatious anti-materialism." [*The Missionary Position* (New York: Verso, 1995), 86]

"There is, especially in the American media, a deep belief that insincerity is better than no sincerity at all. Put a deceitful politician before the cameras, allow a catch to creep into his voice, let him mention his home life and—presto! The next day's polling always shows a rally in public sympathy." ["Clinton—'Like a Gorilla Playing a Violin,'" *Evening Standard*, 8/18/98]

Falwell, Jerry

"I think it's a pity there isn't a hell for him to go to." [*Anderson Cooper 360*, CNN, 5/15/07]

"The empty life of this ugly little charlatan proves only one thing—that you can get away with the most extraordinary offenses to morality and to truth in this country if you will just get yourself called 'Reverend.' Who would, even at your network, have invited on such a little toad to tell us that the attacks of September the 11th were the result of our sinfulness and were God's punishment if they hadn't got some kind of clerical qualification? People like that should be out in the street, shouting and hollering with a cardboard sign and selling pencils from a cup." [*Anderson Cooper 360*, CNN, 5/15/07]

"He woke up every morning, as I say, pinching his chubby little flanks and thinking, 'I have got away with it again.'" [*Anderson Cooper 360*, CNN, 5/15/07]

"Like many fanatical preachers, Falwell was especially disgusting in exuding an almost sexless personality while railing from dawn to dusk about the sex lives of others." ["Faith-Based Fraud," *Slate*, 5/16/07]

"The evil that he did will live after him." ["Faith-Based Fraud," *Slate*, 5/16/07]

"For a vulgar fraud and crook like the Reverend Falwell, it's an obligation to say what one thinks about him or be left off the air and have people like yourselves broadcasting only piety." [*Hannity & Colmes*, Fox News Channel, 5/16/07]

"I think we have been rid of an extremely dangerous demagogue who lived by hatred of others and prejudice and who committed treason by saying that the United States deserved the attack upon it and its civil society of September of 2001 by other religious nutcases like himself." [*Hannity & Colmes*, Fox News Channel, 5/16/07]

"If you gave Falwell an enema, he'd be buried in a matchbox." [*Hannity & Colmes*, Fox News Channel, 5/16/07]

"Jerry Falwell—another man who managed to get away with murder by getting himself called 'Reverend'—dies without being bodily 'raptured' into the heavens. Indeed, his heavy carcass is found on the floor of his Virginia office. The cable shows start to call and I have a book to sell: Maybe someone up there does love me after all." ["God Bless Me, It's a Best-Seller!," *Vanity Fair*, September 2007]

Family
" . . . A family is collectivist as a society and socialist as an economy. It reveres the individual but it operates, approximately, on the principle 'from each according to his or her ability and to each according to his or her need.' If these socialist values are good enough for the rearing of American children, why are they not good enough for American society?" ["Minority Report," *Nation*, 11/05/83]

" . . . The lowest form of American rhetoric . . . is the exploitation of family sentiment." ["Officer Material," *Times Literary Supplement*, 11/03/00]

Family Planning
"In every developing country that has been studied, a clear correlation can be found between the limitation of family size and the life chances of the family members." [*The Missionary Position* (New York: Verso, 1995), 54]

Family Values
"At the present rate, there can't be much family left to devalue." ["Minority Report," *Nation*, 2/21/94]

"It strikes one more than ever that there is something not quite grown-up about the 'family values' crowd." ["Its Own Reward?," *Times Literary Supplement*, 12/08/95]

Fantasy
"The investment in fantasy, and the collusion in it by very down-to-earth operators, is a perpetual source of wonder and revulsion." ["American Notes," *Times Literary Supplement*, 3/06/87]

Farrakhan, Louis
"Some radicals can't see it, because they believe that a man so harshly denounced must be on to something, but Farrakhan is more a black Reagan than a black

Falwell or Kahane. His vision is one of backward, utopian, simpleminded 'self-help,' a half-assed free enterprise backed up by subsidies to the few." ["Minority Report," *Nation*, 10/26/85]

"Farrakhan has no claim on the rhetoric of liberation because he is an unabashed reactionary. But as the right has proved again and again, those slogans and emblems can be picked up by anybody once they are discarded by those who should uphold them." ["Minority Report," *Nation*, 10/26/85]

"Like Jesus, with whom he frequently compares himself, Farrakhan has not read the New Testament." ["The Charmer," *Grand Street*, Winter 1986]

" . . . I laid out a buck for a copy of Farrakhan's newspaper, *The Final Call*. . . . I opened to a page with an article titled 'America: The Big Jewry Heist,' by one Abdul Allah Muhammad. The ensuing essay imparted that warm, rich sensation you get when you allow yourself to think that the whole laborious business of human civilization has been a hilarious waste of time." ["The Tribes of Walter Mosley," *Vanity Fair*, February 1993]

Fascism

"Anti-plutocratic, often anti-clerical, contemptuous of the hereditary principle, possessed of certain utopian and idealist myths—it has been known to fool credulous customers who think they dislike the Establishment." ["Something about the Poems: Larkin and 'Sensitivity,'" *New Left Review*, July 1993]

" . . . A fascist is a fascist and should be called by his or her rightful name." ["The Blind Leading the Dumb," *Nation*, 4/01/96]

"Fascism at home sooner or later means fascism abroad. Face it now or fight it later." ["Don't Call What Happened in Iran Last Week an Election," *Slate*, 6/14/09]

"The curse-word 'fascism' is easily enough thrown around, including by me on occasion, but I give you my oath that it makes a difference to you when you see the real thing at work." [*Hitch-22* (New York: Twelve, 2010), 292]

Fashion and Dress

"One reason that I try never to wear a tie is the advantage that it so easily confers on anyone who goes berserk on you. There you are, with a ready-made noose already fastened around your neck. All the opponent needs to do is grab hold and haul." ["One Angry Man," *Slate*, 4/28/08]

" . . . Wearing dark glasses indoors: a thoroughly bad sign." [*Hitch-22* (New York: Twelve, 2010), 283]

Fast, Howard

"Fast also differs from the classic pattern of the ex-Communist stereotype, made notorious by James Burnham and Whittaker Chambers. He left the Communist Party for the same reason that he joined it—which is to say he left it because he was interested in social justice and historical truth." ["Citizen Howard Fast," *Washington Post*, 11/25/90]

"Love him or hate him, it's very difficult to read him. . . . Hold it right there, one wants to exclaim, except that this is the opening sentence." ["Citizen Howard Fast," *Washington Post*, 11/25/90]

Fatherhood

" . . . Fatherhood precisely insists that you will be outlived, or that it's your duty to ensure that you are. Without premeditation, you realize that you are ready to die for someone as well as live for them." ["Even an Old Renegade Like Me Was Changed by Fatherhood," *Evening Standard*, 6/14/02]

"There was a time, it seemed, when I couldn't sneeze on a woman without becoming a potential father." ["Fetal Distraction," *Vanity Fair*, February 2003]

Faux Pas

"A tendency to gaffe and an inability to get on good terms with the language can become part of your likable, human persona if you are in power." ["The Repackaging of Dan Quayle," *Harper's*, April 1990]

"A tumbril remark doesn't work if it's conscious or deliberate." ["Let Them Eat Pork Rinds," *Vanity Fair*, December 2005]

Fear

"In our more advanced epoch, the *grande peur* need not just be exploited by unscrupulous politicians. It can actually be invented and managed by them." ["Minority Report," *Nation*, 1/09/89–1/16/89]

"People who are constantly afraid have lost their self-respect." ["Minority Report," *Nation*, 1/24/94]

" . . . Fear is the mother of superstition." ["Why Women Aren't Funny," *Vanity Fair*, January 2007]

Feet

"To be truly barefoot is to be truly innocent or truly poor, as well as totally unhygienic. But a fine pair can be among a girl's best friends." ["Why Men Love Toe Cleavage," *Evening Standard*, 8/28/02]

Fellatio

"I once heard it said that one should pity the atheists because they had no one to talk to while receiving a blowjob. Alas, this limitation applies (moan devoutly though they may) to believers also." ["Mr. Universe," *Vanity Fair*, December 1992]

Ferraro, Geraldine

" . . . Geraldine Ferraro, who seems only to have the cowardice of her convictions and who says, in effect, that her views on the immortal soul of the unborn are no concern to anyone but herself, except when she votes for abortion." ["Minority Report," *Nation*, 9/22/84]

Fiction

"It no longer seems to matter whether or not a novel, or film, or play carries the conventional disclaimer about 'all persons herein' being fictional, et cetera. People seem determined to discover themselves in fiction—a version of narcissism that might repay study." ["American Notes," *Times Literary Supplement*, 3/06/87]

Final Solution

"In very striking personal testimonies, several of them [members of the Order Police unit] recall the overpowering nausea and revulsion with which they reacted. . . . But their objections, even in retrospect, were prompted not by ethics but by sheer disgust. Blowing out people's brains was revolting work for the perpetrator; the effect on the victim seems never to have been a consideration." ["A Monster Inside the Average Man," *Newsday*, 3/25/92]

"The fact that those who were nauseated at Jozefow went on doing their foul work for several more years . . . is attributable not to intimidation but to peer pressure and the fear of seeming weak or 'unmanly.' This is almost enough to make one conclude that banality is evil." ["A Monster Inside the Average Man," *Newsday*, 3/25/92]

"The worst offenders in the Final Solution were doctors who saw a chance to conduct vile experiments. None was ever threatened by the Church with excommunication (they would have had to assist at a termination of an unwanted pregnancy in order to run such an awful risk)." [Introduction to *The Portable Atheist* (New York: Da Capo Press, 2007), xv]

Firing Line

"Ahh, *Firing Line*! If I leave a TV studio these days with what Diderot termed *l'esprit de l'escalier*, I don't always blame myself. If I wish that I had remembered to make a telling point, or wish that I had phrased something better than I actually did, it's very often because a 'break' was just coming up, or the 'segment' had been shortened at the last minute, or because the host was obnoxious, or because the panel had been over-booked in case of cancellations but at the last minute every egomaniac invited had managed to say 'yes' and make himself available. But on Buckley's imperishable show, if you failed to make your best case, it was your own damn fault." ["A Man of Incessant Labor," *Weekly Standard*, 3/10/08]

First Amendment

" . . . The First Amendment is my life as well as the source of my living. . . ." ["The Flag Fetish," *Wall Street Journal*, 7/03/06]

Fishing

"For me, the life of the angler is an almost flawless example of how not to have a good time." ["Is the Smoking Ban a Good Idea?," *Guardian*, 5/14/07]

Flags

"If you ever catch yourself asserting that concern with flags and emblems is irrelevant, then pause briefly and inquire what you think about the Confederate battlerag. Many citizens believe this symbol of slavery and secession ought not to be flown over state capitols. Are they making a fuss about nothing?" ["Waiving the Flag," *Nation*, 7/21/97]

"Even though Old Glory has since flown over Vietnam and Panama and other disgraceful scenes, it is still the flag of the Emancipation Proclamation." ["Waiving the Flag," *Nation*, 7/21/97]

"Why is it, when I see a Confederate battle flag flapping from the rear of a pickup truck, that I don't axiomatically make the association with courtesy, gentility, chivalry, and hospitality?" ["Rebel Ghosts," *Vanity Fair*, July 1999]

"The flag of the Union has been purged, as the banner under which slavery was objectively if not intentionally defeated. It may not have been an abolitionist flag, but it was a symbol under which abolitionists fought and died. (For this very reason, I winced at seeing it burned even during the Vietnam War. . . .)" ["Scars and Bars," *Nation*, 2/21/00]

"The flag of the Confederate Army is not just unpurged and unwashed—it is quite deliberately flaunted by those who still think that the vilest aspects of the old 'way of life' are the ones to be cherished." ["Scars and Bars," *Nation*, 2/21/00]

"It is precisely because the flag is so important to some people that we must permit its trashing by others. To legislate otherwise would be to instate a taboo, and that is exactly what the First Amendment exists to forestall." ["The Flag Fetish," *Wall Street Journal*, 7/03/06]

"It's easy enough to boast that 'these colors do not run.' However, those who mistake the symbol for the essence are manifesting not a show of spirit for the former but a pathetic lack of confidence in the latter." ["The Flag Fetish," *Wall Street Journal*, 7/03/06]

Fleet Street
"Fleet Street has always been a Conservative slum, and there is little reason to feel sentimental about its passing." ["Minority Report," *Nation*, 2/22/86]

Flynt, Larry
"Take, for example, a cover of *Hustler* magazine showing a naked woman being fed head-first into a grinder, under the catchy title 'Grade *A* Pink.' Where's the redeeming social value in *that*? Yet the pond-scum publisher of that rebarbative glossy—so it turns out—has done rather more than many high-minded civil libertarians to uphold the First Amendment." ["Hustler with a Cause," *Vanity Fair*, November 1996]

Fonda, Jane
"Jane Fonda, who the last I heard was in the throes of a post-orgasmic spiritual transfiguration, was a byword for ditziness even on the left when I was young, and she now issues apologies for her past politics almost as rapidly as Barbarella changed positions." ["George Galloway Is Gruesome, Not Gorgeous," *Slate*, 9/13/05]

Food
" . . . Americans now dine at their best, and their healthiest, when choosing from the international *à la carte*." ["The Extruded Bagel," *Times Literary Supplement*, 5/27/94]

Foreign Policy

"As the Hungarians were to discover anew in 1956, American policy has been a series of oscillations between great causes overseas and the need to avoid quagmires." [*Blood, Class and Empire* (New York: Nation Books, 2004), 240]

"A country that attempted to be in everybody's good books would be quite paralyzed. The last time everybody said they liked the United States (or said that they said they liked the United States) was just after September 11, when the nation was panicked and traumatized and trying to count its dead. Well, no thanks. This is too high a price to be paid for being popular." ["This July Fourth, Ignore Polls on America's Image," *Washington Examiner*, 7/04/06]

"If there was one thing about U.S. foreign policy that used to make one shudder, it was the habit of ruling by proxy through military regimes." ["It Was Right to Dissolve the Iraqi Army," *Slate*, 9/17/07]

" . . . If the world was already programmed to respond to love and warmth and enthusiasm and mutuality, it would not be necessary to have a foreign or defense policy in the first place." ["Dear Mr. President . . . ," *World Affairs*, Winter 2009]

Foster, Vince

"Those who believe he was killed by Clinton have, I think, a paranoid view, but not as stupid as the view of those who think he was killed by the *Wall Street Journal*. And that last is not considered a paranoid view at all. It's almost orthodoxy among Washington liberals." [Quoted in Michael Rust, "Clinton's Lies Stopped at Hitchens' Door," *Insight on the News*, 6/28/99]

Foxhunting

"Leaving to one side the number of peasants and coal miners who hunt on the weekends, the abolition of the fox chase would neither diminish the power of the ruling class nor improve the condition of the toiling masses by one iota." ["We Know Best," *Vanity Fair*, May 2001]

" . . . The idea that the contest itself should be abolished strikes me as grotesque. Nobody disputes the banal fact that foxes and some other wild predators need to be culled or controlled; it has to be done one way or another. The small achievement of the English rural types (not the most fascinating people in the world, all in all) is that over the centuries they have managed to transform this chore into an art form." ["We Know Best," *Vanity Fair*, May 2001]

" . . . The sound of the horn, the red coats through the mist, the dogs in full cry—it's a spectacle and a thrill that is worth the life of the odd chicken stealer. Some of the ends to which foxes come are sad; some are glorious; some are messy. But these are not herbivores who could look forward to a peaceful retirement. Nor is England a vegetarian society that prohibits the taking of animal life. Foxhunting, I conclude, is therefore being banned for populist and political reasons, disguised as humane and 'concerned' ones." ["We Know Best," *Vanity Fair*, May 2001]

France

"If there is a truly 'unilateralist' government on the Security Council, it is France." ["The Rat That Roared," *Wall Street Journal*, 2/06/03]

Franco, Francisco

"Spanish politics has become an exercise in making up for the wasted time of his era." ["Francisco Franco, with Precious Little Rancor," *Newsday*, 3/02/88]

Francophobia

"An arsenal of Francophobic clichés lies ready to hand, like a pile of rocks and rotten eggs stacked by a pillory. . . . During the argument over the Gulf War, certain turkey-wattled Congressmen drew on this folkloric store of imagery to urge boycotts of the wine and brie that they never actually drank or ate and drew nearer to what they truly knew by trying to rename *pommes frites* as 'Freedom Fries'. . . . Not since the xenophobic patriots of World War I took to roughing up German waiters and announcing that sauerkraut was henceforth to be 'Liberty Cabbage' has there been such a fiesta of all-American bullshit. . . ." ["Garrison Keillor, Vulgarian," *Slate*, 2/13/06]

Franken, Al

"He is really quite witty—which is much better than being funny—when he is being purely political. But he is barely even funny when funny is all he is trying to be." ["Cheap Laughs," *Atlantic Monthly*, October 2009]

Free Market

"The general theory of the free market depends quite largely on the concept of 'consumer sovereignty': the intelligent dollar taking its custom from place to place until it finds value and satisfaction. When this doesn't work as a model—as with savings-and-loans, junk bonds, dream holidays from brochures, irradiated real estate, gift subscriptions to the *New Republic*, gambling in Las Vegas, and a host of other things—it's because of crookery or rashness or poor information or all three. But it isn't terminal." ["Bitter Medicine," *Vanity Fair*, August 1998]

"In the market, we are told, the consumer is sovereign by virtue of choice. But can you 'choose' to travel by train, or 'choose' to have health coverage? Not in any meaningful sense of the term. Well then, how many choices do you have about how, or for whom, and on what conditions, you will work? You must first answer Willy Loman's question from *Death of a Salesman*: What have you got to sell?" ["On the Prole," *Village Voice*, 11/23/99]

Free Speech

"There is therefore no obligation, in defending or asserting the right to speak, to pass any comment on the truth or merit of what may be, or is being, said." ["The Chorus and Cassandra," *Grand Street*, Autumn 1985]

"It is not enough to 'have' free speech. People must learn to speak freely." ["Minority Report," *Nation*, 10/21/91]

"There is a utilitarian case for free expression. It recognizes that the freedom to speak must also be insisted on for the person who thinks differently, because it is pointless to support only free speech for people who agree with you. It is not only unprincipled to want that, but also self-defeating. For your own sake, you need to know how other people think." [Quoted in "Forbidden Thoughts: A Roundtable on Taboo Research," *American Enterprise*, January/February 1995]

" . . . Civil society means that free expression trumps the emotions of anyone to whom free expression might be inconvenient." ["Cartoon Debate," *Slate*, 2/04/06]

Free Will
"Well, one may be genetically programmed for a certain amount of aggression and hatred and greed, and yet also evolved enough to beware of following every prompting. If we gave into our every base instinct every time, civilization would have been impossible and there would be no writing in which to continue this argument." [*God Is Not Great* (New York: Twelve, 2007), 214]

Freedom and Security
"The trade-off between freedom and security, so often proposed so seductively, very often leads to the loss of both." ["Forcing Freedom," *Reason* magazine, August 2003]

French Revolution
"The more the cause of revolution advanced in Paris, the more America's old comrades in the city seemed to lose their eminence, or their liberty, or even their heads." [*Thomas Jefferson: Author of America* (New York: HarperCollins, 2005), 90]

Friedman, Milton
"As author of *Capitalism and Freedom* he makes rather a peculiar enthusiast for the new regimes in Brazil and Chile, where torture and execution have variously worked and not worked as cures for inflation or incentives to growth." ["The Road to Serfdom," *New Statesman*, 7/04/75]

Friendship
"A melancholy lesson of advancing years is the realization that you can't make old friends." ["Unmaking Friends," *Harper's*, June 1999]

"Allow a friend to believe in a bogus prospectus or a false promise and you cease, after a short while, to be a friend at all." [*Letters to a Young Contrarian* (New York: Basic Books, 2001), 82]

" . . . Do not worry too much about who your friends are, or what company you may be keeping. . . . Those who try to condemn or embarrass you by the company you keep will usually be found to be in very poor company themselves; in any case they are, as I was once taught to say, tackling the man and not the ball." [*Letters to a Young Contrarian* (New York: Basic Books, 2001), 135]

"If you pay too much attention to the shortcomings of your allies, or if you worry about being lumped together with dubious or unpopular types, you are in effect having your thinking done for you." ["Without Prejudice: Hawks in the Dovecote," *Observer*, 8/25/02]

" . . . Those who offer false consolation are false friends." [*God Is Not Great* (New York: Twelve, 2007), 9]

"I boldly assert, in fact I think I know, that a lot of friendships and connections absolutely depend upon a sort of shared language, or slang. Not necessarily designed to exclude others, these can establish a certain comity and, even after a long absence, re-establish it in a second." [*Hitch-22* (New York: Twelve, 2010), 164]

"If a difference of principle goes undiscussed for any length of time, it will start to compromise and undermine the integrity of a friendship." [*Hitch-22* (New York: Twelve, 2010), 396]

Frontiers
"Frontiers exist to be conquered." ["Why Men Love Toe Cleavage," *Evening Standard*, 8/28/02]

Fukuyama, Francis
"It's not possible that a solipsistic clown like Fukuyama is history's last word." ["Minority Report," *Nation*, 9/25/89]

"There appears to be an arsenal of clichés and stock expressions located somewhere inside his word processor, so that he has only to touch the keyboard for one of them to spring abruptly onto the page." ["The End of Fukuyama," *Slate*, 3/01/06]

Fundamentalism
"They [Christian fundamentalists] do not argue for the study of the Bible, but for its inculcation, and for its inculcation as revealed white Protestant truth at that." ["American Notes," *Times Literary Supplement*, 4/03/87]

" . . . The work of fundamentalism is never done." ["Monotheistic Notes from All Over," *Nation*, 10/19/98]

Funerals
"I'm the authorized, official pisser-on of people's funerals." ["Princess Di, Mother T., and Me," *Vanity Fair*, December 1997]

Fury
"The finest fury is the most controlled." ["America's Poet?," *Weekly Standard*, 7/05/04–7/12/04]

Future
"There must be an unspoken agreement that the future is common property, and that it belongs above all to those who haven't been born yet, or those who've just arrived." ["Ireland," *Critical Quarterly*, Spring 1998]

"Once it is pitilessly conceded that the future has a big future, certain once-epochal events immediately become more manageable and intelligible." ["Imperial Follies," *Atlantic Monthly*, January/February 2007]

Galileo

"Galileo might have been unmolested in his telescopic work if he had not been so unwise as to admit that it had cosmological implications." [*God Is Not Great* (New York: Twelve, 2007), 255]

Galloway, George

"He had had to resign as the head of a charity called 'War on Want,' after repaying some disputed expenses for living the high life in dirt-poor countries. Indeed, he was a type well known in the Labor movement. Prolier than thou, and ostentatiously radical, but a bit too fond of the cigars and limos and always looking a bit odd in a suit that was slightly too expensive. By turns aggressive and unctuous, either at your feet or at your throat; a bit of a backslapper, nothing's too good for the working class: what the English call a 'wide boy.'" ["Unmitigated Galloway," *Weekly Standard*, 5/30/05]

"Galloway is not supposed by anyone to have been an oil trader. He is asked, simply, to say what he knows about his chief fundraiser, nominee, and crony. And when asked this, he flatly declines to answer. . . . If you wish to pursue the matter with Galloway himself, you will have to find the unlisted number for his villa in Portugal." ["Unmitigated Galloway," *Weekly Standard*, 5/30/05]

"His party calls itself RESPECT, which stands for 'Respect, Equality, Socialism, Peace, Environment, Community, Trade Unionism.' (So that really ought to be RESPECTU, except that it would then sound less like an Aretha Franklin song and more like an organ of the Romanian state under Ceausescu.)" ["Unmitigated Galloway," *Weekly Standard*, 5/30/05]

"His chief appeal was to the militant Islamist element among Asian immigrants who live in large numbers in his district, and his main organizational muscle was provided by a depraved sub-Leninist sect called the Socialist Workers party. The servants of the one god finally meet the votaries of the one-party state. Perfect." ["Unmitigated Galloway," *Weekly Standard*, 5/30/05]

"Galloway is an open supporter of the other side in this war, and at least doesn't try very hard to conceal the fact." ["Yes, London Can Take It," *Weekly Standard*, 7/18/05]

"A man who supported the previous oppressors of the region—the Soviet army in Afghanistan and Saddam Hussein in Iraq—who supports its current oppressors— Bashar Assad and his Lebanese proxies—and who still has time to endorse its potential future tyrants in the shape of the jihadists in Iraq and elsewhere. Galloway began his political life as a fifth-rate apologist for the Soviet Union, but he has now diversified into being an apologist for Stalinism, for fascism, and for jihadism all at once!" ["George Galloway Is Gruesome, Not Gorgeous," *Slate*, 9/13/05]

"Unkind nature, which could have made a perfectly good butt out of his face, has spoiled the whole effect by taking an asshole and studding it with ill-brushed fangs." ["George Galloway Is Gruesome, Not Gorgeous," *Slate*, 9/13/05]

Gambling

" . . . When you gamble, you choose freely. If you don't want the rest of life to be a gamble, for yourself or your dependents, then get insurance." ["Bitter Medicine," *Vanity Fair*, August 1998]

Gandhi, Mahatma

"In many ways, India's postcolonial legacy of backwardness and underdevelopment is a gift from Gandhi, and if he had not been an apparently sincere pacifist we would more easily recognize the traits he shares with Khomeini." ["Holy Men," *Nation*, 1/15/83]

"Even as a pacifist, Gandhi was a hypocrite." ["Holy Men," *Nation*, 1/15/83]

"Those who naïvely credit Gandhi with a conscientious or consistent pacifism might wish to ask if this did not amount to letting the Japanese imperialists do his fighting for him." [*God Is Not Great* (New York: Twelve, 2007), 183]

Gay Marriage

"Make no mistake: This is an argument about the socialization of homosexuality, not the homosexualization of society. It demonstrates the spread of conservatism, not radicalism, among gays." ["The Married State," *Wall Street Journal*, 3/03/04]

Generations

"Tell me which decade you love, or hate, and I'll tell you who and what you are." ["Epitomizing the Eighties," *Newsday*, 12/30/90]

"I must say that I've always found the generational emphasis on the way that my youth was covered to be very annoying. There were a lot of other people born in April 1949, and I just don't feel like I have anything in common with most of them." [Quoted in "Free Radical," *Reason* magazine, November 2001]

Genetics

"All societies that have tried to keep themselves 'pure,' from the Confucian Chinese through to the Castilian Spanish to the post-Wilhelmine Germans, have collapsed into barbarism, insularity and superstition. And swiftly enough for us to be certain that the fall was no more connected to the genes than was the rise. There is no gene for I.Q., and there is no genetic or evolutionary timing that is short enough to explain histories or societies." ["Minority Report," *Nation*, 11/28/94]

"The dullest person, after all, has gleaned from mere observation that highly intelligent parents often produce offspring so stupid that they can barely breathe. (And, much more interesting from the eugenic point of view, that the opposite is also true.)" ["The Eggheads and I," *Vanity Fair*, September 1996]

Gentleman

"The idea of the gentleman may seem self-serving and anachronistic, but it is preferable to the outlook and style of many of its successors." ["An Unlikely Gentleman Among the Buccaneers," *Newsday*, 10/24/90]

"An old definition of a gentleman: someone who is never rude except on purpose. I seem to fail this test." [*Letters to a Young Contrarian* (New York: Basic Books, 2001), 69]

Gentrification
" . . . The unavoidable truth is that it's almost invariably a good symptom." [*Hitch-22* (New York: Twelve, 2010), 236]

Germans
" . . . There is always a market for stories about decent Germans." [*Letters to a Young Contrarian* (New York: Basic Books, 2001), 94]

Ghosts
"A ghost is something that is dead but won't lie down." ["Young Men and War," *Vanity Fair*, February 1997]

Gibson, Mel
"A coward, a bully, a bigmouth, and a queer-basher." ["Schlock, Yes; Awe, No; Fascism, Probably," *Slate*, 2/27/04]

" . . . He tearfully told the cops that 'my life is f—ed,' and this inadvertent truth ought to be remembered in all charity as the last words we ever want to hear from him." ["Mel Gibson's Meltdown," *Slate*, 7/31/06]

Gingrich, Newt
"He has a Tyrannosaurus Rex skull in his office. He has a Tyrannosaurus Rex skull in his *skull*. . . ." ["Newtopia," *London Review of Books*, 8/24/95]

Globalization
"Every day one reads meretricious babble about 'globalization' and the abolition of frontiers, most of it amounting to little more than celebration of the worldwide availability of *Wheel of Fortune*." ["A Subverting Sensualist," *Nation*, 1/01/96]

"'Globalization,' usually the company song of the American corporate strategy, stops at the water's edge and turns prickly and isolationist when it comes to the rights of others to judge American actions." [*No One Left to Lie To* (New York: Verso, 2000), 71]

God
"There are as many impressionist arguments for God's existence as there are human moods, and you can't argue with someone's gestalt." ["Mr. Universe," *Vanity Fair*, December 1992]

"If we are indeed created in God's image, as the believers tell us on who knows what or whose authority, then that image must have room for a digestive tract—with all that it entails—for erections (where applicable), for vile thoughts and dubious motives. . . . Much more probable, really, is the countertheory that man created God in *his* image. This would account for there being so many of Him (more than a hundred dead ones included, by H. L. Mencken's famous count) and also for His being such a son of a bitch." ["Mr. Universe," *Vanity Fair*, December 1992]

"It is of course the height of conceit to believe that there is a divine being who takes a personal and immediate interest in your doings (only astrology comes close to this illusion, with its vulgar assertion that the heavens are arranged for our convenience)." ["Minority Report," *Nation*, 7/25/94–8/01/94]

"A man claims to believe that God is everywhere and is ultimate and all-seeing and all-wise. But take away this same man's temporal and tribal claim to some fragment of land or item of wreckage, and he will scream that the same god has been unpardonably evicted from his only home." ["Value in the Wrong Place," *Free Inquiry*, Spring 2001]

" ... What's the point of an ineffable deity if he can be so readily comprehended by banal mammals like ourselves?" ["The Future of an Illusion," *Daedalus*, Summer 2003]

"One is presuming (is one not?) that this is the same god who actually created the audience he was addressing. This leaves us with the insoluble mystery of why he would have molded ('in his own image,' yet) a covetous, murderous, disrespectful, lying, and adulterous species. Create them sick, and then command them to be well? What a mad despot this is, and how fortunate we are that he exists only in the minds of his worshippers." ["Moore's Law," *Slate*, 8/27/03]

" ... If one could presume a just God, what need would there be for human Enlightenment?" [*Thomas Jefferson: Author of America* (New York: HarperCollins, 2005), 48]

"God did not create man in his own image. Evidently, it was the other way about, which is the painless explanation for the profusion of gods and religions, and the fratricide both between and among faiths, that we see all about us and that has so retarded the development of civilization." [*God Is Not Great* (New York: Twelve, 2007), 8]

"Why *do* people keep saying, 'God is in the details'? He isn't in ours, unless his yokel creationist fans wish to take credit for his clumsiness, failure, and incompetence." [*God Is Not Great* (New York: Twelve, 2007), 85]

" ... Though I dislike to differ with such a great man, Voltaire was simply ludicrous when he said that if god did not exist it would be necessary to invent him. The human invention of god is the problem to begin with." [*God Is Not Great* (New York: Twelve, 2007), 96]

"It is absurd, even for a believer, to imagine that god should owe him an explanation." [*God Is Not Great* (New York: Twelve, 2007), 268]

"God Is Great"

" ... People who commit simultaneous suicide and murder while screaming 'God is great': is that taking the Lord's name in vain or is it not?" ["The New Commandments," *Vanity Fair*, April 2010]

Goebbels, Joseph

"Joseph Goebbels was excommunicated for marrying a Protestant. You see—we *do* have our standards!" [Lecture at Georgetown University, Washington, DC, 10/11/07]

" . . . If I were a Catholic, I would do my best to get people to forget about Josef Goebbels. Like many Nazi leaders, he started off as a practicing Catholic and was the only one of them to be excommunicated—not because of his Nazi crimes but because he had married a woman who was not only Protestant but divorced: a double indemnity in the eyes of Rome!" ["Jewbaiter," *Free Inquiry*, August/September 2010]

Gold

"Gold, like politicians, is extremely malleable and extremely ductile. A single ounce of it can be beaten flat over almost half an acre (like Mondale) or drawn out to the length of several miles (like John Glenn)." ["Minority Report," *Nation*, 11/27/82]

"The obsession with gold, actually and politically, occurs among those who regard economics as a branch of morality. Gold is solid, gold is durable, gold is rare, gold is even (in certain very peculiar circumstances) convertible. To believe in thrift, solidity and soundness is to believe in some way in the properties of gold." ["Minority Report," *Nation*, 11/27/82]

Golden Rule

"The so-called Golden Rule . . . simply enjoins us to treat others as one would wish to be treated by them. This sober and rational precept . . . is well within the compass of any atheist and does not require masochism and hysteria, or sadism and hysteria, when it is breached. It is gradually learned, as part of the painfully slow evolution of the species, and once grasped is never forgotten." [*God Is Not Great* (New York: Twelve, 2007), 213–214]

Gorbachev, Mikhail

"Perhaps more than any modern statesman, Gorbachev has demonstrated the old truth that one cannot be heretical in a piecemeal fashion—that small heresies lead ineluctably to grand ones." ["Luther in Moscow," *Independent*, 6/09/91]

Gore, Al

"Where he isn't robotically normal, he is abnormal in an abnormal way." ["Soft Gore," *Village Voice*, 3/07/00]

" . . . A cringing moral defective who will be remembered forever as the man who held Clinton's coat, but who did so without courage and without conviction." ["Beta Male," *Nation*, 8/21/00–8/28/00]

" . . . He actually does resemble a bronze condom stuffed with walnuts." ["Democratic Centralism," *Nation*, 10/19/00]

Gossip Columns

"The Fleet Street gossip column is a hideous invention, at once bullying and sycophantic. Under the pretense of daring exposure and rapier wit lurks a horrid conformism and a lust for easy targets. As for the style necessitated by this kind of journalism, it is typically arch, gushing, and repetitive. Unfunny euphemisms ('confirmed bachelor' for homosexual) are thought of as subversive coinage. The mighty and the famous occasionally use such columns to take revenge on their friends by means of leaks. But for the most part the scandal page is a banal conveyor belt for received ideas, old gags, and witch hunts against the deviant. The really bad gossip writers aren't even reactionary—just boring." ["Earache," *Nation*, 9/11/82]

"In truth, I have seldom met a gossip columnist who wasn't a coward." ["Earache," *Nation*, 9/11/82]

Government Officials

"Irony and a bit of sass, combined with a pugnacious independence, should always stand a chance against bovine officials who have barely learned to memorize such demanding mantras as 'zero tolerance' and 'no exceptions.'" ["I Fought the Law," *Vanity Fair*, February 2004]

Goya, Francisco de

"It is the special achievement of Goya to have been a radical pessimist; to have forced our attention upon the base and the ghastly aspects of the human personality while not surrendering to them or ceasing to protest their official instatement." ["Minority Report," *Nation*, 6/19/89]

Graham, Billy

"Every time that a conflict impends in any formerly Biblical land, this elderly nuisance starts drivelling about the last days and the end of time. . . ." ["Washington Diary," *London Review of Books*, 2/07/91]

"The country's senior Protestant is a gaping and mendacious anti-Jewish peasant. . . ." ["The God Squad," *Nation*, 4/15/02]

Gramm, Phil

" . . . He has made a career of buying other people's votes and selling his own." ["Minority Report," *Nation*, 9/11/95]

The Great Gatsby

"Despair is never very far away, so it's no exaggeration to say that *Gatsby* also achieved and held its strangely contemporary status by anticipating, in an age of relative if aimless cheerfulness, the concept of the existential, the causeless rebel, and indeed the absurd." ["The Road to West Egg," *Vanity Fair*, May 2000]

"Fitzgerald's work captures the evaporating memory of the American Eden while connecting it to the advent of the New World of smartness and thuggery and corruption. It was his rite of passage; it is our bridge to the time before 'dreams' were slogans." ["The Road to West Egg," *Vanity Fair*, May 2000]

"It was nearly entitled just plain *Gatsby*. It remains 'the great' because it confronts the defeat of youth and beauty and idealism, and finds the defeat unbearable, and then turns to face the defeat unflinchingly. With *The Great Gatsby*, American letters grew up." ["The Road to West Egg," *Vanity Fair*, May 2000]

Greece

"In modern Greek history, there is a close relationship between national humiliation and political radicalization." [*Cyprus* (London: Quartet Books, 1984), 131]

"If language, landscape, national consciousness and philosophic and artistic tradition do not amount to continuity, it is difficult to see what does. Certainly no other European people has a comparable claim (though it is fair to say that the extent and nature of the claim are enthusiastically disputed among Greeks—itself a sign of vigor)." [*The Parthenon Marbles: The Case for Reunification* (New York: Verso, 2008), 103]

"Unlike most of the other great and eclipsed civilizations of the past, the Greeks were never notorious for luxury or ostentation. The poverty of their soil and mountains and coasts was the revenge for its beauty, and rather discouraged the ornate." [*The Parthenon Marbles: The Case for Reunification* (New York: Verso, 2008), 104]

Greed

" . . . Nobody is more covetous and greedy than those who have far too much." ["Minority Report," *Nation*, 7/06/92]

" . . . Who but a member of the comfortable or agnostic classes imagines that people need to be brainwashed into being greedy? The acquisitive instinct, perhaps initially supplied by Satan himself in one interpretation, is after all fairly easily engaged." [Foreword to *Brave New World*, by Aldous Huxley (New York: HarperCollins, 2004), xvi]

The Greenbrier

" . . . If things had gone just a teeny, tiny bit the other way during the Cold War, the Capitol of the United States would have been at the Greenbrier. In complete secrecy, during the Eisenhower administration, a provisional Capitol was built in a deep shelter right beside this palatial hotel. The bunker was encased in several feet of reinforced concrete and buried 720 feet into the hillside. . . . There's a power plant that could supply about 1,100 people for up to 40 days—this was as far ahead as planners could think when they contemplated the blast and radiation that would have been twilight's last gleaming. This is where our final laws would have been passed. The Greenbrier would have been the last resort." ["My Red-State Odyssey," *Vanity Fair*, September 2005]

Greene, Graham

"The essence of Greeneland, if one may dare to try and define it, is the combination of the exotic and the romantic with the sordid and the banal." [Introduction to *Orient Express*, by Graham Greene (New York: Penguin Classics, 2004), ix]

Greenspan, Alan

"Greenspan, of course, is an avowed disciple of the late guru Ayn Rand, author of *The Virtue of Selfishness*, but in Washington nobody thinks that's funny, because it's so normal." ["What's Love Got to Do with It?," *Vanity Fair*, September 1993]

"If he walked down the street, it wouldn't surprise me to see sane citizens touching him for luck." ["Greenspan Shrugged," *Vanity Fair*, December 2000]

"Greenspan didn't look very jazzy the first time I met him. He looked as if he'd be the easiest man in the world to persuade, if you were selling the proposition that everything is a different shade of gray." ["Greenspan Shrugged," *Vanity Fair*, December 2000]

Grenada (Invasion of)

"Even if it could be proved that all the students were in danger, that would only justify rescue of the students. . . . It doesn't justify overthrowing the government of Grenada, even if it's a repulsive one." ["Political Discussion," C-SPAN, 11/07/83]

Guevara, Che

"Only Che Guevara retains a hint of charisma, and he made no contribution whatsoever to the battle of theories and ideas." ["The Old Man," *Atlantic Monthly*, July/August 2004]

Gulag

"The slave system of the gulag did not have as its primary objective the turning of living people into corpses. The huge callousness of the system simply allowed vast numbers to be treated as expendable." ["Lightness at Midnight," *Atlantic Monthly*, September 2002]

Gulf War

"I have forgotten too much of the past to have any hope of repeating it, and think Santayana a windbag, but it still alarms me to see the United States embarking on a military journey without maps." ["Diary," *London Review of Books*, 9/13/90]

"There is a sort of vague idea that America will one day have to fight militant Arab nationalism, so why not now? This is just the kind of fatalism that leads to pointless wars, and to the suppression of pointful questioning." ["Minority Report," *Nation*, 9/17/90]

"Most liberal misgivings about the impending war with Iraq are focused, as usual, on the risks of failure. What about the problems of success?" ["Minority Report," *Nation*, 10/29/90]

"If war comes, it will be a contest of weapons systems rather than of ideas and principles, and in the short term some hybrid of capitalism and feudalism will probably be the winner." ["Tio Sam," *London Review of Books*, 12/20/90]

"The confrontation that opened on the Kuwaiti border in August 1990 was neither the first nor the last battle in a long war, but it was a battle that now directly, overtly involved and engaged the American public and American personnel. The call was to an exercise in peace through strength. But the cause was yet another move in the policy of keeping a region divided and embittered, and therefore accessible to the franchisers of weaponry and the owners of black gold." ["Why We Are Stuck in the Sand," *Harper's*, January 1991]

"The political engagement the United States has made is one of appointing itself the arbiter of inter-Arab border disputes and of the Middle East region as a whole—uninvited, in fact, and without a proper debate. I would say, when people ask me how long is this going to go on, I would say something like a hundred years." ["Persian Gulf War," C-SPAN, 2/04/91]

"There was always, and there still is, an alternative to this war, and that is the one that has been proposed by several countries long before the invasion of Kuwait, which is an international conference on the regional problems of the Middle East." ["Persian Gulf War," C-SPAN, 2/04/91]

"In the present crisis, with the hawks talking of war only on terms of massive and overwhelming superiority, and the doves nervously assenting on condition that not too many Americans are hurt, almost everyone either is a summer soldier or a sunshine patriot." ["Washington Diary," London Review of Books, 2/07/91]

"The irony has been that, in order to make their respective cases, both factions have had to exaggerate the military strength and capacity of Iraq: Bush in order to scare people with his fatuous Hitler analogy, and the peace camp in order to scare people with the prospect of heavy losses. Therefore, as I write, American liberals are coming to the guilty realization that unless Saddam Hussein shows some corking battlefield form pretty soon, they are going to look both silly and alarmist. Surely this cannot have been what they intended?" ["Washington Diary," London Review of Books, 2/07/91]

"There were a thousand ways for a superpower to avert war with a mediocre local despotism without losing face. But the syllogisms of power don't correspond very exactly to reason." ["Washington Diary," London Review of Books, 2/07/91]

"The objective of the war is not the recovery of Kuwait. . . . The point is the United States wants to appoint itself the government of Iraq. . . . Their aim is to get Iraq, get Saddam." [Crossfire, CNN, 2/21/91]

"It's a war to prove that America is number one and the only superpower." [McLaughlin's One on One, 2/22/91]

"It now seems that on their way out of Kuwait the Iraqi forces indulged in an additional saturnalia of looting and mayhem. Why should this in retrospect license the turkey shoot? If they had been withdrawing under international guarantee, how would they have dared to behave in this fashion?" ["Minority Report," Nation, 3/25/91]

"There were many liberals and even leftists who, during the run-up to the conflict, pronounced themselves co-belligerents. A popular formulation was 'I prefer imperialism to fascism.' Now, with a ruined Iraq and a strengthened Saddam—not to mention a strengthened al-Saud and al-Sabah—we no longer have to choose between imperialism and fascism. By a near miraculous synthesis, we can have both!" ["Minority Report," Nation, 6/17/91]

"The Gulf War, of course, was intended as therapy for the 'Vietnam syndrome.'" ["Washington Diary," London Review of Books, 8/20/92]

"A qualitative wrong turn was taken during the Gulf War, when most critics and opponents took refuge in the safe option of the 'body bag' argument. This made for an easy appeal to nativist sentiment—no number of Arabs is worth a single American life—and also postponed any serious thinking about the rights of small nations to self-defense versus the God-given right of the United States to intervene wherever it damn well pleases." ["Minority Report," *Nation*, 5/30/94]

"On his way *out* of Kuwait, with nothing left to fight for, Saddam Hussein had given the order to set fire to the oilfields and also to smash the wellheads, and thus allow the crude black stuff to run directly into the waters of the Gulf, and there thickly to coagulate. . . . Yet with the birds and marine animals of the Gulf choked to death *en masse*, and the sky itself full of fumes and specks that sometimes blotted out the sun, the predominantly 'Green' Left and anti-war movements could still not find a voice in which to call this by its right name." [*Hitch-22* (New York: Twelve, 2010), 292]

Guns

" . . . I have, gradually, come to think that there is something truly admirable in a country that codifies the responsibility for self-defense. Pity it doesn't make use of it." ["Minority Report," *Nation*, 1/24/94]

"If you take the Second Amendment as a whole (which the National Rifle Association and the political conservatives generally do not), it can be understood as enshrining the right, if not indeed the duty, of citizens to defend their country, and themselves, from aggression, including aggression from the government. . . . The time might come when the people might have to muster against the state. Well, what's wrong with that?" ["Minority Report," *Nation*, 1/24/94]

"*Of course* guns kill people. That's why the people should take control of the guns." ["Minority Report," *Nation*, 1/24/94]

"Alas for advocates of 'gun control,' the Second Amendment seems to enshrine a 'right of the people to keep and bear arms' irrespective of whether they are militia members or not." [*Hitch-22* (New York: Twelve, 2010), 252]

Habits

"The trouble with bad habits is that they are mutually reinforcing." ["On the Limits of Self-Improvement, Part I," *Vanity Fair*, October 2007]

"In my case, most of my bad habits are connected with the only way I know to make a living. In order to keep reading and writing, I need the junky energy that scotch can provide, and the intense short-term concentration that nicotine can help supply. To be crouched over a book or a keyboard, with these conditions of mingled reverie and alertness, is my highest happiness." ["On the Limits of Self-Improvement, Part I," *Vanity Fair*, October 2007]

"Bad habits have brought me this far: why change such a tried-and-true formula?" ["On the Limits of Self-Improvement, Part I," *Vanity Fair*, October 2007]

"The other problem with giving up a habit is that you don't exactly get to see the results, or not anything like fast enough." ["On the Limits of Self-Improvement, Part II," *Vanity Fair*, December 2007]

Haig, Alexander

"Now, nobody has a higher opinion of Alexander Haig than I do. And I think that he is a homicidal buffoon." ["Minority Report," *Nation*, 4/21/84]

"Indeed, the bulk of Haig's awful political career was an example of banana-republic principles and the related phenomenon of an overambitious man in uniform who mastered the essential art of licking the *derrières* of those above him while simultaneously . . . bullying and menacing those below." ["Death of a Banana Republican," *Slate*, 2/22/10]

Hair

"The rule, if it is a rule, is this: hair should only be abundant or emphasized or present at all on those parts of the female form that are already on public view. Any other hair disclosure is altogether too intimate." ["His View," *Evening Standard*, 1/09/98]

Haiti

"The good Senator Dole does not necessarily reflect rank-and-file opinion when he says that Haiti is not worth a single American life. That's a position that's only compatible with either (a) pacifism or (b) another ism with *ac* as its second and third letters." ["Minority Report," *Nation*, 10/17/94]

" . . . Nothing much will change in Haiti until its people outgrow the ghastly religions that were either brought to them by their original slaveholders or adapted into voodoo from preexisting cults. For that cause, which will take more than money, I'm willing to solicit contributions every day." ["Who Says the Nonreligious Don't Give?," *Free Inquiry*, April/May 2010]

Hangovers

"When you consider how many millions of workdays begin with hangovers great and small, it is mildly surprising to find how few real descriptions of the experience our literature can boast." ["The Teetotal Effect," *Vanity Fair*, August 2004]

"Hangovers are another bad sign, and you should not expect to be believed if you take refuge in saying you can't properly remember last night. (If you *really* don't remember, that's an even worse sign.)" [*Hitch-22* (New York: Twelve, 2010), 352]

Hanukkah

"If one could nominate an absolutely tragic day in human history, it would be the occasion that is now commemorated by the vapid and annoying holiday known as 'Hannukah.' For once, instead of Christianity plagiarizing from Judaism, the Jews borrow shamelessly from Christians in the pathetic hope of a celebration that coincides with 'Christmas,' which is itself a quasi-Christian annexation, complete with burning logs and holly and mistletoe, of a pagan Northland solstice originally illuminated by the Aurora Borealis. Here is the terminus to which banal 'multicul-turalism' has brought us." [*God Is Not Great* (New York: Twelve, 2007), 273]

" . . . At this time of year, any holy foolishness is permitted. And so we have a semi-official celebration of Hanukkah, complete with menorah, to celebrate not the ig-nition of a light but the imposition of theocratic darkness." ["Bah, Hanukkah," *Slate*, 12/03/07]

" . . . To celebrate Hanukkah is to celebrate not just the triumph of tribal Jewish backwardness but also the accidental birth of Judaism's bastard child in the shape of Christianity. You might think that masochism could do no more. Except that it always can." ["Bah, Hanukkah," *Slate*, 12/03/07]

"Every Jew who honors the Hanukkah holiday because it gives his child an excuse to mingle the dreidel with the Christmas tree and the sleigh (neither of these ab-surd symbols having the least thing to do with Palestine two millenniums past) is celebrating the making of a series of rods for his own back." ["Bah, Hanukkah," *Slate*, 12/03/07]

"And, of course and as ever, one stands aghast at the pathetic scale of the sup-posed 'miracle.' As a consequence of the successful Maccabean revolt against Hel-lenism, so it is said, a puddle of olive oil that should have lasted only for one day managed to burn for eight days. Wow! Certain proof, not just of an Almighty, but of an Almighty with a special fondness for fundamentalists. Epicurus and De-mocritus had brilliantly discovered that the world was made up of atoms, but who cares about a mere fact like that when there is miraculous oil to be goggled at by credulous peasants?" ["Bah, Hanukkah," *Slate*, 12/03/07]

Hasan, Nidal Malik
"By the time the mushy '*pre*-post-traumatic' school was done with the story, Maj. Hasan was not just acquitted of being a bad Muslim. He was more or less exoner-ated of having even done a bad deed." ["Hard Evidence," *Slate*, 11/16/09]

Hatred
"For a lot of people, their first love is what they'll always remember. For me, it's al-ways been the first hate. And I think that hatred, though it provides often rather junky energy, is a terrific way of getting you out of bed in the morning [and] keep-ing you going." ["Booknotes," C-SPAN, 9/01/93 (first aired: 10/17/93)]

"Since it's not really avoidable, I think the question is how to—if you like—turn it to advantage. . . . It's a bit like alcohol, if you like. It's a good servant, but it's a bad master." ["Q&A with Christopher Hitchens," C-SPAN, 1/14/11 (first aired: 1/23/11)]

Hawking, Stephen
" . . . One page, one paragraph, of Hawking is more awe-inspiring, to say nothing of being more instructive, than the whole of Genesis and the whole of Ezekiel." [Quoted in "The Future of the Public Intellectual: A Forum," *Nation*, 2/12/01]

Hayden, Tom

"Nobody would now trouble to read Hayden on anything if it were not for his record as an opponent of imperialist war in Indochina thirty years ago." ["Port Huron Piffle," *Nation*, 6/14/99]

Health

"There are some things more important than the fabled 'healthy lifestyle.'" ["Put That Out or Else," *Evening Standard*, 12/30/97]

"My doctor keeps asking me how I do it. And that's the relationship I want to have with my doctor—giving him advice instead of taking it from him." ["I Don't Do Diets," *Mirror*, 8/18/03]

"There's nothing amiss that a solid martini, followed by a thick sirloin and some crusty bread—washed down with some fine, old bloodstained Burgundy—wouldn't cure." ["I Don't Do Diets," *Mirror*, 8/18/03]

"Now, I don't know about you, but with me a feeling of fitness and well-being always lends extra zest to the cocktail hour. And what's a cocktail without a smoke?" ["On the Limits of Self-Improvement, Part I," *Vanity Fair*, October 2007]

"It could be argued that those who seek to make themselves over into a finer state of health and physique and fitness should not put off the job until they are in their fifty-ninth summer." ["On the Limits of Self-Improvement, Part III," *Vanity Fair*, September 2008]

Health Care

"The HMOs know the economics as well as anybody, and better than most. But it may not be they who have to foot those later and larger bills. Deny a treatment at the initial or emergency stage and the patient may go away, or seek another and more expensive policy. Or die—thus conclusively tidying up the books on the right side of the ledger." ["Bitter Medicine," *Vanity Fair*, August 1998]

"I've always thought that deep down, Americans do not want to be covered. They just don't want national health. They say they do when they're asked. They put it quite high up on the list. They feel they ought to say yes, but they don't really. . . . I sometimes think Americans want to live dangerously. They think this wouldn't be America if you had health coverage." [*Hugh Hewitt Show*, 1/20/10]

Heaven and Hell

" . . . Just consider for a moment what their [Christians'] heaven looks like. Endless praise and adoration, limitless abnegation and abjection of self; a celestial North Korea." [*Letters to a Young Contrarian* (New York: Basic Books, 2001), 64]

"Nothing proves the man-made character of religion as obviously as the sick mind that designed hell, unless it is the sorely limited mind that has failed to describe heaven—except as a place of either worldly comfort, eternal tedium, or (as Tertullian thought) continual relish in the torture of others." [*God Is Not Great* (New York: Twelve, 2007), 219]

"Whether it was a hellishly bad party or a party that was perfectly heavenly in every respect, the moment that it became eternal and compulsory would be the precise moment that it began to pall." [*Hitch-22* (New York: Twelve, 2010), 337]

Heaven's Gate
"The pathetic solipsism of the 'Heaven's Gate' zombies, who thought a comet and a UFO would come just for them, is of course not different in kind from that of the bumper sticker that reads 'Jesus Is My Best Friend.' But a difference does lie in the degree of literal belief, and in the willingness to act upon same. (The Jesus bumper sticker is often placed next to the one that reads 'Oliver North for Senate,' and the driver is generally keenly interested in the things of this world, while the followers of Do had given up everything except their in-flight bags and probably took even less interest in the outcome of the last election than did the remainder of the electorate.)" ["Heavenly Hoax," *Nation*, 5/12/97]

Hell's Angels
"Very much against my will, the network that broadcast my documentary on Mother Teresa decided to entitle it *Hell's Angel*, a rather cheap and sophomoric name. And it's under that unfortunate title that it has since been screened at some film festivals and other locales. When I went to introduce it a few years ago at a showing on the campus of the University of Rochester, I was picketed furiously by a group called the New York Lambs of Christ, a distinctly sheep-like organization. But then the police arrived and told me that I'd require a full security escort because some very dangerous criminal elements had been spotted in the crowd. I didn't believe that the Lambs would resort to bloodshed, and declined the protection. So I was amazed to see, as I pushed toward the hall, a gang of hirsute, leather-jacketed roughnecks yelling at me. The penny didn't drop, so I approached them and asked what they wanted. With some awkwardness, they handed me a notarized 'cease and desist' order, claiming that I had violated their trademark. This was the local chapter of the Hell's Angels. Their honor satisfied, they bestrode their bikes and roared away, leaving me clutching the writ and thinking, It's finally happened. Everybody in this country is a fucking lawyer." ["The Devil and Mother Teresa," *Vanity Fair*, October 2001]

Hellman, Lillian
" . . . Lillian Hellman—surely one of the least attractive women produced by the American 'progressive' culture in this century." ["Rebel in Evening Clothes," *Vanity Fair*, October 1999]

Helms, Jesse
"He used to remind me of an uneasy lesbian trapped in the body of a shifty boxing-gym trainer, but that was when he still had some wit and some wits. Now he looks like a desperate old tortoise." ["Minority Report," *Nation*, 3/27/95]

Heredity
" . . . All things predicated on the hereditary principle are by accident. . . ." [*The Monarchy: A Critique of Britain's Favorite Fetish* (London: Chatto & Windus Ltd, 1990), 21]

"The hereditary principle is a peculiar thing. The laws of nature ensure that it will throw up reprobates, incompetents, villains, and madmen, of the sort that make the works of William Shakespeare imperishable. Yet by some alchemy, a principle so vulnerable to disaster is also the guarantee of tradition, continuity, breeding, and other English hallmarks." ["Windsor Knot," *New York Times Magazine*, 5/12/91]

"Nothing is more human and fallible than the dynastic or hereditary principle. . . ." [*God Is Not Great* (New York: Twelve, 2007), 135]

" . . . Heredity can be destiny." ["A Little Night Music," *Men's Vogue*, May 2008]

Heresy
"It is difficult if not absolutely impossible to imbibe heresy in small doses. Either the system is in need of rapid, total change, or it is not." ["Thousands of Cans and Cartons," *London Review of Books*, 5/24/90]

"One little heresy soon leads to another. . . ." ["Minority Report," *Nation*, 11/14/94]

" . . . It is not possible for long to be just a little bit heretical." [*Hitch-22* (New York: Twelve, 2010), 295]

Heritage Foundation
"The Heritage Foundation isn't funny even when, in its heavily unironic way, it tries to be." [Letter, *Nation*, 4/20/85]

Heroes
" . . . All human achievement must also be accomplished by mammals and this realization . . . puts us on a useful spot. It strongly suggests that anyone could do what the heroes have done." [*Letters to a Young Contrarian* (New York: Basic Books, 2001), 92–93]

"Our heroes and heroines are those who managed, from Orwell through Camus and Solzhenitsyn, to be both intellectual and engaged." ["Susan Sontag," *Slate*, 12/29/04]

Hezbollah
"Many Sunni Arabs hate and detest Hezbollah, but none fail to fear and thus to respect it. . . ." ["Hezbollah's Progress," *Slate*, 10/18/10]

Hilton, Paris
"Not content with seeing her undressed and variously penetrated, it seems to be assumed that we need to watch her being punished and humiliated as well. The supposedly 'broad-minded' culture turns out to be as prurient and salacious as the elders in *The Scarlet Letter*. Hilton is legally an adult, but the treatment she is receiving stinks—indeed it reeks—of whatever horrible, buried, vicarious impulse underlies kiddie porn and child abuse." ["Siege of Paris," *Slate*, 6/11/07]

Hindsight

" . . . Not much is ever learned from hindsight, even if reputations can be founded upon it." ["Minority Report," *Nation*, 3/19/90]

Emperor Hirohito

"So imposing and hysterical was the cult of this god-king that it was believed that the whole Japanese people might resort to suicide if his person was threatened at the end of the war. It was accordingly decided that he could 'stay on,' but that he would henceforward have to claim to be an emperor only, and perhaps somewhat divine, but not strictly speaking a god. This deference to the strength of religious opinion must involve the admission that faith and worship can make people behave very badly indeed." [*God Is Not Great* (New York: Twelve, 2007), 241–242]

Hiss, Alger

"I met Alger Hiss a few times and was impressed, as it seems most people were, by his manners and bearing and address. On the last occasion on which I saw him, the dinner table was a convention of all that is noblest in the New York left-wing tradition. (I do not name names.) As coffee-time drew near, I whispered sarcastically to the hostess: 'Why don't we secure the doors and say: "Look, Alger, it's just us. Come on. You're among friends. Tell us why you really did it."' She gave me a look, and a pinch, which eloquently conveyed the words Don't Even *Think* About It. And it's true that this has long been, for many people, a loyalty oath of its own. If Hiss was wrong, then Nixon and McCarthy were right. And that could not be." ["A Regular Bull," *London Review of Books*, 9/18/97]

Historical Materialism

"The essential element of historical materialism as applied to ethical and social matters was (and actually still is) this: it demonstrated how much unhappiness and injustice and irrationality was man-made." [*Letters to a Young Contrarian* (New York: Basic Books, 2001), 98]

History

" . . . History is very often made, even if only by accident, by men and women who draw a line beyond which they will not be pushed." ["Going Home with Kim Dae Jung," *Mother Jones*, May 1985]

"History does not, in fact, repeat itself (though historians repeat one another)." ["Minority Report," *Nation*, 1/01/90]

" . . . The past is another country, and it can be a big mistake to try to revisit or recapture it." ["Last Orders Catch for Catch-22," *Daily Mail*, 9/24/94]

"As ever, one discovers that those who boast of taking the long view of history are hopelessly wedded to the short-term." ["A Regular Bull," *London Review of Books*, 9/18/97]

" . . . History really begins where evolution ends, and where we gain at least a modicum of control over our own narrative." ["The Medals of His Defeats," *Atlantic Monthly*, April 2002]

"History is more of a tragedy than it is a morality tale." ["Lightness at Midnight," *Atlantic Monthly*, September 2002]

"Hard work is involved in the study of history. Hard moral work, too. We don't get much assistance in that task from mushy secondhand observations. . . ." ["Lightness at Midnight," *Atlantic Monthly*, September 2002]

"You don't get that many measurable historical moments in your life, but you must recognize them when they come." [Interview with *Washington Prism*, 7/21/05]

" . . . Since history is often recounted by the victors, why not have it related for once by one who is something worse than a loser?" ["Scoundrel Time," *Vanity Fair*, March 2006]

"If you can't have a sense of policy, you should at least try to have a sense of history." ["The End of Fukuyama," *Slate*, 3/01/06]

"A highly irritating expression in Washington has it that 'hindsight is always 20–20.' Would that it were so. History is not a matter of hindsight and is not, in fact, always written by the victors." ["A Loser's History," *Slate*, 4/30/07]

"History cannot be unmade." [*The Parthenon Marbles: The Case for Reunification* (New York: Verso, 2008), 25]

" . . . Those who bang their heads against history's wall had better be equipped with some kind of a theoretical crash helmet." [*Hitch-22* (New York: Twelve, 2010), 89]

"Attempts to locate oneself within history are as natural, and as absurd, as attempts to locate oneself within astronomy." [*Hitch-22* (New York: Twelve, 2010), 331–332]

"It is not so much that there are ironies of history, it is that history itself is ironic." [*Hitch-22* (New York: Twelve, 2010), 420]

"If you're saying you are changing history, you're probably not." [*Charlie Rose Show*, 8/13/10]

Hitchens, Christopher

"By instinct, I am a conservative. It's only reason that keeps me from joining them." [Quoted in Don Kowet, "Christopher Hitchens, Drawing Room Marxist," *Washington Times*, 1/02/90]

"I am, I hope, never offensive by accident." [Letter, *Nation*, 3/27/95]

"I don't like to see myself described as a liberal because that seems to me too easy a position." [Quoted in Michael Rust, "Clinton's Lies Stopped at Hitchens' Door," *Insight on the News*, 6/28/99]

"Those who know me will confirm that while I may not be tidy, I am so clean you could eat your dinner off me." ["The Real David Brock," *Nation*, 5/27/02]

"I spent most of my life, three decades or more, as a convinced socialist. I don't repudiate that—I'm not ashamed of it—but I don't find it useful to call myself that any more. Is there now an international working-class movement that has a feasible idea for a better society? No, there isn't. Will it revive? The answer is clearly no. Is there a socialist critique of the capitalist world order? No. Realizing that, to call myself a socialist would be a sentimental thing." [Quoted in Neil Munro, "Leaving the Left," *National Journal*, 4/05/03]

"He [George Galloway] says that I am an ex-Trotskyist (true), a 'popinjay' (true enough, since its original Webster's definition means a target for arrows and shots), and that I cannot hold a drink (here I must protest)." ["George Galloway Is Gruesome, Not Gorgeous," *Slate*, 9/13/05]

"So call me a neo-conservative if you must: anything is preferable to the rotten unprincipled alliance between the former fans of the one-party state and the hysterical zealots of the one-god one." ["At Last Our Lefties See the Light," *Sunday Times* (London), 4/30/06]

"My own opinion is enough for me, and I claim the right to have it defended against any consensus, any majority, anywhere, any place, any time. And anyone who disagrees with this can pick a number, get in line, and kiss my ass." [Debate ("Be It Resolved: Freedom of Speech Includes the Freedom to Hate"), University of Toronto, Toronto, Canada, 11/15/06]

"If I search my own life for instances of good or fine behavior I am not overwhelmed by an excess of choice." [*God Is Not Great* (New York: Twelve, 2007), 188]

"One of these days, having in the course of my life been an Anglican, educated at a Methodist school, converted by marriage to Greek Orthodoxy, recognized as an incarnation by the followers of Sai Baba, and remarried by a rabbi, I shall be able to try and update William James's *The Varieties of Religious Experience*." [*God Is Not Great* (New York: Twelve, 2007), 195]

"Do I consider myself more of an entertainer than an intellectual? Well, I don't know which I want to be, but I'm pretty sure I know at what I'm probably better. And I'm much better at stand-up comedy and telling limericks and doing karaoke than I am at any of the other stuff. I just don't get enough opportunity." ["In Depth with Christopher Hitchens," C-SPAN, 9/02/07]

"Something in me evidently resists, or wants to resist, joining any good-behavior club that will have me as a member." ["On the Limits of Self-Improvement, Part II," *Vanity Fair*, December 2007]

"The world I live in is one where I have five quarrels a day, each with someone who really takes me on over something; and if I can't get into an argument, I go looking for one, to make sure I trust my own arguments, to hone them." [Quoted in "Christopher Hitchens," *Prospect Magazine*, May 2008]

"I've never wanted a political job, but if I was to be given grace in favor by the president it would be the Bureau of Alcohol, Firearms and Tobacco." [Festival of Dangerous Ideas, Australian Broadcasting Corporation, Sydney, Australia, 10/06/09]

"I speak as one who was recently invited to lecture at the Sydney Opera House. I had not thought of myself as spectacularly fat until I made my appearance, but it remains the case that the audience would not leave until I had sung. True fact." ["Dust in the Wind," *Slate*, 10/12/09]

Hitchens, Christopher and Alcohol

"It's a master-servant relationship. I'll leave it to you which is which." [Quoted in Peter Carlson, "The Journalist's Sharpened Pen," *Washington Post*, 2/12/99]

"I'll be fifty-four in April, and everyone keeps asking how I do it. How I do what? I'm never completely sure what the questioner means. I *hope* they mean how do I manage to keep producing books, writing essays, making radio and television appearances at all hours, traveling all over the place with no sign of exhaustion, teaching classes, and giving lectures, while still retaining my own hair and teeth and a near-godlike physique that is the envy of many of my juniors. Sometimes, though, I suppose they mean how do I do all this and still drink enough every day to kill or stun the average mule?" ["Living Proof," *Vanity Fair*, March 2003]

"I follow medical advice in only one respect, which is to make sure that I swallow the two shots of alcoholic medicine that doctors now agree is essential for the heart and the arteries." ["I Don't Do Diets," *Mirror*, 8/18/03]

"Nobody who knows me thinks that I drink too little, and I could probably stand to imbibe less. It's both an advantage and a disadvantage to have a tolerance for alcohol. But I sometimes wonder what those who don't know me must think. The reputation now approaches the legendary." ["Open Letter to Readers and Letter Exchange with Victor Navasky," Christopher Hitchens Web, 2003]

"It wasn't all that easy to get a reputation for boozing when you worked in and around old Fleet Street, where the hardened hands would spill more just getting the stuff to their lips than most people imbibe in a week, but I managed it." [*Hitch-22* (New York: Twelve, 2010), 150–151]

Hitchens, Christopher and the Left

"I learn with complacency that I have been excommunicated from the left." ["The Ends of War," *Nation*, 12/21/01]

"Yet now, it is those on the Left who have come to offend and irritate me the most, and it is also their crimes and blunders that I feel myself more qualified, as well as more motivated, to point out." [*Hitch-22* (New York: Twelve, 2010), 408–409]

"So I didn't so much repudiate a former loyalty, like some attention-grabbing defector, as feel it falling away from me. On some days, this is like the phantom pain of a missing limb. On others, it's more like the sensation of having taken off a needlessly heavy overcoat." [*Hitch-22* (New York: Twelve, 2010), 411–412]

"I do know what it's like, however, to mourn the passing of a love, and I remember Sarajevo for that reason. By the end of that conflict, I was being called a traitor and a warmonger by quite a lot of the Left and was both appalled and relieved to find that I no longer really cared." [*Hitch-22* (New York: Twelve, 2010), 414]

Hitchens, Peter

"My brother, Peter, is, like all bearers of the family name, highly—nay, mysteriously—intelligent and a writer of unusual verve and range. Here, all resemblance ends. He is a staunch Christian and an abstainer from alcohol and tobacco. He lacks also, I sometimes think, my strange, hypnotic power over women." ["O, Brother, Why Art Thou?," *Vanity Fair*, July 2005]

Hitler, Adolf

"The man's opinions are trite and bigoted and deferential, and the prose in *Mein Kampf* is simply laughable in its pomposity." ["Imagining Hitler," *Vanity Fair*, February 1999]

Hoffer, Eric

"Eric Hoffer . . . was to American ideas what Norman Rockwell was to American painting. Defiantly ordinary, he seems able to rise just above kitsch and to reflect something of the elusive 'national character.'" ["American Notes," *Times Literary Supplement*, 6/10/83]

"Born of immigrant parents, overcoming childhood blindness, working on the waterfront while reading Montaigne, he eventually caught the eyes of presidents and academics. At that point, his writing started to become bland and trite." ["American Notes," *Times Literary Supplement*, 6/10/83]

Hollings, Ernest

"The remaining speakers [at the Democratic Party's 1982 midterm conference] were a torment to hear, except for Ernest Hollings, who was incomprehensible when he wasn't inaudible." ["Fashion Parade in Philadelphia," *Nation*, 7/10/82–7/17/82]

Hollywood

"Once you begin to notice that special set of ethics known as Hollywood exceptionalism, you may find yourself seeing it everywhere." ["Save the Children," *Slate*, 10/05/09]

Holmes, Oliver Wendell

" . . . The celebrated phrase about shouting 'Fire!' in a crowded theater comes from Oliver Wendell Holmes, one of the most overrated and hypocritical legal figures in modern American history. He evolved that cute notion—of a definition of limits—while condemning some Socialist dissidents to prison for opposing the First World War." ["Hustler with a Cause," *Vanity Fair*, November 1996]

Holy Place

" . . . The concept of the 'holy place' makes its loud claim in the register of foolish and dangerous ideas. The folly ought to be doubly self-evident even to the faithful, since, while a benevolent deity might perhaps wish to 'intervene' every now and then with a miracle here, a plague or earthquake there, if only in order to keep up morale or show who is boss, the same lofty he or she cannot possibly have any interest in the preservation of any man-made structure or man-maintained site." ["Value in the Wrong Place," *Free Inquiry*, Spring 2001]

Holy Writ

"Holy writ may indeed be employed for literary purposes. Holy writ is probably fiction, of a grand sort, to begin with." ["Siding with Rushdie," *London Review of Books*, 10/26/89]

Homeland Security [See: Security]

Homosexuality

"There is no such thing as a coterie or conspiracy of declared homosexuals. Bigotry and denial are apparently opposing sides of an identical coin. The fear of being exposed is what spurs the witchhunter." ["It Dare Not Speak Its Name," *Harper's*, August 1987]

"I say that homosexuality is not just a form of sex. It's a form of love, and it deserves our respect for that reason." [Intelligence Squared Debate ("The Catholic Church Is a Force for Good in the World"), Methodist Central Hall Westminster, Oxford, UK, 10/19/09]

Homosexuality and the Right

"Why does the right torture itself about homosexuality? The flagellation is partly a consequence of the overlap between extreme conservatives and the more traditional wing of the Roman Catholic Church. Then there is self-protection—honesty means loss of power, so gays on the right toe the line and gay bash. . . . There is of course self-hatred in all this, personal but perhaps ideological. The latter stems from the neurotic identification by some conservatives of homosexual conduct with weakness, cowardice, and even treason. To these people, the gay world is a lethal compound of E. M. Forster's morality, Guy Burgess's loyalty, and John Maynard Keynes's economics." ["It Dare Not Speak Its Name," *Harper's*, August 1987]

" . . . History speaks of a long and not so surprising connection between homosexuality and the right. One can look to the church and the military. 'Gay' has never necessarily meant 'left.'" ["It Dare Not Speak Its Name," *Harper's*, August 1987]

"Whether you are a creationist like Pat Robertson, or a Catholic like Pat Buchanan, or a materialist believer in 'Natural Law' like [Harry] Jaffa and others, you can't avoid the salient fact that the Creator, or the Divinity, or Nature, or Evolution, has evidently mandated that there be a certain quite large number of homosexuals." ["Bloom's Way," *Nation*, 5/15/00]

Hook, Sidney

"Hook may have been in many ways anti-McCarthy but anti-McCarthyite he famously was not." ["A Political Pundit Who Need Never Dine Alone," *Newsday*, 11/07/90]

Hope

"To wait is to hope, of course, and in some ways to hope is to wait." ["Havana Can Wait," *Vanity Fair*, March 2000]

Hope, Bob

" . . . Bob Hope devoted a fantastically successful and well-remunerated lifetime to showing that a truly unfunny man can make it as a comic." ["Hopeless," *Slate*, 8/01/03]

Hostility

" . . . If you radiate hostility, you also tend to attract it." ["The Best Woman?," *Slate*, 9/08/08]

Huckabee, Mike

" . . . A moon-faced true believer and anti-Darwin pulpit-puncher from Arkansas who doesn't seem to know the difference between being born again and born yesterday." ["Holy Nonsense," *Slate*, 12/06/07]

Hugging

"Sudden, spontaneous hugging of strangers is . . . permitted to all Americans on one condition: They should, for maximum sympathy, be celebrating a forthcoming execution." ["Dirty Stories," *Nation*, 7/07/97]

Hughes, Robert

"Robert Hughes is the most successful art historian, or explainer of art, of his time. . . . In an age of credentials and specialization, Hughes is a polymath of a distinct type. He has made amateurism professional. He is the marsupial critic." ["Angel in the Outback," *Vanity Fair*, May 1997]

Human Nature

"The 'human nature' argument has been allowed to waste a lot of liberal time, and keeps emerging as the subtext of contemporary arguments about crime, race, evil, and other areas where reactionaries feel that the instinctive gives them the upper hand." ["Minority Report," *Nation*, 6/19/89]

"It is only those who hope to *transform* humans who end up by burning them, like the waste product of a failed experiment." [*Letters to a Young Contrarian* (New York: Basic Books, 2001), 32]

Humanism

"Just as you discover that stupidity and cruelty are the same everywhere, you find that the essential elements of humanism are the same everywhere, too." [*Letters to a Young Contrarian* (New York: Basic Books, 2001), 111]

"Humanism has many crimes for which to apologize. But it can apologize for them, and also correct them, in its own terms and without having to shake or challenge the basis of any unalterable system of belief." [*God Is Not Great* (New York: Twelve, 2007), 250]

Humanitarian Intervention

"Debates and discussions about humanitarian intervention tend (for good reasons) to be about American intervention. They also tend to share the assumption that the United States can afford, or at any rate has the power, to take or leave the option to get involved. On some occasions, there may seem to be overwhelming moral grounds to quit the sidelines and intervene. On others, the imperatives are less clear-cut. In all instances, nothing exceptional should be contemplated unless it has at least some congruence with the national interest." ["Just Causes," *Foreign Affairs*, September/October 2008]

Humanity

"Those who are being enjoined to remember their humanity are being urged to remember Quite A Lot." ["Ireland," *Critical Quarterly*, Spring 1998]

Humans

" . . . We are mammals and the prefrontal lobe (at least while we wait for genetic engineering) is too small while the adrenaline gland is too big." [*Letters to a Young Contrarian* (New York: Basic Books, 2001), 32]

"Those who need or want to think for themselves will always be a minority; the human race may be inherently individualistic and even narcissistic, but in the mass it is quite easy to control. People have a need for reassurance and belonging." [*Letters to a Young Contrarian* (New York: Basic Books, 2001), 95–96]

"Most important of all, the instinct for justice and for liberty is just as much 'innate' in us as are the promptings of tribalism and sexual xenophobia and superstition. People know when they are being lied to, they know when their rulers are absurd, they know they do not love their chains; every time a Bastille falls one is always pleasantly surprised by how many sane and decent people were there all along." [*Letters to a Young Contrarian* (New York: Basic Books, 2001), 111–112]

"With a part of themselves, humans relish cruelty and war and absolute capricious authority, are bored by civilized and humane pursuits and understand only too well the latent connection between sexual repression and orgiastic vicarious collectivized release." [*Why Orwell Matters* (New York: Basic Books,2002), 191]

"Paradoxically, it is those who calmly recognize that we are alone [in the universe] who may have the better chance of investing human life with such meaning as it might be made to possess." ["The Future of an Illusion," *Daedalus*, Summer 2003]

"The plain fact is that the physical structure of the human being is a joke in itself: a flat, crude, unanswerable disproof of any nonsense about 'intelligent design.'" ["Why Women Aren't Funny," *Vanity Fair*, January 2007]

" . . . It is a fact of nature that the human species is, biologically, only partly rational. Evolution has meant that our prefrontal lobes are too small, our adrenal glands are too big, and our reproductive organs apparently designed by committee; a recipe that, alone or in combination, is very certain to lead to some unhappiness and disorder." [*God Is Not Great* (New York: Twelve, 2007), 8]

"It is because we evolved from sightless bacteria, now found to share our DNA, that we are so myopic." [*God Is Not Great* (New York: Twelve, 2007), 82]

Humility

"There is a trick to getting people to do things for you . . . and that trick consists in pretending to be humble and impressed." ["Pretending to Write 'Vile Bodies,'" *London Review of Books*, 1/09/92]

Humor

" . . . A sense of humor is not the definition of a person's mood when he is off duty from being serious." ["American Notes," *Times Literary Supplement*, 5/30/86]

"One is made to appreciate yet again the apparent paradox that links comic genius to the most bitter and pessimistic view of the human condition." ["Evelyn Waugh's War with the Present Tense," *Newsday*, 8/26/92]

"Mere industry and effort . . . will not make up for a humor deficit. (At least, not for a humorist.)" ["O'Rourke's Drift," *Mail on Sunday*, 12/10/95]

" . . . The ability to laugh is one of the faculties that defines the human and distinguishes the species from other animals. (With the other higher mammals, which I do not in the least wish to insult, there may be high levels of playfulness and even some practical jokes, but no irony.) An individual deficient in the sense of humor represents more of a challenge to our idea of the human than a person of subnormal intelligence. . . ." [*Letters to a Young Contrarian* (New York: Basic Books, 2001), 115–116]

"It's therefore not true to say, as some optimists do, that humor is essentially subversive. It can be an appeal to the familiar and the clichéd, a source of reassurance through shared hilarity." [*Letters to a Young Contrarian* (New York: Basic Books, 2001), 116]

" . . . The sophisticated element in humor is exactly its capacity to shock, or to surprise, or to occur unintentionally." [*Letters to a Young Contrarian* (New York: Basic Books, 2001), 116]

" . . . The sharp aside and the witty nuance are the consolation of the losers and are the one thing that pomp and power can do nothing about. The literal mind is baffled by the ironic one, demanding explanations that only intensify the joke." [*Letters to a Young Contrarian* (New York: Basic Books, 2001), 117–118]

"Humor is easily enough definable as a weapon of criticism and subversion, but it is very often a mere comfort or survival technique." [*Letters to a Young Contrarian* (New York: Basic Books, 2001), 119]

"Humor ought to be pointed—ought to preserve its relationship to wit—and it ought to be fearless. The easiest forms it takes are those of caricature (the clever politician already knows enough to make an offer for the original cartoon, as a show of his good-heartedness and tolerance) and associated forms of mimicry. The mordant forms it takes are the ironic and the obscene. Probably only the latter two forms can be revolutionary." [*Letters to a Young Contrarian* (New York: Basic Books, 2001), 121]

"A rule of thumb with humor; if you worry that you might be going too far, you have already not gone far enough. If everybody laughs, you have failed." [*Letters to a Young Contrarian* (New York: Basic Books, 2001), 122]

"Nothing so much empowers a magazine or a movement as an ability to be witty and sarcastic; nothing condemns a regime so much as a fear of laughter." [Introduction to *Left Hooks, Right Crosses: A Decade of Political Writing*, ed. Christopher Caldwell and Christopher Hitchens (New York: Nation Books, 2002), 209]

" . . . Any act that depends too much on the scatological is in some kind of trouble. . . . This isn't unfunny just because it's infantile and repetitive and doesn't know when to stop; it's unfunny because the revulsion produced by feces is universal and automatic and thus much too easy to exploit." ["Kazakh Like Me," *Slate*, 11/13/06]

"Male humor prefers the laugh to be at someone's expense and understands that life is quite possibly a joke to begin with—and often a joke in extremely poor taste. Humor is part of the armor-plate with which to resist what is already farcical enough." ["Why Women Aren't Funny," *Vanity Fair*, January 2007]

"Humor, if we are to be serious about it, arises from the ineluctable fact that we are all born into a losing struggle." ["Why Women Aren't Funny," *Vanity Fair*, January 2007]

"A saving grace of the human condition (if I may phrase it like that) is a sense of humor. Many writers and witnesses, guessing the connection between sexual repression and religious fervor, have managed to rescue themselves and others from its deadly grip by the exercise of wit." [Introduction to *The Portable Atheist* (New York: Da Capo Press, 2007), xxv]

Humor (British)
" . . . My theory of British, or English, humor, which is that its charm (without defining it out of existence) lies in the fact that it is more subversive and obscene than the general run of American comedy, while hailing from a culture that Americans regard as more venerable, staid, and traditional." ["Kings of Comedy," *Vanity Fair*, December 1995]

Hunting
" . . . 'Canned hunting': the can't-miss virtual safaris that charge a fortune to fly bored and overweight Americans to Africa and 'big game' destinations on other continents for an air-conditioned trophy trip and the chance to butcher a charismatic animal in conditions of guaranteed safety." ["Political Animals," *Atlantic Monthly*, November 2002]

Hussein, Saddam
"It is quite clear that Saddam Hussein had by the late 1980s learned, or been taught, two things. The first is that the United States will intrigue against him

when he is weak. The second is that it will grovel before him when he is strong." ["Why We Are Stuck in the Sand," *Harper's*, January 1991]

"There is not the least doubt that he has acquired some of the means of genocide and hopes to collect some more; there is also not the least doubt that he is a sadistic megalomaniac. Some believe that he is a rational and self-interested actor who understands 'containment,' but I think that is distinctly debatable: Given a green light by Washington on two occasions—once for the assault on Iran and once for the annexation of Kuwait—he went crazy both times and, knowing that it meant disaster for Iraq and for its neighbors, tried to steal much more than he had been offered." ["Taking Sides," *Nation*, 10/14/02]

" . . . To the extent that the United States underwrote Saddam in the past, this redoubles our responsibility to cancel the moral debt by removing him." ["So Long, Fellow Travelers," *Washington Post*, 10/20/02]

"Saddam Hussein is a bad guy's bad guy. He's not just bad in himself but the cause of badness in others." ["Machiavelli in Mesopotamia," *Slate*, 11/07/02]

"Even though he doesn't look quite the same without his uniform, and in off-moments resembles a man who talks too much on a park bench, he can remind you of what it would have been like to live under him." ["Saddam in the Dock: Invulnerable? We'll See About That," *Mirror*, 7/02/04]

"Everywhere I have been in Iraq, I have noticed that the bravest person betrays a slight change of expression when the name Saddam Hussein is mentioned. Just a flicker in the eye, perhaps, but pure fear. The sort of fear you can bottle." ["Saddam in the Dock: Invulnerable? We'll See About That," *Mirror*, 7/02/04]

" . . . It's very incautious to doubt any atrocity story, however lurid, if it is laid to the charge of Saddam Hussein." [*Hitch-22* (New York: Twelve, 2010), 294]

"'All right, we agree that Saddam was a bad guy.' Nobody capable of uttering that commonplace has any conception of radical evil." [*Hitch-22* (New York: Twelve, 2010), 299]

Huxley, Aldous
"We should, I think, be grateful that Aldous Huxley was such a mass of internal contradictions. These enabled him to register the splendors and miseries, not just of modernity, but of the human condition." [Foreword to *Brave New World*, by Aldous Huxley (New York: HarperCollins, 2004), xx]

Hygiene
"There are those of us who do not choose to live in some huge, wholesome happy-camper Disneyland of hygiene and pumped-up enthusiasm. . . ." ["Smoke and Mirrors," *Vanity Fair*, October 1994]

"You will be glad to hear . . . that I high-mindedly declined the Chardonnay-Clay Body Wrap: it savored too much of yet another method of taking in booze, through the pores. Instead, I opted for a punishing session on the Biltmore's immaculate croquet lawn." ["On the Limits of Self-Improvement, Part I," *Vanity Fair*, October 2007]

Hype

"'Hype' is when a publisher gets Michael Herr to use the words 'Great American Novel.' That's hype." ["Excuse Me But I Think You Just Dropped This Name," *Evening Standard*, 12/11/97]

Hypocrisy

"But everybody agrees, somewhere in his heart, that there ought to be *some* connection between what you believe and how you behave, what you advocate for others and how you live yourself." ["The Hawks with White Feathers," *Spectator*, 8/10/85]

"There is an obvious connection to be intuited between the grossly moralizing and repressive and the grossly prurient." ["At the Scamulator," *Times Literary Supplement*, 11/30/90–12/06/90]

"You don't say 'they all do it' unless you know you've been doing it too." ["Bodies Everywhere, No 'Smoking Gun,'" *Nation*, 9/08/97–9/15/97]

"I always take it for granted that sexual moralizing by public figures is a sign of hypocrisy or worse, and most usually a desire to perform the very act that is most being condemned." [*Hitch-22* (New York: Twelve, 2010), 78]

" . . . Whenever I hear some bigmouth in Washington or the Christian heartland banging on about the evils of sodomy or whatever, I mentally enter his name in my notebook and contentedly set my watch. Sooner rather than later, he will be discovered down on his weary and well-worn knees in some dreary motel or latrine, with an expired Visa card, having tried to pay well over the odds to be peed upon by some Apache transvestite." [*Hitch-22* (New York: Twelve, 2010), 78]

Iceland

"They say that if you take Icelanders away from their ancestral terrain, they are liable to pine and even to die from homesickness. Perhaps that's why one meets so few of them." ["Iceland Reminds Us Nature Is Boss," *Slate*, 4/19/10]

Idealism

"There is a kind of intensity that marks the exquisitely fine line between idealism and fanaticism. The only thing to do in these cases is to try and go for the lucid interval." ["Vintage Vanessa," *Vanity Fair*, December 1994]

"I suspect that the hardest thing for the idealist to surrender is the teleological, or the sense that there is some feasible, lovelier future that can be brought nearer by exertions in the present, and for which 'sacrifices' are justified. With some part of myself, I still 'feel,' but no longer really think, that humanity would be the poorer without this fantastically potent illusion. . . . I have actually seen more prisons broken open, more people and territory 'liberated,' and more taboos broken and censors flouted, since I let go of the idea, or at any rate the plan, of a radiant future." [*Hitch-22* (New York: Twelve, 2010), 420]

Identity Politics

"Identity politics are a drag, aren't they, forcing people to think with their genitalia or their epidermis?" ["Sensitive to a Fault," *Vanity Fair*, April 1994]

"This tendency has often been satirized—the overweight caucus of the Cherokee transgender disabled lesbian faction demands a hearing on its needs—but never satirized enough." [*Letters to a Young Contrarian* (New York: Basic Books, 2001), 113]

" . . . It was the dense and boring and selfish who had always seen identity politics as their big chance." [*Letters to a Young Contrarian* (New York: Basic Books, 2001), 113]

"People who think with their epidermis or their genitalia or their clan are the problem to begin with. One does not banish this specter by invoking it. If I would not vote against someone on the grounds of 'race' or 'gender' alone, then by the exact same token I would not cast a vote in his or her favor for the identical reason." ["The Peril of Identity Politics," *Wall Street Journal*, 1/18/08]

Ideology

"A feature, not just of the age of the end of ideology, but of the age immediately preceding the age of the end of ideology, is that of the dictator who has no ideology at all." ["Tio Sam," *London Review of Books*, 12/20/90]

"Once you define yourself as emancipated from dogma and ideology, and you can hope to live a life of unexamined lightness." ["Goodbye to Berlin," *Nation*, 12/08/97]

" . . . Every position including the ostensibly neutral is in the last instance ideological." [*Why Orwell Matters* (New York: Basic Books, 2002), 196]

"Coexistence with totalitarian, expansionist, one-man-state, one-god-state ideologies is impossible. And it's good, because it's not desirable." [*Charlie Rose Show*, 7/15/05]

"There are days when I miss my old convictions as if they were an amputated limb. But in general I feel better, and no less radical, and you will feel better, too, I guarantee, once you leave hold of the doctrinaire and allow your chainless mind to do its own thinking." [*God Is Not Great* (New York: Twelve, 2007), 153]

Illiteracy

" . . . The slump in reading cannot be unrelated to the awful statistics on the ability to read." ["American Notes," *Times Literary Supplement*, 5/11/84]

" . . . It is plain that the schools are graduating thousands of analphabetic students each year. Many of them are obviously not stupid. It takes cunning and ingenuity to conceal illiteracy into adulthood and to fool employers, bureaucrats, and fellow-workers (if any). One young man asked for help simply to write his name—he didn't want to become literate, but he did want to be able to open a bank account." ["American Notes," *Times Literary Supplement*, 5/11/84]

Illness

"The absorbing fact about being mortally sick is that you spend a good deal of time preparing yourself to die with some modicum of stoicism (and provision for loved ones), while being simultaneously and highly interested in the business of survival. This is a distinctly bizarre way of 'living'—lawyers in the morning and doctors in the afternoon—and means that one has to exist even more than usual in a double frame of mind." ["Unanswerable Prayers," *Vanity Fair*, October 2010]

"One almost develops a kind of elitism about the uniqueness of one's own personal disorder. So, if your own first- or secondhand tale is about some other organs, you might want to consider telling it sparingly, or at least more selectively. This suggestion applies whether the story is intensely depressing and lowering to the spirit . . . or whether it is intended to convey uplift and optimism: 'My grandmother was diagnosed with terminal melanoma of the G-spot and they just about gave up on her. But she hung in there and took huge doses of chemotherapy and radiation at the same time, and the last postcard we had was from her at the top of Mount Everest.'" ["Miss Manners and the Big C," *Vanity Fair*, December 2010]

Illusions

"Illusions, of course, cannot be abolished. But they can and must be outgrown." [*The Monarchy: A Critique of Britain's Favorite Fetish* (London: Chatto & Windus Ltd, 1990), 42]

"In the gradual manufacture of an illusion, the conjurer is only the instrument of the audience. He may even announce himself as a trickster and a clever prestidigitator and yet gull the crowd." [*The Missionary Position* (New York: Verso, 1995), 15]

" . . . While people are entitled to their illusions, they are not entitled to a limitless enjoyment of them and they are not entitled to impose them upon others." [*Letters to a Young Contrarian* (New York: Basic Books, 2001), 82]

"I try to deny myself any illusions or delusions, and I think that this perhaps entitles me to try and deny the same to others, at least as long as they refuse to keep their fantasies to themselves." [*Hitch-22* (New York: Twelve, 2010), 342–343]

Image

"Image and perception are everything, and those who possess them have the ability to determine their own myth, to be taken at their own valuation." [*The Missionary Position* (New York: Verso, 1995), 6]

Imagination

" . . . I believe that the human capacity for wonder neither will nor should be destroyed or superseded." ["A Templeton Conversation: Does Science Make Belief in God Obsolete?," John Templeton Foundation, May 2008]

Imitations

"Beware of imitations. But be aware, also, of those moments in public life that you could not hope to make up." [Introduction to *Ancient Gonzo Wisdom: Interviews with Hunter S. Thompson*, ed. Anita Thompson (New York: Da Capo Press, 2009), xviii]

Immigration

" . . . Immigration policy has had certain unintended consequences, or at least consequences unintended by those who profess Statue of Liberty values. It has also succeeded in splitting American conservatives, who have to wonder if their laissez-faire and anti-statist convictions will sit well with the regulatory assumption that must govern population control." ["From Melting Pot to Potpourri," *Los Angeles Times*, 5/21/95]

"Speaking for myself, I didn't come to America in order to join another Anglo-Saxon condominium." ["From Melting Pot to Potpourri," *Los Angeles Times*, 5/21/95]

Impartiality

"In any case, one ought not to quarrel with the aim of impartiality. It is just that, as an objective, it is harder to attain than its advocates imagine." ["Francisco Franco, with Precious Little Rancor," *Newsday*, 3/02/88]

Imperialism

"The term has such a multitude of references, and covers such a complexity of subjects, that no author should permit himself the luxury of using it as a shorthand. . . ." ["The Move Forward," *Times* (London), 6/21/71]

"When it comes to carving up other people's countries, the West is agnostic and, so to speak, value free." ["Minority Report," *Nation*, 7/03/95]

"Historically, 'divide and rule' was the method of colonial governance, so 'divide and quit' became the means of withdrawal." ["Minority Report," *Nation*, 8/14/95–8/21/95]

"To suffer all the consequences of being imperialistic, while acting with all the resolution and consistency and authority of, say, Belgium, is to have failed rather badly." ["Why Is Everything Such a Surprise?," *Wall Street Journal*, 8/03/06]

Impotence

" . . . The question of impotence has always been a matter of laughing at someone else." ["It's Magic Darling," *Evening Standard*, 4/28/98]

Inauguration Day

"A president may by all means use his office to gain reelection, to shore up his existing base, or to attract a new one. But the day of his inauguration is not one of the days on which he should be doing that. It is an event that belongs principally to the voters and to their descendants, who are called to see that a long tradition of peaceful transition is cheerfully upheld, even in those years when the outcome is disputed." ["Three Questions About Rick Warren's Role in the Inauguration," *Slate*, 12/19/08]

Incumbents

"People reelect their own long-term incumbents because they want their own districts to have the pork privilege that comes with seniority. However, they don't want the pork spreading to other districts." ["The Limits of Democracy," *Vanity Fair*, September 2001]

Independence

"Just as one cannot make a child grow smaller, so the momentum and appetite for autonomy increase with the experience of it." ["Thunder in the Black Mountains," *Vanity Fair*, November 1999]

India

"India, through no fault of its own, has many more people than it has indoor plumbing units." ["The Death of Shame," *Vanity Fair*, March 1996]

"One of the curses of India, as of other poor countries, is the quack medicine man, who fleeces the sufferer by promises of miraculous healing." ["Mommie Dearest," *Slate*, 10/20/03]

"India is not a country sizzling with self-pity and self-loathing, because it was never one of our colonies or clients." ["Why Does Pakistan Hate the United States?," *Slate*, 12/21/09]

Indifference

" . . . Anything can be pardoned except utter, ruthless indifference." ["Reader, He Married Her," *London Review of Books*, 5/10/90]

Individualism

"Radicals have been taught to distrust any too-great display of individualism, and where they forget this lesson there are always conservatives to remind them. . . ." ["Minority Report," *Nation*, 2/20/88]

"The twentieth century has taught the Left (has it not?) that 'the masses' are composed of 'individuals' and that any vulgar counterposition of the two will bring forth horrors. (It is invariably the suppression of individuality, for example, that necessitates the equal and opposite *grotesquerie* of the 'cult of personality.')" [Introduction to *Lines of Dissent: Writings from the New Statesman, 1913 to 1988*, ed. Stephen Howe (New York: Verso, 1988), 2–3]

Inferiority Complex

"Teasing is very often a sign of inner misery." ["Demons and Dictionaries," *Atlantic Monthly*, March 2009]

"Just as many of the people who believe in numinous coincidence and supernatural intervention are secretly hoping to prove that it is they themselves who are the pet of the universe, so many of those who overcompensate for inferiority are possessed of titanic egos and regard other people as necessary but incidental." ["The Zealot," *Atlantic Monthly*, December 2009]

Innocence

" . . . Innocence, as we know, can be as dangerous as its cousin, cynicism." ["Newtopia," *London Review of Books*, 8/24/95]

"There comes that awful day when innocence is somehow lost and the Berenstain Bears just won't cut it." ["Welcome to the Dahl House," *Vanity Fair*, September 1997]

" . . . A society can lose its innocence by trying to preserve it." ["Whatever You Do, Don't Mention Sex in America," *Evening Standard*, 1/23/98]

"That phrase 'loss of innocence' has become stale with overuse and diminishing returns; no other culture is so addicted to this narcissistic impression of itself as having any innocence to lose in the first place." ["The Road to West Egg," *Vanity Fair*, May 2000]

" . . . The age of innocence is long over by the time that most of our children have turned sixteen." ["Foley Loaded," *Wall Street Journal*, 10/16/06]

Insults

"Of course, in this country and culture, invective and repartee have almost no pulse at all. On any given day you may read an account of destabilizing 'mud-slinging' that consists of '"This behavior is inappropriate," he thundered' or '"I'll need to see the full text," he shot back.'" ["Satanic Curses," *Nation*, 12/22/97]

"I have a very thick skin and a very broad back, so I think that I shall not complain of being called a redneck mutant, provincial philistine, backwoods dolt, or blood-crazed religious maniac. Insults come with the turf." ["Not So Dumb Then?," *Mirror*, 11/11/04]

Integrity

" . . . Integrity can be as infectious as bullshit." ["Potter's Field," *Vanity Fair*, August 1994]

Intellectuals

"For intellectuals, often the hardest thing is to be unpopular in their own circle." ["Signature Sontag," *Vanity Fair*, March 2000]

" . . . Intellectuals never sound more foolish than when posing as the last civilized man." ["The Egg-Head's Egger-On," *London Review of Books*, 4/27/00]

"It's actually quite a common failing among Washington intellectuals. They wish to prove that they are not just ivory-tower or pointy-headed; that they can be tough and practical and even, when occasion may demand it, ruthless." ["Thinking Like an Apparatchik," *Atlantic Monthly*, July/August 2003]

"Between the word 'public' and the word 'intellectual' there falls, or ought to fall, a shadow. The life of the cultivated mind should be private, reticent, discreet: Most of its celebrations will occur with no audience, because there can be no applause for that moment when the solitary reader gets up and paces round the room, having just noticed the hidden image in the sonnet, or the profane joke in the devotional text, or the secret message in the prison diaries. Individual pleasure of this kind is only rivaled when the same reader turns into a writer, and after a long wrestle until daybreak hits on his or her own version of the *mot juste*, or the unmasking of pretension, or the apt, latent literary connection, or the satire upon tyranny." ["Susan Sontag," *Slate*, 12/29/04]

"Many scholars are intelligent and highly regarded professors, but they are somehow not public intellectuals. . . . In some sense, then, it is a title that has to be earned by the opinion of others." ["The Plight of the Public Intellectual," *Foreign Policy*, May/June 2008]

"Indeed, one might do worse than to say that an intellectual is someone who does not, or at least does not knowingly and obviously, attempt to soar on the thermals of public opinion. There ought to be a word for those men and women who do their own thinking; who are willing to stand the accusation of 'elitism' (or at least to prefer it to the idea of populism); who care for language above all and guess its subtle relationship to truth; and who will be willing and able to nail a lie." ["The Plight of the Public Intellectual," *Foreign Policy*, May/June 2008]

"An intellectual need not be one who, in a well-known but essentially meaningless phrase, 'speaks truth to power.' . . . However, the attitude toward authority should probably be skeptical, as should the attitude toward utopia, let alone to heaven or hell. Other aims should include the ability to survey the present through the optic of a historian, the past with the perspective of the living, and the culture and language of others with the equipment of an internationalist. In other words, the higher one comes in any 'approval' rating of this calling, the more uneasily one must doubt one's claim to the title in the first place." ["The Plight of the Public Intellectual," *Foreign Policy*, May/June 2008]

"I am sometimes asked about the concept or definition of a 'public intellectual,' and though I find the whole idea faintly silly, I believe it should ideally mean that the person so identified is self-sustaining and autonomously financed." [*Hitch-22* (New York: Twelve, 2010), 235]

"The usual duty of the 'intellectual' is to argue for complexity and to insist that phenomena in the world of ideas should not be sloganized or reduced to easily repeated formulae. But there is another responsibility, to say that some things are simple and ought not to be obfuscated. . . ." [*Hitch-22* (New York: Twelve, 2010), 418]

Intelligence Community
"Incidentally, when is anyone at the CIA or the FBI going to be *fired*?" ["Taking Sides," *Nation*, 10/14/02]

"Our intelligence 'community,' with its multibillion-dollar secret budget, left us under open skies on 9/11. The only born-and-raised American who had infiltrated the Taliban was John Walker Lindh of Marin County." ["Power Suits," *Vanity Fair*, April 2006]

Intelligent Design
"'Intelligent design' is not even a theory. It is more like a mentality. It admits of no verification or falsity and does not deserve to be mentioned in the same breath as a series of hypotheses and experiments that have served us well in analyzing the fossil record, the record of molecular biology, and—through the unraveling of the DNA strings—our kinship with other species." ["Equal Time," *Slate*, 8/23/05]

"The 'design' of the world is conspicuous for its lack of natural bridges. The 'designer' didn't bother to connect Marin with the San Francisco peninsula, or Manhattan with Brooklyn. That had to be left to mere evolved humans, operating with hard-won scientific rules." ["My Red-State Odyssey," *Vanity Fair*, September 2005]

" . . . Of the other bodies in our own solar system alone, the rest are all either far too cold to support anything recognizable as life, or far too hot. The same, as it happens, is true of our own blue and rounded planetary home, where heat contends with cold to make large tracts of it into useless wasteland, and where we have come to learn that we live, and have always lived, on a climatic knife edge. Meanwhile, the sun is getting ready to explode and devour its dependent planets like some jealous chief or tribal deity. Some design!" [*God Is Not Great* (New York: Twelve, 2007), 80]

International Socialists

" . . . A feature of the IS, as it called itself, was that it was inoculated against certain sixties fads in advance." ["In the Bright Autumn of My Senescence," *London Review of Books*, 1/06/94]

Internationalism

"The notion of 'internal affairs' has become prehistoric." ["Minority Report," *Nation*, 5/17/86]

"However ill it may sound when proceeding from the lips of George Bush, internationalism has a clear advantage in rhetoric and principle over the language of America First." ["Washington Diary," *London Review of Books*, 2/07/91]

Interventionism

"What is not decent or practical is to pretend concern, or to fake an interest, and then to walk away from it." ["Betrayal Becomes Farce," *Washington Post*, 8/15/93]

"Intervention, whether moral or political, is always and everywhere a matter of the most exquisite timing. The choice of time and the selection of place can be most eloquent. So indeed may be the moments when nothing is said or done." [*The Missionary Position* (New York: Verso, 1995), 86]

"It has always to be remembered that such regimes will not last forever, and that one day we will be asked, by their former subjects, what we were doing while they were unable to speak for themselves. Better to have the answer ready now and to consider American influence in a country as the occasion for leverage rather than as the occasion for awkward silence." ["The Brother Karimov," *Slate*, 6/01/05]

"Nonintervention does not mean that nothing happens. It means that something else happens." ["Realism in Darfur," *Slate*, 11/07/05]

Interviews

"The very thing that you feel that people are least likely to want to disclose is actually the thing that's nearest the front of their mind." ["Political Books," C-SPAN2, 10/26/97]

Invitations

"I once asked the Veep [Al Gore] to a birthday dinner for his sixth or seventh cousin Gore Vidal; he fell down on that occasion by saying that he had to go to the Baltimore airport to greet the Pope. This was the rudest excuse for declining an invitation that I have ever heard." ["Beta Male," *Nation*, 8/21/00–8/28/00]

Iowa Caucuses

"I was in Des Moines and Ames in the early fall, and I must say that, as small and landlocked and white and rural as Iowa is, I would be happy to give an opening bid in our electoral process to its warm and generous and serious people. But this is not what the caucus racket actually does. What it does is give the whip hand to the moneyed political professionals, to the full-time party hacks and manipulators, to the shady pollsters and the cynical media boosters, and to the supporters of fringe and crackpot candidates." ["The Iowa Scam," *Slate*, 12/31/07]

I.Q.

"There is, and there always has been, an unusually high and consistent correlation between the stupidity of a given person and that person's propensity to be impressed by the measurement of I.Q." ["Minority Report," *Nation*, 11/28/94]

Iran

"Nobody has ever used the term 'Iranian street,' at least in print or on broadcast news, if only because everyone knows that Iranian opinion, as registered during the mock elections or voiced to visiting hacks, is strongly against the reigning theocracy." ["The Arab Street," *Slate*, 2/28/05]

"Why is Iran not in the family of nations? Because it's an Islamic Republic." [Sydney Writers' Festival, Sydney, Australia, 6/01/10]

Iran-Contra Affair

"What was being tried, by the deniable offices and operations set up by Oliver North and William Casey and covered up by Edwin Meese, was a consistent attempt at permanent, secret government." ["Making and Unmaking a Secret Government," *Newsday*, 9/21/88]

"On its own, this is not the nightmare of 'Seven Days in May.' But taken together with much other evidence, it is as near to a state-within-a-state and a takeover of the latter by the former as one would want to come." ["Making and Unmaking a Secret Government," *Newsday*, 9/21/88]

"'Affair' is too bland a word for the Iran-Contra connection. Remember that it involved the use of skimmed profits from one outrageous policy—hostage-trading with Iran—to finance another: the illegal and aggressive destabilization of Nicaragua. This necessitated the official cultivation of contempt for American law and of impatience, to put it no higher, with the Constitution." ["On the Imagining of Conspiracy," *London Review of Books*, 11/07/91]

"It's an amazing bestiary of characters. . . . Adnan Khashoggi, Oliver North, Amiram Nir, Michael Ledeen, Robert MacFarlane—the sweepings of the Levant meet the white trash of Washington." ["On the Imagining of Conspiracy," *London Review of Books*, 11/07/91]

"In the late eighties, when official Washington was striving to 'put Iran-Contra behind us,' it was common to hear the pundits saying that there was 'zero public support' for prolonging or deepening the inquiry, or for letting it become a threat to a president 'perceived' as popular. Analyses of this sort had their basis in polls that found a majority of interviewees assenting to questions such as 'Is Colonel North a real patriot?' But no pollster ever asked a sample group: 'If you were asked to choose between Ronald Reagan and the United States Constitution, which would you rather sacrifice?'" ["Voting in the Passive Voice," *Harper's*, April 1992]

" . . . The Senate and House inquiry into Iran-contra decided in advance to concern itself only with 'the diversion'—the illegal transfer of funds from one bunch of thugs and torturers in Iran to another bunch in Central America. It's as if, in considering the implications of the whole term 'Iran-contra,' the lawyers had decided to play it safe and concentrate only on the hyphen." ["Untrue North," *Vanity Fair*, March 1994]

Iraq

"Partly as a 'counterweight' to Iran, partly as a rich sponge for the finest products of the military-industrial complex, partly because of its oil and partly because of its 'strategic position,' Iraq under Saddam became a particular pet of the contractors and salesmen who were such a feature of Washington life in those years [of the Reagan administration]." ["When Inhumanity Rode Side by Side with Profit," *Newsday*, 12/04/91]

"The very concept of 'human rights violations' is almost absurd in Saddam's Iraq, which recognizes no right except that of the ruling party." ["When Inhumanity Rode Side by Side with Profit," *Newsday*, 12/04/91]

" . . . Iraq has become an immiserated society about which the empire cares nothing, visiting it with warplanes and missiles every five years or so and only consulting the remnants of its own 'vibrant democracy' when the actual choices have narrowed to nil." ["Iraq & the Visitations of Empire," *Nation*, 3/16/98]

"Actually, the best case for a regime change in Iraq is that it is the lesser evil: better on balance than the alternatives, which are to confront Saddam later and at a time of his choosing, trust him to make a full disclosure to inspectors or essentially leave him alone." ["So Long, Fellow Travelers," *Washington Post*, 10/20/02]

"Whatever you do about Iraq, or in Iraq, please don't use 'Desert' in the code name." ["Saddam's Long Goodbye," *Vanity Fair*, June 2003]

" . . . The signature features of Iraq under the Saddam regime were the killing field abroad and the mass grave at home. . . ." ["The *Lancet*'s Slant," *Slate*, 10/16/06]

" . . . If Churchill as a postwar colonial secretary had not been forced to make economies and to find Arab leaders to whom Britain could surrender responsibility, there would have been no Iraq." ["The Woman Who Made Iraq," *Atlantic Monthly*, June 2007]

"In Saddam's Iraq, if you wanted to cover yourself, the best thing was to propose the most exorbitantly cruel and extreme measures." [*Hitch-22* (New York: Twelve, 2010), 317]

Iraq and Inspections
"Those who are calling for 'more time' in this process should be aware that they are calling for more time for Saddam's people to complete their humiliation and subversion of the inspectors." ["Inspecting 'Inspections,'" *Slate*, 2/13/03]

"To call for real inspections was actually to demand regime change." [*Hitch-22* (New York: Twelve, 2010), 302]

Iraq and the Left
"The left has betrayed the Iraqi people, including the Iraqi left, which was the original opposition to Saddam. There is quite a number of people on the left who agree with me, but the preponderance of people on the left seem to think the main danger is the global power of the United States." [Quoted in Neil Munro, "Leaving the Left," *National Journal*, 4/05/03]

"On the left, [Bush's arguments on Iraq] could have carried the day if they weren't being put by Bush." [Quoted in Neil Munro, "Leaving the Left," *National Journal*, 4/05/03]

"I don't know anyone on the left who wouldn't rather have Saddam back. This is psychopathically crazy, it seems to me." ["Start the Week," BBC Radio 4, 5/30/05]

"The bad faith of a majority of the left is instanced by four things (apart, that is, from mass demonstrations in favor of prolonging the life of a fascist government). First, the antiwar forces never asked the Iraqi left what it wanted, because they would have heard very clearly that their comrades wanted the overthrow of Saddam. . . . Second, the left decided to scab and blackleg on the Kurds, whose struggle is the oldest cause of the left in the Middle East. Third, many leftists and liberals stressed the cost of the Iraq intervention as against the cost of domestic expenditure, when if they had been looking for zero-sum comparisons they might have been expected to cite waste in certain military programs, or perhaps the cost of the 'war on drugs.' This, then, was mere cynicism. Fourth . . . their humanitarian talk about the sanctions turned out to be the most inexpensive hypocrisy." ["Unmitigated Galloway," *Weekly Standard*, 5/30/05]

Iraq and Sanctions
"The sanctions policy, which was probably always hopeless, is now quite indefensible. If lifted, it would only have allowed Saddam's oligarchy to re-equip. But once imposed, it was immoral and punitive without the objective of regime change. Choose." ["Chew on This," *Stranger*, 1/16/03–1/22/03]

"Sanctions plus Saddam or no sanctions and no Saddam? No contest." ["Countdown to War: Two Mirror Writers with Opposing Views," *Mirror*, 3/18/03]

"It was said during the time of sanctions on that long-suffering country that the embargo was killing, or had killed, as many as a million people, many of them infants. . . . Saying farewell to the regime was, evidently, too high a price to pay for relief from sanctions." ["Unmitigated Galloway," *Weekly Standard*, 5/30/05]

"Those who had alleged that a million civilians were dying from sanctions were willing, nay eager, to keep those same murderous sanctions if it meant preserving Saddam!" ["Unmitigated Galloway," *Weekly Standard*, 5/30/05]

Iraq War

"The decision to put an end to the regime of Saddam Hussein is the right one, and was also the only one. It is not, really, a declaration of war. It is, rather, the resolve to bring a long and sordid war to an overdue conclusion." ["Countdown to War: Two Mirror Writers with Opposing Views," *Mirror*, 3/18/03]

"Those of us who support this intervention do so precisely because we are scrupulous about human life and reverent when it comes to its protection." ["Countdown to War: Two Mirror Writers with Opposing Views," *Mirror*, 3/18/03]

" . . . There is both honor and glory in being able to demolish the palaces and cellars of a murdering dictatorship, inflicting so few incidental casualties (and taking such obvious care to minimize them) that the propaganda of Saddam's goons can produce almost no genuine victims to gloat over. I feel disgust for those who blame this week's deaths on the intervention and not on its sole target: Saddam Hussein." ["Gulf War 2: Christopher Hitchens on Why We Must Keep Our Nerve," *Mirror*, 3/25/03]

"This battle . . . has always seemed to me to be a just one. Perhaps for that reason, as well as doubtless for other ones, it received almost zero support from organized religion." ["Public Solidarity Does Not Help Humanism," *Free Inquiry*, Summer 2003]

"It may be a war waged by generally conservative tacticians, but it is a project designed by internationalist and liberal minds." ["Rumble on the Right," *Vanity Fair*, July 2004]

"Unless the United States chooses to be defeated in Iraq, it cannot be." ["Tariq Ali v. Christopher Hitchens: A Debate on the U.S. War on Iraq, the Bush-Kerry Race and the Neo-Conservative Movement," *Democracy Now!*, 10/12/04]

"Yes, we did indeed underestimate the ferocity and ruthlessness of the jihadists in Iraq. Where, one might inquire, have we *not* underestimated those forces and their virulence?" ["The End of Fukuyama," *Slate*, 3/01/06]

"As one who used to advocate strongly for the liberation of Iraq (perhaps more strongly than I knew), I have grown coarsened and sickened by the degeneration of the struggle: by the sordid news of corruption and brutality . . . and by the paltry politicians in Washington and Baghdad who squabble for precedence while lifeblood is spent and spilled by young people whose boots they are not fit to clean." ["A Death in the Family," *Vanity Fair*, November 2007]

"I still reel when I remember how many supposedly responsible people advocated surrendering Iraq without a fight." ["Iraq's Budget Surplus Scandal," *Slate*, 8/11/08]

"I think it's a certainty that historians will not conclude that the removal of Saddam Hussein was something that the international community ought to have postponed any further. (Indeed, if there is a disgrace, it is that previous administrations left the responsibility undischarged.)" ["No Regrets," *Slate*, 1/19/09]

Iraq War: The Surge
"It makes no sense to announce that the more we surge, the faster we can be out of there; everybody knows that unless the United States affirms its iron determination to stick around and to hold the ring, every faction in Iraq will start making its accommodations to a future that will be arbitrated instead by local militias and cross-border neighbors." ["It Was Right to Dissolve the Iraqi Army," *Slate*, 9/17/07]

Ireland
"One of the reasons for fear of a United Ireland has always been that the pond will get too big for the fish." ["King Billy's Scattered Legions," *New Statesman*, 10/27/72]

"How much the British have suffered from their fatuous belief that the Irish are stupid!" [*Thomas Paine's Rights of Man: A Biography* (New York: Atlantic Monthly Press, 2006), 141]

Irony
"The struggle for a free intelligence has always been a struggle between the ironic and the literal mind." ["Now, Who Will Speak for Rushdie?," *New York Times*, 2/17/89]

"Irony is for losers." ["The Children of '68," *Vanity Fair*, June 1998]

"In our native terms, the ironic style is often compounded with the sardonic and the hard-boiled; even the effortlessly superior. But irony originates in the glance and the shrug of the loser, the outsider, the despised minority. It is a nuance that comes most effortlessly to the oppressed." ["Moderation or Death," *London Review of Books*, 11/26/98]

"It's the gin in the Campari, the X-factor, the knight's move on the chessboard, the cat's purr, the knot in the carpet. Its elusive and allusive nature is what makes it impossible to repress or capture. It has a relationship to the unintended consequence. One of its delights is that it can be deployed literally." [*Letters to a Young Contrarian* (New York: Basic Books, 2001), 122]

"Since irony is always ready to jog the elbow and spoil the plan of anyone engaged in a high task, and since, if it can be detected at work anywhere, its fingerprints can be found on history, it will have its say most firmly but delicately with anyone claiming to have 'history' on his or her side. Bear this ever and always in mind when you hear the tuneful heralds of any grand new epoch." [*Letters to a Young Contrarian* (New York: Basic Books, 2001), 122]

"If I have it right, the special signature of today's media-savvy writer is his or her capacity for 'irony.' (This noble and elusive term has now been reduced to a signature wink, or display of the fingertips as if to signal quotation marks, though conceivably that is better than nothing.)" ["Theater of War," *Claremont Review of Books*, Winter 2006]

" . . . The literal mind does not understand the ironic mind, and sees it always as a source of danger." [*God Is Not Great* (New York: Twelve, 2007), 29]

"A sense of irony is to be carefully, indeed strictly, distinguished from the possession of a funny bone. Irony is not air-quote finger-marks, as if to say 'Just kidding' when in fact one is not quite kidding. (Does anyone ever say 'Just kidding' when in fact only kidding?)" ["Cheap Laughs," *Atlantic Monthly*, October 2009]

Irving, David
"David Irving is not just a Fascist historian. He is also a great historian of Fascism. . . . It's unimportant to me that Irving is my political polar opposite. If I didn't read my polar opposites, I'd be even stupider than I am." ["Hitler's Ghost," *Vanity Fair*, June 1996]

Islam
"Islam is at once the most and the least interesting of the world's monotheisms. It builds upon its primitive Jewish and Christian predecessors, selecting a chunk here and a shard there, and thus if these fall, it partly falls also." [*God Is Not Great* (New York: Twelve, 2007), 123]

"Even if god is or was an Arab (an unsafe assumption), how could he expect to 're-veal' himself by way of an illiterate person who in turn could not possibly hope to pass on the unaltered (let alone unalterable) words?" [*God Is Not Great* (New York: Twelve, 2007), 124]

"Only in Islam has there been no reformation, and to this day any vernacular version of the Koran must still be printed with an Arabic parallel text. This ought to arouse suspicion even in the slowest mind." [*God Is Not Great* (New York: Twelve, 2007), 125]

"There has never been an attempt in any age to challenge or even investigate the claims of Islam that has not been met with extremely harsh and swift repression. Provisionally, then, one is entitled to conclude that the apparent unity and confidence of the faith is a mask for a very deep and probably justifiable insecurity." [*God Is Not Great* (New York: Twelve, 2007), 125–126]

" . . . Islam when examined is not much more than a rather obvious and ill-arranged set of plagiarisms, helping itself from earlier books and traditions as occasion appeared to require. . . . Islam in its origins is just as shady and approximate as those from which it took its borrowings. It makes immense claims for itself, invokes prostrate submission or 'surrender' as a maxim to its adherents, and demands deference and respect from nonbelievers into the bargain. There is nothing—absolutely nothing—in its teachings that can even begin to justify such arrogance and presumption." [*God Is Not Great* (New York: Twelve, 2007), 129]

"Quite rightly, Islam effectively disowns the idea that it is a new faith, let alone a cancellation of the earlier ones, and it uses the prophecies of the Old Testament and the Gospels of the New like a perpetual crutch or fund, to be leaned on or drawn upon. In return for this derivative modesty, all it asks is to be accepted as the absolute and final revelation." [*God Is Not Great* (New York: Twelve, 2007), 133]

"As one who has occasionally challenged Islamic propaganda in public and been told that I have thereby 'insulted 1.5 billion Muslims,' I can say what I suspect—which is that there is an unmistakable note of menace behind that claim. . . . [T]he plain fact is that the believable threat of violence undergirds the Muslim demand for 'respect.'" ["God-Fearing People," *Slate*, 7/30/07]

"You may, if you wish, try to make a case for cultural relativism—different standards for different societies and traditions—but the plain fact is that the Prophet Mohammed was betrothed to his favorite wife Aisha when she was six and took her as his wife when she was nine, and this gives an 'empowering' effect to those who like things to be this way and to keep it legal." ["Save the Children," *Slate*, 10/05/09]

"What is needed from the supporters of this very confident faith is more self-criticism and less self-pity and self-righteousness." ["Free Exercise of Religion? No, Thanks.," *Slate*, 9/06/10]

"In reading the Koran, I can't tell if it's the word of god, but I can hope it's a sign of god having a bad day." [Debate with Tariq Ramadan ("Is Islam a Religion of Peace?"), 92nd Street Y, New York City, NY, 10/05/10]

Islam and Sex

"I simply laugh when I read the Koran, with its endless prohibitions on sex and its corrupt promise of infinite debauchery in the·life to come: it is like seeing through the 'let's pretend' of a child, but without the indulgence that comes from watching the innocent at play." [*God Is Not Great* (New York: Twelve, 2007), 55]

"The homicidal lunatics—rehearsing to be genocidal lunatics—of 9/11 were perhaps tempted by virgins, but it is far more revolting to contemplate that, like so many of their fellow jihadists, they *were* virgins. Like monks of old, the fanatics are taken early from their families, taught to despise their mothers and sisters, and come to adulthood without ever having had a normal conversation, let alone a normal relationship, with a woman. This is disease by definition." [*God Is Not Great* (New York: Twelve, 2007), 55]

Islamofascism

"Even as we worry about what they may intend for our society, we can see very plainly what they have in mind for their own: a bleak and sterile theocracy enforced by advanced techniques." ["Let's Not Get Too Liberal," *Guardian*, 9/21/01]

" . . . The bombers of Manhattan represent fascism with an Islamic face, and there's no point in any euphemism about it. What they abominate about 'the west,' to put it in a phrase, is not what Western liberals don't like and can't defend about their own system, but what they do like about it and must defend: its eman-

cipated women, its scientific inquiry, its separation of religion from the state."
["Let's Not Get Too Liberal," *Guardian*, 9/21/01]

" . . . Islamic fascism is an enemy for life, as well as an enemy of life." ["Let's Not Get Too Liberal," *Guardian*, 9/21/01]

"Never forget that the Muslim fundamentalists are not against 'empire.' They fight proudly for the restoration of their own lost caliphate." ["Chew on This," *Stranger*, 1/16/03–1/22/03]

"'Does Bin Ladenism or Salafism or whatever we agree to call it have anything in common with fascism? I think yes. The most obvious points of comparison would be these: Both movements are based on a cult of murderous violence that exalts death and destruction and despises the life of the mind. . . . Both are hostile to modernity (except when it comes to the pursuit of weapons), and both are bitterly nostalgic for past empires and lost glories. Both are obsessed with real and imagined 'humiliations' and thirsty for revenge. Both are chronically infected with the toxin of anti-Jewish paranoia (interestingly, also, with its milder cousin, anti-Freemason paranoia). Both are inclined to leader worship and to the exclusive stress on the power of one great book. Both have a strong commitment to sexual repression—especially to the repression of any sexual 'deviance'—and to its counterparts the subordination of the female and contempt for the feminine. Both despise art and literature as symptoms of degeneracy and decadence; both burn books and destroy museums and treasures." ["Defending *Islamofascism*," *Slate*, 10/22/07]

Islamophobia
"A phobic is a person suffering from irrational or uncontrollable dread. I don't choose to regard my own apprehensiveness about Muslim violence as groundless or illusory." ["Fundamentals," *Tablet Magazine*, 5/24/10]

"This is why the fake term *Islamophobia* is so dangerous: It insinuates that any reservations about Islam must *ipso facto* be 'phobic.' A phobia is an irrational fear or dislike. Islamic preaching very often manifests precisely this feature, which is why suspicion of it is by no means irrational." ["A Test of Tolerance," *Slate*, 8/23/10]

Isolationism
"The blunt fact is that the tradition of Lindbergh and Buchanan would not have kept America out of World War II or innocent of overseas adventures. But it would have pledged a not-so-surreptitious neutrality to the other side in that conflict, and perhaps come by its empire that way." ["Buchanan's Twisted History," *Nation*, 11/01/99]

"I respect those who say that the United States should simply withdraw from the Middle East, but I don't respect them for anything but their honesty." ["Machiavelli in Mesopotamia," *Slate*, 11/07/02]

Isolationism vs. Interventionism
" . . . The celebrated distinction between interventionist and isolationist turns out upon examination to be a distinction about whether or not to intervene in *Europe*,

or in wars being fought by others." ["Farewell to the Helmsman," *Foreign Policy*, September/October 2001]

Israel

"It is indecent and illiterate to compare Israel to Nazi Germany. But not all those who do this can possibly be ill intentioned." ["On Anti-Semitism," *Nation*, 10/09/82]

"'Genocide,' along with 'Final Solution' and 'Holocaust,' is a term not to be lightly used for propaganda. By the same token, it is wrong for the Israeli government to speak of the Palestinians as neo-Nazis, and for Israeli apologists to invoke the Holocaust against every criticism. If the moral chaos exists, it is partly because of Israeli special pleading." ["On Anti-Semitism," *Nation*, 10/09/82]

"And the wider attempt—to classify all critics of Israel as infected or compromised with anti-Semitism—is, of course, itself a trivialization of the Holocaust." ["The Chorus and Cassandra," *Grand Street*, Autumn 1985]

"If you ever feel like a good laugh, just tell yourself that things would improve if only the Israeli government would be more Orthodox." ["Peanut Envy," *Slate*, 5/21/07]

"Israel will never be accepted as a state for Jews, let alone as a Jewish state, until it ceases to govern other people against their will." ["Israel and Turkey: It's Complicated," *Slate*, 6/07/10]

Jackson, Jesse

"Jesse Jackson was never more instructive or more honest than when he said that he was tired of hearing about the Holocaust." ["The Charmer," *Grand Street*, Winter 1986]

James, C. L. R.

"The tall and handsome James went through white women like an avenging flame." ["Mid Off, Not Right On," *Times Literary Supplement*, 1/18/02]

" . . . C. L. R. James, one of the moral titans of twentieth-century dissent." [*Hitch-22* (New York: Twelve, 2010), 90]

James, Clive

"Then there was Clive James, dressed as usual like someone who had assembled his wardrobe in the pitch dark. . . ." [*Hitch-22* (New York: Twelve, 2010), 156]

James I

"James I was known to be very ugly and somewhat bloodthirsty (he liked hunting both witches and deer)." ["Blessed Are the Phrasemakers," *New York Times*, 5/18/03]

Jefferson, Thomas

"The real symptom of a PC bore, by the way, is a tendency to stress the fact that Thomas Jefferson was a slaveholder." ["The Cruiser," *London Review of Books*, 2/22/96]

"Modern and postmodern historians are fond of using terms such as 'inventing America' or 'imagining America.' It would be truer to say, of Thomas Jefferson, that he *designed* America, or that he authored it." [*Thomas Jefferson: Author of America* (New York: HarperCollins, 2005), 5]

"He seemingly never tired of having to be persuaded and cajoled to take high office." [*Thomas Jefferson: Author of America* (New York: HarperCollins, 2005), 42]

"Jefferson's view was that those who shouted the loudest about 'foreign influence' were themselves the principal agents of it." [*Thomas Jefferson: Author of America* (New York: HarperCollins, 2005), 111]

" . . . The record as it comes down to us makes it possible to state that without Thomas Jefferson as president, it is in the highest degree improbable that the United States would exist as we know it today, or even as we knew it a century ago." [*Thomas Jefferson: Author of America* (New York: HarperCollins, 2005), 125]

"Jefferson is one of the few figures in our history whose absence simply cannot be imagined: his role in the expansion and definition of the United States is too considerable, even at this distance, to be reduced by the passage of time." [*Thomas Jefferson: Author of America* (New York: HarperCollins, 2005), 187]

"Not without wit, but without humor." [*Charlie Rose Show*, 7/15/05]

Jefferson, Thomas and the Barbary War
" . . . In essence Jefferson's policy was an unalloyed triumph for peace, and the freedom of trade from blackmail, through the exercise of planned force." [*Thomas Jefferson: Author of America* (New York: HarperCollins, 2005), 135]

Jefferson, Thomas and the Bible
" . . . Thomas Jefferson took a razor to the New Testament and cut out everything that was evil, silly, or mythical. This left him with a very short edition." ["My Red-State Odyssey," *Vanity Fair*, September 2005]

Jefferson, Thomas and Sally Hemings
"Part of my education in the subtleties of racism had been learning to cope with American historians who could easily accept that Jefferson had *owned* Sally Hemings and had indeed acquired her as a wedding present from a man who was his father-in-law and her actual *father*—this making the girl his wife's half-sister—but who could not bring themselves to believe that in addition to inheriting her and owning her, our third president had also gone so far as to have fucked her." [*Hitch-22* (New York: Twelve, 2010), 256]

Jefferson, Thomas and Slavery
" . . . Jefferson took the same view of Haiti as he had of Virginia: the abolition of slavery could be as dangerous and evil as slavery itself." [*Thomas Jefferson: Author of America* (New York: HarperCollins, 2005), 101]

Jerusalem

"Jerusalem may not be a 'holy city' at all, but just an archaeological site that inspires bad behavior." ["The Gospel According to Mel," *Vanity Fair*, March 2004]

". . . Jerusalem—that birthplace of all our dreams and graveyard of all our hopes." ["The Blair-Hitch Project," *Vanity Fair*, February 2011]

Jews

"The Jews have seen through Jesus and Mohammed. . . . May this always be the case, whenever any human primate sets up, or is set up by others, as a Messiah." [*Hitch-22* (New York: Twelve, 2010), 379]

"Leo Strauss was right. The Jews will not be 'saved' or 'redeemed.' (Cheer up: neither will anyone else.) They/we will always be in exile whether they are in the greater Jerusalem area or not, and this in some ways is as it should be." [*Hitch-22* (New York: Twelve, 2010), 384]

"A critical register of the general health of civilization is the status of 'the Jewish question.' No insurance policy has ever been devised that can or will cover this risk." [*Hitch-22* (New York: Twelve, 2010), 384]

Jews and Irony

" . . . Jewishness contrives irony at its own expense. If there is one characteristic of Jews that I admire, it is that irony is seldom if ever wasted on them." [*Hitch-22* (New York: Twelve, 2010), 378]

Jobs

"When did the term 'job-creating' become an excuse for almost anything and a charitable description for any employer?" ["Minority Report," *Nation*, 5/08/95]

John Paul II

"He openly announced that the bullet that hit him was prevented from taking his life not because of the skill of his physicians, but because its trajectory had been guided by Our Lady. She let the assassin fire and hit, in other words, and only then took action." ["On Not Mourning the Pope," *Slate*, 4/08/05]

" . . . A brave and serious person capable of displaying both moral and physical courage." [*God Is Not Great* (New York: Twelve, 2007), 193]

Johnson, Paul

"Long before he made his much-advertised stagger from left to right, Johnson had come to display all the lineaments of the snob, the racist and the bigot." ["Minority Report," *Nation*, 4/10/89]

"It's difficult to know whom Johnson admires more: the Prussian police spy or the Earl of Westmoreland, whose mere name is a magic caress to him." ["Minority Report," *Nation*, 4/10/89]

"Something occurred to me as I put *Intellectuals* on the chuck-out shelf. It is a book so sordid and comical that it discredits even its ridiculous author. Yet apparently nobody—family member, colleague, publisher, drinking companion—told Johnson to pull the chain on it. It seems, then, that he can't have a true friend in all the world." ["Minority Report," *Nation*, 4/10/89]

"He's probably the classic instance of the guy who, having lost his faith, believes that he's found his reason—in other words, a defector." ["Booknotes," C-SPAN, 9/01/93 (first aired: 10/17/93)]

"In a puerile novel which is hard to obtain, but which still repays the attention of the specialist, he wrote a heavy-breathing, man-on-woman spanking scene that takes its place among the collectors' items. Compared to these episodes, it almost counts as normal that he should, over the past eleven years, have arranged regular meetings with a lady who would give him a good smacking in his turn. This week, the lady in question sold herself to the tabloids. But then so does Johnson." ["Spectator Sport: Hit and Myth," *Observer*, 5/17/98]

"Johnson has made a career as an especially bilious and persecuting moralizer. . . . With sermonizers like this, it's just a matter of setting one's watch. Give it time, just a little time, and—presto! We open the tabloids to see their withered haunches bared to the slipper, and the haggard remnants of their Johnsons exposed to the cruel light of day." ["Johnson & Johnson," *Nation*, 6/29/98]

"It's both satisfying and unsatisfying that Spanker Johnson is now, conclusively and forever, a figure of ridicule and contempt. . . . [N]ot all the potions of the Pfizer Corp. can make this Johnson rise again." ["Johnson & Johnson," *Nation*, 6/29/98]

Jokes
"A joke isn't a joke if it has to be explained, let alone justified, and the same goes for many sorts of allusion, nuance, and affect—the invisible bits of writing and conversation that actually make it possible." ["Sensitive to a Fault," *Vanity Fair*, April 1994]

"It's interesting and rather frightening when people ignore, or don't understand, jokes made at their expense." ["Diary," *London Review of Books*, 4/20/95]

" . . . If you have to signal a joke, then it is a weak one. Any audience that is being cued or prompted to applaud is also likely to say to itself, 'Actually, we'll be the judge of that.'" ["Obama's Court Jesters," *Slate*, 5/18/09]

Journalism
" . . . There is more to journalism than pleasing the public and winning political squabbles." ["Shotgun Wedding for a *Grande Dame*," *Los Angeles Times*, 2/01/81]

"In my wasted youth as a Fleet Street hack, I was instructed in several journalistic principles, viz., lay off the Royal Family, don't take drinks from policemen, don't buy drinks for Members of Parliament (they've had enough and we're paying anyway), try to justify your expenses in the first paragraph and, when covering a foreign conflict, always ask for someone who's been raped and speaks English." ["Minority Report," *Nation*, 11/09/85]

" . . . They [journalists] are incredibly easy to gull. A bit of flattery, a touch of 'access' and presto—you have your own personal journalist." ["Political Curve Balls Thrown from the Hill," *Newsday*, 8/31/88]

" . . . An empty mind in the world of consensus journalism will not stay vacant for long but be swiftly filled up—with platitude." ["Heart of Darkness," *London Review of Books*, 6/28/90]

"In 'the old days' the editorialist and columnist, and very likely the reporter, too, were inclined to be clubbable with the powerful. Now, with journalism a fast-paced pack activity, deference has become the most noticeable thing about the profession. . . . Honorifics like 'Sir' and 'Mr. President' are never omitted. If anyone uses a first name, it is the interviewee bestowing a mark of favor on some network nobody—a gesture always requited by an abject flush of pleasure on the part of the recipient." ["Diary," *London Review of Books*, 9/13/90]

"There's no reason to be snobbish or prudish about British popular journalism and its appeal to the newly or the not-very literate." ["At the Scamulator," *Times Literary Supplement*, 11/30/90–12/06/90]

"The reformist journalist's mission is not to speak truth coolly but rather to speak it forcefully in the face of hostile power—while partly hoping for power to be exercised by people more like, say, himself." ["Missionary Positions," *Wilson Quarterly*, Winter 1991]

"An honestly expressed prejudice, well-written and heedless of consequence, usually supplies the most memorable journalism. Those who fear to be thought 'offensive' or 'elitist' are as indentured as those who tremble at the proprietor or the advertiser or—often the worst enemy—the circulation department." ["Missionary Positions," *Wilson Quarterly*, Winter 1991]

"Too much of today's dissenting journalism forgets that consensus is the enemy to begin with." ["Missionary Positions," *Wilson Quarterly*, Winter 1991]

"Most instant reporters are so wised-up that they become innocent: taking politicians at their own valuation." ["On the Imagining of Conspiracy," *London Review of Books*, 11/07/91]

"I'm often surprised by the low price at which a Washington journalist will sell out, and become an insider or a diplomat instead of a truth seeker and truth teller. All it takes, in very many cases, is the dangled offer of 'access' to those in power, or the lure of a supposedly 'exclusive' interview." ["The Media's Illicit Affair with the Power Structure," *Newsday*, 7/08/92]

"If the press were as ill briefed as the readers it claims to instruct, it would be too dumb to bring out tomorrow's edition." ["Minority Report," *Nation*, 3/29/93]

"No one who wasn't skeptical of the official story or the conventional wisdom would want to be a journalist in principle. . . . 'Journalist' means being interested in everything—someone who wants to continue their own education while claiming at any rate to improve other people's." [Quoted in Bill Steigerwald and Bob Hoover, "Objectivity and Other Lies," *Pittsburgh Post-Gazette*, 4/27/97]

"If ever you criticize the prevailing news values, whether to a booker or a researcher or a pre-interviewer or a presenter, you will always be told that the public wants it this way, and is only being given what it wants, and indeed likes what it gets. . . . But news can't be made to fit a profile, because news by definition involves telling people what they don't know, and may not even 'like.' That in turn is why so much trouble is taken, in designing news coverage, to put the emphasis on what people know, or think they know, already." ["Princess Di, Mother T., and Me," *Vanity Fair*, December 1997]

"I became a journalist because I didn't want to rely on the press for information. Imagine being a reader rather than a writer of newspapers—you would never know what was going on." [Quoted in Judy Stoffman, "Loving Rumpled Hitchens for His Mind," *Toronto Star*, 5/15/99]

"In the old days, true enough, the Washington press corps was a megaphone for 'official sources.' Now, it's a megaphone for official sources *and* traders from the toilet." [*No One Left to Lie To* (New York: Verso, 2000), 4]

"The pact that a journalist makes is, finally, with the public." [*No One Left to Lie To* (New York: Verso, 2000), 147]

" . . . Why does the profession of journalism have such a low reputation? The answer: because it has such a bad press." ["Fleet Street's Finest," *Guardian*, 12/03/05]

" . . . If you sometimes find the responses of public officials at press conferences to be stupid or inarticulate, you should always make a point of looking up the original journalistic questions." ["Theater of War," *Claremont Review of Books*, Winter 2006]

"Allowance made for heroic exaggeration, this is the way in which many of us have imagined the craft of journalism: as a way of forcing the general public to continue paying for our free education indefinitely." [Introduction to *Ancient Gonzo Wisdom: Interviews with Hunter S. Thompson*, ed. Anita Thompson (New York: Da Capo Press, 2009), xvi]

Judaism

"A tiny preference for Judaism has occasionally stirred in my breast, because (a) Judaism does not proselytize, (b) Judaism does not bang on unnecessarily about the afterlife and (c) Judaism does not make the idiotic claim that the essential revelation has already taken place." ["Minority Report," *Nation*, 7/25/94–8/01/94]

Judges

"In the country of my birth, which is England, a judge is someone who comes at you from antiquity but still has a reasonable chance of being on the bench after you are dead. . . . A wretch who died in the time of Dickens would easily recognize the legal procedure of the ancien regime in the present day." ["Reflections on the Bork Nomination," *Newsday*, 11/08/89]

Judgment

"Snap judgments are so often the best." ["Joseph Heller," *Nation*, 1/03/00]

"The admonition not to rush to judgment or jump to conclusions might sound fair and prudent enough, perhaps even statesmanlike when uttered by the president, as long it's borne in mind that such advice is itself a judgment that is more than halfway to a conclusion." ["Hard Evidence," *Slate*, 11/16/09]

Justice

"The prompting of justice, like the voice of reason, is quiet but very persistent." [*The Parthenon Marbles: The Case for Reunification* (New York: Verso, 2008), xxvi]

KAL 007

"It doesn't matter what you think happened to KAL 007. Whatever the truth may be, it can now be stated with confidence that everything said by the [Reagan] Administration was a lie." ["Minority Report," *Nation*, 1/09/89–1/16/89]

Hurricane Katrina

"Those who find themselves in the midst of a ruined city may be excused some but not all of their hysteria. Those who blog about it from dry land have no such excuse." ["Iraq and Katrina," *Slate*, 9/06/05]

Kelly, Michael

"His curiosity and his humor, and his quick impatience with bullshit, were all of a piece. I often thought he was wrong, but I never knew him to be wrong for an ignoble or cowardly reason." ["Michael Kelly," *New York Observer*, 4/13/03]

Kennedy, John F.

"It may be, and it probably is, a complete waste of time trying to undo the grandiose absurdity of the Kennedy myth. If Americans knew then what they know now about JFK . . . they might not have trusted him as they did. But, knowing all this now, they cannot quite relate it to the man they think they remember. Somehow, the drama of Dallas has sanctified and cancelled everything." ["Kennedy Lies," *Spectator*, 11/19/83]

"Mr. Kennedy remains a veritable Siegfried to many ignorant liberals." ["Minority Report," *Nation*, 4/04/94]

"His was the worst hard-cop/soft-cop routine ever to be attempted, and it suffered from the worst disadvantages of both styles." ["Where's the Aura?," *Wall Street Journal*, 11/21/03]

"The Kennedy interlude was a flight from responsibility, and ought to be openly criticized and exorcised rather than be left to die the death that sentimentality brings upon itself." ["Where's the Aura?," *Wall Street Journal*, 11/21/03]

"At practically all material times, the Galahad of Camelot was pumped full of drugs that affected his mental and physical ability, and was concomitantly obsessed with a need to demonstrate 'potency.' That this led him to adopt something like a Marilyn Monroe doctrine is indubitable." ["Feckless Youth," *Atlantic Monthly*, September 2006]

" . . . Kennedy was the first of the absolutely image-conscious, media-savvy, sales-oriented generation. Those of us who hate the dull and sordid world of the professional 'handler' must date our mourning from the moment when the TV camera decided that it loved JFK." ["Feckless Youth," *Atlantic Monthly*, September 2006]

"If this vulgar hoodlum president had not been survived by a widow of exceptional bearing and grace, his reputation would probably now be dirt." ["Feckless Youth," *Atlantic Monthly*, September 2006]

"One of the many dreadful aspects of the Kennedy 'legacy' is the now-unbreakable grip of celebrity politics, image-doctoring, stage management, and 'torch passing' rhetoric in general." ["Redemption Song," *Slate*, 8/31/09]

Kennedy, John F.: The Assassination
"November 22, 1963, was the psychic moment at which 'The Sixties' began." ["If JFK Had Lived Much Longer, He'd Have Been Puffy, Poxy, Jumpy and Incontinent," *Mirror*, 11/22/03]

Kennedy, John F. and Cuba
"Like every one else of my generation, I can remember exactly where I was standing and what I was doing on the day that President John Fitzgerald Kennedy nearly killed me. In October 1962 I was in my first term at an English boarding school and was at least as ignorant of Cuba as Kennedy was." ["Kennedy Lies," *Spectator*, 11/19/83]

"The attempt to take over and run Cuba, to enlist the support of the Mafia in the assassination of Castro, to poison and devastate Cuban crops, and to land a mercenary army on Cuban shores would have been much more disastrous if it had succeeded than if it had failed." ["Kennedy Lies," *Spectator*, 11/19/83]

Kennedy, Paul
"Like many other think-tank artists, he seems to have imbibed the lesson that if you are going to be wrong, you might as well be heroically and laughably so." ["Who Would the Prophet Be," *Daily Mail*, 3/25/93]

Kennedy, Ted
"Kennedy is the most popular Democrat and the most unpopular one. (Of course, the same could have been said about Reagan.)" ["Minority Report," *Nation*, 12/11/82]

Kennedy Family
" . . . Rites of passage in the Kennedy family always turn out to be laden with complexity. Everybody is living for somebody else." ["Curse of the Kennedys Alights on the Smith Boy," *Independent*, 4/07/91]

" . . . If you really want to find out what trouble is, try taking on the myth of the Kennedy dynasty." ["Whose History Is It?," *Vanity Fair*, December 1993]

" . . . As anyone who has ever argued with a fan will swiftly appreciate, nothing is wrong if a Kennedy does it." ["National Treasure," *London Review of Books*, 11/14/96]

"It's conventional to refer to the Kennedys as America's royal family, and they are indeed almost dysfunctional enough to deserve the title." ["A Good Man, Very Fair, Very Witty, Very Loyal," *Salon*, 7/17/99]

" . . . The funeral has been the measure and benchmark of the Kennedy family re-union." ["A Good Man, Very Fair, Very Witty, Very Loyal," *Salon*, 7/17/99]

"There are too damn many of them, and many of them are not much damn good. It really is uncomfortably like the House of Windsor, in other words." ["If JFK Had Lived Much Longer, He'd Have Been Puffy, Poxy, Jumpy and Incontinent," *Mirror*, 11/22/03]

"There was a time when the high casualty rate among Kennedys made foolish people talk about a family 'curse.' On the contrary, the Kennedys were extremely lucky." ["If JFK Had Lived Much Longer, He'd Have Been Puffy, Poxy, Jumpy and Incontinent," *Mirror*, 11/22/03]

Kennedy Onassis, Jacqueline

" . . . One of those women who can do nothing wrong whatever their 'fashion statement.' At JFK's inaugural, she had an accidental dent in her pillbox hat; women everywhere copied the affectation. On the day of his murder, she refused to change her blood-and-brain spattered clothes and that, too, seemed right." ["National Treasure," *London Review of Books*, 11/14/96]

"As a thirty-one-year-old First Lady she had a Tiffany-style team of designers, a personal dresser, the first press secretary in the history of First Ladyhood, and a Frank Sinatra–hosted inaugural party. All the things, in short, for which Nancy Reagan was later to be lampooned." ["National Treasure," *London Review of Books*, 11/14/96]

Kentucky

"A bit like Cuba's, Kentucky's economy depends almost entirely on things that are good for you but are said to be bad for you: Cuba has sugar, rum, and tobacco, and Kentucky has bourbon, tobacco, and horse racing." ["My Red-State Odyssey," *Vanity Fair*, September 2005]

Kerry, John

"If you slightly stifled a yawn when you first saw Kerry give a speech, get ready to be comatose by November." ["Why Kerry Isn't the Man to Beat Bush," *Mirror*, 3/08/04]

"Anything he might say can be countered with things he's already said, or things he's said and then changed his mind about." ["Why Kerry Isn't the Man to Beat Bush," *Mirror*, 3/08/04]

"He has a choice of several houses he can live in, but I hope in each of these houses there is only one bathroom. Because if there were two, I wouldn't back him to be able to make up his mind which one to use." [Quoted in "Christopher Hitchens: Off the Cuff, in His Own Words," *Georgetowner*, 5/27/04]

"He must be the only Catholic Jew with Mayflower-Winthrop roots to have sought the highest office." ["A War Hero and an Antiwar Hero," *New York Times*, 8/15/04]

"If Kerry is dogged and haunted by the accusation of wanting everything twice over, he has come by the charge honestly." ["A War Hero and an Antiwar Hero," *New York Times*, 8/15/04]

"Kerry is against the death penalty, except in cases where the perpetrator has done something really heinous or unpopular." ["A War Hero and an Antiwar Hero," *New York Times*, 8/15/04]

" . . . There is the pleasure of seeing him take every side on abortion and gay marriage, while waving deer-rifles in swing states, and getting names of local teams and stadiums just that little bit wrong." ["Neck and Neck," *Mirror*, 10/21/04]

"I knew that John Kerry was through when a friend of mine looked up from the *New York Times* and said, 'Oh dear. He's gone goose hunting again.'" ["Let Them Eat Pork Rinds," *Vanity Fair*, December 2005]

KGB
"There are a number of reasons why one ought not, perhaps, on mature reflection, to take money and favors from the KGB. There's—oh, I don't know—the fact that it's a secret police organization that conducts kidnappings and assassinations, and confines sane protestors in mental hospitals." ["Gotterdämmerung," *London Review of Books*, 1/12/95]

Khrushchev, Nikita
"In spite of much boorishness and demagoguery—partly undertaken to conceal the increasing lack of confidence that the USSR and the Communist movement felt after his own 'secret speech' concerning the crimes of Stalinism—Khrushchev was, probably no less than his eventual successor Gorbachev, a man with whom, at a minimum, business could be done." ["Feckless Youth," *Atlantic Monthly*, September 2006]

King Jr., Martin Luther
"In no real as opposed to nominal sense, then, was he a Christian. This does not in the least diminish his standing as a great preacher any more than does the fact that he was a mammal like the rest of us, and probably plagiarized his doctoral dissertation, and had a notorious fondness for booze and for women a good deal younger than his wife. He spent the remainder of his last evening in orgiastic dissipation, for which I don't blame him." [*God Is Not Great* (New York: Twelve, 2007), 176]

"Martin Luther King was a distinguished preacher who inspired genuine uplift, but his 'dream' rhetoric has long been a refuge for the lazy and the demagogic and for all those who prefer feeling to thinking." ["The Democrats' Rising Star," *Sunday Times* (London), 5/06/07]

Kissinger, Henry

"When I had finished digesting *The White House Years*, I was so replete with its mendacity and conceit that I took a vow. I swore that I would never read another work by Henry Kissinger until the publication of his prison letters." ["Shock Value," *Nation*, 6/05/82]

"One of the privileges of a ruling class is that it can treat public property as private. This is what Kissinger has done with the archives of his time in power." ["Minority Report," *Nation*, 6/05/89]

"There is something about Kissinger that registers a natural affinity with anything cruel or ruthless or atrocious." ["Diary," *London Review of Books*, 12/14/95]

"It took Henry Kissinger to ensure that a war of atrocity, which he had helped prolong, should end as furtively and ignominiously as it had begun." [*The Trial of Henry Kissinger* (New York: Verso, 2002), 24]

"It's very hard to identify the most revolting moment in Henry Kissinger's life." [Quoted in "'Don't Cross Over if You Have Any Intention of Going Back,'" *Common Review*, Summer 2005]

"A president who says, 'I'd like Henry Kissinger to chair an inquiry,' is saying, 'I want a cover-up.'" ["In Depth with Christopher Hitchens," C-SPAN, 9/02/07]

"He is that rare and foul beast, a man whose record shows sympathy for communism *and* fascism. It comes from a natural hatred of the democratic process, which he has done so much to subvert and undermine at home and abroad, and an instinctive affection for totalitarians of all stripes." ["How Can Anyone Defend Kissinger Now?," *Slate*, 12/13/10]

Knowledge

"There is a sense in which all of us are prisoners of knowledge." [*Cyprus* (London: Quartet Books, 1984), 19]

"It is enough to know that we do not know enough." ["Political Animals," *Atlantic Monthly*, November 2002]

" . . . The most educated person in the world now has to admit—I shall *not* say confess—that he or she knows less and less but at least knows less and less about more and more." [*God Is Not Great* (New York: Twelve, 2007), 9]

" . . . One must never forget how recent most of our knowledge really is. . . ." [*God Is Not Great* (New York: Twelve, 2007), 93]

Koestler, Arthur

"Far from being a 'skeptic,' Arthur Koestler was a man not merely convinced but actively enthused by practically any intellectual or political or mental scheme that came his way." ["The Zealot," *Atlantic Monthly*, December 2009]

"Otto Katz once said to him, 'We all have inferiority complexes of various sizes, but yours isn't a complex—it's a cathedral.' Koestler liked this remark so much that he included it in his autobiography, thus attaining the status of one who could actually brag about his inferiority complex as if size mattered." ["The Zealot," *Atlantic Monthly*, December 2009]

Kosovo

"NATO's torpid indifference to Kosovo is yet another way of teaching the Muslim world about our unshakable attachment to pluralism." ["Monotheist Notes from All Over," *Nation*, 10/19/98]

"There *are* free-fire zones and strategic hamlets in Kosovo: They are the work not of NATO but of Serbian death squads." ["Port Huron Piffle," *Nation*, 6/14/99]

"There is no need to romanticize the Kosovo state." ["Why Kosovo Still Matters," *Slate*, 7/26/10]

"We lose something important if we forget Kosovo and the harrowing events that finally led to the self-determination of its nearly 2 million inhabitants. Long deprived of even vestigial national and human rights, then forced at gunpoint onto deportation trains and threatened with the believable threat of mass murder, these people were belatedly rescued by an intervention that said, fairly simply, there is a limit beyond which law cannot be further broken and conscience further outraged." ["Why Kosovo Still Matters," *Slate*, 7/26/10]

Krauthammer, Charles

"In common with most but not all of his conservative columnist colleagues, Krauthammer does not write very well, reason very well or know very much about anything." ["Blunt Instruments," *Nation*, 11/16/85]

"Charles Krauthammer used to work as a speechwriter for the ridiculous Mondale. Ordinarily, he underlines this bit of his resumé in order to show that he is a former bleeding heart, knows the score, has been an insider, has seen the light, has lost his faith and therefore found his reason—all the familiar or predictable panoply of the careerist defector." ["Blunt Instruments," *Nation*, 11/16/85]

Kristol, Irving

"Irving Kristol's great charm . . . was that he didn't care overmuch for the charm business." ["Farewell to the Godfather," *Slate*, 9/20/09]

Kurds

"Lacking an alternative homeland of any kind, Kurds can emigrate, but they can't escape." ["The Struggle of the Kurds," *National Geographic*, August 1992]

"The Kurds are homeless even at home, and stateless abroad. Their ancient woes are locked inside an obscure language. They have powerful, impatient enemies and a few rather easily bored friends. Their traditional society is considered a nuisance at worst and a curiosity at best. For them the act of survival, even identity itself, is a kind of victory." ["The Struggle of the Kurds," *National Geographic*, August 1992]

"In the area of Iraq that was liberated from Saddam Hussein's control the earliest—the Kurdish provinces in the northeast part of the country—all objective observers seem to agree that an unprecedented prosperity has replaced what was once an unimaginable wasteland of misery. With their head-start of liberation beginning in 1992, the Kurds (who still have no refineries and little infrastructure) have nonetheless set an example for the rest of the region as well as of the country." ["Iraq: Worth the Price," *Washington Post*, 3/11/08]

Labor Party
"Internationalism is something that the British Labor Party is prepared to spend a great deal of time not bothering about." ["Socialism from St. John's Wood," *New Statesman*, 7/21/72]

" ... The Labor Party, in its present form and in any likely future one, offers an image of Britain's decline rather than an answer to it." ["Haven for British Dissent Is in Full Eclipse," *Los Angeles Times*, 6/19/83]

"In the coverage of the Tony Blair 'New Labor' phenomenon—coverage that I can hardly believe will go on being so uncritical—the entire operating assumption of every article is that Labor as a party only has one thing to live down—and that is its Red past! It is enough to make a cat laugh." ["All Aboard the Bland Wagon," *Observer*, 11/19/95]

"A party with a history of radicalism, however attenuated, simply cannot afford to present itself as the party of safety first and a steady hand on the Treasury tiller." ["*Au Revoir* to the Status Quo," *Slate*, 5/03/10]

Laden, Osama bin
"As with every big-mouth cleric who ululates to an imaginary heaven about the bliss of suicide-murder, he preferred (and nominated) others to do the dying." ["It's a Good Time for War," *Boston Globe* (online), 9/08/02]

"When I analyze the sermons of bin Laden, I cannot see how his claim to divine authority and prompting is any better or any worse than anybody else's." ["The Future of an Illusion," *Daedalus*, Summer 2003]

"Wherever bin Laden is now, it cannot be where he wanted or hoped to be four and a half years ago." ["Al-Qaida Is Losing," *Slate*, 1/24/06]

Language
"Just as those who call for 'English Only' believe themselves to be speaking English when they are mounting a mediocre patois, and just as those who yell for

'Western civilization' cannot tell Athens, Georgia, from Erasmus Darwin, so those who snicker at the latest 'PC' gag are generally willing slaves to the most half-baked jargon." ["Minority Report," *Nation*, 10/21/91]

" . . . When every newscaster in the country uses the knee-jerk term 'peace process,' or discourses about 'credibility,' or describes some blood-soaked imposter as 'a moderate,' the deadening of language has gone so far that it's almost impossible to ironize." ["Minority Report," *Nation*, 10/21/91]

"Clogged language usually expresses confused thought." ["The Wrong Questions," *Washington Post*, 11/09/97]

"People who say that terminology isn't worth fighting over are saying in effect that language doesn't matter. The latter proposition is much more dangerous than the former." ["Ireland," *Critical Quarterly*, Spring 1998]

"There is true power in really good bad English. . . ." ["Thunder in the Black Mountains," *Vanity Fair*, November 1999]

"But [Winston] Smith, though he does not mention Newspeak in his litany, is clear that one does not need a new language with which to oppose doublethink and lies. What one needs is a pure speech that means what it says, and that can be subjected to refutation in its own terms. This will very often be an *old* speech, organically connected to the ancient truths preserved and transmitted by literature." [*Why Orwell Matters* (New York: Basic Books, 2002), 198]

Larkin, Philip
"Even while he was still ambulant and breathing, Philip Larkin was a Dead White European Male." ["D.W.E.M. Seeks to R.I.P.," *Vanity Fair*, April 1993]

"The PC warriors are so fixated on such frantically earnest 'now' terms as 'racism-sexismisogyny,' and so set on employing Larkin's case to discredit Englishness, that they have failed to register his most salient and atypical delinquency. As far as the letters can speak, they instruct us that, in the period 1940 to 1945, Larkin expected Hitler to win the war or half hoped he would, or both." ["D.W.E.M. Seeks to R.I.P.," *Vanity Fair*, April 1993]

"Our [Martin Amis's and my] common admiration for Larkin, as a poet if not as a man, arose from the bleak honesty with which he confronted the fucked-up—the expression must be allowed—condition of the country in those years. . . . Larkin's innate pessimism, his loyalty to the gritty northern town of Hull (where lay the provincial university that employed him), and his hilarious interest in filth of all kinds were attractive to all of us; likewise his very moving, deliberate refusal of the false consolations of religion (beautifully captured by his 'Aubade' and 'Church-going') on which not even Kingsley disagreed. However, Larkin's pungent loathing for the Left, for immigrants, for striking workers, for foreigners and indeed 'abroad,' and for London showed that you couldn't have everything." [*Hitch-22* (New York: Twelve, 2010), 171]

Las Vegas

"... A city hewn out of an arid wilderness, consecrated to the tough-minded idea that there will be winners and losers, with rewards for risktaking and initiative and much garish amusement on the side. A certain harshness and vulgarity, to be sure, and even a certain undertone of the ruthless." ["Bitter Medicine," *Vanity Fair*, August 1998]

Laughter

"Laughter can be the most unpleasant sound; it's an essential element in mob conduct and is part of the background noise of taunting and jeering at lynchings and executions. Very often, crowds or audiences will laugh complicitly or slavishly, just to show they 'see' the joke and are all together. (The worst case here is the unfunny racist joke, requiring the least effort to trigger a laugh response. But there are also consensus comedies so awful that they require the post-Pavlovian imposition of a dubbed-in 'laugh track.')" [*Letters to a Young Contrarian* (New York: Basic Books, 2001), 116]

Law

"An authoritarian law, giving the state the right to pronounce on truth, is an authoritarian law whoever invokes it." ["The Chorus and Cassandra," *Grand Street*, Autumn 1985]

"It's salutary to find that the law operates on big questions as it does on little ones. That is to say, it displays tremendous deference to the views and the needs of the rich and the well-placed." ["A Post-Law Education in Irangate," *Newsday*, 2/24/91]

"Truly is it written that hard cases make bad law." ["Minority Report," *Nation*, 2/01/93]

Law and Order

"There's nobody as innocent as a law-and-order man who is just doing his job." ["Minority Report," *Nation*, 2/01/93]

Lawbreaking

"The lawbreaking itch is not always an anarchic one. In the first place, the human personality has (or ought to have) a natural resistance to coercion. We don't like to be pushed and shoved, even if it's in a direction we might choose to go. In the second place, the human personality has (or ought to have) a natural sense of the preposterous." ["I Fought the Law," *Vanity Fair*, February 2004]

Laws of Nature

"... The laws of nature do not respond to petitions...." ["Less than Miraculous," *Free Inquiry*, February/March 2004]

Lawyers

"Since we presently have a government of lawyers rather than laws, it's necessary to pay attention to the views of the lowliest pinstripe performer." ["A Post-Law Education in Irangate," *Newsday*, 2/24/91]

" . . . Everything went wrong when lawyers began to be praised for trial-strategies, including jury-tampering, that got high-profile defendants off the hook." ["'It's Our Turn,'" *American Enterprise*, May/June 1999]

"Poor people can't get lawyers in a country that is glutted with them. . . ." ["On the Prole," *Village Voice*, 11/23/99]

Leadership
" . . . Wartime leaders often seem more statesmanlike and decisive than they really are, because of their ability to make and to enforce decisions." ["FDR as the Premier Leader of World War II," *Newsday*, 10/26/88]

Leaking
"The art of leaking and influencing depends upon deniability. . . ." [*Thomas Jefferson: Author of America* (New York: HarperCollins, 2005), 81]

The Left
"There's something vaguely creepy about the compulsion to chuck 'Old Left' causes over the side." ["Re-Bunking," *Grand Street*, Summer 1986]

"In order to avoid the taunt that he is merely utopian or irrelevant, the 'progressive' must at times be arrogant and even *dirigiste*, if not actually authoritarian. (Anybody who has spent time on the Left knows that those supporting the status quo always seem to be smugly waiting to consign him to one pit or the other—that of the authoritarian or of the irrelevant.)" ["Missionary Positions," *Wilson Quarterly*, Winter 1991]

"It's easy enough, for leftists, to imagine confronting a mob of racial bigots, McCarthyites, or religious fundamentalists. The harder test is resistance to 'public opinion' in one's own camp." ["Missionary Positions," *Wilson Quarterly*, Winter 1991]

"Probably everyone on the left has had a similar experience: the unpleasing sensation of hearing your own slogans twisted against you." ["Minority Report," *Nation*, 9/21/92]

"One of these days I'm going to write a book called 'Guilty as Hell: A Short History of the American Left.' Revisionism has cut great roads through the *causes célèbres* of the *bien pensants*. Where are we now? Joe Hill probably guilty as charged, according to Wallace Stegner. Sacco and Vanzetti darker horses than we thought. The Rosenbergs at least half-guilty. Most of the Black Panthers (always excepting those murdered by the FBI) amazingly guilty. The McNamara brothers certainly guilty. The Haymarket martyrs probably innocent, and the later Chicago conspiracy defendants also, even if they tried their best to be guilty. . . . There is also my companion volume to bear in mind. (It's to be called 'Soft on Crime: The American Right from Nixon to North.')" ["A Regular Bull," *London Review of Books*, 9/18/97]

" . . . There is also a special *ad hominem* venom on the left, and an extreme willingness to attribute the very lowest motives to those who transgress its codes. . . .

Having come across this syndrome more than once, I have learned to regard it with resignation, as yet one more aspect of radical impotence in America." ["Unmaking Friends," *Harper's*, June 1999]

"Looking at some of the mind-rotting tripe that comes my way from much of today's left, I get the impression that they go to bed saying: what have I done for Saddam Hussein or good old Slobodan or the Taliban today?" ["Ha Ha Ha to the Pacifists," *Guardian*, 11/14/01]

"Members of the left, along with the far larger number of squishy 'progressives,' have grossly failed to live up to their responsibility to think; rather, they are merely reacting, substituting tired slogans for thought. The majority of those 'progressives' who take comfort from [Oliver] Stone and [Noam] Chomsky are not committed, militant anti-imperialists or anti-capitalists. Nothing so muscular. They are of the sort who, discovering a viper in the bed of their child, would place the first call to People for the Ethical Treatment of Animals." ["Stranger in a Strange Land," *Atlantic Monthly*, December 2001]

" . . . Quarrels on the left have a tendency to become miniature treason trials, replete with all kinds of denunciation. There's a general tendency—not by any means confined to radicals but in some way specially associated with them—to believe that once the lowest motive for a dissenting position has been found, it must in some way be the real one." ["Left-Leaving, Left-Leaning," *Los Angeles Times*, 11/16/03]

"There is a noticeable element of the pathological in some current leftist critiques, which I tend to attribute to feelings of guilt allied to feelings of impotence. Not an attractive combination, because it results in self-hatred." [Quoted in Jamie Glazov, "Frontpage Interview: Christopher Hitchens," *FrontPage Magazine*, 12/10/03]

"One of the many problems with the American left, and indeed *of* the American left, has been its image and self-image as something rather too solemn, mirthless, herbivorous, dull, monochrome, righteous, and boring." ["Unfairenheit 9/11," *Slate*, 6/21/04]

"How shady it is that our modern leftists and peaceniks can detect fascism absolutely everywhere except when it is actually staring them in the face." ["Abu Ghraib Isn't Guernica," *Slate*, 5/09/05]

"To many callow leftists, the turbulent masses of the Islamic world are at once a reminder of the glory days of 'Third World' revolution, and a hasty substitute for the vanished proletariat of yore." ["At Last Our Lefties See the Light," *Sunday Times* (London), 4/30/06]

" . . . Once you decide that American-led 'globalization' is the main enemy, then any revolt against it is better than none at all. In some way yet to be determined, al-Qaeda might be able to help to stave off global warming." ["At Last Our Lefties See the Light," *Sunday Times* (London), 4/30/06]

"It is a deformity in some 'radicals' to imagine that, once they have found the lowest or meanest motive for an action or for a person, they have correctly identified the authentic or 'real' one. Many a purge or show trial has got merrily under way in this manner." [*Thomas Paine's Rights of Man: A Biography* (New York: Atlantic Monthly Press, 2006), 71]

"It's strange to think that many on the left have been slow to see the menace of one-party, one-state, or messianic systems." ["Farewell to the Godfather," *Slate*, 9/20/09]

" . . . The half-baked view of many on the Left [is] that there must be *something* of value in any movement that hates Zionism and globalization." ["Fundamentals," *Tablet Magazine*, 5/24/10]

The Left and Islamofascism

"From the first day of the immolation of the World Trade Center, right down to the present moment, a gallery of pseudointellectuals has been willing to represent the worst face of Islam as the voice of the oppressed. . . . If this is liberal secularism, I'll take a modest, God-fearing, deer-hunting Baptist from Kentucky every time, as long as he didn't want to impose his principles on me (that our Constitution forbids him to do)." ["Bush's Secularist Triumph," *Slate*, 11/09/04]

"A large tranche of the once-secular liberal left has disqualified itself by making excuses for jihad and treating Osama bin Laden as if he were advocating liberation theology." [" . . . And Why I'm Most Certainly Not!," *Wall Street Journal*, 5/05/05]

"Of course, the most flagrant offenders against morality and common sense are still the nihilistic pseudo-leftists, who claim to see no real difference between Western democracy and those who desire to murder its voters at random." ["Young Brit Defends American People, Politics and Policies," *Washington Examiner*, 8/30/06]

The Left and Religion

"Piety on the left is a terrible thing to behold." ["The Lord and the Intellectuals," *Harper's*, July 1982]

"In most developed countries, the left and the workers' movement begin by affirming that they are not religious. They don't expect bishops and clergymen to stay out of politics because they already know that the church is part of the material reality of the ruling order. How different it is in the United States. Here, the left is either actually religious or secular in a semi-apologetic way." ["Minority Report," *Nation*, 9/22/84]

"What is needed is not a thin and permeable wall between church and state but a realization on the left that in any argument involving blind faith, it is the right that has the whip hand." ["Minority Report," *Nation*, 9/22/84]

"Only one faction in American politics has found itself able to make excuses for the kind of religious fanaticism that immediately menaces us in the here and now.

And that faction, I am sorry and furious to say, is the left." ["Bush's Secularist Triumph," *Slate*, 11/09/04]

The Left and September 11, 2001

"I was apprehensive from the first moment about the sort of masochistic email traffic that might start circulating from the Noam Chomsky–Howard Zinn–Norman Finkelstein quarter, and I was not to be disappointed." ["Let's Not Get Too Liberal," *Guardian*, 9/21/01]

"Every liberal twit talks about the danger of 'over-reaction' to the Taliban, when the actual danger is, and has for some time been, one of under-reaction." ["Why Can't Rushdie Fly?," *Guardian*, 9/26/01]

"What is known in American psycho-babble as 'denial' strikes in many insidious forms. It can express itself as the simple refusal to admit that a painful event has occurred. It may manifest itself as a cheery rationalization of something ghastly. Or it can involve a crude shifting of blame. It's actually a more useful term than it sometimes looks. The reaction of much of the Left to the human and moral catastrophe at the World Trade Center, and to the aggression that lies behind it, has partaken of all three variants." ["The Fascist Sympathies of the Soft Left," *Spectator*, 9/29/01]

"The September 11 attacks were one of those rare historical moments, like 1933 in Germany or 1936 in Spain or 1968, when you are put in a position to take a strong stand for what is right. The left failed this test." [Interview with *Washington Prism*, 7/21/05]

" . . . I didn't have long to wait for my worst fears about the Left to prove correct." [*Hitch-22* (New York: Twelve, 2010), 244]

Legacy

" . . . A legacy is either something you owned yourself (and thus could not disown) or else it is some cause or issue henceforward inseparable from yourself." ["The Clinton Legacy: The Peronista Presidency," *Wall Street Journal*, 1/16/01]

Lesser Evil

"The argument for a lesser evil, then, has one sure effect. It guarantees that the choice will be between greater evils next time around." ["Minority Report," *Nation*, 8/22/94–8/29/94]

"If the 'lesser evil' argument is not an axiom, it is nothing. It cannot be true only some of the time, without losing all or most of its force." ["Against Lesser Evilism," *Dissent*, Fall 1996]

"Here, stated in its full masochistic form, is the very essence of 'lesser evilism.' If it were a doctrine, instead of a reflex or a dogma, it would be a doctrine without limits. Try rephrasing it. 'We have already made the decision that they can do this to us and get away with it. We have made this decision known in advance. *Ergo* they can and will get away with it.'" ["Against Lesser Evilism," *Dissent*, Fall 1996]

"There is an undistributed middle in the lesser-evil syllogism, and a rather indigestible one at that. It suggests that we are not responsible for what we *do* vote for, only for what we vote against. . . . It commits us in advance to underwrite those who have an objective quite different from our own, and methods entirely different." ["Against Lesser Evilism," *Dissent*, Fall 1996]

"To persist in saying that you didn't vote wholeheartedly but merely as a confirmed lesser-evilist is as useful (and as original) as saying that you didn't inhale." ["The Greater Evil," *Nation*, 11/18/96]

"Only the liberals and soft-leftists persist in agonizing as they give their (actually unqualified) loyalty, in advance, to people who publicly spit on them. I don't know whether the masochist or the sadist commits the greater evil, but I do know that you can't have one without the other." ["The Greater Evil," *Nation*, 11/18/96]

"The reservation or stipulation that the evil must of course be 'lesser' is a mental exercise on your part alone. You have already conceded the evil; you leave it to the party to determine if it's 'lesser' or not." ["Democratic Centralism," *Nation*, 10/19/00]

Lewinsky, Monica
"Had she not had Clinton's horrid leavings on her garments, she would now be in a world of pain and distress." ["What Really Happened," *Nation*, 3/01/99]

Libel
"The 'trickle down' use of libel suits has . . . become a handy weapon for the well-off." ["Minority Report," *Nation*, 9/04/82]

Liberalism
"Muddled thinking? In the same breath as the word liberal? Never!" ["Divine Right of Liberals and Other Misjudgments," *Newsday*, 1/15/92]

"In the end, the liberals always do what the empire wants." ["Minority Report," *Nation*, 5/24/93]

"When official liberalism decides to award itself a pat on the back, it thumps away unstintingly." ["Goodbye to Berlin," *Nation*, 12/08/97]

"Liberalism is for those who don't need it; free to those who can afford it and very expensive—if even conceivable—to those who cannot." ["Moderation or Death," *London Review of Books*, 11/26/98]

"I think we may have to face the fact that there is something in the whole liberal makeup at the moment that is masochistic." [*Hardball with Chris Matthews*, MSNBC, 7/01/99]

"It is only in liberal circles that one hears party pluralism denounced as something akin to treason or sabotage." ["Dirty Rotten Scoundrels," *Observer*, 11/12/00]

" . . . American liberalism shows no sign of abandoning its comfortable role as an essentially status quo force, at home and abroad. . . ." ["American Conservatism: A View from the Left," *Wall Street Journal*, 1/13/03]

"There's no intolerance like liberal intolerance, no closed-mindedness like the closed-mindedness of liberals." [Quoted in "Christopher Hitchens," *Prospect Magazine*, May 2008]

"Some American liberals, in my opinion, worry too much about whether or not the rest of the world likes them." ["Obamamania Deux," *Mirror*, 7/28/08]

Liberals and Humor
"I've been on the Jon Stewart show. I've been on your show. I've seen you make about five George Bush I.Q. jokes per night. There's no one I know who can't do it. You know what I think? This is now the joke that stupid people laugh at. It's a joke that any dumb person can laugh at because they think they can prove they're smarter than the president—like the people who make booing and mooing noises in your audience." [*Real Time with Bill Maher*, HBO, 8/25/06]

"Baudelaire wrote that the devil's greatest achievement was to have persuaded so many people that he doesn't exist: liberal platitudinousness must be a bit like that to those who suffer from it without quite acknowledging that there is such a syndrome to begin with." ["Cheap Laughs," *Atlantic Monthly*, October 2009]

"A liberal joke, at present, is no laughing matter." ["Cheap Laughs," *Atlantic Monthly*, October 2009]

Liberals and Intelligence
" . . . Michael Moore, Jesse Jackson, Jon Bon Jovi, Ben Affleck, and Bill Clinton (who left my university without being able to take his degree) strike me as having a long way to go before they even attain intellectual mediocrity." ["Not So Dumb Then?," *Mirror*, 11/11/04]

Liberals and War
"Few if any things are more pitiable and ridiculous than the spectacle of liberal Democrats on the verge of military intervention." ["Minority Report," *Nation*, 5/24/93]

Liberation
"I am sorry for those who have never had the experience of seeing the victory of a national liberation movement, and I feel cold contempt for those who jeer at it." [*Hitch-22* (New York: Twelve, 2010), 318]

Libertarianism
"Why, then, are the libertarians so authoritarian? Why, when it comes to questions like police power and civil liberty, industrial relations discipline, sexual morality, foreign and defense policy, crime and punishment, above all perhaps, immigration, do they reach so swiftly for the knout?" ["The Road to Serfdom," *New Statesman*, 7/04/75]

"It seems trite, then, to say that their freedom is intended for limited consumption only, but so it is." ["The Road to Serfdom," *New Statesman*, 7/04/75]

"I have not . . . abandoned all the tenets of the Left. . . . But I have learned a good deal from the libertarian critique of this worldview, and along with this has come a respect for those who upheld that critique when almost all the reigning assumptions were statist." [*Letters to a Young Contrarian* (New York: Basic Books, 2001), 102]

"Libertarianism often feels like an optional philosophy for citizens in societies or cultures that are already developed or prosperous or stable." [Quoted in "Free Radical," *Reason* magazine, November 2001]

Life

" . . . The unlived life is not worth examining." ["Nixon: Maestro of Resentment," *Dissent*, Fall 1990]

"Here is the very factor that the one-dimensional Puritans and Prohibitionists and health-measurement experts are doomed to overlook. They cannot allow, in their calculations, for the fact that all of life is a wager." ["Why Genius Cries Out for a Drink," *Evening Standard*, 4/02/92]

" . . . Human life can and should be respected whether or not it is constituted by a creator with an immortal soul; to make the one position dependent upon the other is to make the respect in some way contingent." [*The Missionary Position* (New York: Verso, 1995), 52–53]

" . . . A totally unblemished life is only for saints. . . ." ["Orwell on Trial," *Vanity Fair*, October 1996]

"We are born into a losing struggle, and nobody can hope to come out a winner, and much of the intervening time is crushingly tedious in any case. Those who see this keenly, or who register the blues intently, are not to be simplistically written off as 'dysfunctional' cynics or lushes." ["Living Proof," *Vanity Fair*, March 2003]

"The best way of getting through [life] is to eat and drink heartily, in order to keep up your strength, and to ask yourself why it is that you meet more old drunks than old doctors." ["I Don't Do Diets," *Mirror*, 8/18/03]

" . . . We do not have all our lives to waste simply in growing up. . . ." [*God Is Not Great* (New York: Twelve, 2007), 265]

"It could be that all existence is a pointless joke, but it is not in fact possible to live one's everyday life as if this were so." [*Hitch-22* (New York: Twelve, 2010), 331]

Light

"What needs to be combated is the idea, so often and so worthily expressed—and so stultifying—that 'light' is to be preferred to 'heat.' Heat . . . is the only possible source of light." ["Goodbye to All That," *Harper's*, November 1998]

Limericks
"Those who think of the humble, unassuming limerick as a trivial or vulgar thing are making a serious mistake. Its capacity and elasticity can contain multitudes." ["My Week," *Observer*, 8/16/09]

Lincoln, Abraham
"Yes, Virginia, it is true that Lincoln would have retained slavery if it had suited him, and was probably a morose and tortured syphilitic. But this doesn't diminish him as an overcoming man, unless you wanted a saintly illusion in the first place." ["Subversive Dispatches from the Outside In," *Independent*, 11/10/91]

Literary Theory and Criticism
"The proceedings of the Modern Language Association, in particular, have furnished regular gag material (gag in the sense of the guffaw, rather than the less common puke reflex) for solemn papers on 'Genital Mutilation and Early Jane Austen: Privileging the Text in the World of Hampshire Feudalism.' (I paraphrase only slightly.)" ["Transgressing the Boundaries," *New York Times*, 5/22/05]

"The study of literature as a tradition, let alone as a 'canon,' has in many places been deposed by an emphasis on deconstruction, postmodernism, and the nouveau roman. The concept of authorship itself has come under scornful scrutiny, with the production of 'texts' viewed more as a matter of social construct than as the work of autonomous individuals. Not surprisingly, the related notions of objective truth or value-free inquiry are also sternly disputed; even denied." ["Transgressing the Boundaries," *New York Times*, 5/22/05]

Literature
" . . . It would be nice to hear more about principles and less about ruffled feelings. What thoughtful person has not felt the hurt expressed by the Jews over some performances of the *Merchant of Venice*? A whole anthology of black writing exists in the United States, protesting with quite unfeigned horror about the teaching of *Huckleberry Finn* in the schools, for the good and sufficient reason that the book employs the word 'nigger' as natural. A mature and sensitive response to such tenderness of feeling and consciousness of historic wrong would run much like this, and could be uttered by a person of any race or religion. . . . We know why you feel as you do, but—too bad. Your thinness of skin, however intelligible, will not be healed by the amputation of the literary and theatrical and musical canon." ["Siding with Rushdie," *London Review of Books*, 10/26/89]

"Literature, not scripture, sustains the mind and—since there is no other metaphor—also the soul." [*God Is Not Great* (New York: Twelve, 2007), 5]

" . . . As a source of ethical reflection and as a mirror in which to see our human dilemmas reflected, the literary tradition is infinitely superior to the childish parables and morality tales, let alone the sanguinary and sectarian admonitions, of the 'holy' books." [Introduction to *The Portable Atheist* (New York: Da Capo Press, 2007), xxiv]

Literature vs. Art

"The 'literary' world is scornful, and perhaps a bit jealous, of the pelf and promotion enjoyed by the 'art' world. Glamour and instant success seem more available to the dauber than to the scribbler. Moreover, the art reviews and magazines have become shameless puff-papers. Unlike writers, New York's artists seem to function as a flock, migrating together to exhibitions in California and Europe, and burying each other in bouquets." ["American Notes," *Times Literary Supplement*, 4/13/84]

Los Angeles

"Clinton, meanwhile, thought of trying to restage Bobby Kennedy's famous visit to Watts but called off the idea because of 'logistical difficulties.' Just as well. You can't hang around South Central these days and talk about passing the torch." ["Minority Report," *Nation*, 6/22/92]

"It's full of nonsense and delusion and egomania, but I'm sort of glad to know it's there." ["City of Cults," *Guardian*, 8/19/93]

"If you can fake it here, you can fake it anywhere." ["It Happened on Sunset," *Vanity Fair*, April 1995]

"Lost Angeles. That's it in a phrase." ["It Happened on Sunset," *Vanity Fair*, April 1995]

Lott, Trent

"Having warmly praised the Dixie record of the old segregationist and paternity-suit miscegenation artist Strom Thurmond, Lott sweatily resorted to an appearance on Black Entertainment Television to promise support for affirmative-action programs if he was allowed to stay on. For a number of neocon pundits, that was it. You can perhaps fail to be color-blind once, but not twice—or not twice in the same news cycle." ["Rumble on the Right," *Vanity Fair*, July 2004]

Love

" . . . In each expired partnership, there is always one who is secretly hungry for love." ["Party of Two," *Vanity Fair*, December 1999]

"I really very much need to be loved. I just don't want to be popular." [Hay Festival of Literature & Arts, Hay-on-Wye, Powys, Wales, 5/31/05]

"We are not so made as to love others as ourselves. . . ." [*Is Christianity Good for the World?* (Moscow, ID: Canon Press, 2008), 44]

"The idea of compulsory love has always struck me as a bit shady, especially if you're ordered to love someone who you absolutely must fear." [Intelligence Squared Debate ("The Catholic Church Is a Force for Good in the World"), Methodist Central Hall Westminster, Oxford, UK, 10/19/09]

Lowest Common Denominator

"The lowest common denominator is a simple and humble achievement, and in politics it is always the chief goal of the mediocre." ["Fashion Parade in Philadelphia," *Nation*, 7/10/82–7/17/82]

" . . . There is a limit to gullibility and a diminishing return even on the lowest common denominator." ["At the Scamulator," *Times Literary Supplement*, 11/30/90–12/06/90]

Luck
"It's one thing to be lucky: it's another thing to admit that luck has been yours." ["Across the Great Divide," *Guardian*, 5/01/10]

Lying
"The telling of a serious lie presumably necessitates the use of prepositions and conjunctions." ["American Notes," *Times Literary Supplement*, 7/15/83]

"Re-lying is no better than the original lie." [Letter, *Nation*, 10/28/96]

"Just as the necessary qualification for a good liar is a good memory, so the essential equipment of a would-be lie detector is a good timeline, and a decent archive." [*No One Left to Lie To* (New York: Verso, 2000), 19]

Machismo
"Machismo is most often a sign of insecurity. . . ." ["If JFK Had Lived Much Longer, He'd Have Been Puffy, Poxy, Jumpy and Incontinent," *Mirror*, 11/22/03]

Magnanimity
"In general, it is the stronger or the victorious side that should inaugurate the magnanimous gestures." ["Who's Sorry Now?," *Nation*, 5/29/00]

Major, John
"Major is more like a traditional Labor prime minister (or opposition leader) eagerly assuring the Americans that they can count on him no matter what. That of course is just what they then proceed to do." ["Washington Diary," *London Review of Books*, 2/07/91]

Man-Made
"To say that something is 'man-made' is not always to say that it is stupid." [*God Is Not Great* (New York: Twelve, 2007), 117]

Mandela, Nelson
" . . . Political courage and moral and physical courage are not axiomatically linked, and Mandela has a surplus only of the last two." ["Race and Rescue," *Slate*, 2/01/03]

Martinis
"On the whole, observe the same rule about gin martinis—and all gin drinks—that you would in judging female breasts: one is far too few, and three is one too many. Do try to eat the olives: they can be nutritious." ["Living Proof," *Vanity Fair*, March 2003]

Marx, Karl
" . . . Many people who dismiss Marx as a 'determinist' and an 'economic materialist' or as the grandpapa of Stalinism are actually using his lines all the time." ["Minority Report," *Nation*, 4/02/83]

"Marx's paradox, then, is the love-hate attitude he manifests toward the achievements of the bourgeoisie. That distinguished class has never produced or paid anyone who could sing its praises as he did." ["Minority Report," *Nation*, 4/02/83]

"Socialism was an idea before Marx. Democracy was an idea before Marx. Social revolution was an idea before Marx. What he showed was that you can't have any of the above until you are ready for them, and that you can't have one without the others." ["Minority Report," *Nation*, 4/02/83]

"It's always a pleasure to hear Karl Marx quoted correctly, to say nothing of hearing him quoted appositely. . . ." ["Minority Report," *Nation*, 1/30/95]

"He and Engels, throughout the latter part of the nineteenth century, looked on America as the country of liberty and revolution, and on Russia as the source of despotism and darkness. This must count as a genuine irony of history." ["On the Prole," *Village Voice*, 11/23/99]

"If ruling elites and powerful states only squabbled over identifiable interests and privileges, there would have been no need for Marxist analysis. The genius of the old scribbler was to see how often the sheerly irrational intruded upon the material and utilitarian world of our great-grandfathers." ["The Grub Street Years," *Guardian*, 6/16/07]

Marx, Karl and Sigmund Freud
"Marx and Freud, it has to be conceded, were not doctors or exact scientists. It is better to think of them as great and fallible imaginative essayists." [*God Is Not Great* (New York: Twelve, 2007), 10]

Marx, Karl and Religion
"What Marx meant is that there is a chord of credulity waiting to be struck in all of us. It is most likely to be struck successfully if the stroke comes concealed as an argument for moral and humane behavior." ["The Lord and the Intellectuals," *Harper's*, July 1982]

Marxism
"The core of Marxist thought, and the reason for its stubborn survival, is the enduring conflict between the *forces* and the *relations* of production." ["Minority Report," *Nation*, 4/02/83]

"The eggs were broken, but the omelette was not made. Yet Marxism summons people to regard themselves as the subject, not the object of history." ["Minority Report," *Nation*, 2/27/89]

"When I try to make sense of the garish way the twentieth century has turned out, by bad luck Marxists always seem to be on the losing end. But not forever!" [Quoted in Don Kowet, "Christopher Hitchens, Drawing Room Marxist," *Washington Times*, 1/02/90]

"From each according to his ability, I would mutter [in the 1960s]—but what about my needs?" ["The Children of '68," *Vanity Fair*, June 1998]

"Marxism in the twentieth century did produce its Andrés Nins as well as its Kim Il-sungs. It's something more than an irony that so many calling themselves left-ists have been either too stupid or too compromised to recognize this, or have ac-tually been twisted enough to prefer the second example to the first." [*Why Orwell Matters* (New York: Basic Books, 2002), 78]

"I learned a great deal from Marxism (and I hope it shows), but as a prescription, it seems to have run completely out of steam." [Quoted in Neil Munro, "Leaving the Left," *National Journal*, 4/05/03]

"When I was a Marxist, I did not hold my opinions as a matter of faith, but I did have the conviction that a sort of unified field theory might have been discovered. The concept of historical and dialectical materialism was not an absolute and it did not have any supernatural element, but it did have its messianic element in the idea that an ultimate moment might arrive, and it most certainly had its mar-tyrs and saints and doctrinaires and (after a while) its mutually excommunicating rival papacies. It also had its schisms and inquisitions and heresy hunts." [*God Is Not Great* (New York: Twelve, 2007), 151]

The Masses
"Corrupt, sleazy, mendacious . . . it's about time we threw the masses out of office and found a new lot." ["Never Mind the President, Impeach the American Elec-torate," *Observer*, 3/22/98]

"People in the mass or the aggregate often have a lower intelligence than their constituent parts." [*Letters to a Young Contrarian* (New York: Basic Books, 2001), 75]

Masturbation
" . . . Men produce infinitely more seminal fluid than is required to build a human family, and are tortured—not completely unpleasantly—by the urgent need to spread it all over the place or otherwise get rid of it. (Religions have needlessly added to the torture by condemning various simple means of relieving this pre-sumably 'designed' pressure.)" [*God Is Not Great* (New York: Twelve, 2007), 88]

" . . . There can be no question that a human being, whether standing up or lying down, finds his or her hand resting just next to the genitalia. . . . Now: who de-vised the rule that this easy apposition between the manual and the genital be for-bidden, even as a thought? To put it more plainly, who ordered that you *must* touch (for other reasons having nothing to do with sex or reproduction) but that you also *must not*? There does not even seem to be any true scriptural authority here, yet almost all religions have made the prohibition a near-absolute one." [*God Is Not Great* (New York: Twelve, 2007), 214–215]

Maxims
"Never overestimate your enemy. Never despise the obvious. These are among the maxims I mutter to myself as I pad around the nation's capital." ["Minority Re-port," *Nation*, 5/11/85]

McCain, John

"John McCain—nobody's idea of an intellectual but likes to talk dirty and got himself shot down while scattering high explosives over someone else's country. (People keep describing him as a POW, but I think that there must be some mistake—no war on Vietnam was ever declared.)" ["Diary," *London Review of Books*, 1/06/00]

McCarthy, Eugene J.

"Staunch fighter that he is, McCarthy has in many ways the character of a poet—reflective, ironic, and attendant on longer-term rhythms." [Foreword to *1968: War & Democracy*, by Eugene J. McCarthy (Petersham, MA: Lone Oak Press, 2000), 10]

McCarthy, Joseph

"A lasting consequence of the McCarthy period is the penumbra of discredit and revulsion that still surrounds all attempts at political invigilation." ["American Notes," *Times Literary Supplement*, 1/10/86]

"The McCarthy period is doubly ridiculous . . . because it involved apparently intelligent people in contending, as a matter of principle, either that American liberals were really Communists or that American Communists were really liberals." ["A Regular Bull," *London Review of Books*, 9/18/97]

" . . . The slobbering bigmouth who still helps us to make the distinction between the crowd-pleaser and the democrat." [Foreword to *1968: War & Democracy*, by Eugene J. McCarthy (Petersham, MA: Lone Oak Press, 2000), 8–9]

Mecca

"Like many but not all of Islam's principal sites, Mecca is closed to unbelievers, which somewhat contradicts its claim to universality." [*God Is Not Great* (New York: Twelve, 2007), 136]

Media Bias

"We live in a period when a chat show that includes Morton Kondracke considers that it has filled the liberal slot." ["Blunt Instruments," *Nation*, 11/16/85]

"And then there's the Cable News Network's *Crossfire*, which awakes the adrenaline of millions of citizens each weekday evening—and is yet another phony *hommage* to the notion of unfettered exchange. . . . The conservative or the administration case is put by people who believe in or are paid by it, respectively. 'Balance' is satisfied by inviting an obscure radical onto the set when there has been a hijacking, say, or a Russian atrocity. 'Now, Mr. Lefty, you're an apologist for the Soviets. What do you have to say about that?'" ["Blabscam," *Harper's*, March 1987]

" . . . It's amazing to see how hesitantly most TV and radio and print people approach the very idea that there could be another side to a question." ["Princess Di, Mother T., and Me," *Vanity Fair*, December 1997]

"The overall bias of the American press is towards consensus, and the overwhelming bias of its proprietors is towards profit and entertainment, but the stuff still has to be written by somebody, and thus a man like Seymour Hersh can be a hero to a young *New York Times* reporter in a way that William F. Buckley, for example, was never likely to become." [Introduction to *Left Hooks, Right Crosses: A Decade of Political Writing*, ed. Christopher Caldwell and Christopher Hitchens (New York: Nation Books, 2002), 208]

Medicine

"If you set out to master a filthy and lethal disease, you may not find what you are looking for. But if you look in the right way, you may find something even more startling." ["Forging the Magic Bullet," *Vanity Fair*, November 1993]

Memory

"We must bear in mind that, in demotic speech, forgetting is a close ally of forgiving." ["Ireland," *Critical Quarterly*, Spring 1998]

"The responsibility of the memory you assume, like the guilt you accept, must be your own." ["Ireland," *Critical Quarterly*, Spring 1998]

" . . . A person who is unable to flush and void his or her memory can only be one kind of savant, and an idiotic one at that. To say that memory is selective is not in principle a condemnation—because the forgetting faculty must know how to discriminate, just as the aware and conscious faculties must know how to discriminate also." ["Ireland," *Critical Quarterly*, Spring 1998]

"It's very important to remember what everybody else chooses to forget. . . ." ["What Clinton and Lewinsky Really Got Down To," *Independent*, 8/16/98]

Men

"One lesson seems to be that men and boys behave worse—a good bit worse—when they travel in packs." ["Call of the Wilding," *Vanity Fair*, July 1993]

"It's men, not women, who need to practice saying 'No.'" ["Call of the Wilding," *Vanity Fair*, July 1993]

"Men may seem insufferable when they are confident, but they do not behave better when they are sexually insecure." ["Viagra Falls," *Nation*, 5/25/98]

"Men have prostate glands, hysterically enough, and these have a tendency to give out, along with their hearts and, it has to be said, their dicks." ["Why Women Aren't Funny," *Vanity Fair*, January 2007]

Mencken, H. L.

"The special signifier of his independence was an unslackening scorn of the religious; then as now America's most salient taboo." ["Critic of the Booboisie," *Dissent*, Summer 1994]

"He was scrupulous and mannerly in his dealings with individual Jews and African Americans, while apparently harboring crass suspicions of them in the mass, so to speak. Among some hypocrites of today, the paradox is more commonly met with the other way about. I know this is progress." ["Critic of the Booboisie," *Dissent*, Summer 1994]

"With Mencken, the face grew to fit the mask, and the playful *Prejudices* became the drone of authentic prejudice." ["Critic of the Booboisie," *Dissent*, Summer 1994]

Mensa
"The standing joke about Mensa people is that if you didn't know they were so all-get-out brilliant you would never guess. Many of them have trouble remembering to put the curtain *inside* the tub before turning on the shower." ["The Eggheads and I," *Vanity Fair*, September 1996]

"Mensa exists in part to separate the supposedly intelligent from their money." ["The Eggheads and I," *Vanity Fair*, September 1996]

"Yes, I think I get the picture. A singles club for nerds. Or, as a recent issue of the Mensa newsletter so carefully phrased it: 'Where eggheads go to get laid.' ... Actually, it appears to be a club where eggheads go to get laid—and then don't. What other explanation can there be for the recent announcement of a Mensa sperm bank?" ["The Eggheads and I," *Vanity Fair*, September 1996]

"It comes back to me that the first Mensa type I met was a boy at school with the name of Coffin. He was forever tearing open his wallet and accidentally displaying his membership card." ["The Eggheads and I," *Vanity Fair*, September 1996]

Milford Family
"And how many families could you conjure to mind, one of whose female scions or scionettes wrote a brilliant early novel satirizing fascism, one of whom had Josef Goebbels as her best man when married, one of whom attempted suicide for love of the Führer, and one of whom seriously plotted to get close to the Führer and shoot him dead?" [Introduction to *Hons and Rebels*, by Jessica Milford (New York: New York Review of Books, 2004), x]

Militarism
"You can learn a lot in a short time when there are tanks in the street." ["The Greek Lesson," *New Statesman*, 12/14/73]

" ... The weeks between Memorial Day and July 4 are looking like a banana republic or 'people's democracy' fiesta, with heavy weaponry being trucked past schoolchildren." ["Minority Report," *Nation*, 6/17/91]

"A system in which nothing really works except the military and the police will, like North Korea, end up producing somewhat spastic missiles and low-yield nukes, as well." ["Why Wait to Disarm Iran?," *Slate*, 10/19/09]

Military

"The open secret about the American Armed Forces is that, by rank and file, they are composed of poor blacks, Hispanics, and rural whites." ["The Hawks with White Feathers," *Spectator*, 8/10/85]

"I have always felt a little queasy when elderly militaristic politicians refer sob-bingly to soldiers as 'Our Boys.'" ["Scout's Honor," *Washington Post*, 6/22/86]

"As students of the original Julius Caesar will know, generals thrive on defeat." ["An Old Soldier Who Wouldn't Fade Away," *Newsday*, 5/03/89]

" . . . The armed services . . . have been one of our society's principal organs and en-gines of ethnic and religious integration." ["Hard Evidence," *Slate*, 11/16/09]

Military-Industrial Complex

"If there were any real conflict of interest, Congress would by now have voted against at least one missile appropriation. It's never happened, and it probably never will. While the rest of us worry about the nuclear winter, the contractors and their bought politicians are celebrating a nuclear spring." ["Minority Report," *Nation*, 5/11/85]

Millennium

"As the year 2000 approaches, it is a safe bet that we will be treated to more super-stition and barbarism of the [Pat] Robertson sort, and that other unscrupulous demagogues will try to canalize the fears and doubts of those who have been let down by the education system." ["Minority Report," *Nation*, 10/04/86]

"At the turn of the year 1999 into 2000, many educated people talked and pub-lished infinite nonsense about a series of possible calamities and dramas. . . . The occasion was nothing more than an odometer for idiots, who sought the cheap thrill of impending doom." [*God Is Not Great* (New York: Twelve, 2007), pp. 59–60]

Milosevic, Slobodan

" . . . He looks like the sort of faceless uniformed dolt who stamps your passport in a banana republic." ["Saddam in the Dock: Invulnerable? We'll See About That," *Mirror*, 7/02/04]

Miracles

"Many popes have been slow to canonize, as the Church is generally slow to vali-date miracles and apparitions, because if divine intervention in human affairs is too promiscuously recognized, then an obvious danger arises. If one leper can be cured, the flock may inquire, then why not all lepers? Allow of a too-easy miracle and it becomes harder to answer questions about infant leukemia or mass poverty and injustice with unsatisfying formulae about the Lord's preference for moving in mysterious ways." [*The Missionary Position* (New York: Verso, 1995), 13–14]

"When we read accounts of miracles—the sorcerer Jesus of Nazareth casting out devils, for instance, and causing them to enter the bodies of pigs—we do so through the numinous prism of a remote and mythical past. . . . It's much more difficult to picture the actual scene as it was: a bunch of stupefied Galilean peasants watching the convulsions of an epileptic and then seeing some pigs behave oddly on a neighboring slope, and being induced to draw the connection by an exorcist on the make." ["Mother Teresa on a Roll," *Nation*, 3/17/97]

"Just as the Virgin Mary seems to appear only to believing Catholics, so miracles tend to occur only when a requirement for them is specified." ["Less than Miraculous," *Free Inquiry*, February/March 2004]

"If you seem to witness such a thing, there are two possibilities. The first is that the laws of nature have been suspended (in your favor). The second is that you are under a misapprehension, or suffering from a delusion. Thus the likelihood of the second must be weighed against the likelihood of the first." [*God Is Not Great* (New York: Twelve, 2007), 141]

"Miracles in any case do not vindicate the truth of the religion that practices them. . . ." [*God Is Not Great* (New York: Twelve, 2007), 142]

"And remember, miracles are supposed to occur at the behest of a being who is omnipotent as well as omniscient and omnipresent. One might hope for more magnificent performances than ever seem to occur." [*God Is Not Great* (New York: Twelve, 2007), 150]

Mirren, Helen
"You don't notice that she's acting at all, and you can forget (unlike with, say, Debra Winger or Meryl Streep) that you have ever seen her before. I even forgot that I'd seen her romping naked through *Caligula* and had to go out and rent it all over again just to remind myself." ["Mirren and 'Middlemarch,'" *Vanity Fair*, May 1994]

Misfortune
"When confronted with the misfortune of others, we are all supposed to reflect, if only for a fleeting instant, that there but for the grace of God could be ourselves. This thought has degenerated from a platitude to a superstition and now means little more than a blessing on one's own luck. Most people, I suspect, do not see themselves even for an instant in the features of a panhandler, a bagperson or a grating-sleeper. A society that teaches that everybody can be a success can hardly avoid the corollary that those who fail are in some fashion to blame for their own plight." ["America's Inescapable Crisis—the Homeless," *Newsday*, 2/24/88]

"Laughing at the misfortunes of others—that gets me through a lot of the day." [Interview with Jian Ghomeshi, "Q TV," CBC Radio 1, 9/20/09]

Missile Defense
"The American people are once again being sold a bill of goods, and for once the term 'astronomical' is an appropriate one." ["Minority Report," *Nation*, 3/16/85]

"In a way, the mentality of the NMD [National Missile Defense] partisans is a perfect fusion of isolationist and interventionist psyches: We can build a shield over 'our' country while reserving the right to intervene at will around the globe. In this way, the parochial and the imperial instincts are jointly served." ["Farewell to the Helmsman," *Foreign Policy*, September/October 2001]

Mitterrand, François

"One cannot eat enough to vomit enough at the mention of Mitterrand's name." ["Minority Report," *Nation*, 4/12/93]

Moderates

" . . . That magic class of people who oscillate between the foreign office and the *Economist*. I mean no disrespect by this—such people are often very well informed, after all—but only someone from this provenance could be so sincere about squaring an apparent circle. . . . They are incapable of hearing or speaking the word 'moderate' without undergoing a near-religious ecstasy." ["An Informed View of the Post-Apartheid Era," *Newsday*, 4/01/92]

Modernity

"Modernity can be wrenching, as indeed can capitalism, and there will always be 'out' groups who feel themselves disrespected or left behind." ["Palin's Base Appeal," *Newsweek*, 11/23/09]

Monarchy

"Just as the holy men will tell us to thank god for our many blessings and to put the many things that are *not* blessings down to the undoubted fact that god moves in a mysterious way, so the monarchy is praised and extolled for all the honorable and admirable aspects of the country which it symbolizes, while avoiding even a whisper of blame for anything that might have gone, or be going, amiss." [*The Monarchy: A Critique of Britain's Favorite Fetish* (London: Chatto & Windus Ltd, 1990), 5]

"Those who say that without the monarchy Britain would be a banana republic are closing their eyes to the banana republic features that the cult of monarchy necessitates." [*The Monarchy: A Critique of Britain's Favorite Fetish* (London: Chatto & Windus Ltd, 1990), 13–14]

" . . . Under the influence of monarchic hysteria it [human reason] seems sometimes to evaporate like a gas for whole weeks at a time. . . ." [*The Monarchy: A Critique of Britain's Favorite Fetish* (London: Chatto & Windus Ltd, 1990), 15]

"The British monarchy inculcates unthinking credulity and servility. It forms a heavy layer on the general encrustation of our unreformed political institutions. It is the gilded peg from which our unlovely system of social distinction and hierarchy depends. It is an obstacle to the objective public discussion of our own history. It tribalizes politics. It entrenches the absurdity of the hereditary principle. It contributes to what sometimes looks like an enfeeblement of the national intelligence, drawing from our press and even from some of our poets the sort of degrading and abnegating propaganda that would arouse contempt if displayed in Zaïre or Romania. It is, in short, neither dignified nor efficient." [*The Monarchy: A Critique of Britain's Favorite Fetish* (London: Chatto & Windus Ltd, 1990), 19]

"Subliminal association with English history and valor can make opposition to the throne seem almost akin to self-hatred. The British do not argue for their monarchy, or attempt to rationalize it. For most of them, it just is, and they affirm it with the same relish as some early church fathers affirmed the Trinity—'Credo quia absurdum,' I believe because it is absurd." ["Windsor Knot," *New York Times Magazine*, 5/12/91]

"To them [the British], the monarchy is the special symbol of nationhood, the emblem of historical continuity, the seal on the unbroached integrity of the Isles, the elusive ghost in the national machine, the hint of magic at the heart of the unwritten constitution, and also the consolation for the rude decline in the value of the pound sterling." ["Bourgeois Blues," *Vanity Fair*, November 1992]

" . . . The Crown in England has always been the secret weapon of the oligarchy, in alliance with the mob, against democracy and the intelligentsia." ["Bourgeois Blues," *Vanity Fair*, November 1992]

" . . . Monarchy, by its reliance on heredity, guarantees absurdity and recurrent succession crises." ["Tarnished Crown," *Vanity Fair*, September 1997]

"The maintenance of the monarchy has become a form of human sacrifice." ["Tarnished Crown," *Vanity Fair*, September 1997]

"Whichever direction we may be taking, there is a monarchy-shaped blur that obscures the view. More worrying in a way, there seems to be a fear of what might be revealed if that blur was dispelled." ["End of the Line," *Guardian*, 12/06/00]

"It can't be good for people to lead vicarious lives, made up partly of prurience and partly of deference, and fixated on the doings of an undistinguished and spoiled family." ["End of the Line," *Guardian*, 12/06/00]

"What one wants to propose . . . is not that we abolish monarchy but that we transcend it or, to put it in more old-fashioned terms, that we grow out of it. To remove the Windsors by the stroke of a legislative pen would be highly satisfying in one way, but disappointing in another. The infantilism and cretinism of the press, for example, can't be cured just by a fiat. What should now begin is the process of emancipating ourselves from the mental habits of royalism, and the many supports it provides to unthinking attitudes and dysfunctional practices." ["End of the Line," *Guardian*, 12/06/00]

"The latent power of the monarchy is obscured by the widespread belief that it has no power at all." ["Throne of Contention," *Vanity Fair*, March 2001]

"In the UK, the Queen is the head of the church and head of state, as well as the Armed Forces—a state of affairs that is so ridiculous that many people hardly notice it." ["Not So Dumb Then?," *Mirror*, 11/11/04]

Monarchy and Breeding

"The breeding of a 'master family' is not much different in principle from the breeding of a master race; it involves much the same combination of the ridiculous and the sinister, and is every bit as incompatible with democracy and civilization." ["Mourning Will Be Brief," *Guardian*, 4/01/02]

Monarchy and Tourism

"Indeed, if it weren't for the tourist trade the British might already have gotten rid of their monarchy." ["Mirren and 'Middlemarch,'" *Vanity Fair*, February 1994]

"I hate the tourist trade, which has turned large tracts of beautiful England into a mediocre royalist theme park, so I don't give a damn if it suffers. But I resent the insulting suggestion that the British have nothing else to offer foreign visitors, and nothing else in which to take pride." ["Tarnished Crown," *Vanity Fair*, September 1997]

Monarchy vs. Republic

"To be a republican is not at all—not any more, anyway—to be a mere anti-royalist. It is to propose republican ideas and republican virtues, not against this royal house only, but against all man-made conceptions of supernatural and overweening power. As the arguments for monarchy dissolve of their own accord, one can begin to advance a case that is assertive and even optimistic." ["Away with Them and Their Overweening Power," *Independent*, 6/02/93]

"The republican case is and always has been complete on its own terms. It argues that even a happy and successful monarchy inculcates deference, hallows the hierarchy of class, dangerously confuses church with state and sanctifies privy politics and elitist secrecy." ["Our Martyred Monarchy," *Guardian*, 10/17/94]

Money

" . . . The power of money—which is the only thing that born-again conservatives really worship." ["Minority Report," *Nation*, 1/22/83]

Monotheism

"I would not want the job of deciding which monotheism, let alone which faith, was 'the stupidest.' For one thing, one becomes lost in an Aladdin's cave of multiple choice." ["The Stupidest Religion," *Free Inquiry*, Fall 2002]

"From a plurality of prime movers, the monotheists have bargained it down to a single one. They are getting ever nearer to the true, round figure." [*God Is Not Great* (New York: Twelve, 2007), 87]

"The syncretic tendencies of monotheism, and the common ancestry of the tales, mean in effect that a rebuttal to one is a rebuttal to all." [*God Is Not Great* (New York: Twelve, 2007), 98]

" . . . Monotheistic religion is a plagiarism of a plagiarism of a hearsay of a hearsay, of an illusion of an illusion, extending all the way back to a fabrication of a few nonevents." [*God Is Not Great* (New York: Twelve, 2007), 280]

"If all the official stories of monotheism, from Moses to Mormonism, were to be utterly and finally discredited, *we would be exactly where we are now*. All the agonizing questions that we face, from the idea of the good life and our duties to each other to the concept of justice and the enigma of existence itself, would be just as difficult and also just as fascinating. It takes a totalitarian mind-set to claim that only one Bronze Age Palestinian revelation or prophecy or text can be our guide through this labyrinth." ["'Tis the Season to Be Incredulous," *Slate*, 12/15/08]

Montenegro

"It's the place that god forgot, the end of the earth, a wasteland of violence and poverty given over to lupine copulation." ["Thunder in the Black Mountains," *Vanity Fair*, November 1999]

Mood

"Then there is the question of mood. The oppositional and critical mind need not always be one of engagement and principle; it has to deal with a considerable quantity of discouragement and there are days, even years, when Diogenes has much more appeal than Wilde." [*Letters to a Young Contrarian* (New York: Basic Books, 2001), 85]

Moon, Rev. Sun Myung

"Despite indictments and a conviction for all kinds of tax fiddling, despite his known connections with the subversive activities of a foreign power, despite a record of kidnapping and coercion and despite his openly fascistic opinions and practices, this hateful person has a whole clutch of eminent Reaganites eating almost literally from his hand. . . . What is depressing is not just the scandal of Moon's activity, but the apparent impunity with which it is conducted." ["Minority Report," *Nation*, 1/22/83]

Moore, Dudley

"Like any self-respecting satirist, he pretends to be embarrassed by any serious talk of 'satire.' That would run the risk of seeming to take oneself unforgivably seriously." ["Kings of Comedy," *Vanity Fair*, December 1995]

Moore, Michael

"The laugh here is on the polished, sophisticated Europeans. They think Americans are fat, vulgar, greedy, stupid, ambitious, and ignorant and so on. And they've taken as their own, as their representative American, someone who actually embodies all of those qualities." [*Scarborough Country*, MSNBC, 5/18/04]

"I never quite know whether Moore is as ignorant as he looks, or even if that would be humanly possible." ["Unfairenheit 9/11," *Slate*, 6/21/04]

" . . . Moore is a silly and shady man who does not recognize courage of any sort, even when he sees it because he cannot summon it in himself. To him, easy applause, in front of credulous audiences, is everything." ["Unfairenheit 9/11," *Slate*, 6/21/04]

Moral Equivalence

"But the point of protesting about 'moral equivalence' is surely not to blur moral choices on 'our side.' Is it?" ["Gotterdämmerung," *London Review of Books*, 1/12/95]

Morality

"There seems to be a sort of iron rule at work here—true for all countries—that morality campaigners need to bust loose even more often than the rest of us." ["Scandals as Part of Politics," *Los Angeles Times*, 7/08/82]

"For now, official morality distrusts the orgasm and experiences cathartic relief in the lethal chamber." ["Dirty Stories," *Nation*, 7/07/97]

"Everybody knows that morality is indissoluble from the idea of conscience and that something innate in us will condemn murder and theft without having to have the lesson pedantically inculcated." ["'Evil,'" *Slate*, 12/31/02]

" . . . A high moral character is not a precondition for great moral accomplishments." [*God Is Not Great* (New York: Twelve, 2007), 176]

"The moral basis of action is quite robust. If we all did a bit more of it, and things like it, the world would be no worse. If the prompting to do such things was not innate in us, we would never have evolved this far." ["Finding Morals Under Empty Heavens," *Science & Spirit*, July/August 2007]

"Do not swallow your moral code in tablet form." ["The New Commandments," *Vanity Fair*, April 2010]

Mormons

" . . . To the extent that we view latter-day saints as acceptable, and agree to overlook their other quaint and weird beliefs, it is to the extent that we have decidedly *limited* them in the free exercise of their religion." ["Free Exercise of Religion? No, Thanks.," *Slate*, 9/06/10]

Morris, Dick

"Yes, you too may be a mediocre, flaky-scalped, pudgy sycophant. But, with the right 'skills,' you also can possess a cellular phone and keep a limo on call and 'take meetings' and issue terse directives like 'I want this *yesterday*, understand.' Unfortunately, the women you meet in the politics biz will tend to be rather too much like yourself. But, hey, bimbos can be rented! And won't they just be impressed to death when you pass them the bedroom telephone extension and it's the Prez talking." ["Bill and Dick's Excellent Adventure," *London Review of Books*, 2/20/97]

"There may be some right-wing creeps behind Paula Jones and even Linda Tripp, but they can't be as right-wing or as creepy as Dick Morris." ["Clinton's Comeuppance," *Nation*, 2/16/98]

"Like the scandal—and like the president—he is part absurd and part sinister." ["It's Not the Sin. It's the Cynicism," *Vanity Fair*, December 1998]

Moses

"Apart from the absurdity of claiming to be meek in such a way as to assert superiority in meekness over all others, we have to remember the commandingly authoritarian and bloody manner in which Moses is described, in almost every other chapter, as having behaved. This gives us a choice between raving solipsism and the falsest of modesty." [*God Is Not Great* (New York: Twelve, 2007), 104]

Mother Teresa (Agnes Bojaxhiu)

" . . . With M. T. one sees yet again the alliance between ostentatious religiosity and the needs of crude secular power. This is of course a very old story indeed, but when one surveys the astonishing, abject credulity of the media in the face of the M. T. fraud, it becomes easier to understand how the sway of superstition was exerted in medieval times." ["Minority Report," *Nation*, 4/13/92]

"It is probably true that people need saints, and that some historical figures have demonstrated great modesty, humility, and simplicity. But Mother Teresa lays claim to the mandate of heaven, which is hardly modest. She acts as spiritual camouflage for dictators and wealthy potentates—hardly the essence of simplicity. And she preaches surrender and fatalism to the poor, which a truly humble person would scarcely have the nerve to do." ["The Glow Goes from Mother Teresa," *Guardian*, 11/08/94]

"Only an absence of scrutiny has allowed her to pass unchallenged as a force for pure goodness, and it is high time that this suspension of our critical faculties was itself suspended." ["The Glow Goes from Mother Teresa," *Guardian*, 11/08/94]

"In her dealings with pelf, as in her transactions with power, Mother Teresa reigns in a kingdom that is very much of this world." [*The Missionary Position* (New York: Verso, 1995), 71]

" . . . Mother Teresa, one of the few untouchables in the mental universe of the mediocre and the credulous." [*The Missionary Position* (New York: Verso, 1995), 96]

"She merely desires to be taken at her own valuation and to be addressed universally as 'Mother Teresa.' Her success is not, therefore, a triumph of humility and simplicity. It is another chapter in a millennial story that stretches back to the superstitious childhood of our species, and which depends on the exploitation of the simple and the humble by the cunning and the single-minded." [*The Missionary Position* (New York: Verso, 1995), 98]

"Here is a woman who has already achieved canonization. This state of living sainthood might be defined as the miraculous condition of having all your actions judged by your reputation, instead of your reputation by your actions." ["Mother Teresa on a Roll," *Nation*, 3/17/97]

"Never happier than when providing photo-ops for the powerful and the great, she runs a multinational missionary operation that is impossible to audit but that has, by her own admission, opened many more convents than clinics." ["Mother Teresa on a Roll," *Nation*, 3/17/97]

" . . . Her reputation for modesty was not the least inflated thing about her." ["Throne & Altar," *Nation*, 9/29/97]

"Agnes Bojaxhiu was very fond of saying that her work was religious and not humanitarian, that suffering and disease were gifts from God, that family planning was morally equivalent to abortion and that all abortion was murder. But, by some similar charismatic knack, she couldn't get anyone to believe her either." ["Throne & Altar," *Nation*, 9/29/97]

"Mother Teresa was no stranger to might and pomp—it was the press that was a stranger to the evidence of it." ["Princess Di, Mother T., and Me," *Vanity Fair*, December 1997]

"Her famous Calcutta clinic was in fact nothing more than a primitive hospice—a place for people to die, and a place where medical treatment was vestigial or nonexistent. (When she became ill herself, she flew first-class to a private clinic in California.) The vast sums of money she raised were spent mainly on building convents in her own honor. And she had befriended a whole series of rich crooks and exploiters, ranging from Charles Keating of the Lincoln Savings & Loan to the hideous Duvalier dynasty in Haiti, having accepted from both large donations of money that had actually been stolen from the poor." ["The Devil and Mother Teresa," *Vanity Fair*, October 2001]

"What is so striking about the 'beatification' of the woman who styled herself 'Mother' Teresa is the abject surrender, on the part of the church, to the forces of showbiz, superstition, and populism." ["Mommie Dearest," *Slate*, 10/20/03]

"The rich world has a poor conscience, and many people liked to alleviate their own unease by sending money to a woman who seemed like an activist for 'the poorest of the poor.' People do not like to admit that they have been gulled or conned, so a vested interest in the myth was permitted to arise, and a lazy media never bothered to ask any follow-up questions." ["Mommie Dearest," *Slate*, 10/20/03]

"Millions of people are poorer or sicker or have died because of Mother Teresa's campaign against the empowerment of women in the Third World. She has gigantically increased the amount of poverty and misery in the world. And she was on the take from the vilest elements of the rich. . . . She was a terrible person." [*Scarborough Country*, MSNBC, 12/18/04]

"She was not a friend of the poor. She was a friend of poverty. She liked poverty. She thought it was good for people. She told people to think of it as a gift from God, and she made sure that they stayed poor." ["In Depth with Christopher Hitchens," C-SPAN, 9/02/07]

"One couldn't exactly *hate* her, because in a way she was a pathetic figure." ["Q&A with Christopher Hitchens," C-SPAN, 1/14/11 (first aired: 1/23/11)]

Mother Teresa and Princess Diana
"Both had spent their careers in the service and the pursuit of the rich and powerful. Both had used poor and sick people as 'accessories' in their campaigns. And both had succeeded in pulling off the number-one triumph offered by the

celebrity culture—the achievement of a status where actions are judged by reputation and not the other way around." ["Throne & Altar," *Nation*, 9/29/97]

"It was the mutually perfect photo op." ["Throne & Altar," *Nation*, 9/29/97]

"Whereas the princess was promoted from human to martyr all in one go, and proposed for metaphorical or media canonization at warp speed, Mother Teresa has been drowning in 100 percent adoring and favorable publicity for twenty-five years." ["Princess Di, Mother T., and Me," *Vanity Fair*, December 1997]

"By the way, what have we 'chosen' for our idols and icons? A simpering Bambi narcissist and a thieving, fanatical Albanian dwarf. Nice going." ["Princess Di, Mother T., and Me," *Vanity Fair*, December 1997]

Motherhood
"Is there anything so utterly lacking in humor as a mother discussing her new child? She is unboreable on the subject." ["Why Women Aren't Funny," *Vanity Fair*, January 2007]

Moynihan, Daniel Patrick
"Is there anybody for whom he has not worked? Is there anything that he would not do? A man who has labored for L.B.J. and for Richard Nixon, and who has held Henry Kissinger's coat, needs to be judged by rather stricter standards than other mortals." ["Minority Report," *Nation*, 5/19/84]

Mugabe, Robert
"The president-for-life of Zimbabwe may have many charms, but spare cash is not among them. His treasury is as empty as the stomachs of his people." ["The Rat That Roared," *Wall Street Journal*, 2/06/03]

"Mugabe has been a devout Catholic ever since his days in a mission school in what was then colonial Rhodesia, and one is forced to wonder what he tells his priest when he is asked if he has anything he'd like to confess." ["The Lion Who Didn't Roar," *Slate*, 6/09/08]

Muggeridge, Malcolm
"Here was a man ever-ready to uncork a sermon about the fallen state of the species and the pathetic vanity of our earthly desires—all while he was notorious as an apostle of carnality and a ringmaster at the circus of his own self-promotion." ["A Hundred Years of Muggery," *Weekly Standard*, 5/05/03]

Muhammad
"As with the lineage of the isnads, a direct kinship line with the Prophet can be established if one happens to know, and be able to pay, the right local imam." [*God Is Not Great* (New York: Twelve, 2007), 135]

Multiculturalism
"Those who speak about the importance of 'multiculturalism' in their own case should not forget it when it comes to others." ["Weapons in Caches Under Mosques, Mass Graves, Secret Prisons," *Mirror*, 1/16/03]

Murdoch, Rupert

" . . . That sultan of sleaze and titan of trash. . . ." ["Minority Report," *Nation*, 2/22/86]

" . . . Rupert Murdoch, the most deft practitioner yet evolved in the art and science of blending the known requirements of populism to the immediate needs of the elite." ["Secular Values and Republican Virtues," *Salmagundi*, Spring/Summer 1998]

Muslim Grievances

"Amid all our loose talk about Muslim 'grievances,' have we even noticed that no such bill of grievances has ever been published, let alone argued and defended?" ["Reflections on Political Violence," *Slate*, 1/10/11]

Names

"We ought to beware of too easy a surrender to the vicarious identification that makes us address people whom we have never met ('Di,' 'O. J.,' 'Ollie') by their first names. This synthetic informality may mask hysterical symptoms." ["Mother Teresa or Mrs. Simpson: Which Was the Real Diana?," *Los Angeles Times*, 9/01/97]

"There is almost no English surname, however ancient and dignified, that cannot be instantly improved by the prefix 'Spanker.'" ["Johnson & Johnson," *Nation*, 6/29/98]

Nanny State

"In the space of a few hours late in November, I managed to break a whole slew of New York laws. That is to say, I sat on an upended milk crate, put my bag next to me on a subway seat, paused to adjust my shoe on a subway step, fed some birds in Central Park, had a cigarette in a town car, attempted to put a plastic frame around a vehicle license plate, and rode a bicycle without keeping my feet on the pedals at all times." ["I Fought the Law," *Vanity Fair*, February 2004]

NASCAR

"In the environs of the Richmond International Raceway, stretching to the horizon, are great tracts of pickups and trailers, fuming with barbecue and hot dogs and surmounted by flags. Old Glory predominates, but quite often the Stars and Bars is flown as well (though always underneath) or separately. . . . The tailgates groan with huge coolers, and groan even more when proud, gigantic rear ends are added. People wear shorts who shouldn't even wear jeans." ["My Red-State Odyssey," *Vanity Fair*, September 2005]

"Should you desire to remove the right to bear arms from these people, you might well have to prize away a number of cold, dead, chubby fingers. Bailey's cigarettes ('Smooth Start! Smokin' Finish!') are advertised and endorsed by NASCAR celebrities. The whole NASCAR tradition actually began with the drivers of souped-up cars who raced on dirt roads through the night, outrunning the authorities in the scramble to bring moonshine liquor to all who desired it. . . . Agents of the Bureau of Alcohol, Tobacco and Firearms—the only Washington job I ever wanted—must find NASCAR weekends their busiest time." ["My Red-State Odyssey," *Vanity Fair*, September 2005]

The Nation

" . . . Because the *Nation* is not 'mainstream,' it fails the only test that the mainstream can set—that of being in the mainstream—and is thus not much quoted or cited beyond its own borders." ["All Aboard the Bland Wagon," *Observer*, 11/19/95]

"When I began work for the *Nation* over two decades ago, Victor Navasky described the magazine as a debating ground between liberals and radicals, which was, I thought, well judged. In the past few weeks, though, I have come to realize that the magazine itself takes a side in this argument, and is becoming the voice and the echo chamber of those who truly believe that John Ashcroft is a greater menace than Osama bin Laden. (I, too, am resolutely opposed to secret imprisonment and terror-hysteria, but not in the same way as I am opposed to those who initiated the aggression, and who are planning future ones.) In these circumstances it seems to me false to continue the association, which is why I have decided to make this 'Minority Report' my last one." ["Taking Sides," *Nation*, 10/14/02]

Nationalism

"Nationalism is often strongest at its periphery." [*Cyprus* (London: Quartet Books, 1984), 52]

"Small nations have the right to insist on their freedom from imperial control, and intellectuals should not be trying to think up excuses for the big battalions. But nationalism is always finally unsatisfying because it elevates the claims of a single group over all others, and makes a virtue of doing so." ["Minority Report," *Nation*, 5/14/90]

Natural Disasters

"Natural disasters are actually not violations of the laws of nature, but rather are part of the inevitable fluctuations within them, but they have always been used to overawe the gullible with the mightiness of god's disapproval." [*God Is Not Great* (New York: Twelve, 2007), 148]

"Some ancient Egyptians believed that sodomy was the cause of earthquakes: I expect this interpretation to revive with especial force when the San Andreas Fault next gives a shudder under the Gomorrah of San Francisco." [*God Is Not Great* (New York: Twelve, 2007), 149]

Nazism and Art

"Nazism was obsessed by art and 'culture' but was almost by definition incapable of creating anything that could be recognized as such. It was, however, capable both of destroying art and of plundering it." ["Art in Peril: The Third Reich and the Old Masters," *Washington Post*, 6/05/94]

Neoconservatives

"What is it that makes a neoconservative anyway? Typically, the product is an ex-socialist, often an ex-Marxist, who has passed through some testing experience of disillusion with the Communist or Moscow line. In domestic affairs, he or she will profess the virtues of some kind of welfare capitalism. On the international scene, the neoconservative organizes everything around the need to resist the Soviet design—everything including the possession of and the readiness to use nuclear weapons. The state of Israel is regarded as an especially important Western commitment. 'Excesses' on our own side in the *Kulturkampf* are not so much excused as expected, and discounted in advance." ["An Exchange on Orwell," *Harper's*, February 1983]

"The neocons do not *have* a style or a mood; they *are* a style and a mood. From the 'tough-minded' realism of *Commentary* and the *Public Interest* to the muscular 'family values' aesthetic of the *New Criterion*, the tone is one of 'I don't care if self-interest *is* unfashionable; I'm brave enough to affirm it.' And what holds for individuals and nations may be said, in this galère, to hold for ideas: the more strenuous the better, even if this means the more circular." ["How Neoconservatives Perish," *Harper's*, July 1990]

" . . . It was the demise of 'totalitarianism' as a useful term—useful in petrifying political opponents, in giving watery notions the strength of concrete—that meant the demise of neoconservatism. . . ." ["How Neoconservatives Perish," *Harper's*, July 1990]

"The neoconservative movement is really a mentality, a mentality of refined pessimism about politics and rancid pessimism about human nature. As such, it is more or less impervious to new evidence or new experience and increasingly obsessed with refighting battles of the past—such as the great triumph over George McGovern or the stab in the back over Vietnam or the moral depredations of the counterculture. It has also been centrally preoccupied with power and more explicitly concerned with its cultivation and exercise than any comparable intellectual movement." ["How Neoconservatives Perish," *Harper's*, July 1990]

"If you take the version [of neoconservatism] offered by its acolytes, you discover a group of New York Jewish intellectuals who decided that duty, honor, and country were superior, morally and mentally, to the bleeding-heart allegiances of their boy- and girlhoods. If you take the version offered by its critics, you stumble on an old Anglo-Saxon definition of the upper crust: 'A load of crumbs held together by dough.' They just might have set out to do good, but there is no question that they ended up doing well." ["Unmaking Friends," *Harper's*, June 1999]

" . . . The so-called neo-conservatives are attacked most of all for their impetuous radicalism and their willingness to 'destabilize'; if this is not exactly Left, it is certainly not Right, either, as the paleolithic Right is the first to point out." ["What's Left?," *Atlantic Monthly*, March 2006]

"A faction willing to take the risks of making war on the ossified status quo in the Middle East can be described as many things, but not as conservative." [Quoted in George Eaton, "Interview: Christopher Hitchens," *New Statesman*, 7/12/10]

Neoconservatives and Iraq

"It wasn't that the Middle East 'lacked democracy' so much that one of its keystone states was dominated by an unstable and destabilizing dictatorship led by a psychopath. And it wasn't any illusion about the speed and ease of a transition so much as the conviction that any change would be an improvement. The charge that used to be leveled against the neoconservatives was that they had wanted to get rid of Saddam Hussein (pause for significant lowering of voice) *even before* Sept. 11, 2001. And that 'accusation' . . . was essentially true—and to their credit." ["The End of Fukuyama," *Slate*, 3/01/06]

Neoliberals

"It's all too easy to sneer at neoliberals. But it is, I'm afraid, all too necessary." ["Minority Report," *Nation*, 11/05/83]

" . . . What is neoliberalism? Its adherents beam with false modesty when they are asked. They will not be so dogmatic as to attempt a definition. . . . Neoliberals are like that. They have a sort of pious earnestness. They hold opinions rather than convictions. They wear their lightness learnedly. They are easily disappointed by the efforts and the antics of common people. They have a slightly feigned nostalgia for the times of FDR and JFK. They practice risk-free iconoclasm. Their idea of bravery is to speak the unsayable, shocking thing. For example: 'I know it's not fashionable to say this, but a lot of people really do cheat on welfare.' Some of them actually want Ernest Hollings to be President. To spend a weekend with them was like living through, rather than sitting through, the *Big Chill*." ["Minority Report," *Nation*, 11/05/83]

" . . . This bright-eyed group, mugged as they are by unreality." ["Minority Report," *Nation*, 11/05/83]

"The neoliberal style is a smart-ass one, and not without its effectiveness. The core of it is a species of gutless irony. . . . Neoliberals like to puncture illusions, and one wishes them luck in that enterprise. But they never take aim at the huge, gaseous balloon that supports their own basket." ["Minority Report," *Nation*, 11/05/83]

" . . . Neoliberals have, at best, only the cowardice of their convictions." ["Minority Report," *Nation*, 11/05/83]

Neoliberals vs. Neoconservatives

"Cynics have compared the neoliberal tendency to the neoconservative one. I think that comparison must be counted as unfair. For one thing, neoconservatives are much more rigorous. For another, they are much more interesting. Neoconservatives believe in original sin, while neoliberals believe in the enervating effect of public spending programs. . . . Neoconservatism could occur in any country. Neoliberalism could, really, only occur in a country like America, which combines abundance with *angst* and has a vast population of overqualified graduate students, some of whom wish they had, after all, served in Vietnam." ["Minority Report," *Nation*, 11/05/83]

Nevada

"Beautiful as Salt Lake City was, with its street plan leading to white-topped horizons in every direction, and lovely as Utah was, with its main church having only just had the needful 'revelation' that black people might have human souls after all, it was a slight relief to cross the frontier of Nevada and breathe the bracingly sordid and amoral air of Reno and Las Vegas." [*Hitch-22* (New York: Twelve, 2010), 215]

The New Republic

"It moved from being unpredictably silly to being predictably silly, which isn't the thing to be if you want to be predictable." [Quoted in Don Kowet, "Christopher Hitchens, Drawing Room Marxist," *Washington Times*, 1/02/90]

"A blow from the *New Republic* has a tendency to be a low one." [Letter, *New Republic*, 5/09/94]

New Statesman

"[It] really ought to change its name, and stop trading under the same title as the fine paper for which [Martin] Amis and I, as well as Julian Barnes and James Fenton, once wrote. . . ." ["Stalin's Crimes Deserve Better Than This Book," *Evening Standard*, 9/02/02]

New York

"It was from New York that the British finally departed and the city was for a brief time the capital of the United States—as, in everything but politics, it still is." ["American Notes," *Times Literary Supplement*, 4/15/83]

"New York barmen, taxi drivers, and policemen may labor too hard to give the impression of having seen it all before. But there is always the nagging suspicion that they actually *have*." ["Bites from the Big Apple," *Times Literary Supplement*, 9/30/83]

"In fact, the law these days is very clear. It states that New York City is now the domain of the mediocre bureaucrat, of the inspector with too much time on his hands, of the anal-retentive cop with his nose in a rule book, of the snitch willing to drop a dime on a harmless fellow citizen, and of a mayor who is that most pathetic and annoying figure—the micro-megalomaniac." ["I Fought the Law," *Vanity Fair*, February 2004]

New York Intellectuals

"Every time another book about 'the New York intellectuals' makes an appearance, there is a feeling that it must be the last. This feeling is entirely mistaken. Not until the last surviving participant has penned his or her account will there be any release." ["American Notes," *Times Literary Supplement*, 2/10/84]

New York Times

"Every day, the *New York Times* carries a motto in a box on its front page. 'All the News That's Fit to Print,' it says. It's been saying it for decades, day in and day out.

I imagine that most readers of the canonical sheet have long ceased to notice this bannered and flaunted symbol of its mental furniture. I myself check every day to make sure that the bright, smug, pompous, idiotic claim is still there. Then I check to make sure that it still irritates me. If I can still exclaim, under my breath, *why* do they insult me and *what* do they take me for and what *the hell* is it supposed to mean unless it's as obviously complacent and conceited and censorious as it seems to be, then at least I know that I still have a pulse." [*Letters to a Young Contrarian* (New York: Basic Books, 2001), 53]

"When the *New York Times* scratches its head, get ready for total baldness as you tear out your hair." ["History and Mystery," *Slate*, 5/16/05]

Newspapers
"American newspapers have long failed to answer the question, 'where is the knowledge we have lost in information?'" ["American Notes," *Times Literary Supplement*, 7/06/84]

"Only the aspirants for president are fool enough to believe what they read in the newspapers." ["News Review," C-SPAN, 3/14/88]

"In dealing with newspaper proprietors, it is essential to know a great deal about vagary and conceit." ["Heart of Darkness," *London Review of Books*, 6/28/90]

"The curse of American newspapers is not so much their belief in objectivity but their belief in *their own* objectivity—a word that they confuse with fairness, impartiality, neutrality, and equal space." ["These Glittering Prizes," *Vanity Fair*, January 1993]

Newspeak
"The disquieting thing about newscaster-babble or editorial-speak is its ready availability as a serf idiom, a vernacular of deference. 'Mr. Secretary, are *we* any nearer to bringing about a *dialogue* in this *process*?' Here is the politically correct language of the consensus, which can be spoken while asleep or under hypnosis by any freshly trained microphone-holder." ["Minority Report," *Nation*, 10/21/91]

"Pretty soon, we should be able to get electoral politics down to a basic newspeak that contains perhaps ten keywords: Dream, Fear, Hope, New, People, We, Change, America, Future, Together." ["Words Matter," *Slate*, 3/03/08]

Nicaragua
"It is hard to imagine U.S. troops landing in Nicaragua, unless you are a Nicaraguan who is more than sixty years of age." ["Minority Report," *Nation*, 2/28/87]

Niebuhr, Reinhold
"Niebuhr knew well how to condense the 'Judeo' with the 'Christian' in order to arrive at the decaffeinated hybrid that has since become fashionable." ["What's Love Got to Do with It?," *Vanity Fair*, September 1993]

Night

"For those of us fated to lead smaller and less portentous existences, it is still the gathering shade of evening that very often gives rise to our most intense, and sometimes necessarily our most melancholy, moments of reflection and retrospect." ["Fade to Black," *New York Times*, 10/04/09]

Nihilism

"The nihilist cannot be placated or satisfied. Like the Party of God, he wants nothing less than the impossible or the unthinkable. This is what distinguishes him from the revolutionary. And this is what he has in common with the rulers of our world, who subject us to lectures about the need to oppose terrorism while they prepare, daily and hourly, for the annihilation of us all." ["Minority Report," *Nation*, 8/03/85–8/10/85]

Nitze, Paul

"One can understand that he was the American of choice during negotiations in the Brezhnev period. Not even the sycophancy and repetition of Pravda would have bored him." ["Four Decades Near the Center of Power," *Newsday*, 10/18/89]

"When he is interesting, it is by accident." ["Four Decades Near the Center of Power," *Newsday*, 10/18/89]

Nixon, Richard

"Well we knew, didn't we, that Nixon had a brimming toilet for a mind and that he suffered from anti-Semitic paranoia?" ["Minority Report," *Nation*, 6/13/94]

"Say what you like about Dick, there was nothing of the cock-teaser about him." ["Diary," *London Review of Books*, 12/14/95]

"Nixon was scum, from top to bottom and from beginning to end, and through and through. Even by our degraded standard for the professional pol, he managed to be both howlingly empty and screamingly foul. His choice of associates tells you everything you need to know, about both them and him." ["Nixon's Tapes & the 'Greek Connection,'" *Nation*, 11/24/97]

" . . . One of the many things I found loathsome about Richard Nixon (at whose gravesite Clinton 'forgave' so exorbitantly) was the too obvious fact that he *didn't* have a sex life." ["It's Not the Sin. It's the Cynicism," *Vanity Fair*, December 1998]

" . . . In the Nixon era the United States was, in essence, a 'rogue state.' It had a ruthless, paranoid and unstable leader who did not hesitate to break the laws of his own country in order to violate the neutrality, menace the territorial integrity or destabilize the internal affairs of other nations." ["Let Me Say This About That," *New York Times*, 10/08/00]

"Like many law-and-order types, Nixon had a relish for rough stuff and police provocation. . . . As president, he can be heard on tape agreeing to the employment of Teamster bullies to batter antiwar demonstrators ('Yeah. . . . They've got guys who'll go in and knock their heads off'). . . . A small man who claimed to be for the little guy, but was at the service of the fat cats. A pseudo-intellectual who hated and resented the real thing." ["Let Me Say This About That," *New York Times*, 10/08/00]

Nixon Administration (1969–1974)

" . . . The thought of the Nixon gang in the White House still infuses me with a pure and undiluted hatred and makes me consider throwing up things that I don't even remember having eaten." ["Caught on Tape," *Slate*, 6/29/09]

Noblesse Oblige

"Perhaps, then, there are times when noblesse oblige is a better principle than mere populism and compromise." ["Feckless Youth," *Atlantic Monthly*, September 2006]

Noncombatants

" . . . Why do we employ the word 'innocent' only for those out of uniform?" ["Gulf War 2: Christopher Hitchens on Why We Must Keep Our Nerve," *Mirror*, 3/25/03]

"I distrust anyone who claims to speak for the fallen, and I distrust even more the hysterical noncombatants who exploit the grief of those who have to bury them." ["Cindy Sheehan's Sinister Piffle," *Slate*, 8/15/05]

Non-Events

"Nothing that *has* to be done every year is . . . likely to be much good. (Think of Christmas.) And now, the Oscars themselves are starting to bore people. When the original non-event goes stale, then the society of spectacle is in serious trouble." ["Diary," *London Review of Books*, 4/20/95]

North, Oliver

"Men like North can be found at gun clubs, beer-belly reunions, and charismatic tent meetings from sea to polluted sea. He is of the type that formed the *Freikorps* and took part in the march on Rome." ["Minority Report," *Nation*, 8/01/87–8/08/87]

"Oliver North, with his puffed-out chest and his lachrymose style, his awful martial ardor and his no less awful sentimentality, is the perfect example of a [Norman] Mailer figure—a superstitious fascist, whose whole entourage was full of self-hating, uniform-loving homosexuals." ["On the Imagining of Conspiracy," *London Review of Books*, 11/07/91]

"North could sure be tough when it came to scaring some uninformed congressmen before the cameras. But leave him alone with a gun-running middleman for hostage takers and he was more than a patsy and somewhat more than eager to please." ["Untrue North," *Vanity Fair*, March 1994]

" . . . A drug-running, blood-encrusted pathological liar and proto-fascist. . . ." ["Minority Report," *Nation*, 8/22/94–8/29/94]

North Korea

"One evening I gave in and tried a bowl of dog stew, which at least tasted hearty and spicy—they wouldn't tell me the breed—but then found my appetite crucially diminished by the realization that I hadn't seen a domestic animal, not even the merest cat, in the whole time I was there. (In a Pyongyang restaurant, don't ever ask for a doggie bag.)" ["Visit to a Small Planet," *Vanity Fair*, January 2001]

"Often referred to as 'the world's last Stalinist state,' it might as easily be described as the world's prototype Stalinist state." [*Why Orwell Matters* (New York: Basic Books, 2002), 73]

" . . . A society where individual life is *absolutely pointless*, and where everything that is not absolutely compulsory is absolutely forbidden." [*Why Orwell Matters* (New York: Basic Books, 2002), 75]

" . . . North Korea is unique in having a dead man as head of state: Kim Jong-il is the head of the party and the army, but the presidency is held in perpetuity by his deceased father, which makes the country a necrocracy or mausolocracy as well as a regime that is only one figure short of a Trinity." [*God Is Not Great* (New York: Twelve, 2007), 248]

"Unlike previous racist dictatorships, the North Korean one has actually succeeded in producing a sort of new species. Starving and stunted dwarves, living in the dark, kept in perpetual ignorance and fear, brainwashed into the hatred of others, regimented and coerced and inculcated with a death cult: This horror show is in our future, and is so ghastly that our own darling leaders dare not face it and can only peep through their fingers at what is coming." ["A Nation of Racist Dwarves," *Slate*, 2/01/10]

" . . . We become accomplices in evil every time we seek to soothe the unslakable appetites of the crime family that sits in Pyongyang." ["Kim Jong-il's Willing Accomplices," *Slate*, 5/24/10]

Northern Ireland

"The international community, especially the United States, would be well within its rights if it made Northern Ireland its business and ignored Britain's claim to exclusive sovereignty. As for the view that such an initiative would be a victory for the terrorist gunmen, it doesn't hold water. The gunmen are only made possible by the unique insensitivity of British policy, and an influx of international credit and concern would do much to isolate them." ["The Way to Rescue Britain," *New York Times*, 7/04/79]

"Most American politicians I have met are a good deal better informed about Northern Ireland than their British counterparts." ["The Way to Rescue Britain," *New York Times*, 7/04/79]

Nostradamus

"People who have read nothing, and who can barely crack a book or a comic without frowning deeply, are signaling wildly about the latest rumor they picked up (no doubt in the original medieval Latin) from Nostradamus. I am tired of this already." ["Pre-Millennial Syndrome," *Salmagundi*, Summer 1996]

Not in Our Name

"I don't think the administration is going to war in the name of Ed Asner or Marisa Tomei. . . ." ["So Long, Fellow Travelers," *Washington Post*, 10/20/02]

Nothing

"To do nothing is a policy." [*Cyprus* (London: Quartet Books, 1984), 138]

Novak, Robert

"Novak is one of those ultrarightists who have made a good thing of Reaganism but still regard themselves as members of an oppressed and ignored minority." ["Blabscam," *Harper's*, March 1987]

Novelists

"Novelists can be lucky in their editors, in their friends, in their mentors, and even in their pupils. Sometimes they are generous or sentimental enough to fictionalize the relationship." ["The Egg-Head's Egger-On," *London Review of Books*, 4/27/00]

Nuclear War

" . . . Or 'nuclear exchange' as the experts and pseudo-intellectuals of extinction used to put it so prettily, as if we were to hand mushroom clouds to one another in a display of mutuality." ["How I Became a Neoconservative," *La Règle du Jeu*, 9/15/05]

Nuclear Weapons

"When I was a lad, the call was to ban the bomb. Now it's to freeze it and, as a special favor, not to use it first. I know we're supposed to be grateful for small mercies, but only a liberal could call this progress." [Letter, *Nation*, 5/29/82]

"Like an empire, a nuclear state cannot be a democracy. . . . Just as 'our own' governments can be terrorists, so 'our own' nuclear systems represent the threat of and not the defense against the totalitarian temptation." ["Minority Report," *Nation*, 9/14/85]

"The sure sign of a moral idiot is a person who discourses about nuclear weapons as if they were bigger and more powerful versions of conventional weapons." ["Collected Thoughts on the Evolution of War," *Newsday*, 3/30/88]

"Nuclear bases endanger civilians in time of 'peace' as well as giving them the dubious opportunity to watch their governments commit simultaneous suicide and genocide in time of war." ["Minority Report," *Nation*, 4/16/90]

"The whole case against nuclear weapons is that *they* threaten to melt everything and make everything disappear, and thus that their use in geopolitical contests is or would be unpardonable. There was always another essential element to the critique: namely, that 'nuclearism' creates an unaccountable and secret priesthood or élite that doesn't just think it 'knows better' than the man and woman in the street but is prepared to annihilate all of them, including all non-combatants in all other countries and indeed all people who have been born or might be born." ["Moderation or Death," *London Review of Books*, 11/26/98]

Nudity

" . . . Nakedness, whether visited on presidents or emperors or fathers—as in the story of the horrid shock inflicted by Noah on his sons—imposes shame not just upon the unclad but upon the witnesses and spectators." ["It's a Scandal, but Nothing Like the One About to Break," *Independent*, 9/13/98]

Obama, Barack

"One might have hoped, in short, for a little more audacity." ["The Democrats' Rising Star," *Sunday Times* (London), 5/06/07]

"Senator Obama cannot possibly believe, and doesn't even act as if he believes, that he can be elected president of the United States next year." ["Run, Al, Run," *Slate*, 9/24/07]

"The more that people claim Obama's mere identity to be a 'breakthrough,' the more they demonstrate that they have failed to emancipate themselves from the original categories of identity that acted as a fetter upon clear thought." ["Identity Crisis," *Slate*, 1/07/08]

" . . . The problem is that Senator Obama wants us to transcend something at the same time he implicitly asks us to give that same something as a reason to vote for him." ["The Peril of Identity Politics," *Wall Street Journal*, 1/18/08]

"Not to dampen any parade, but if one asks if there is a single thing about Mr. Obama's Senate record, or state legislature record, or current program, that could possibly justify his claim to the presidency one gets . . . what? Not much." ["The Peril of Identity Politics," *Wall Street Journal*, 1/18/08]

"I shall not vote for Senator Obama, and it will not be because he—like me and like all of us—carries African genes." ["The Perils of Identity Politics," *Wall Street Journal*, 1/18/08]

"To have accepted Obama's smooth apologetics is to have lowered one's own pre-existing standards for what might constitute a post-racial or a post-racist future." ["Blind Faith," *Slate*, 3/24/08]

"Obama is greatly overrated in my opinion, but the Obama-Biden ticket is not a capitulationist one, even if it does accept the support of the surrender faction, and it does show some signs of being able and willing to profit from experience." ["Vote for Obama," *Slate*, 10/13/08]

"On the right, where febrile talk of Obama's 'Marxism' is still to be heard, the rage and frustration reminds me of the way some on the left used to talk about Ronald Reagan in the age of 'Teflon': a politician seemingly immune from consequences and benefiting even from his own mistakes." ["Cool Cat," *Atlantic Monthly*, January/February 2009]

"Our new president's charm is not merely superficial. It is compounded of two qualities that are distinctly rare in the political class: an apparently very deep internal equanimity, and an ability to employ irony at his own expense." ["Cool Cat," *Atlantic Monthly*, January/February 2009]

"The political rhetoric of Obamaism, alas, is even more bloviating at times than Camelot was. . . ." ["Redemption Song," *Slate*, 8/31/09]

Obama, Barrack—Winning the Nobel Peace Prize

"It would be like giving someone an Oscar in the hope that he would one day make a good motion picture. It's a virtual award. It's for good intent." [*Hardball with Chris Matthews*, MSNBC, 10/12/09]

"We thus find ourselves in a rather peculiar universe where good intentions are rewarded before they have undergone the strenuous metamorphosis of being translated into good deeds, or hard facts." ["Underqualified for the Overrated," *Newsweek*, 10/19/09]

Objectivism

" . . . The striking thing about objectivism, and the thing that distinguishes it from the mainstream of American conservatism, is exactly its disgust with religion. Belief in God is equated with mental slavery." ["Greenspan Shrugged," *Vanity Fair*, December 2000]

Objectivity

"The ideology of objectivity denominates the press itself not as the gatekeeper of any one party or issue but as the generalized guardian of the consensus." ["Covering Politics in the '90s," C-SPAN2, 6/19/93]

"Objectivity means the search for the truth no matter what. It's a very, very great responsibility to say that's what you're seeking or that's what you're practicing." [Quoted in Bill Steigerwald and Bob Hoover, "Objectivity and Other Lies," *Pittsburgh Post-Gazette*, 4/27/97]

"Objectivity is a wholly new, denatured idea. It's like decaf coffee or beer for pregnant women." [Quoted in Bill Steigerwald and Bob Hoover, "Objectivity and Other Lies," *Pittsburgh Post-Gazette*, 4/27/97]

"A knowledge of one's own subjectivity is necessary in order even to contemplate the 'objective'. . . ." [*Why Orwell Matters* (New York: Basic Books, 2002), 205]

O'Brien, Conor Cruise

" . . . O'Brien himself has made the transition all the way from Red and Green—via a slightly empurpled phase—to flag-waving Orange." [*Why Orwell Matters* (New York: Basic Books, 2002), 45]

Obscenity

" . . . He [Simon Leys] describes the title of my book [*The Missionary Position: Mother Teresa in Theory and Practice*] as 'obscene,' and complains that it attacks someone who is 'elderly.' Would he care to say where the obscenity lies?" [Letter, *New York Review of Books*, 12/19/96]

The Obvious

"Never overlook the obvious." ["Demystifying the Breakthroughs," *Nation*, 4/04/81]

"It's very important never to ignore what's staring you in the face." ["Covering Politics in the '90s," C-SPAN2, 6/19/93]

"Loud, overconfident dismissals of obvious qualms betray the stirrings of an uneasy conscience." ["Political Animals," *Atlantic Monthly*, November 2002]

"The obvious is sometimes the most difficult thing to discern, and few things are more amusing than the efforts of our journals of record to keep 'open' minds about the self-evident, and thus to create mysteries when the real task of reportage is to dispel them." ["Inconvenient Truths," *Slate*, 12/08/08]

Occam's Razor

"The principle of Occam's razor is attractive and useful because it can dispose of unnecessary assumptions." ["Minority Report," *Nation*, 3/14/87]

"When two explanations are offered, one must discard the one that explains the least, or explains nothing at all, or raises more questions than it answers." [*God Is Not Great* (New York: Twelve, 2007), 148]

Official Secrets Act

"If you tangle with the Official Secrets Act, even a teeny-weeny little bit, make sure to keep a toothbrush in your top pocket." ["Minority Report," *Nation*, 11/09/85]

"The Official Secrets Act is the only piece of Western democratic legislation that stands comparison with the much-cited fictions of Franz Kafka and Joseph Heller. Its operative, central function is totalitarian. If charged, you must be guilty of *something*." ["Minority Report," *Nation*, 11/09/85]

"British law features an Official Secrets Act, allowing the government to decide that even public information is secret, which in the United States would be a violation of the First Amendment. Another reason, it occurred to me, why I had changed countries to begin with." ["Power Suits," *Vanity Fair*, April 2006]

Oil

"What a curse the stuff is, and how wretchedly distributed. Arab nationalists are rightly fond of recalling the glories of Arab civilization, but these glories pre-date the discovery of the region's greatest resource." ["Washington Diary," *London Review of Books*, 2/07/91]

"How strange that the anti-war left should have forgotten all of its Marxism and superciliously ignored the fact that oil is blood: lifeblood for Iraqis and others. Under Saddam it was wholly privatized; now it can become more like a common resource." ["The Perils of Withdrawal," *Slate*, 11/29/05]

"Control over the production and distribution of oil is the decisive factor in defining who rules whom in the Middle East." ["Blood and Oil," *Slate*, 3/12/07]

Olympics

"Though I didn't think the story belonged in the news section at all, I did learn today that there's not enough snow for this bloately funded spitefest in Vancouver and so they'll be choppering some white stuff in from the north. That at least might be momentarily interesting to watch (Haitians in particular would, I bet, be riveted to see it). Meanwhile, with millions of other don't-care people, I won't be able to escape the pulverizing tedium of the events themselves. Global warming never seemed a more inviting prospect." ["Fool's Gold," *Newsweek*, 2/15/10]

O'Neill, Eugene

"It's true that O'Neill did his best stuff after he sobered up, but he had obviously learned a lot from the years when he couldn't remember which train he had boarded, or why." ["Living Proof," *Vanity Fair*, March 2003]

O'Neill, Tip

"O'Neill seems to think that if you add the word 'football' to the word 'political' and if you use the phrase 'the American people' as often as seems bearable, you have disgraced dissent and made conformity into a patriotic virtue." ["Minority Report," *Nation*, 3/10/84]

"If some deplorable accident ever befell the Speaker (which Heaven forfend), the chief mourner would have to be Ronald Reagan. And for once, his emotion would be genuine. Tip O'Neill has been Reagan's most valued collaborator." ["Minority Report," *Nation*, 3/10/84]

Open-Mindedness

"The problem with open-mindedness is that it can become empty-mindedness." [Sydney Writers' Festival, Sydney, Australia, 6/01/10]

Oratory

"A literary test of those who can say things forcibly and out loud is whether they are capable of understatement." ["Martin Luther King: Genesis of the Dream," *Newsday*, 2/19/92]

"People who can't get along without 'um' or 'er' or 'basically' (or, in England, 'actually') or 'et cetera et cetera' are of two types: the chronically modest and inarticulate, such as Ms. [Caroline] Kennedy, and the mildly authoritarian who want to make themselves un-interruptible." ["The *Other* L-Word," *Vanity Fair* (online), 1/13/10]

"When a charge against me of 'incitement to riot' was eventually dropped, I was slightly crestfallen because I had thought it a back-handed tribute to my abilities as an orator." [*Hitch-22* (New York: Twelve, 2010), 108]

" . . . If you can give a decent speech in public or cut any kind of figure on the podium, then you need never dine or sleep alone." [*Hitch-22* (New York: Twelve, 2010), 124]

Original Sin

"Of course, original sin would be just as persuasive a verdict as any other the Church might offer. But tautology is the enemy of historical inquiry: if we are all evil, then everything becomes a matter of degree. . . . Incidentally, do not the

Churches also insist on trying to perfect the imperfectible, and on forcing the human shape into unnatural attitudes? Surely the 'totalitarian' impulse has a common root with the proselytizing one." ["Lightness at Midnight," *Atlantic Monthly*, September 2002]

Originality
"Originality is a quality so rarely met with in humans that when it does occur it is often disputed." ["Steal This Article," *Vanity Fair*, May 1996]

O'Rourke, P. J.
"The essential P. J. joke is fairly easy to 'get.' It consists in waiting for the punchline." ["O'Rourke's Drift," *Mail on Sunday*, 12/10/95]

"O'Rourke may indeed have been a smelly, lecherous, doped-out mess when he was a Sixties baby. I have a distinct suspicion that he never took as many drugs, or as many liberties with the Flag, or the fair sex, as he now claims he did." ["O'Rourke's Drift," *Mail on Sunday*, 12/10/95]

Orwell, George
"Now, George Orwell was opposed to capitalism and its values, whether the system was prospering or not, and believed in common ownership. He never had any illusions to lose about the Soviet system, and spent almost half his life exposing and ridiculing them in others (Left and Right). He was deeply and personally opposed to making Stalinism a pretext for 'imperialist' conduct by the democracies. He was very suspicious of the growing power of the United States. He was against nuclear weapons. He was opposed to Zionism. He was as far from being a neoconservative, or the model for a neoconservative, as it is feasible to be. Many times he was offered the chance, and just as many times he pushed the poisoned chalice from his lips." ["An Exchange on Orwell," *Harper's*, February 1983]

"Almost by definition, then, the name 'Orwell' and the term 'apologist' do not belong in the same sentence." ["Orwell on Trial," *Vanity Fair*, October 1996]

"His very ordinariness is the sterling guarantee that we need no saintly representative consciences. We would do better to make sterner use of our own." ["Prophet with a Typewriter," *Wilson Quarterly*, Autumn 2000]

"A striking fact about Orwell, a tribute to his 'power of facing,' is that he never underwent a Stalinoid phase, never had to be cured or purged by sudden 'disillusionment.' It is also true that he was somewhat impatient with those who pleaded their original illusions as excuses for later naïveté. This—with its potential hint of superiority—is certainly part of the reason for the intense dislike he aroused then and arouses still." [*Why Orwell Matters* (New York: Basic Books, 2002), 56]

"At best it could be asserted, even by an atheist admirer, that he took some of the supposedly Christian virtues and showed how they could be 'lived' without piety or religious belief." [*Why Orwell Matters* (New York: Basic Books, 2002), 211]

"Orwell's 'views' have been largely vindicated by Time, so he need not seek any pardon on that score. But what he illustrates, by his commitment to language as the partner of truth, is that 'views' do not really count; that it matters not what you think, but *how* you think; and that politics are relatively unimportant, while principles have a way of enduring, as do the few irreducible individuals who maintain allegiance to them." [*Why Orwell Matters* (New York: Basic Books, 2002), 211]

"Born one hundred years ago, Orwell died an almost Dickensian death, of combined 'consumption' and poverty, in the first month of the second half of the last century. He is almost as far from us, chronologically, as he himself was from Dickens. Yet he owns the twentieth century, as a writer about fascism and communism and imperialism, in a way that no other writer in English can claim." ["Dragon Slayer," *Washington Post*, 9/28/03]

"Orwell was interested above all not in the rationalizations of the dominant, but in the excuses and whimperings of the submissive. Hence his fascination with the role of religion, in both confirming and denying the role of the autonomous, defiant individual." ["Dragon Slayer," *Washington Post*, 9/28/03]

"A short word of advice: In general, it's highly unwise to quote Orwell if you are already way out of your depth on the question of moral equivalence. It's also incautious to remind people of Orwell if you are engaged in a sophomoric celluloid rewriting of recent history." ["Unfairenheit 9/11," *Slate*, 6/21/04]

Orwell, George and the Left
"There isn't much room for doubt about the real source of anti-Orwell resentment. In the view of many on the official Left, he committed the ultimate sin of 'giving ammunition to the enemy.'" [*Why Orwell Matters* (New York: Basic Books, 2002), 58–59]

Outrage
"There are a lot of things about the 1960s that I don't miss. But . . . one thing we seem to have lost is the ability to be shocked—morally shocked—by politicians. There has been a dulling of the nerve of outrage." ["Shock Value," *Nation*, 6/05/82]

"The nerve of outrage is not an incidental part of the body politic, like an appendix. It's a vital piece of equipment." ["Here's the Beef," *Newsday*, 10/16/88]

Oxford University
"I utterly neglected the studies that I was being subsidized by the taxpayers to pursue, at a great university which many less fortunate people would have given a limb to attend. I may have used my limited gifts as a public speaker in order to make loud and simplistic statements and even, on at least one occasion, to get a member of the audience to disrobe. (No, you fool, not at the meeting itself.)" ["The Children of '68," *Vanity Fair*, June 1998]

"The Oxford debating tradition does possess one great strength, drawn indirectly from the *Symposium*. You are supposed to be able to give an honest account of an opposing or different worldview, and even as an exercise to be able to present it as if you believed it yourself." ["Moderation or Death," *London Review of Books*, 11/26/98]

"[James] Fenton swears that I even donned a beret to lead a demonstration [at Oxford University]: he is quite incapable of an untruth, but I am sure I didn't do it more than once." [*Hitch-22* (New York: Twelve, 2010), 102]

"Let us say one quarter of the time allotted to political confrontations and dramas, another devoted to reading books on any subject except the ones I was supposed to be studying, another quarter on seeking out intellectual heavyweights who commanded artillery superior to my own, with the residual 25 percent being consumed by the polymorphous perverse." [*Hitch-22* (New York: Twelve, 2010), 123]

Pacifism
"The serious pacifist objects not to dying but to killing." ["The Hawks with White Feathers," *Spectator*, 8/10/85]

Pain
"If you're in pain and being tortured, and you felt it was helping the liberation of humanity, then you can bear it better." [Interview with Melissa Block, *All Things Considered*, National Public Radio, 10/29/10]

Paine, Thomas
"Of *Common Sense* it can be said, without any risk of cliché, that it was a catalyst that altered the course of history." [*Thomas Paine's Rights of Man: A Biography* (New York: Atlantic Monthly Press, 2006), 30]

"Thomas Paine was one of the first to experience the full effect of modern absolutist ideology in all of its early forms: his life could be seen as a prefiguration of what would happen to idealists and revolutionaries in the following century." [*Thomas Paine's Rights of Man: A Biography* (New York: Atlantic Monthly Press, 2006), 68]

"In a time when both rights and reason are under several kinds of open and covert attack, the life and writing of Thomas Paine will always be part of the arsenal on which we shall need to depend." [*Thomas Paine's Rights of Man: A Biography* (New York: Atlantic Monthly Press, 2006), 142]

Paine, Thomas and Edmund Burke
"This classic exchange between two masters of polemic is rightly considered to be the ancestor of all modern arguments between Tories and radicals, or between those who believe in tradition and property and heredity and those who distrust or abhor them." [*Thomas Paine's Rights of Man: A Biography* (New York: Atlantic Monthly Press, 2006), 69]

Pakistan
"Whenever there is a crisis on the eastern frontiers of the empire, some group of thugs decides to abolish democracy in Pakistan." ["Minority Report," *Nation*, 10/15/90]

Paleoconservatives
"If you want a picture of a 'paleoconservative'—someone who is a bred-in-the-bone all-American hard-liner and enjoys reminiscing about the great days of

Barry Goldwater and Ronald Reagan, with a side bet on Joe McCarthy—just keep the image of Patrick Buchanan in your mind." ["Rumble on the Right," *Vanity Fair*, July 2004]

Palestine and Palestinians

" . . . Where else, one wonders, are the Palestinian people to live? Under occupation? In camps? In exile?" [*No One Left to Lie To* (New York: Verso, 2000), 127]

"One people lives, without its consent, under the rule of another. This unjust and unwanted rule is guaranteed, militarily and economically, by a Pax Americana. And this was the case long before bin-Ladenism became the latest excuse for it. A Pax Americana cannot long endure half-slave and half-free." ["American Conservatism: A View from the Left," *Wall Street Journal*, 1/13/03]

"The sooner there is a Palestinian state with a share of Jerusalem as its capital, the safer Israel will be." ["Don't Let Iran Blackmail the World," *Slate*, 5/17/10]

Palestine Liberation Organization

"The PLO is regarded as a terrorist organization by the United States government, and that has the effect of making distinction and discrimination impossible. Is it possible that this is the intention of the term?" ["Wanton Acts of Usage," *Harper's*, September 1986]

Palin, Sarah

"It is not snobbish to harbor grave doubts about somebody who seems uninterested in reading for pleasure or recreation and whose only interest in her local public library is sniffing round its shelves for books that ought to be removed for expressing impure ideas." ["Speak Up!," *Slate*, 10/20/08]

"On the witch-exorcism stuff, not even her stoutest apologists have been able to help her out: it's all on YouTube, as is the quasi-coherent speech with which she bid farewell to her governorship without a word of warning to her voters or backers. I would urge you to scan both links and see if they don't make you feel suddenly much more elitist." ["Palin's Base Appeal," *Newsweek*, 11/23/09]

"Sarah Palin appears to have no testable core conviction except the belief (which none of her defenders denies that she holds, or at least has held and not yet repudiated) that the end of days and the Second Coming will occur in her lifetime. This completes the already strong case for allowing her to pass the rest of her natural life span as a private citizen." ["Palin's Base Appeal," *Newsweek*, 11/23/09]

" . . . An unscrupulous and uncultured political neophyte who will happily act as a megaphone for any kind of libel and insinuation—Obama's 'palling around with terrorists' was, I suppose, the money shot of the last campaign—and then later revise and extend her remarks." ["Palin's Pals," *Slate*, 12/07/09]

"At least Richard Nixon had the ill fortune to look like what he was: a haunted scoundrel and repressed psychopath. Whereas the usefulness of Sarah Palin to the right-wing party managers is that she combines a certain knowingness with a feigned innocence and a still-palpable blush of sex." ["Palin's Pals," *Slate*, 12/07/09]

"The most arresting thing about Palin, indeed, is the absolutely unbreachable serenity of her ignorance. She already has all the information she requires. She knows, for example, how heaven fine-tunes employment practices in the Alaskan oil industry. ('As the months went by, [her husband] Todd's prayer was answered by an offer for a permanent position with BP.') This would be laughable if it weren't creepy." ["When Ignorance Is Bliss," *Sunday Times* (London), 12/13/09]

"She's got no charisma of any kind. I can imagine her being mildly useful to a low-rent porn director." [*Leonard Lopate Show*, WNYC, 6/04/10]

Pantheism
"And if there is a pervasive, preexisting cosmic deity, who is part of what he creates, then there is no space left for a god who intervenes in human affairs, let alone for a god who takes sides in vicious hamlet-wars between different tribes of Jews and Arabs. No text can have been written or inspired by him, for one thing, or can be the special property of one sect or tribe." [*God Is Not Great* (New York: Twelve, 2007), 262]

Paranoia
"To the paranoid mind, all things are connected." ["Minority Report," *Nation*, 7/17/89]

Pardons
" . . . Guiltless men are in no need of pardons." ["Minority Report," *Nation*, 1/18/93]

The Parthenon
"A pagan shrine, a church, a mosque, an arms dump, a monument to Nazi profanity, and a target for promiscuous collectors of all kinds. . . . It is a wonder that the Parthenon still stands." [*The Parthenon Marbles: The Case for Reunification* (New York: Verso, 2008), 23]

Partisanship
"Our culture uses 'partisan' as a term of opprobrium, and 'bipartisan' as a term of praise. Implicit is the understanding that real opposition politics would be dangerous. Implicit in *that* is the admission that we have a one-party system enclosed in a two-party form." ["Minority Report," *Nation*, 8/22/94–8/29/94]

Partition
"In the first place, people are partitioned, not maps. . . . In the second place, partition always leads to another war. . . . In the third place, it 'empowers' not the disparate or diverse populations but the most hectically nationalist and religious elements of their leaderships, who really believe in exclusivity and purity as goods in themselves." ["Minority Report," *Nation*, 8/14/95–8/21/95]

Pascal, Blaise
"Pascal reminds me of the hypocrites and frauds who abound in Talmudic Jewish rationalization. Don't do any work on the Sabbath yourself, but pay someone else to do it. You obeyed the letter of the law: who's counting?" [*God Is Not Great* (New York: Twelve, 2007), 212]

The Passion of the Christ
"A few years ago, Mel Gibson got himself into an argument after uttering a series of crude remarks that were hostile to homosexuals. Now he has made a film that principally appeals to the gay Christian sado-masochistic community: a niche market that hasn't been sufficiently exploited. If you like seeing handsome young men stripped and tied up and flayed with whips, *The Passion of the Christ* is the movie for you." ["I Detest This Film . . . With a Passion," *Mirror*, 2/28/04]

Paternalism
" . . . There is always some mediocre jerk who knows what's best for you." ["Living Proof," *Vanity Fair*, March 2003]

Patriotism
" . . . Patriotism and jingoism are not by any means the same thing." ["The Hawks with White Feathers," *Spectator*, 8/10/85]

"Above me was emblazoned a grand banner that said: 'Patriotism not Politics.' A very old and cherished illusion, dear to the heart of all those who think conservatism and jingoism are common sense. Lucky is the man who has found novelty in this stale idea. Innocent—or deeply cynical—is the man who takes his politics from it." ["Minority Report," *Nation*, 7/06/92]

Patterns
" . . . The hasty search for 'patterns' is an essential element in the inflation of a *grande peur*." ["Minority Report," *Nation*, 1/09/89–1/16/89]

"If you look for them, you find them." ["My Red-State Odyssey," *Vanity Fair*, September 2005]

Peace Through Strength
"Josef Stalin, as it happened, also believed in peace through strength." ["Collected Thoughts on the Evolution of War," *Newsday*, 3/30/88]

The People vs. Larry Flynt
"The story of this film is the story of an intrepid immigrant, a vulgar sleazebag, a two-faced businessman, a crusading lawyer, a drug-sodden, AIDS-infected starlet, and a serial killer. Didn't I say it was all-American?" ["Hustler with a Cause," *Vanity Fair*, November 1996]

"Cameo parts are played by Flynt himself, as the judge who once gave him a quarter-century in the slammer, and James Carville, as the prosecutor in that very case and looking every inch like the product of the love scene in *Deliverance*." ["Hustler with a Cause," *Vanity Fair*, November 1996]

Perception
"Perception modifies reality. . . ." [*Hitch-22* (New York: Twelve, 2010), 342]

Perjury
" . . . The offense of perjury has been so downwardly defined by the Clintonoids that it can't seriously be charged against a perjurer's apprentice. Morally, also, it

has been defined by the Democratic leadership as an offense only slightly worse than telling the truth." ["I'll Never Eat Lunch in This Town Again," *Vanity Fair*, May 1999]

"Human society is inconceivable unless words are to some extent bonds, and in legal disputes we righteously demand the swearing of oaths that entail severe penalties for perjury. . . . Nothing focuses the attention more than a reminder that one is speaking on oath. The word 'witness' expresses one of our noblest concepts. 'Bearing witness' is a high moral responsibility." ["The New Commandments," *Vanity Fair*, April 2010]

Perot, Ross

"The affection of certain 'progressives' for the bat-eared czar conceals and in some cases reveals a species of moral exhaustion with democracy." ["Minority Report," *Nation*, 7/06/92]

"Perot emerges . . . more as a man who keeps the secrets in a blackmailer's safe than as one who wants to tell the citizens where the bodies are buried." ["Minority Report," *Nation*, 7/06/92]

"In the course of my day spent among the Ross-fanciers, I found that despite their many charms and courtesies, they want a revolution that is painless to them. They have the self-pity of the self-satisfied. They have no conception of self-criticism. They are, for the most part, those who thought Richard Nixon and Ronald Reagan were the tribunes of the little guy. One might call this the elitism of fools." ["Minority Report," *Nation*, 7/06/92]

" . . . A man who proudly and unoriginally shouts for the United States to be run like a private corporation without having the wit to appreciate that, as his own mediocre career testifies, it is run like one already." ["Minority Report," *Nation*, 7/06/92]

"The Personal Is Political"

"The idea that 'the personal is political'—an idea that emerged in an era of post-1960s depoliticization—has come to mean that personal identity or preference is a sufficient political commitment." ["Missionary Positions," *Wilson Quarterly*, Winter 1991]

"In the meanwhile, of course, the political has conversely become personalized, with the result that public affairs are dominated by celebrity-style posturing." ["Radical Pique," *Vanity Fair*, February 1994]

"I remember very well the first time I heard the saying 'The Personal Is Political.' It began as a sort of reaction to the defeats and downturns that followed 1968: a consolation prize, as you might say, for people who had missed that year. I knew in my bones that a truly Bad Idea had entered the discourse. Nor was I wrong. People began to stand up at meetings and orate about how they *felt*, not about what or how they thought, and about who they were rather than what (if anything) they had done or stood for. It became the replication in even less interesting form of the narcissism of the small difference, because each identity group begat its subgroups and 'specificities.'" [*Letters to a Young Contrarian* (New York: Basic Books, 2001), 112–113]

"From now on, it would be enough to be a member of a sex or gender, or epidermal subdivision, or even erotic 'preference,' to qualify as a revolutionary. In order to begin a speech or to ask a question from the floor, all that would be necessary by way of preface would be the words: 'Speaking as a . . .' Then could follow any self-loving description." [*Hitch-22* (New York: Twelve, 2010), 121]

Pessimism

"For those facing a long haul and a series of defeats, pessimism can be an ally." [*Letters to a Young Contrarian* (New York: Basic Books, 2001), 86]

Philosophy

" . . . One does not scan the works of professional philosophers in order to come across tautologies. One scans them to see tautologies exposed." ["Scorched Earth," *Weekly Standard*, 7/31/06]

"Philosophy begins where religion ends, just as by analogy chemistry begins where alchemy runs out, and astronomy takes the place of astrology." [*God Is Not Great* (New York: Twelve, 2007), 256]

Pigs

"The more one reflects on the national trough and its imagery, the more one wants to spring to the defense of the maligned pig. . . . Pigs have a fine ratio of brain-to-body weight, almost the equal of dolphins. They do, if left to themselves, know how to keep clean. They possess many intelligent and humorous faculties. Can the same be said of, say, the members of the Senate and House Appropriations Committees? I rest my case." ["It's Everybody's Trough in Wonderful Pork World," *Newsday*, 9/09/92]

"It would be merely boring and idiotic to wonder how the designer of all things conceived such a versatile creature and then commanded his higher-mammal creation to avoid it altogether or risk his eternal displeasure." [*God Is Not Great* (New York: Twelve, 2007), 38]

Pinter, Harold

"Even in his increasingly lame and slovenly literary output, Mr. Pinter always married politicization to illiteracy." ["The Sinister Mediocrity of Harold Pinter," *Wall Street Journal*, 10/17/05]

Plagiarism

" . . . If you think you know what plagiarism is, you are making a very large claim—the claim that you know originality when you see it." ["Steal This Article," *Vanity Fair*, May 1996]

"'Plagiarism,' that most obvious and banal discovery of the literary sleuth. . . ." [Introduction to *The Mating Season*, by P. G. Wodehouse (New York: Penguin Classics, 1999), ix]

"The rules of borrowing are that some interest, or some gesture of gratitude, should accompany the repayment." [Introduction to *The Mating Season*, by P. G. Wodehouse (New York: Penguin Classics, 1999), x]

Pledge of Allegiance

"I am a strict constructionist and a firm believer in original intent. This is why I believe that the Pledge of Allegiance, in its current phrasing, is two words too long." ["God and Man in the White House," *Vanity Fair*, August 2003]

Pluralism

"Pluralism is a means as well as an end." ["Goodbye to All That," *Harper's*, November 1998]

Podhoretz, Norman

" . . . Norman Podhoretz, another moral and intellectual hooligan who wishes he had the balls to be a real-life rat fink." ["Minority Report," *Nation*, 4/10/89]

"True, the former editor of the supposedly solemn *Commentary* magazine has always himself sought to ease the life of the book reviewer. He does this small but welcome favor by making all his faults crashingly apparent from the very first page, sometimes even from the opening paragraph." ["Unmaking Friends," *Harper's*, June 1999]

"As a literary critic, he rather resembles an undertaker scanning the obits for trade." ["Unmaking Friends," *Harper's*, June 1999]

" . . . A crass power worshiper whose only regrets are for himself, and who can conceive of no cause larger than his own esteem." ["Unmaking Friends," *Harper's*, June 1999]

Podhoretz, Norman vs. Gore Vidal

"You could say, very approximately, that the contending styles were represented by Gore Vidal and Norman Podhoretz. Vidal is cynical, patrician, and assured. Podhoretz is sarcastic, demotic, and, in the old sense of the term, enthusiastic. Vidal tends to approach matters with the maddening *de haut en bas*, ludic approach. Podhoretz takes a more pugnacious and protesting stance, insisting on the word 'seriousness' at all times and punctuating it with the word 'moral.' Vidal pities those who take him too seriously, and Podhoretz resents those who fail to pay him the same compliment. If ever there was a Roundhead and Cavalier confrontation in the American culture, it would be drawn from characters of this kind." ["American Notes," *Times Literary Supplement*, 5/30/86]

Poetry

"Poetry . . . is morally proof against censorship." ["Minority Report," *Nation*, 10/23/89]

"Who seriously wishes that Coleridge's 'Kubla Khan' was even one stanza longer?" ["Why Genius Cries Out for a Drink," *Evening Standard*, 4/02/92]

" . . . The most generous verdict [of poets] is arguably the most durable." ["D.W.E.M. Seeks to R.I.P.," *Vanity Fair*, April 1993]

" . . . Hesitate once, hesitate twice, hesitate a hundred times before employing political standards as a device for the analysis and appreciation of poetry." ["How Unpleasant to Meet Mr. Eliot," *Nation*, 8/12/96]

Political Action Committees

"The PACs . . . don't care about parties as such; they care about incumbents, about those who remain on the Hill and roll up seniority and get to be key lawmakers on key committees." ["The Loyally Complicit," *Harper's*, July 1991]

Political Correctness

"The beauty of consensus PC is that it makes differences on matters of principle almost unsayable." ["Minority Report," *Nation*, 10/21/91]

"In the nondebate over nonissues that goes on here, the hands-down winner is the culture of euphemism. . . . One is almost rejoiced to hear a stupid, meaningless, barbarous emphasis—'Fuck this shit' springs to mind—merely for the sake of its unadorned clarity." ["Minority Report," *Nation*, 10/21/91]

" . . . The trend of their emaciated terminology leads in the direction of a mini-consensus that does not welcome dissent. The fact that this consensus is mostly a laugh doesn't make it, as an effort, any less potentially sinister." ["Minority Report," *Nation*, 10/21/91]

"Morally, it may pose as a complement to pluralism and 'divesity,' which makes it feel superior to its white-bread senior partner. But politically and socially, it translates as 'watch what you say and don't give offense to anybody,' which isn't a serious definition of diversity." ["Minority Report," *Nation*, 10/21/91]

"For the first time, those who seek an extension of 'rights' also argue for an abridgement of 'speech.' . . . The novel and surreptitious arguments for censorship and for linguistic conformism come tricked out in the language of 'empowerment' and of civil rights. In plain words, they come from a bastardized or mutated grammar of the American Left. . . . 'Sensitivity training' seminars, and something-for-everyone hiring practices, have themselves become additional instruments of power and control, with the loser being the secular and the color-blind. Empowerment is now an etiquette and a reinforcement of authority, backed up by constant reminders of what may happen to those who speak freely or out of turn. . . . It is an authoritarian, language-murdering enforcement of official liberalism." ["Words Fail Us," *Independent*, 6/13/93]

" . . . One cannot write about PC without draining the last ironic drop from the use of quotation marks." ["Words Fail Us," *Independent*, 6/13/93]

" . . . A paraplegic demands to join the Marine Corps, and cries discrimination when turned down. At once, you can predict three things. First, the majority will weary of the good cause of the disabled. Second, the paraplegic will come up with a euphemism for his or her condition. Third, there will be those who say that the issue of Cherokee paraplegics has not yet been addressed as a specific 'agenda.'" ["Words Fail Us," *Independent*, 6/13/93]

"The cult of PC, in fact, is probably best understood as a sort of mutation of the sixties, in which all the crappy aspects of that decade have been fused. The idealism and élan are defunct, while in hybrid form all the sectarian hysteria, all the juvenile intolerance, and all the paranoia and solipsism have been retained." ["Radical Pique," *Vanity Fair*, February 1994]

" . . . The great fallacy at the heart of today's political correctitude—that in order to secure something vaguely termed 'diversity' it insists on something definitely recognizable as conformity." ["Radical Pique," *Vanity Fair*, February 1994]

"Claim that something is 'offensive,' and it is as if the assertion itself has automatically become an argument." ["Mau-Mauing the Mosque," *Slate*, 8/09/10]

Political Parties

"A national political party can suffer intermittent trouble with either its spine or its brain, but it cannot long persist as mindless and invertebrate." ["The Loyally Complicit," *Harper's*, July 1991]

"At the risk of tautology, the two-party system requires two parties." ["The Loyally Complicit," *Harper's*, July 1991]

"It is difficult, as recent elections prove, to motivate voters to vote without some appeal to what they understand to be their better selves. Young voters—whom the Democrats, as recently as the 1960s, knew grew up to be the most consistent voters—are in particular drawn to a party with a Big Picture. Not surprisingly, that party today is the Republican." ["The Loyally Complicit," *Harper's*, July 1991]

"Notoriously, if two parties say very much the same thing, the palm tends to go to the party that said it first, and most convincingly." ["Washington Diary," *London Review of Books*, 8/20/92]

" . . . The rules of the two-party pendulum mandate that the other party is always the greater evil." ["Minority Report," *Nation*, 8/22/94–8/29/94]

"If you announce in advance that whatever a party does it will have your vote, then you surrender your right to choose and your right to think, and in effect hand your hard-won ballot to someone else." ["Minority Report," *Nation*, 8/22/94–8/29/94]

"Once concede that you are with party B, and that's all anyone wants to know about you." ["Against Lesser Evilism," *Dissent*, Fall 1996]

Political Police

"Nations that allow a secret political police, and that allow them great latitude on the ground of national security, are famously asking for trouble. As with most important lessons, this one is easy to learn if you confine it to the experience of others." ["Minority Report," *Nation*, 9/12/87]

Politicians

"The most deplorable politicians are the ones who vote even against their own speeches and against the remnants of their own principles, selling themselves for an imagined 'leverage' in order to 'send a signal.'" ["Minority Report," *Nation*, 6/22/85]

"A truly substantial politician, who has convictions and the wit to express them, as well as the nerve to express them when they are unpopular, will ipso facto have style. A stylish politician, by the same token, may be precisely the one who has dash and confidence because he knows and cares what he is talking about." ["The Merchandising of Our Candidates," *Newsday*, 11/02/88]

"Beware of those resentful nonentities who enter politics for therapeutic reasons." ["No Sympathy for Slobo," *Slate*, 3/13/06]

"The most insulting thing that a politician can do is to compel you to ask yourself: 'What does he take me for?'" ["Vote for Obama," *Slate*, 10/13/08]

"To kindle a smidgeon of faith in a mere politician after the Nixon debacle was an almost touching display of something like innocence. . . ." [Introduction to *Ancient Gonzo Wisdom: Interviews with Hunter S. Thompson*, ed. Anita Thompson (New York: Da Capo Press, 2009), xix]

"I really think that people who look for heroism among politicians are probably looking for love in all the wrong places." [*Charlie Rose Show*, 8/13/10]

Politics

"Most of the buying and selling of our national political process is legal, and the corruption is so routine that it barely raises a bump of outrage." ["A Bipartisan Congress with Votes for Sale," *Newsday*, 6/29/88]

"One sometimes wonders—do Americans know how their politics look to outsiders who are already suspicious of Hollywood?" ["The Merchandising of Our Candidates," *Newsday*, 11/02/88]

"Every once in a while, a political campaign or a political candidate bursts the constraints of 'ordinary,' business-as-usual routine and becomes recognizable as authentic. People differ over these magic moments. . . . There's always one infallible sign, however. The pundits and the political establishment never see it coming." ["Our Political Style's Debt to Hollywood Hysteria," *Newsday*, 4/22/92]

" . . . To be an apolitical animal is to leave fellow citizens at the mercy of ideology." [Introduction to *For the Sake of Argument* (New York: Verso, 1993), 3]

" . . . The only people truly bound by campaign promises are the voters who believe them." ["Inaugural Closeout," *Nation*, 2/17/97]

"The highest art in low politics is to be able to induce the masses to invest their own sense of dignity in yours. Then, if you are exposed as a fraud, they will be exposed as credulous: a conclusion they approach with a natural human reluctance." ["Clinton—'Like a Gorilla Playing a Violin,'" *Evening Standard*, 8/18/98]

"We are of course accustomed to hear that we should concentrate on 'issues' instead of personalities, and this distinction often sounds suitably serious. But experience teaches us that it can be a false one, or a distinction without a difference. Who would say that the personality of Lyndon Johnson or Robert Kennedy—perhaps especially the personality of the latter—was not a factor in prolonging the war? Who would argue that the personality of the Republican nominee of that year was not a political consideration on its own?" [Foreword to *1968: War & Democracy*, by Eugene J. McCarthy (Petersham, MA: Lone Oak Press, 2000), 10]

"I cringe every time I hear denunciations of 'the politics of division'—as if politics was not division by definition." [*Letters to a Young Contrarian* (New York: Basic Books, 2001), 31]

" . . . The attention of Congress and the public has been easier to engage than to maintain." [*Blood, Class and Empire* (New York: Nation Books, 2004), 240]

"You may think you can give up politics, but you can't. Politics will come and find you." [Quoted in Mindy Belk, "The World According to Hitch," *World Magazine*, 6/03/06]

" . . . The prevailing drivel assumes that every adult in the country is a completely illiterate jerk who would rather feel than think and who must furthermore be assumed, for a special season every four years, to imagine that everyone else 'in America' or in 'this country' is unemployed or starving or sleeping under a bridge." ["Words Matter," *Slate*, 3/03/08]

"Consider: What normal person would consider risking their career and their family life in order to undergo the incessant barrage of intrusive questioning about every aspect of their lives since well before college? . . . Then comes the treadmill of fundraising and the unending tyranny of the opinion polls, which many media systems now use as a substitute for news and as a means of creating stories rather than reporting them. And, even if it 'works,' most of your time in Washington would be spent raising the dough to hang on to your job. No wonder that the best lack all conviction." ["The Politicians We Deserve," *Slate*, 10/11/10]

Politics (British)

"The winner-take-all rules of a British election mean that a party leader can become Prime Minister simply by waiting for the incumbent Government to decompose." ["Downstairs Upstairs," *New York Times Magazine*, 6/01/75]

"Rebellious declarations of independence from the British Crown are the very stuff of politics." ["The Way to Rescue Britain," *New York Times*, 7/04/79]

"The accepted categories of British politics show a stubborn resistance to redefinition." ["Choosing Between Clichés," *Times Literary Supplement*, 6/25/82]

"Britain's politicians may be Lilliputian, but the problems they face are Brobdingnagian." ["Choosing Between Clichés," *Times Literary Supplement*, 6/25/82]

"It would be a mistake to assume that the British people are necessarily becoming more conservative. . . . It is just that Britain no longer possesses a party that organizes dissent, unites the poor, and has a vision of the future." ["Haven for British Dissent Is in Full Eclipse," *Los Angeles Times*, 6/19/83]

"Parliament trains its sons in a hard school of debate and unscripted exchange, and so does the British Labor movement. You get your retaliation in first, you rise to a point of order, you heckle and you watch out for hecklers." ["Unmitigated Galloway," *Weekly Standard*, 5/30/05]

"If you exempt the appeal of strictly local nationalist parties in Scotland, Wales, and Northern Ireland, British society is actually a three-party system stitched and corseted into a two-party duopoly." ["*Au Revoir* to the Status Quo," *Slate*, 5/03/10]

Politics and Hypocrisy

"Public, political life, as we understand it, is an exercise in hypocrisy, and that's necessary for the thing to go on." [CNN, 5/21/92]

"Have we not learned by now that the propensity of politicians to rave on about morality is often in direct proportion to their hypocrisy on the point?" ["Foley Loaded," *Wall Street Journal*, 10/16/06]

"Anyone who has studied the fate of leading gay-bashers in American politics will know that the danger-signs are there from the start. Set your watch, and sure enough that fervent campaigner will be arrested kneeling abjectly on the men's-room floor. If the campaigner is an evangelist for purity and abstinence, he is booked to keep an early and certain date in a dreary motel, beseeching a drab hooker with an expired MasterCard." ["Foley Loaded," *Wall Street Journal*, 10/16/06]

Polls

"Polls are deployed only when they might prove *useful*—that is, helpful to the powers that be in their quest to maintain their position and influence. Indeed, the polling industry is a powerful ally of depoliticization and its counterpart, which is consensus. The polls undoubtedly help decide what people think, but their most important long-term influence may be on *how* people think." ["Voting in the Passive Voice," *Harper's*, April 1992]

"A good pollster is like a good attorney, and fights for the result that the commissioning party expects or needs. . . ." ["Voting in the Passive Voice," *Harper's*, April 1992]

"In alliance with the new breed of handlers, fundraisers, spin-specialists, and courtier journalists, [polling] has become both a dangerous tranquilizer and an artificial stimulant." ["Voting in the Passive Voice," *Harper's*, April 1992]

"The one measurement of the pace and rhythm of events that is absolutely no good at all is the opinion poll. This must be why it is featured in the headline of every newspaper." ["Washington Diary," *London Review of Books*, 8/20/92]

" . . . Most polling data is abject rubbish collected by morons from morons. . . ." ["Mr. Universe," *Vanity Fair*, December 1992]

"By no means . . . are polls the instrument of the mob. The mob would not know how to poll itself, nor could it afford the enormous outlay that modern polling requires. . . . Instead, the polling business gives the patricians an idea of what the mob is thinking, and of how that thinking might be changed or, shall we say, 'shaped.' It is the essential weapon in the mastery of populism by the elite." [*No One Left to Lie To* (New York: Verso, 2000), 28–29]

"When President Reagan was discovered to have cancer in his colon, one major newspaper printed a poll in which people were solemnly asked if they thought the cancer would be cured, would recur, or would go into remission. Now, not even the enthusiasts of ultrademocracy would maintain that there could be any popular insight into the state of affairs in Reagan's bottom." [*Letters to a Young Contrarian* (New York: Basic Books, 2001), 79]

"To be able to cite a poll is now the shortest cut to economizing both on thought and on research." ["All the Views Fit to Print," *Slate*, 11/01/10]

Popular Culture

"There is a huge trapdoor waiting to open under anyone who is critical of so-called 'popular culture' or (to redefine this subject) anyone who is uneasy about the systematic, massified cretinization of the major media. If you denounce the excess coverage, you are yourself adding to the excess. If you show even a slight knowledge of the topic, you betray an interest in something that you wish to denounce as unimportant or irrelevant." ["Siege of Paris," *Slate*, 6/11/07]

Population

"Anyone whose major concern is the sanctity of human life is in effect, by leaving population growth unchecked, ensuring death by famine. Nature is pitiless, and if humans will not themselves limit population then they will have it done for them." ["A Gloomy Forecast for a Crowded Planet," *Newsday*, 4/05/90]

"Clearly there are many ways of getting the population question wrong. On the other hand, there is no rational way of saying that the question does not arise." [*The Missionary Position* (New York: Verso, 1995), 30]

"'Population bomb' theorists, most notably Paul Ehrlich, have seen their extrapolated predictions repeatedly fail to come true—at least partly because they are extrapolations." [Foreword to *Brave New World*, by Aldous Huxley (New York: HarperCollins, 2004), xviii]

Populism

"No American politician would risk an unexplained reference to a chess move." ["Thousands of Cans and Cartons," *London Review of Books*, 5/24/90]

"Populism, which is in the last instance always an illiberal style, may come tricked out as folkish emancipation. That is when it most needs to be satirized." ["Critic of the Booboisie," *Dissent*, Summer 1994]

"But the problem with populism is not just that it stirs prejudice against the 'big cities' where most Americans actually live, or against the academies where many of them would like to send their children. No, the difficulty with populism is that it exploits the very 'people' to whose grievances it claims to give vent." ["Palin's Base Appeal," *Newsweek*, 11/23/09]

"In my own not-all-that-humble opinion, duping the hicks is a degree or two worse than condescending to them." ["Palin's Base Appeal," *Newsweek*, 11/23/09]

"Populism imposes its own humiliations on anyone considering a run [for political office]. How many times can you stand in front of an audience and state: 'I will always put the people of X first'? (Quite a lot of times, to judge by recent campaigns.) This is to say no more than that you will be a megaphone for sectional interests and regional mood swings and resentment, a confession that, to you, all politics is yokel." ["The Politicians We Deserve," *Slate*, 10/11/10]

Pornography
"There will always appear to be something bizarre about those who campaign against pornography. Something, if you like, a little too *interested*." ["American Notes," *Times Literary Supplement*, 6/27/86]

Port Huron Statement
"If you look back to the founding document of the sixties left, which was the Port Huron statement (also promulgated in Michigan), you will easily see that it was in essence a conservative manifesto. It spoke in vaguely Marxist terms of alienation, true, but it was reacting to bigness and anonymity and urbanization, and it betrayed a yearning for a lost agrarian simplicity." ["Where Aquarius Went," *New York Times*, 12/19/04]

Postmodernism
"Postmodernism à la Warhol or indeed à la Baudrillard is very often another way, as if we needed one, of saying 'I don't care' or 'Who cares?' or 'It doesn't matter.' Nothing fresh or original or worthwhile is likely to happen again." ["Diary," *London Review of Books*, 10/12/89]

"In one important respect, indeed, Fascist thinking is already upon us. Young people are being taught that reason itself is suspect. Abstract theory and knowledge are not, however, described any longer as 'Jewish science' or 'rootless rationalism.' Instead, they are denounced without irony or elegance as 'constructs' of patriarchy, phallocracy, or whatever. (Since when did the *penis*, of all organs, have a monopoly on *reason*, of all things?)" ["Radical Pique," *Vanity Fair*, February 1994]

Pound, Ezra
" . . . Shelley wanted poets to be 'the unacknowledged legislators' of the world, while Pound sought hectically for acknowledgment, not just for poetry but for himself, and lost the sense of both in the process." ["A Revolutionary Simpleton," *Atlantic Monthly*, April 2008]

Poverty

" . . . Poverty and underdevelopment are not God-given but are man-made, and can be unmade by man." ["The Move Forward," *Times* (London), 6/21/71]

"The world of municipal poverty provision is a world of almost weird extravagance." ["America's Inescapable Crisis—the Homeless," *Newsday*, 2/24/88]

"Either one eschews luxury and serves the poor or one does not. If the poor are always with us, on the other hand, then there is no particular hurry, and they can always be used to illustrate morality tales. In which case, it might be more honest for their prophetic benefactors to admit that the poor have *us* always with *them*." [*The Missionary Position* (New York: Verso, 1995), 29]

"If anyone's interested in the alleviation of poverty . . . the only thing we know definitely works is giving women control over their own reproduction." ["In Depth with Christopher Hitchens," C-SPAN, 9/02/07]

Power

"I believe that those who wield power are implicitly capable of anything, which makes me even keener than the next person to be absolutely specific and certain about what they did this time or that time." ["Minority Report," *Nation*, 7/17/89]

"The end of power, in short, becomes power itself." ["Two Monsters in an Aristotelian Mold," *Newsday*, 3/18/92]

"The arrogance of power is boundless, but it mustn't deprive us of that great consolation of the underdog—the presumption of guilt." ["Conspiracies with Sidney," *Nation*, 3/30/98]

"Dogma in power does have a unique chilling ingredient not exhibited by power, however ghastly, wielded for its own traditional sake." ["Moderation or Death," *London Review of Books*, 11/26/98]

"Ruthless and arrogant though power can appear, it is only ever held by mere mammals who excrete and yearn, and who suffer from insomnia and insecurity. These mammals are also necessarily vain in the extreme, and often wish to be liked almost as much as they desire to be feared." [*Letters to a Young Contrarian* (New York: Basic Books, 2001), 87]

Prayer

"As in medieval Europe, those who wanted to impose prayer on others are demonstrating not their confidence in their own faith, but their lack of confidence in it." ["Why Copy Our British Folly?," *Washington Post*, 3/18/84]

" . . . A Jerry Falwell clone named Bailey Smith observed that 'God Almighty does not hear the prayers of a Jew.' This is the only instance known to me of an anti-Semitic remark having a basis in fact. After all, there is no such person as God Almighty, and thus all prayer by all denominations has the same moral effect as aerobic dancing, if not less." ["The Stupidest Religion," *Free Inquiry*, Fall 2002]

"The positions for prayer are usually emulations of the supplicant serf before an ill-tempered monarch. The message is one of continual submission, gratitude, and fear." [*God Is Not Great* (New York: Twelve, 2007), 73–74]

"After all, if one was not a mammal, and could get erections on demand, there'd be no need for prayer in the first place." [Quoted in Boris Kachka, "Are You There, God? It's Me, Hitchens," *New York*, 5/07/07]

"If people got well by praying . . . we wouldn't be in the case that we are, with so many people desperately sick." ["In Depth with Christopher Hitchens," C-SPAN, 9/02/07]

Precedent
"Precedent, after all, connotes precedence." [*The Monarchy: A Critique of Britain's Favorite Fetish* (London: Chatto & Windus Ltd, 1990), 24]

Predictability
"I have never been able, except in my lazier moments, to employ the word 'predictable' as a term of abuse. Nor has the expression 'knee-jerk' ever struck me as a witty way of denigrating a set of strongly held convictions. . . . Speaking purely for myself, I should be alarmed if my knee failed to respond to certain stimuli. It would warn me of a loss of nerve." ["Blunt Instruments," *Nation*, 11/16/85]

Prescience
"Prescience, like every other science, requires a sense of history." ["Minority Report," *Nation*, 6/07/93]

Presidents
"The ratio between presidential 'credibility' and foreign crisis is so well-understood that it has become worn smooth by repetition. What Nixon lost at home, he nearly recouped in China: what Carter lost in Iran, he never regained on the domestic front." ["The Luck That Does No One Any Good but Clinton," *Evening Standard*, 8/10/98]

"American history may one day read: 1988–2008: Bush-Clinton-Bush-Clinton. Unbelievable? The first three phases of it have tested our credulity enough." ["Going All the Way," *Evening Standard*, 12/20/00]

Presidents and Comedians
"When comedians flatter the president, they become court jesters, and the country becomes a banana republic." ["Obama's Court Jesters," *Slate*, 5/18/09]

Presidents and the Press
" . . . You still read articles about the 'adversary relationship' between the press and the presidency. I'll start to believe that on the day that Ted Koppel forgets to call Henry Kissinger 'Doctor.'" ["Blabscam," *Harper's*, March 1987]

"Every year in Washington there is a grisly evening known as the Gridiron Club dinner. It rivals other such soirées in raising the question: which is the more painful and degrading spectacle, to see the president fawning on the press or the press fawning on the president?" ["A Smart Set of One," *New York Times*, 11/17/02]

Pride

"In the end, even when it takes a vain form or a truculent or sullen shape, pride is an essential part of self-respect." ["Saddam's Long Goodbye," *Vanity Fair*, June 2003]

Privacy

"Perhaps we should agree on a recognized code of conduct. A politician's private life should be his or her own affair if (a) there is no graft or selling of office, (b) there is no risk to state or national security, (c) the partner is above the age of consent, (d) the general atmosphere is decorous and tasteful, (e) there is no flaunting of privilege and (f) there is no conflict of interest and no hypocrisy." ["Scandals as Part of Politics," *Los Angeles Times*, 7/08/82]

Privilege

"To be a spoiled person is not to be well-off or favored by fortune or protected from brute realities. It is to be well-off and favored by fortune and protected from brute realities *and not to know it*." ["The Baby-Boomer Wasteland," *Vanity Fair*, January 1996]

Pro-Choice Movement

"It's just my impression, but the idea that a fetus is 'only' a growth in, or appendage to, the female body seems to be advanced with less conviction than was once the case. . . . [T]o its credit the 'pro-choice' school has turned queasy and shifted to the ironic or . . . the merely sarcastic. Thus it's more often argued that the so-called right to life movement is, generally speaking, led by people who support capital punishment, endorse imperialist war, fetishize nuclear weapons, and detest women's liberation. The abortion issue, in this analysis, is an opportunistic conscription of the emotions for the purpose of retarding or negating the gains made by women since the 1960s." ["Minority Report," *Nation*, 4/24/89]

Pro-Life Movement

"The leading element in the 'right to life' movement is indeed composed of hypocrites, who are either indifferent to the suffering of others or in some cases positively enthusiastic about it; who are marketers of religious cretinism; and who have been thoroughly and revealingly unsettled by one of the century's most positive developments, the sexual autonomy of women. As has been said before, the 'lifers' pretend concern for humanity before it is born and after it is dead, and contribute mightily to the preventable bits of misery in between." ["Minority Report," *Nation*, 4/24/89]

"If you care to spend a few minutes talking with the people who attend 'right to life' events, the active majority of them working-class women, you will encounter all kinds of what I am still arrogant or confident enough to call illusions. But you will also encounter a genuine, impressive, unforced revulsion at the idea of the disposable fetus. This revulsion would deserve respect even if it were 'only' emotional." ["Minority Report," *Nation*, 4/24/89]

"I can't help noticing that quite a few pro-life activists revere the fetus second only to the way in which they cherish the Confederate flag." ["Fetal Distraction," *Vanity Fair*, February 2003]

Prohibition

"The Prohibitionist instinct did not and does not really care whether my smoke affects other people 'second hand' or any other way. It wants to stop me smoking, just as it once would have wanted to stop me drinking. And with about as much success, I might add." ["Why I Blow Smoke at This Moral Frenzy," *Evening Standard*, 4/15/94]

"Sensing the coming of a brash new world, the traditionalists of Puritan America mounted their last great stand in 1919 by passing the 18th Amendment, or Prohibition. Their target was not just the demon drink but really the whole phenomenon of modernism, with its sexual freedom, motorcars, and migration from the small and simple town to the big and clever city. . . ." ["The Road to West Egg," *Vanity Fair*, May 2000]

Promise Keepers

"Unless you find mass credulity upsetting, what's not to like about huge drifts of mostly unerotic, mostly white guys carrying coolers, putting up 'prayer tepees' and wearing unfunny shirts that read 'Too Blessed to Be Stressed' or 'If God Is Your Father—Call Home'? This was MMM as Mass Movement of the Mediocre. You could see why they wouldn't object to being called a flock." ["Another March, Another Prick in the Wall," *Nation*, 10/27/97]

"I can't say I care for the new mode of ostentatiously self-abasing prayer, Islamic style, with steatopygous mounds thrust directly skyward. 'Creepy' might also be the term for the addiction to hugging and the enthusiasm for the raised-arm salute (which I mentally caption 'Hands up, all those who jerked off last night,' in order to make it all go away)." ["Another March, Another Prick in the Wall," *Nation*, 10/27/97]

Propaganda

"You don't draw the sting from a brainless propaganda word merely by turning it around." ["Wanton Acts of Usage," *Harper's*, September 1986]

Prophets

"We shall have no more prophets or sages from the ancient quarter, which is why the devotions of today are only the echoing repetitions of yesterday, sometimes ratcheted up to screaming point so as to ward off the terrible emptiness." [*God Is Not Great* (New York: Twelve, 2007), 7]

"Scripture warns gloomily that prophets are not honored in their own countries, and given the record of many prophets, that's very probably a good thing." ["The Blair-Hitch Project," *Vanity Fair*, February 2011]

Prostitution

"Once removed to her sinister cubicle, we commenced to bargain. Or rather, in a sort of squalid reverse-haggle, every time I agreed to the price she added some tax or impost or surcharge and bid me higher. . . . I wearily started to count out the ever-steepening fee, which was the only thing in the room that showed any sign of enlarging itself." [*Hitch-22* (New York: Twelve, 2010), 166]

Proust, Marcel

"To be so perceptive and yet so innocent—that, in a phrase, is the achievement of Proust." ["The Acutest Ear in Paris," *Atlantic Monthly*, January/February 2004]

Public Opinion

"There is something touching, as well as something stupid, in the desperate effort to discover and predict the public taste." ["Minority Report," *Nation*, 5/11/92]

"If you want to know what people think, go out and ask them, and then you'll find out how they think as well, which is far more valuable as well as far more interesting." ["America's Last Real Journalist," *Evening Standard*, 5/27/98]

"If you say that you are very often pretty sure that it's the majority who is wrong and the way the public opinion is constructed that's wrong, the way that popular mandates are construed that's wrong, then you can be accused of being an elitist or a snob and so on, and then you know you're on to something." [Interview with Harry Kreisler, "Conversations with History: A Dissenting Voice," 4/25/02]

"I do not believe any of the statistical claims that are made about public opinion. I don't see why anybody does." [Quoted in Boris Kachka, "Are You There, God? It's Me, Hitchens," *New York*, 5/07/07]

Puns

"Puns are the lowest form of verbal facility." ["The Eggheads and I," *Vanity Fair*, September 1996]

Puritanism

"Step outside the inner cities of the nation—where, thanks in part to the heroic war on drugs, pretty much anything goes—and you can find yourself confronted by the friendly and insidious personality of the authoritarian. At a bar at the top of a ski lift in Aspen, Colorado, I was denied a gin and tonic because, 'at this altitude, sir, it would be twice as strong.' Hot dog! Bring it over!" ["Smoke and Mirrors," *Vanity Fair*, October 1994]

" . . . Something in the Puritan soul is committed to making and keeping people miserable, even when it is *not* for their own good." ["Living Proof," *Vanity Fair*, March 2003]

Quayle, Dan

"Watching and listening up close, I saw nothing to suggest that if his brains were made of TNT they would generate enough explosive power to disarrange his hair." ["The Repackaging of Dan Quayle," *Harper's*, April 1990]

Questions

"It's a true sign of nervousness to answer a question that you have not been asked." ["Why Starr Is Determined to Nail Clinton," *Evening Standard*, 7/29/98]

Quotations

"No letters, please, about 'quoting out of context.' One does not have to be a deconstructionist to know that quotation *is* out of context." ["American Notes," *Times Literary Supplement*, 3/04/83]

" . . . If I write an article and I quote somebody and for space reasons put in an ellipsis like this (. . .), I swear on my children that I am not leaving out anything that, if quoted in full, would alter the original meaning or its significance. Those who violate this pact with readers or viewers are to be despised." ["Unfairenheit 9/11," *Slate*, 6/21/04]

Race and Racism

"The point about racists and fascists. . . is that they don't have to win many votes to do their damage." ["Britain's Punks Go Fascist," *Mother Jones*, August 1978]

"Those who flirt with race theory should learn to beware their own dominant gene." ["Critic of the Booboisie," *Dissent*, Summer 1994]

"Linguistics, genetics, paleontology, anthropology: All are busily demonstrating that we as a species have no objective problem of 'race.' What we still do seem to have are all these racists." ["Minority Report," *Nation*, 11/28/94]

"One reason to be a decided antiracist is the plain fact that 'race' is a construct with no scientific validity. DNA can tell who you are, but not what you are." ["Minority Report," *Nation*, 10/23/95]

"For years, when I went to renew my annual pass at the United States Senate, I was made to fill in two forms. The first asked me for my biographical details, and the second stipulated that I had signed the former under penalty of perjury. I was grateful for the latter form, because when asked to state my 'race' I always put 'human' in the required box." [*Letters to a Young Contrarian* (New York: Basic Books, 2001), 110]

"If white people call black people niggers, they are doing their very best to hurt and insult them, as well as to remind them that their ancestors used to be property. If black people use the word, they are either uttering an obscenity or trying to detoxify a word and rob it of its power to wound them. Not quite the same thing." ["Eschew the Taboo," *Slate*, 12/04/06]

"Racism is totalitarian by definition: It marks the victim in perpetuity and denies him, or her, the right to even a rag of dignity or privacy, even the elemental right to make love or marry or produce children with a loved one of the 'wrong' tribe, without having love nullified by law." [*God Is Not Great* (New York: Twelve, 2007), 251]

"The number of subjective definitions of 'racist' is almost infinite, but the only objective definition of the word is 'one who believes that there are human races.'" ["The Peril of Identity Politics," *Wall Street Journal*, 1/18/08]

"In this country, it seems that you can always get an argument going about 'race' as long as it is guaranteed to be phony, but never when it is real." ["Huck's Free Pass," *Slate*, 1/21/08]

"The one thing that the racist can never manage is anything like discrimination: He is indiscriminate by definition." [*Hitch-22* (New York: Twelve, 2010), 266]

"It would be or ought to be dangerous if we ever get to the point where the charge of racism becomes so overused and hackneyed as to be meaningless. Such a term ought to retain its potency as a weapon of shame and disapproval." ["From the N-Word to Code Words," *Slate*, 9/20/10]

Radicals

"The real test of a radical or a revolutionary is not the willingness to confront the orthodoxy and arrogance of the rulers but the readiness to contest illusions and falsehoods among close friends and allies." ["Minority Report," *Nation*, 7/03/89]

". . . In order to be a 'radical' one must be open to the possibility that one's own core assumptions are misconceived." [*Letters to a Young Contrarian* (New York: Basic Books, 2001), 102]

"The only real radicalism in our time will come as it always has—from people who insist on thinking for themselves and who reject party-mindedness." [Quoted in Jamie Glazov, "Frontpage Interview: Christopher Hitchens," *FrontPage Magazine*, 12/10/03]

Radicals and Humor

"It's often said that radicals are humorless; this is certainly not intended as a compliment to the seriousness that they must affect. . . . (By the way, what is often really meant by the supposed humorlessness of their [*sic*] radicals is their supposed inability to laugh at themselves. But why should they accept an invitation to consider their grand schemes absurd?)" [*Letters to a Young Contrarian* (New York: Basic Books, 2001), 119]

"There are times when one wants to hold society's feet to the fire, and to force a confrontation, and to avoid the blandishments of those who always call upon everyone to 'lighten up' and change the subject. I think that many great and stern radicals did not *lack* a sense of humor. . . so much as they felt themselves obliged to be serious." [*Letters to a Young Contrarian* (New York: Basic Books, 2001), 120-121]

Ramadan, Tariq

". . . It's hardly possible to read of a media appearance with Tariq Ramadan that does not describe him as arrestingly handsome and charismatic. No disrespect, of course, but I'd be the first to agree that it can't be his writing that draws the crowd." ["Fundamentals," *Tablet Magazine*, 5/24/10]

Rand, Ayn

". . . The mad philosopher Ayn Rand—a woman who in real life did take and keep a number of younger male disciples, running them ragged until an advanced stage of the game. She wasn't as old as she felt—by the time she had finished she was as old as they felt." ["She's the Real Thing," *Evening Standard*, 8/24/99]

"Nathaniel Branden, it turned out, had been having a torrential affair with Rand, of which both their spouses knew and approved. But then Rand discovered that Branden—'Ben Rand' himself—was having yet another sizzling relationship with a much younger woman. In an epic fury, she covered Branden's face with weals,

excommunicated him from the cult, and put a twenty-year curse on his penis."
["Greenspan Shrugged," *Vanity Fair*, December 2000]

Rationalization

"To be against rationalization is not the same as to be opposed to reasoning." ["A Rejoinder to Noam Chomsky," *Nation* (online), 10/15/01]

Reactionaries

"Reactionaries have a tendency to stick together (and I don't mean 'guilt by association' here. I mean GUILT)." ["Chew on This," *Stranger*, 1/16/03–1/22/03]

Reagan, Ronald

"Ronald Reagan is doing to the country what he can no longer do to his wife." ["Minority Report," *Nation*, 10/30/82]

"It's been obvious for some time that Reagan believes democracy and public scrutiny are incompatible with his foreign policy. There is every reason to suspect that he's right. . . ." ["Minority Report," *Nation*, 4/21/84]

"Even more than his ghastly predecessor, Richard Nixon, the man is a sponge, a fantasist, an obedient projection of the aims and wishes of others. He repeatedly romances even his own petty life story. He's an apology for the autonomous individual, and so are his cronies and his few remaining friends. He represents no saga of Americanism, no test of character, no enduring set of values. Family and church, those recurring standbys of the demagogue, are neglected by him except as rhetorical opportunities. He is a hollow man, and he has been stuffed." ["Minority Report," *Nation*, 10/20/84]

"There may be—there must be—many people who feel that America needed Reagan's kind of shot in the arm. It will take time for them to feel and to recognize it as a shot in the back." ["Minority Report," *Nation*, 10/20/84]

"The essence of the Reagan era has been a combination of unexampled slap-happy greed at home and squalid, surreptitious violence overseas." ["Minority Report," *Nation*, 1/17/87]

"To listen even very briefly to Ronald Reagan is to realize that here is a man upon whose synapses the termites have dined long and well." [*Observer*, 9/13/87]

"Among the many reliefs of a Reagan-free Washington is the relief from having to pretend that Ronald Wilson Reagan was, whatever else you might think of him, a nice guy." ["Nothing Positive," *Times Literary Supplement*, 4/21/89]

"The king of Saudi Arabia knew a great deal more about the working of the Reagan foreign policy and the Reagan White House than any senator or elected official did." ["Tilting Democracy," *Middle East Report*, January/February 1992]

"The fox, as has been pointed out by more than one philosopher, knows many small things, whereas the hedgehog knows one big thing. Ronald Reagan was neither a fox nor a hedgehog. He was as dumb as a stump. He could have had anyone in the world to dinner, any night of the week, but took most of his meals on a White House TV tray. He had no friends, only cronies. His children didn't like him all that much. He met his second wife—the one that you remember—because she needed to get off a Hollywood blacklist, and he was the man to see. Year in and year out in Washington, I could not believe that such a man had even been a poor governor of California in a bad year, let alone that such a smart country would put up with such an obvious phony and loon." ["Not Even a Hedgehog," *Slate*, 6/07/04]

"He wondered aloud about Biblical prophecies of the end of the world, and Armageddon. But his legacy was to have postponed Armageddon, almost without meaning to." ["Movie Star Who Became U.S. President: Impossible to Hate This Lying Crook," *Mirror*, 6/07/04]

Reagan, Ronald and Alzheimer's
"So Reagan has Alzheimer's. How could they tell?" ["Minority Report," *Nation*, 11/28/94]

"Nobody was less surprised than I when Reagan was later found to be suffering from Alzheimer's disease: I believe it will one day be admitted that some of his family and one or two of his physicians had begun to suspect this as early as his first term." [*Hitch-22* (New York: Twelve, 2010), 233]

Reagan, Ronald and Executive Power
"You can read the entire 'Reagan revolution' as a concerted attempt to roll back the gains made by the Fulbright and Church committees in the seventies." ["Reality Time," *Spectator*, 11/29/86]

Reagan, Ronald and John F. Kennedy
". . . The truth is that Reagan has not, in his entire presidency to date, acted with anything like the gun-slinging idiocy that the boy-hero did." ["Kennedy Lies," *Spectator*, 11/19/83]

Reagan, Ronald and Lying
"He lies with such ease and artistry that it has almost become part of his notorious charm." ["'A Bodyguard of Lies,'" *Spectator*, 10/25/86]

". . . Every word he says is a lie, including the words 'and' and 'but.'" ["Minority Report," *Nation*, 11/26/90]

Reagan Administration (1981–1989)
"The Reaganites are naturally strong on law and order—Meese conspicuously so—but when it comes to themselves, they regard the law as a rough guide." ["Minority Report," *Nation*, 4/07/84]

"By the standards of the Reagan administration, it appears that an act is not immoral if it is not illegal." ["Minority Report," *Nation*, 10/06/84]

"As a general rule, they take international condemnation as a compliment." ["Minority Report," *Nation*, 2/28/87]

Reagan Doctrine

"The Reagan doctrine, once so fiercely promulgated, now looks like the pathetic remnant of an era of opportunism." ["Minority Report," *Nation*, 3/05/90]

"There is a persistent, stupid argument about the present wave of human and political emancipation coursing through the Communist world, to the effect that it represents the paternity and posterity of the Reagan doctrine. If that were true, one would expect to see the *contras* and Unita and the Afghan fundamentalists—the only admitted and claimed descendants of a doctrine that can hardly boast of having invented Vaclav Havel—doing very well. Yet the diametrical opposite is the case." ["Minority Report," *Nation*, 3/05/90]

Reaganomics

". . . Reagan's economic policy is not a racialist one. It demoralizes and damages *all* poor people regardless of color, creed, or national origin." ["Minority Report," *Nation*, 10/16/82]

"For them [Reaganites], economics is not so much a branch of morality as morality is a branch of economics. Some would say that that was capitalism for you." ["Minority Report," *Nation*, 11/27/82]

"Reaganism, already a waning memory, was never much more than a fraud, based on a three-credit-card trick and appealing principally to hedonism and credulity. Taxes would not go up, but everybody would be better-off, and there would be a morale-boosting boom in military spending." ["Credibility Brown," *London Review of Books*, 8/31/89]

Realism and Realpolitik

"Generally, it must be said that realpolitik has been better at dividing than at ruling. Take it as a whole since Kissinger called on the Shah in 1972, and see what the harvest has been." ["Why We Are Stuck in the Sand," *Harper's*, January 1991]

"States and superpowers cannot only be moral individuals, and even moral individuals may need to make shabby compromises for survival, and there may be an occasional need to practice realpolitik for pressing military reasons, but in all cases it is necessary to be aware that one is doing so. Don't make a habit of it, in other words." ["The Brother Karimov," *Slate*, 6/01/05]

"Any critique of realism has to begin with a sober assessment of the horrors of peace." ["Realism in Darfur," *Slate*, 11/07/05]

Reason

". . . If you can't reason from effect to cause, you will lose the ability to reason from cause to effect." ["Whatever You Do, Don't Mention Sex in America," *Evening Standard*, 1/23/98]

Redgrave, Vanessa

"In the popular mind, Vanessa Redgrave is probably the archetypal Cannes-one-minute-and-Nicaragua-the-next, Oscar-ceremony-grandstanding, petition-signing Hecuba and banshee of all time. Groupie of the Palestinians; sob sister for

this and that; daughter of privilege; can't be content with unpublicized opinions."
["Vintage Vanessa," *Vanity Fair*, December 1994]

Reed, Ralph
". . . A youth who combines a gender-free appearance with a seductive line in Insincerity 101. . . ." ["Minority Report," *Nation*, 10/09/95]

Regan, Donald
"Donald Regan differs from me in that he thinks that astrology discredits the First Family rather than the other way around." ["Muddy Insights from an Ex-Grand Vizier," *Newsday*, 5/25/88]

"Donald Regan can't write, and neither can his 'collaborator' Charles McCarry. What's more, Donald Regan can barely think and can scarcely read." ["Muddy Insights from an Ex-Grand Vizier," *Newsday*, 5/25/88]

Regan, Donald and Ronald Reagan
". . . Regan thinks Reagan is a poor henpecked sleepwalker and Reagan thinks Regan is an opportunist, nasty coward. I predict with confidence that both men will turn out to be absolutely right." ["Muddy Insights from an Ex-Grand Vizier," *Newsday*, 5/25/88]

Regime Change
"It is now quite well understood that those who wish to replace a popular government by force must proceed carefully." [*Cyprus* (London: Quartet Books, 1984), 67]

"You want to change our regime? No, we'll change yours." [Quoted in "Christopher Hitchens: Off the Cuff, in His Own Words," *Georgetowner*, 5/27/04]

". . . Once one has announced that someone is another Hitler, further coexistence with him becomes impossible, and the overthrow of his regime is morally necessitated." ["Theater of War," *Claremont Review of Books*, Winter 2006]

Regulation
". . . Regulation is the engine of influence-peddling and backstairs dealing in the capital because it furnishes business and politics with a nexus of rules and fine print that it takes an expert to violate." ["Dissecting America's Sullied Democracy," *Newsday*, 4/15/92]

Reincarnation
"The most fashionable new delusion involves one or another form of belief in reincarnation. Karma is big these days, and those who regard their bodies and brains as disposable and replaceable 'vehicles'. . . are as goofily sincere as those who believe they get a better model with each trade-in from Detroit." ["Heavenly Hoax," *Nation*, 5/12/97]

Relativism
"In the mind of many socialists, cultural relativism has become such an anchor of certainty and principle that it would be physically painful to haul it in." ["Siding with Rushdie," *London Review of Books*, 10/26/89]

Religion

"... Many people will deride a man's tendency to wishful thinking until they reach the 'private matter' of his religion." ["The Lord and the Intellectuals," *Harper's*, July 1982]

"Since it is obviously inconceivable that all religions can be right, the most reasonable conclusion is that they are all wrong." ["The Lord and the Intellectuals," *Harper's*, July 1982]

"What we have to face as an enemy is not any particular religion but the slavish, credulous mentality upon which all religious and superstitious movements feed." [*In These Times*, 11/16/83–11/22/83]

"If only religion *were* an opiate. No known narcotic rots the brain so fast." ["Extremists on Whose Side?," *Nation*, 3/18/96]

"If you have ever argued with a religious devotee... you will have noticed that his self-esteem and pride are involved in the dispute, and that you are asking him to give up something more than a point in argument." [*Letters to a Young Contrarian* (New York: Basic Books, 2001), 28]

"Religion of every kind involves the promise that the misery and futility of existence can be overcome or even transfigured. One might suppose that the possession of such a magnificent formula, combined with the tremendous assurance of a benevolent God, would make a person happy. But such appears not to be the case: unease and insecurity and rage seem to keep up with blissful certainty, and even to outpace it." ["Holy Writ," *Atlantic Monthly*, April 2003]

"There still remain four irreducible objections to religious faith: that it wholly misrepresents the origins of man and the cosmos, that because of this original error it manages to combine the maximum of servility with the maximum of solipsism, that it is both the result and the cause of dangerous sexual repression, and that it is ultimately grounded on wish-thinking." [*God Is Not Great* (New York: Twelve, 2007), 4]

"Religious faith is, precisely *because* we are still-evolving creatures, ineradicable. It will never die out, or at least not until we get over our fear of death, and of the dark, and of the unknown, and of each other. For this reason, I would not prohibit it even if I thought I could. Very generous of me, you may say. But will the religious grant me the same indulgence?" [*God Is Not Great* (New York: Twelve, 2007), 12]

"Religion comes from the period of human prehistory where nobody... had the smallest idea what was going on. It comes from the bawling and fearful infancy of our species, and is a babyish attempt to meet our inescapable demand for knowledge (as well as for comfort, reassurance, and other infantile needs)." [*God Is Not Great* (New York: Twelve, 2007), 64]

"The brilliant Schiller was wrong in his *Joan of Arc* when he said that 'against stupidity the gods themselves contend in vain.' It is actually by *means* of the gods that we make our stupidity and gullibility into something ineffable." [*God Is Not Great* (New York: Twelve, 2007), 77]

"Those who become bored by conventional 'Bible' religions, and seek 'enlightenment' by way of the dissolution of their own critical faculties into nirvana in any form, had better take a warning. They may think they are leaving the realm of despised materialism, but they are still being asked to put their reason to sleep, and to discard their minds along with their sandals." [*God Is Not Great* (New York: Twelve, 2007), 204]

"One definite way to prove that we are half a chromosome away from being chimpanzees is to look at our religious practices." [Quoted in Gregg LaGambina, "Christmas with Christopher Hitchens," *A. V. Club*, 12/20/07]

"If we stay with animal analogies for a moment, owners of dogs will have noticed that, if you provide them with food and water and shelter and affection, they will think you are god. Whereas owners of cats are compelled to realize that, if you provide them with food and water and shelter and affection, they draw the conclusion that *they* are god. (Cats may sometimes share the cold entrails of a kill with you, but this is just what a god might do if he was in a good mood.) Religion, then, partakes of equal elements of the canine and the feline. It exacts maximum servility and abjection, requiring you to regard yourself as conceived and born in sin and owing a duty to a stern creator. But in return, it places you at the center of the universe and assures you that you are the personal object of a heavenly plan." [Introduction to *The Portable Atheist* (New York: Da Capo Press, 2007), xvi]

"The theist can opt to be a mere deist, and to say that the magnificence of the natural order strongly implies an ordering force. . . . But the religious person *must* go further and say that this creative force is also an intervening one: one that cares for our human affairs and is interested in what we eat and with whom we have sexual relations, as well as in the outcomes of battles and wars. To assert this is quite simply to assert more than any human can possibly claim to know, and thus it fails, and should be discarded, and should have been discarded long ago." [Introduction to *The Portable Atheist* (New York: Da Capo Press, 2007), xviii-xix]

"We are unlikely to cease making gods or inventing ceremonies to please them for as long as we are afraid of death, or of the dark, and for as long as we persist in self-centeredness. That could be a lengthy stretch of time." [Introduction to *The Portable Atheist* (New York: Da Capo Press, 2007), xxiii]

"Religion is, after all, more than the belief in a supreme being. It is the cult of that supreme being and the belief that his or her wishes have been made known or can be determined." [Introduction to *The Portable Atheist* (New York: Da Capo Press, 2007), xxiii]

"But the original problem with religion is that it is our first, and our worst, attempt at explanation. It is how we came up with answers before we had any evidence. It belongs to the terrified childhood of our species, before we knew about germs or could account for earthquakes. It belongs to our childhood, too, in the less charming sense of demanding a tyrannical authority: a protective parent who demands compulsory love even as he exacts a tithe of fear." ["A Templeton Conversation: Does Science Make Belief in God Obsolete?," John Templeton Foundation, May 2008]

"With religious people it is possible to spend a long time in discussion without ever discovering precisely what role they believe the supernatural to play in our lives. And no two claims are ever quite the same—further proof that the whole religious enterprise is improvised by primates." [Debate with Kenneth R. Miller ("Does Science Make Belief in God Obsolete?"), John Templeton Foundation, 2008]

"People ask, do you mean religion poisons aerobic dancing? Chess? Tantric sex? And I say yes—it does. Religion attacks us in our deepest integrity by saying we wouldn't be able to make a moral decision without it, and that a supernatural dictatorship is our only hope. That makes us all into serfs. And chess and Tantric sex and Chinese food are pointless if you must enjoy them as a serf." [Quoted in "Heathens Above," *Sydney Morning Herald*, 10/02/09]

"We are pattern-seeking primates, and religion was our first attempt to make sense of nature and the cosmos. This does not give us permission, however, to go on pretending that religion is other than man-made." ["What We Were Reading: 2006," *Guardian*, 12/05/09]

"Religion forces nice people to do unkind things and also makes intelligent people say stupid things. Handed a small baby for the first time, is it your first reaction to think, 'Beautiful, almost perfect—now please hand me the sharp stone for its genitalia that I may do the work of the Lord'?" [Debate with Tony Blair ("Be it resolved, religion is a force for good in the world"), Roy Thomson Hall, Toronto, Canada, 11/26/10]

Religion (Arguments for)

"Like elements of the same universe flying apart, the arguments for God and the arguments in favor of religion are now almost completely separated from their origins and from each other. There are those who believe in God but not in religion, and those who believe in religion but not in God. Many people who belong to no church, and who are even hostile to organized faith, profess a belief in God because, in the usual phrase, it gives their life meaning. (This is of course subject to the same grand regress as the creationist argument: just as we have to ask who then created the Creator, so we're bound to ask if God's life has meaning and, if so, from what deity He or She derives it.)" ["Mr. Universe," *Vanity Fair*, December 1992]

"If I made a concession in an argument with the religious, it would be this: I am willing to admit that there may be unknowable things." ["The Future of an Illusion," *Daedalus*, Summer 2003]

"The charitable instinct, or the prompting of compassion, is one thinkable defense of the religious mentality. But this is undermined and corrupted by definition if it solicits money that's already been compulsorily raised by law." ["God and Man in the White House," *Vanity Fair*, August 2003]

"The best ones [arguments for religion] argue that there can't be an uncaused cause. But even if it was valid, this wouldn't get you further than deism." [Quoted in George Eaton, "Interview: Christopher Hitchens," *New Statesman*, 7/12/10]

Religion and Bigotry

"For most of human history, religion and bigotry have been two sides of the same coin, and it still shows." ["Cartoon Debate," *Slate*, 2/04/06]

". . . The very most that can be said for religion in the grave matter of abolition [of slavery] is that after many hundreds of years, and having both imposed and postponed the issue until self-interest had led to a horrifying war, it finally managed to undo some small part of the damage and misery that it had inflicted in the first place." [*God Is Not Great* (New York: Twelve, 2007), 179]

"The chance that someone's religious belief would cause him or her to take a stand against slavery and racism was statistically quite small. But the chance that someone's religious belief would cause him or her to uphold slavery and racism was statistically extremely high, and the latter fact helps us to understand why the victory of simple justice took so long to bring about." [*God Is Not Great* (New York: Twelve, 2007), 180]

". . . If someone publicly charges that 'Mormonism is a cult,' it is impossible to say that the claim by itself is mistaken or untrue. However, if the speaker says that heaven is a real place but that you will not get there if you are Jewish, or that Mormonism is a cult and a false religion but that other churches and faiths are the genuine article, then you know that the bigot has spoken." ["Three Questions About Rick Warren's Role in the Inauguration," *Slate*, 12/19/08]

Religion and Censorship

"The force that is the main source of hatred is also the main caller for censorship." [Debate ("Be It Resolved: Freedom of Speech Includes the Freedom to Hate"), University of Toronto, Toronto, Canada, 11/15/06]

"All religions take care to silence or to execute those who question them (and I choose to regard this recurrent tendency as a sign of their weakness rather than their strength)." [*God Is Not Great* (New York: Twelve, 2007), 125]

"I have no right to claim past philosophers as putative ancestors of atheism. I do, however, have the right to point out that because of religious intolerance we cannot know what they really thought privately, and were very nearly prevented from learning what they wrote publicly." [*God Is Not Great* (New York: Twelve, 2007), 263–264]

Religion and Charity

". . . When the requirements of dogma clash with the needs of the poor, it is the latter that give way." [*The Missionary Position* (New York: Verso, 1995), 46]

"Nine times out of ten, in debate with a cleric, one will be told not of some dogma of religious certitude but of some instance of charitable or humanitarian work undertaken by a religious person. . . . My own response has been to issue a challenge: name me an ethical statement made or an action performed by a believer that could not have been made or performed by a non-believer. As yet, I have had no takers. (Whereas, oddly enough, if you ask an audience to name a wicked statement or action directly attributable to religious faith, nobody has any difficulty in finding an example.)" [Introduction to *The Portable Atheist* (New York: Da Capo Press, 2007), xiii-xiv]

Religion and Children

". . . The religious want religion in the schools because there, unlike the *milieux* of adult life, they can hope for a captive and malleable audience of the sort on which they have traditionally relied." ["God at Work," *Free Inquiry*, Spring 2000]

". . . To become a hardened exploiter of children as part of your vocation, and to be defended by a coalition of stone-faced, ignorant patriarchs and hysterical virgins, is a privilege known only to the most devout." ["Pedophilia's Double Standard," *Free Inquiry*, Summer 2002]

". . . Both in theory and in practice, religion uses the innocent and the defenseless for the purposes of experiment." [*God Is Not Great* (New York: Twelve, 2007), 51]

"Indoctrination of the young often has the reverse effect, as we also know from the fate of many secular ideologies, but it seems that the religious will run this risk in order to imprint the average boy or girl with enough propaganda. What else can they hope to do? If religious instruction were not allowed until the child had attained the age of reason, we would be living in a quite different world." [*God Is Not Great* (New York: Twelve, 2007), 219-220]

"If anyone came to my door as a babysitter wearing holy orders, I'd call first a cab and then the police." [Intelligence Squared Debate ("The Catholic Church Is a Force for Good in the World"), Methodist Central Hall Westminster, Oxford, UK, 10/19/09]

Religion and Death

"Religion will die out when we stop worrying about death." [Quoted in Gregg LaGambina, "Christmas with Christopher Hitchens," *A. V. Club*, 12/20/07]

Religion and Freedom

"Freedom from religion is also a fundamental right—the right to be secular, not to be bothered by it." [*Scarborough Country*, MSNBC, 12/18/04]

"All major confrontations over the right to free thought, free speech, and free inquiry have taken the same form—of a religious attempt to assert the literal and limited mind over the ironic and inquiring one." [*God Is Not Great* (New York: Twelve, 2007), 258]

"Any fool can think of an example where freedom exists without religion—and even more easily of an instance where religion exists without (or in negation of) freedom." ["Holy Nonsense," *Slate*, 12/06/07]

Religion and Health

"The connection between religious faith and mental disorder is, from the viewpoint of the tolerant and the 'multicultural,' both very obvious and highly unmentionable." [*God Is Not Great* (New York: Twelve, 2007), 53]

Religion and Hypocrisy

"Nothing optional—from homosexuality to adultery—is ever made punishable unless those who do the prohibiting (and exact the fierce punishments) have a repressed desire to participate." [*God Is Not Great* (New York: Twelve, 2007), 40]

"Bishop Eddie Long of the New Birth Missionary Baptist Church in Georgia preaches that Bayard Rustin was a vile sinner who suffered from the curable 'disease' of homosexuality. I have a rule of thumb for such clerics and have never known it to fail: Set your watch and sit back, and pretty soon they will be found sprawling lustily on the floor of the men's room." ["God's Bigmouths," *Slate*, 9/27/10]

Religion and Law

"Religion is the worst possible excuse for any exception to the common law. Mormons may not have polygamous marriage, female circumcision is a federal crime in this country, and in some states Christian Scientists face prosecution if they neglect their children by denying them medical care." ["In Your Face," *Slate*, 5/10/10]

Religion and Morality

". . . Religion is not just incongruent with morality but in essential ways incompatible with it." ["Moore's Law," *Slate*, 8/27/03]

". . . Religion has caused innumerable people not just to conduct themselves no better than others, but to award themselves permission to behave in ways that would make a brothel-keeper or an ethnic cleanser raise an eyebrow." [*God Is Not Great* (New York: Twelve, 2007), 6]

". . . Religion is—because it claims a special divine exemption for its practices and beliefs—not just amoral but immoral." [*God Is Not Great* (New York: Twelve, 2007), 52]

"All three monotheisms, just to take the most salient example, praise Abraham for being willing to hear voices and then to take his son Isaac for a long and rather mad and gloomy walk. And then the caprice by which his murderous hand is finally stayed is written down as divine mercy." [*God Is Not Great* (New York: Twelve, 2007), 53]

". . . It is surely insulting to the people of Moses to imagine that they had come this far under the impression that murder, adultery, theft, and perjury were permissible." [*God Is Not Great* (New York: Twelve, 2007), 99]

"The argument that religious belief improves people, or that it helps to civilize society, is one that people tend to bring up when they have exhausted the rest of their case." [*God Is Not Great* (New York: Twelve, 2007), 184]

". . . Virtuous behavior by a believer is no proof at all of—indeed is not even an argument for—the truth of his belief." [*God Is Not Great* (New York: Twelve, 2007), 184–185]

"The worse the offender, the more devout he turns out to be." [*God Is Not Great* (New York: Twelve, 2007), 192]

"Human decency is not derived from religion. It precedes it." [*God Is Not Great* (New York: Twelve, 2007), 266]

"If you credit any one religion with motivating good deeds, how (without declaring yourself to be sectarian) can you avoid crediting them all?" ["An Atheist Responds," *Washington Post*, 7/14/07]

"Yet, I keep being asked, by good and anxious people, how we would teach morality in the absence of God. This question has two minor implications. It first shows a lack of confidence among believers, as if they half know that faith is weak, and suspect that morality might also be so. Second, it insults unbelievers, as if we infidels might at any moment give ourselves over to slaughter and rapine." ["Finding Morals Under Empty Heavens," *Science & Spirit*, July/August 2007]

"Can you name any right action or moral thought, performed or uttered by a religious person, which could not have been performed or uttered by an unbeliever? So far, I have had no takers." ["Finding Morals Under Empty Heavens," *Science & Spirit*, July/August 2007]

". . . The working assumption is that we should have no moral compass if we were not somehow in thrall to an unalterable and unchallengeable celestial dictatorship. What a repulsive idea! . . . [I]t constitutes a radical attack on the very concept of human self-respect. It does so by suggesting that one could not do a right action or avoid a wrong one, except for the hope of a divine reward or the fear of divine retribution." [Introduction to *The Portable Atheist* (New York: Da Capo Press, 2007), xvi]

"It is belief in the supernatural that can make otherwise decent people do things that they would otherwise shrink from—such as mutilating the genitals of children, frightening infants with talk of hellfire, forbidding normal sexual practices, blaming all Jews for 'deicide,' applauding suicide-murderers, and treating women as Paul or Muhammad thought they should be treated." [*Is Christianity Good for the World?* (Moscow, ID: Canon Press, 2008), 36]

"All deities have been hailed by their subjects as the fount of good behavior, just as they have been used as the excuse for inexcusable behavior." [*Is Christianity Good for the World?* (Moscow, ID: Canon Press, 2008), 59]

". . . It is precisely those who think they have divine permission who are truly capable of any atrocity. . . ." [*Hitch-22* (New York: Twelve, 2010), 331]

Religion and Natural Disasters

"When the earthquake hits, or the tsunami inundates, or the twin towers ignite, you can see and hear the secret satisfaction of the faithful. Gleefully they strike up: 'You see, this is what happens when you don't listen to us!'" [*God Is Not Great* (New York: Twelve, 2007), 60]

Religion and Peace
"If religion is so goddamned peaceful, then why are we fighting zealots and fundamentalists on so many fronts?" ["God and Man in the White House," *Vanity Fair*, August 2003]

"I want to maintain that there is no such thing as a religion of peace, by definition." [Debate with Tariq Ramadan ("Is Islam a Religion of Peace?"), 92nd Street Y, New York City, NY, 10/05/10]

"Demands that you believe the impossible do not lead to peaceful outcomes." [Debate with Tariq Ramadan ("Is Islam a Religion of Peace?"), 92nd Street Y, New York City, NY, 10/05/10]

Religion and Politics
"Yes. Religion helped Bobby Kennedy win votes. The trouble is that George Wallace was also forever using his flock." ["The Lord and the Intellectuals," *Harper's*, July 1982]

"Religious ideas, supposedly private matters between man and god, are in practice always political ideas." [*The Monarchy: A Critique of Britain's Favorite Fetish* (London: Chatto & Windus Ltd, 1990), 26]

"Humans should not worship other humans at all, but if they must do so it is better that the worshipped ones do not occupy any positions of political power." [*The Monarchy: A Critique of Britain's Favorite Fetish* (London: Chatto & Windus Ltd, 1990), 39]

Religion and Populism
"Almost all religions from Buddhism to Islam feature either a humble prophet or a prince who comes to identify with the poor, but what is this if not populism? It is hardly a surprise if religions choose to address themselves first to the majority who are poor and bewildered and uneducated." [*God Is Not Great* (New York: Twelve, 2007), 115]

Religion and Power
"Religion, in some form, is necessary to temporal ruling elites, so that they can convince themselves that they rule in the interest of all." ["Minority Report," *Nation*, 9/22/84]

"Religion is, and always has been, a means of control. Some of those who recommend religion—I am thinking of the school of Leo Strauss—are blunt enough to make this point explicit: it may be myth and mumbo-jumbo, but it's very useful for keeping order." [*Letters to a Young Contrarian* (New York: Basic Books, 2001), 64–65]

"His [God's] kingdom, as the Christians say, is not of this world. But in which world does religion actually exact the demand for obedience? In this one. How confoundedly odd." ["The Future of an Illusion," *Daedalus*, Summer 2003]

"It [religion] *must* seek to interfere with the lives of nonbelievers, or heretics, or adherents of other faiths. It may speak about the bliss of the next world, but it wants power in this one." [*God Is Not Great* (New York: Twelve, 2007), 17]

"And the worst excuse ever invented for the exertion of power by one primate over another is the claim that certain primates have God on their side. It is not only justifiable to be impatient and contemptuous when such tyrannies are proposed; it's more like a duty." ["What We Were Reading: 2006," *Guardian*, 12/05/09]

Religion and Race

"The unspoken agreement to concede the black community to the sway of the pulpit is itself a form of racist condescension." ["Identity Crisis," *Slate*, 1/07/08]

"The easiest way to gain instant acceptance as a black 'leader' these days is to shove the word *Reverend* in front of your name. Or, if you are really greedy and ambitious, the word *Bishop*." ["God's Bigmouths," *Slate*, 9/27/10]

". . . There is something especially horrible about the way in which the black pulpit gets a sort of free pass, almost as if white society has assured itself that black Americans just love them some preaching. In this fog of ethnic condescension, it is much easier for mountebanks and demagogues to get away with it." ["God's Bigmouths," *Slate*, 9/27/10]

Religion and Science

". . . What a difference when one lays aside the strenuous believers and takes up the no less arduous work of a Darwin, say, or a Hawking or a Crick. These men are more enlightening when they are wrong, or when they display their inevitable biases, than any falsely modest person of faith who is vainly trying to square the circle and to explain how he, a mere creature of the Creator, can possibly know what that Creator intends. . . . If you read Hawking on the 'event horizon,' that theoretical lip of the 'black hole' over which one could in theory plunge and see the past and the future. . . I shall be surprised if you can still go on gaping at Moses and his unimpressive 'burning bush.'" [*God Is Not Great* (New York: Twelve, 2007), 8]

"A modern believer can say and even believe that his faith is quite compatible with science and medicine, but the awkward fact will always be that both things have a tendency to break religion's monopoly, and have often been fiercely resisted for that reason." [*God Is Not Great* (New York: Twelve, 2007), 47]

"Thanks to the telescope and the microscope, it [religion] no longer offers an explanation of anything important. Where once it used to be able, by its total command of a worldview, to *prevent* the emergence of rivals, it can now only impede and retard—or try to turn back—the measurable advances that we have made." [*God Is Not Great* (New York: Twelve, 2007), 282]

Religion and Sex

". . . Merely to survey the history of sexual dread and proscription, as codified by religion, is to be met with a very disturbing connection between extreme prurience and extreme repression. Almost every sexual impulse has been made the occasion for prohibition, guilt, and shame. Manual sex, oral sex, anal sex, non-missionary position sex: to name it is to discover a fearsome ban upon it." [*God Is Not Great* (New York: Twelve, 2007), 53–54]

"Clearly, the human species is designed to experiment with sex. No less clearly, this fact is well-known to the priesthoods." [*God Is Not Great* (New York: Twelve, 2007), 54]

"This is a thing that almost all religions have in common. There's something they hate about the genitalia, especially the female. I don't share this view." [*Red Eye*, Fox News Channel, 5/12/07]

Religion and the Sexes
"A consistent proof that religion is man-made and anthropomorphic can also be found in the fact that it is usually 'man' made, in the sense of masculine, as well." [*God Is Not Great* (New York: Twelve, 2007), 54]

"Determined women. . . appear far too seldom in the history of religion." [*God Is Not Great* (New York: Twelve, 2007), 163]

Religion and Solipsism
"Somebody claiming to detect a divine design in respect of himself may phrase the idea in terms of humility, even submissiveness. But this false modesty is, as always with false modesty, a symptom of the most majestic self-centeredness. ('Don't mind me—I'm just busy doing god's work.')" ["The Future of an Illusion," *Daedalus*, Summer 2003]

"But there is a reason why religions insist so much on strange events in the sky, as well as on less quantifiable phenomena such as dreams and visions. All of these things cater to our inborn stupidity, and our willingness to be persuaded against all the evidence that we are indeed the center of the universe and that everything is arranged with us in mind." [Introduction to *The Portable Atheist* (New York: Da Capo Press, 2007), xvii]

"I suppose that one reason I have always detested religion is its sly tendency to insinuate the idea that the universe is designed with 'you' in mind or, even worse, that there is a divine plan into which one fits whether one knows it or not. This kind of modesty is too arrogant for me." [*Hitch-22* (New York: Twelve, 2010), 332–333]

Religion and Torture
"In an era where there was little enough by way of public entertainment, a good public burning or disembowelment or breaking on the wheel was often as much recreation as the saintly dared to allow." [*God Is Not Great* (New York: Twelve, 2007), 218–219]

Religion and Truth
". . . One religious fallacy only reinforces other ones." ["Public Solidarity Does Not Help Humanism," *Free Inquiry*, Summer 2003]

"The faithful believe that certain truths have been 'revealed.' The skeptics and secularists believe that truth is only to be sought by free inquiry and trial and error. Only one of these positions is dogmatic." ["Bullshitting about Atheism," *Free Inquiry*, June/July 2007]

Religion and War

"As is customary with religious wars, both sides were wrong because they were both right." ["Minority Report," *Nation*, 2/14/87]

Religious Convictions

"Once allow that 'religious convictions' are admirable in themselves, and where is the limit? It's not denied that the Reverend Jim Jones gave some purpose and meaning to the (abbreviated) lives of his unhappy followers." ["The Lord and the Intellectuals," *Harper's*, July 1982]

Religious Right

"Our indictment of the religious right is not that it is heartless—a tautology in any case—but that it is brainless." ["Minority Report," *Nation*, 9/22/84]

Repentance

"I am sure there are many who feel that a sinner who repents, no matter how late, is better than a sinner who does not repent at all. Ought we not to be grateful for small mercies? I think not. The time is short, and these mercies are much too small." ["Minority Report," *Nation*, 5/19/84]

Republican Party

"There is a paradox at the very core of the 'new' Republicanism. It is a theory and a practice that distrusts, even hates, the state and the government. But it is also a theory and a practice that believes, even religiously affirms, 'States' Rights.' In a bizarre mutation of Federalism, the foes of the state want to multiply its powers by fifty." ["Newtopia," *London Review of Books*, 8/24/95]

Reputation

"Our culture judges actions by reputation and not reputation by actions." ["The Clinton Years: How Was He for You?," *Observer*, 1/07/01]

Responsibility

"These days, if a public figure 'accepts responsibility'—like Janet Reno disingenuously claiming it for the Waco massacre—it is only as a means of evading it." ["The Death of Shame," *Vanity Fair*, March 1996]

Resurrection

"The action of a man who volunteers to die for his fellow creatures is universally regarded as noble. The extra claim not to have 'really' died makes the whole sacrifice tricky and meretricious. (Thus, those who say 'Christ died for my sins,' when he did not really 'die' at all, are making a statement that is false in its own terms.) Having no reliable or consistent witnesses, in anything like the time period needed to certify such an extraordinary claim, we are finally entitled to say that we have a right, if not an obligation, to respect ourselves enough to disbelieve the whole thing." [*God Is Not Great* (New York: Twelve, 2007), 143]

Revelation

"A further difficulty is the apparent tendency of the Almighty to reveal himself only to unlettered and quasi-historical individuals, in regions of Middle Eastern wasteland that were long the home of idol worship and superstition, and in many instances already littered with existing prophecies." [*God Is Not Great* (New York: Twelve, 2007), 98]

Revisionism

"Revisionism, like heresy, is hard to imbibe in small sips. Once get hold of the notion that you alone stand between the public and a falsified history and there are few impermissible vanities." ["Re-Bunking," *Grand Street*, Summer 1986]

"So even on the wilder shores, it remains true that to be a revisionist incurs the risk of being revised." ["Whose History Is It?," *Vanity Fair*, December 1993]

"Cold and detached revision has removed the aura of heroism from many luminous and legendary events, including the storming of the Bastille, the fall of the Winter Palace, and the publication of the Emancipation Proclamation. Yet new tales arise continually to replace the exploded ones." ["The Medals of His Defeats," *Atlantic Monthly*, April 2002]

Revolution

". . . When a subject people believe that they will outlive an oppressive regime, a revolution has begun." ["Minority Report," *Nation*, 12/21/85]

"The revolutions of the twentieth century are, in many ways, their own justification. There is no case, except perhaps Cambodia, where it can be said that the old regime was preferable or could have been preserved without comparable results." ["Minority Report," *Nation*, 1/25/86]

Rhodes, Cecil

"Other nineteenth century tycoons look rather pallid beside him. Newspaper magnate William Randolph Hearst could orchestrate war fever perhaps, but Rhodes could actually declare one." ["The Empire-Builder Who Plundered Africa," *Newsday*, 11/16/88]

The Right

". . . The chief lesson learned and inculcated on the right—the supposed superiority of the American populist Volk over the untrustworthy and even treasonable intellectuals—is easily shown to be silly, and nasty, and void." ["A Regular Bull," *London Review of Books*, 9/18/97]

"Many liberals believe that there is something essentially mean and resentful about the American Right, and there is good historical support for this proposition, as well as plenty of contemporary illustration." [Introduction to *Left Hooks, Right Crosses: A Decade of Political Writing*, ed. Christopher Caldwell and Christopher Hitchens (New York: Nation Books, 2002), 209]

Rights

"Countries cannot for long have human rights without economic rights. They can very easily have neither, which is a common experience, and there can be countries, for example, that have literacy programs but who dare not give people they have taught to read any books or newspapers." [Quoted in "Promoting Democracy: A Panel Discussion," *Temple Law Quarterly*, Winter 1987]

"Inalienable human right is unique in that it needs no super-human guarantee; no 'fount' except itself." [*The Monarchy: A Critique of Britain's Favorite Fetish* (London: Chatto & Windus Ltd, 1990), 42]

"As it happens, there is no solution to the historic contradiction between individual rights and social responsibilities." ["Selfishness Masquerading as Individual Rights," *Newsday*, 8/28/91]

"Either the concept of 'right' has meaning or it is a selfish and solipsistic claim made by needy humans, with no objective basis for its assertion." [*Thomas Paine's Rights of Man: A Biography* (New York: Atlantic Monthly Press, 2006), 90–91]

Roberts, Oral

"One had only to look at the peerlessly fatuous face of an Oral Roberts, for example, to realize that the human race must be the product of evolution. None but the most heartlessly irresponsible deity would have 'created' him like that. . . ." ["Minority Report," *Nation*, 10/04/86]

Robertson, Pat

"'Pat' argues, with complete seriousness, that the numbers 666 will soon be stamped on the hand and forehead of every person on earth, but he urges people to cheer up because the reign of the anti-Christ is the antechamber to the reign of people like himself." ["Minority Report," *Nation*, 10/04/86]

Role Models

"What *is* this expression? Why does it receive such uncritical acceptance? Its whole sound is inauthentic and contrived, and so is its effect. Just like those who believe that religion gives people a 'value system' or a 'meaning' to their lives, the role-model promulgators appear to think that a *Führerprinzip* is necessary for the shaping of the young. So we have a succession of tripwire narcissists being overpaid by their sponsors to act paternal and nurturing for as long as the cameras are switched on. As with religion, in the end this only means that parents have more explaining to do rather than (as they had slothfully hoped) less." ["Minority Report," *Nation*, 7/25/94–8/01/94]

"Our current culture, with its stupid emphasis on the 'role model,' offers as examples the lives of superstars and princesses and other pseudo-ethereal beings whose lives—fortunately, I think—cannot by definition be emulated." [*Letters to a Young Contrarian* (New York: Basic Books, 2001), 93]

Roman Empire

"Much can be divined about any individual, however outwardly complex, from his or her explanation of the decline of the Roman Empire." [*Blood, Class and Empire* (New York: Nation Books, 2004), 22]

Romania

"Timisoara is a superficially uninteresting town with a dull, routine Stalinist design. The box-like buildings even have generic names stencilled on the outside: 'Hotel,' 'Restaurant,' 'Cultural Centre.'. . . What a terrible place to die, I thought grotesquely, especially if you feared you might be doing it for nothing. On the other hand, a perfect place for concluding that you had little or nothing to lose." ["On the Road to Timisoara," *Granta*, Spring 1990]

Romanticism

"There is a protean quality to the 'Romantic' attribution; no sooner is it defined than it begins to dissolve." ["Don't Listen to Reason," *New York Times*, 11/19/00]

"It was an axiom of the Romantics that there were skulls beneath the skin, that flowers sprouted on graves and dunghills, and that good and evil flourished upon the same stem. A very slight kink or flaw in this perspective might allow a man to conclude that, since society was innately hypocritical and two-faced, he was entitled to be the same way himself." ["Bad Guy Number One," *New York Review of Books*, 5/31/01]

". . . The death of the young is the essential ingredient of romanticism." ["If JFK Had Lived Much Longer, He'd Have Been Puffy, Poxy, Jumpy and Incontinent," *Mirror*, 11/22/03]

"Our perhaps forgivable tendency to group the Romantic tribe of early nineteenth-century poets under a single collective title is a disservice both to history and to literature." ["An Introduction to the Poetry of Percy Bysshe Shelley," *Guardian*, 1/28/10]

Roosevelt, Eleanor

"Mrs. Roosevelt was simply introducing principle into politics, always trying to get her husband to do the unpopular or uncommercial thing. Whatever one thinks about Jim Crow or Republican Spain or desegregation of the Armed Forces, these were positions that required courage, and required her urging courage and principle on her husband." ["Is Hillary Clinton Eleanor Roosevelt?," *American Enterprise*, July/August 2000]

Roosevelt, Franklin Delano

"Every time Roosevelt extended the least support to the anti-Hitler policy of his supposed friend, he exacted an immense and immediate price. . . . If you add to this the fact that it was massive rearmament, and not the New Deal, that pulled America out of the slump then you can indeed hold Roosevelt responsible for the empire, the national security state and the military-industrial complex—the foundations of 'big government.' This gave the rest of the globe a bit more to fear than fear itself." ["F.D.R.—the Good, the Bad and the Banal," *Nation*, 5/26/97]

"FDR the good. . . was the friend of collective bargaining, the foe (at least in rhetoric) of the lawless cartels and the hate-object of the Jew-baiters and Nazi fellow travelers. At least he had some of the right enemies, even if he didn't do enough to earn them." ["F.D.R.—the Good, the Bad and the Banal," *Nation*, 5/26/97]

". . . The conservatives thought Franklin Roosevelt was a communist, even as he saved capital from itself by means of the National Recovery Act." [*No One Left to Lie To* (New York: Verso, 2000), 79]

Roswell, New Mexico
". . . Roswell, New Mexico—the crash site of choice for alien craft from all galaxies." ["Airline Insecurity," *Vanity Fair*, June 1997]

Rushdie, Salman
"By his experiments with language and dialect and his conscription of musical themes, he has approached the closest to poetry in prose." [Foreword to *Unacknowledged Legislation* (New York: Verso, 2000), xiv]

"I never understand why his reputation is so grave when he can be, and is, so consistently funny." ["Hobbes in the Himalayas," *Atlantic Monthly*, September 2005]

"For our time and generation, the great conflict between the ironic mind and the literal mind, the experimental and the dogmatic, the tolerant and the fanatical, is the argument that was kindled by *The Satanic Verses*." ["Assassins of the Mind," *Vanity Fair*, February 2009]

Rushdie, Salman and the Fatwa
"It seems that many respectable people are prepared to be more critical of a novel written by a private individual than they are about a murder threat issued so boldly by a man with state power." ["Now, Who Will Speak for Rushdie?," *New York Times*, 2/17/89]

"In the responses of a liberal society to this direct affront, there has been altogether too much about the offended susceptibilities of the religious and altogether too little about the absolute right of free expression and free inquiry. One can and must be 'absolute' about these. Unlike other absolutisms, they guarantee rather than abridge the rights of all—Khomeini included—to be heard and debated." ["Now, Who Will Speak for Rushdie?," *New York Times*, 2/17/89]

". . . The Muslim extremists have, in two vital senses, demanded the impossible. They have asked the slightly lazy but nonetheless conscious heirs of the Enlightenment to adopt, not the practice (which never dies out, as we know to our cost), but the *principle* of censorship. And they have demanded, for themselves, the smashing of a mirror in which they might glimpse their own reflection." ["Siding with Rushdie," *London Review of Books*, 10/26/89]

"If a like threat had been made against a corporation president, fleets would have been moved portentously around and White House briefers would have appeared gravely on the nightly news, pointing at maps and 'evaluating options.'" ["Siding with Rushdie," *London Review of Books*, 10/26/89]

"This is an all-out confrontation between the ironic and the literal mind: between every kind of commissar and inquisitor and bureaucrat and those who know that, whatever the role of social and political forces, ideas and books have to be formulated and written by individuals." ["Siding with Rushdie," *London Review of Books*, 10/26/89]

"One must side with Salman Rushdie, not because he is an underdog but because there is no other side to be on." ["Siding with Rushdie," *London Review of Books*, 10/26/89]

"Freedom of speech and expression did not fall from the sky. They had to be fought for and they have to be defended. This is payback time." ["Round Two on Rushdie," *Newsday*, 12/03/89]

"Many lazy people when asked, and many vulgar editorialists whether asked or not, will say he brought this on himself by insufficient 'sensitivity' to the feelings of Muslims. To me, the case has always seemed exactly the other way around." ["Minority Report," *Nation*, 3/01/93]

"The Khomeini *fatwa*, as it now appears, was an early warning of a new confrontation as well as a reminder of an old one. For the new confrontation, between religious tolerance and religious bigotry, look in any newspaper. For the old one, see under Galileo, Joyce, Voltaire, Spinoza." ["Minority Report," *Nation*, 3/01/93]

"Make the assumption—surely insulting to many Sunni and Shiite Muslims—that the response of the senile despot Ayatollah Khomeini is the considered reaction of 'a great religion.' Assume, too, that the sole purpose of an elaborate work of fiction is an 'insult.' You are left with the assertion that there is no right to criticize theocracy." ["Satanic Curses," *Nation*, 12/22/97]

"So who will now say that a lone novelist 'brought it all on himself' by 'insulting Islam'? The insult to Islam, as Rushdie and his supporters argued all along, was the assumption that the Muslim culture itself demanded blood sacrifice." ["Monotheist Notes from All Over," *Nation*, 10/19/98]

"The 'offending' phrases occur in the course of a nightmare experienced by a madman. All the excitements of a prohibited book had their usual effect, one of which is to expose the fact that censors don't know what they are talking about." ["The Quiet Triumph," *Guardian*, 2/13/99]

". . . In the week when the Ayatollah Khomeini pronounced a life sentence and a death sentence on Salman Rushdie, there was pandemonium of a different sort. Many of those literati who normally sign *bien pensant* petitions were suddenly remembering pressing appointments elsewhere. One day it will be told—the roster of those friends of free speech who coughed and shuffled their feet." ["Signature Sontag," *Vanity Fair*, March 2000]

Russell, Bertrand

"We can be thankful that Russell was not a Victorian, and that he broke not just the injunctions of morality but the injunction to treat women as brainless." ["The Warrior for Peace as a Rebellious Victorian," *Newsday*, 8/05/92]

Sabbath

". . . Rest periods are not exactly an ethical imperative and are mandated by practicality as much as by heaven." ["The New Commandments," *Vanity Fair*, April 2010]

Saber Rattling

"It's eternally fashionable in Washington (and elsewhere) to contrast 'diplomatic' initiatives with 'saber-rattling' ones. What this naïve dichotomy overlooks is the plain fact that without the known quantity of the American saber, few if any diplomatic movements would be possible, either." ["Dear Mr. President. . . ," *World Affairs*, Winter 2008]

"If there's no saber in the scabbard, then at least don't make the vulgar mistake of rattling it." ["Why Wait to Disarm Iran?," *Slate*, 10/19/09]

Sacred

"And, since the Devil can quote Scripture, it's an easy step to mobilizing the profane in defence of the sacred." ["On the Imagining of Conspiracy," *London Review of Books*, 11/07/91]

"'Is nothing sacred?' *Of course not.*" [Foreword to *Unacknowledged Legislation* (New York: Verso, 2000), xiv]

Said, Edward

"It can be said for Edward Said that he helped make us reconsider our perspectives a little." ["East Is East," *Atlantic Monthly*, March 2007]

Saints

". . . To baptise a human being as a saint is to secure for that person a near-absolute immunity from criticism." ["The Glow Goes from Mother Teresa," *Guardian*, 11/08/94]

Sandinistas

"In numerous respects, the Sandinista revolution *is* its own justification. Despite some exaggerated claims, the achievements in social welfare and education are spectacular and moving. So is the fact that, after half a century and more of tutelage, Nicaragua is no longer a mere 'ditto' to the wishes of the United States. But the only way to justify the gradual emergence of a one-party-state is by continual reference to the neighboring fascisms and the menace of imperialist invasion." ["Nicaragua," *Granta*, Summer 1985]

"Support for the violent overthrow of the Sandinista government was almost a loyalty test for good Americans." ["Minority Report," *Nation*, 3/05/90]

Satan
"The ontological proof of Satan's existence is just as good as that of God's, and the reasons for propitiating him are, on one analysis, slightly more compelling." ["The Lord and the Intellectuals," *Harper's*, July 1982]

Satire
". . . Robed sages since the dawn of time have understood that satire is powerless against the brain-dead." ["F.D.R.—the Good, the Bad and the Banal," *Nation*, 5/26/97]

". . . One should beware of one's own tiny satires." ["God at Work," *Free Inquiry*, Spring 2000]

Scalia, Antonin
"Whether for 'Christ' or not, Scalia is certainly a fool. He should have fewer allies and emulators on the court, not more." ["Catholic Justice," *Slate*, 8/01/05]

Scandals
"Americans are oddly ambivalent about the morality of their politicians. The electorate, from saloon to salon, sets itself up as savvy and cynical. It likes to think and to say that politicians are incompetent, self-interested, and corrupt, only in it for what they can get. Yet let any breath of scandal disturb the scene, and there are pained expressions of shock on all sides, usually leading to sullen demands for a full inquiry." ["Scandals as Part of Politics," *Los Angeles Times*, 7/08/82]

"The big difference, of course, is between sexual scandal and financial scandal. These categories are not exclusive—the very best scandals have lots of both ingredients—but gossip divides most scams into one kind or another." ["Scandals as Part of Politics," *Los Angeles Times*, 7/08/82]

"An ideal scandal is the one that reveals to us what our leaders really think of us; the fools they take us to be and the ease with which they get away with things." ["The Perfect Scandal," *Observer*, 11/12/00]

"If we realized that scandals are revelations of business as usual, instead of interruptions to it, we'd be nearer to what we don't seem to want: to be responsible ourselves rather than to chuckle with glee at revelations of the irresponsibility of our masters." ["The Perfect Scandal," *Observer*, 11/12/00]

Schlesinger, Arthur
"Like Will Rogers, Schlesinger seems never to meet anyone for whom he can't find a good word." ["The Courtier," *Atlantic Monthly*, December 2007]

Schröder, Gerhard
". . . Schröder is a man so sensitive that he recently sought an injunction against a London newspaper for printing speculation about his hair color and his notoriously volatile domestic life." ["Cowboy," *Slate*, 1/27/03]

Science

". . . A commitment to experiment and find evidence is no guarantee of immunity to superstition and worse." [Introduction to *The Portable Atheist* (New York: Da Capo Press, 2007), xxi]

"Those who despise science and learning are not anti-elitist. They are morally and intellectually slothful people who are secretly envious of the educated and the cultured." ["Sarah Palin's War on Science," *Slate*, 10/27/08]

Secession

"All secessions and partitions lead to further secessions and partitions." [Quoted in "Excerpts from Conversation with Hitchens," *National Post*, 11/18/06]

Secrecy

"All worthwhile information in Washington is 'classified' one way or another. We have good reason to be grateful to various officials and reporters who have, in our past, decided that disclosure was in the public interest." ["What Goes Around Comes Around," *Wall Street Journal*, 10/31/05]

Sectarianism

"Sectarianism is conveniently self-generating and can always be counted upon to evoke a reciprocal sectarianism." [*God Is Not Great* (New York: Twelve, 2007), 19]

Secularism

"Secularism is not just a smug attitude. It is a possible way of democratic and pluralistic life that only became thinkable after several wars and revolutions had ruthlessly smashed the hold of the clergy on the state." ["Bush's Secularist Triumph," *Slate*, 11/09/04]

"If you want diversity, you need a secular state with a godless constitution. Secularism is the only guarantee of religious freedom." [Debate with Tariq Ramadan ("Is Islam a Religion of Peace?"), 92nd Street Y, New York City, NY, 10/05/10]

Security

"I was asked to produce a photo identification when buying a ticket for a train to New York. It seemed odd that they would want my picture when I had gone to all the trouble of turning up in person, but once I had produced it I was allowed to carry my unsearched bags straight on to the express." ["Security? It Makes Me Nervous," *Guardian*, 10/03/01]

"Neither within our borders nor outside them are we protected by security forces who are trained to recognize an enemy." ["Knowledge (and Power)," *Nation*, 6/10/02]

"We are, in essence, being asked to trust the state to know best. What reason do we have for such confidence? The agencies entrusted with our protection have repeatedly been shown, before and after the fall of 2001, to be conspicuous for their incompetence and venality." ["Statement: Christopher Hitchens, NSA Lawsuit Client," American Civil Liberties Union, 1/16/06]

"Are we certain that our obsession with 'security' is not in fact making us insecure?" ["Prince Valiant," *Slate*, 3/10/08]

Sedgwick, Peter
". . . Someone who was a trained and hardened skeptic about the worst of the Left as well as an advocate for the best of it." [*Hitch-22* (New York: Twelve, 2010), 89]

Self-Criticism
". . . A society that has no means of criticizing itself will obviously be prone to stagnation and inefficiency, and will seek to remedy these by militarizing life and forbidding dissent even more dramatically." [Introduction to *Rudolf Bahro Interviews Himself*, by Rudolf Bahro, trans. David Fernbach (Nottingham, UK: Spokesman for the New Statesman and the Bertrand Russell Peace Foundation, 1978), 2]

Self-Deprecation
"To deprecate self is one thing, while to denigrate self is masochistic. Without self-deprecation much English literary and academic conversation would become difficult to carry on." ["Moderation or Death," *London Review of Books*, 11/26/98]

"The whole point of self-deprecation is that it disarms: You do not have to be a masochist to know how to practice it." ["Obama's Court Jesters," *Slate*, 5/18/09]

Self-Persuasion
". . . If you have to try and persuade yourself of something, you are probably already very much inclined to doubt or distrust it." [*Hitch-22* (New York: Twelve, 2010), 108]

September 11, 2001
"As before, the deed announces and exposes its 'root cause.' The grievances and animosity predate even the Balfour Declaration, let alone the occupation of the West Bank. They predate the creation of Iraq as a state. The gates of Vienna would have had to fall to the Ottoman jihad before any balm could begin to be applied to these psychic wounds." ["The Fascist Sympathies of the Soft Left," *Spectator*, 9/29/01]

"I am beginning to get irritated by the public-service announcements recorded by various pop-culture icons that implore me not to go out and burn my neighborhood mosque or lynch my local Sudanese grocer. . . . The public doesn't expect praise for refraining from pogroms, but nor does it expect ceaseless injunctions to abstain from them. It's now been three weeks since the United States took a terrific physical and emotional blow; that means it's not a moment too soon to say that the general response has been exemplary." ["We're Not All Stupid," *Guardian*, 10/03/01]

"Anybody could have been a victim of the death-squad attack on the most cosmopolitan city in the world, and thus we must think and act as if we have all been hit." ["Why Blair Has Hit Precisely the Right Note," *Mirror*, 10/04/01]

"... Todd Beamer and a few of his co-passengers, shouting 'Let's roll,' rammed the hijackers with a trolley, fought them tooth and nail, and helped bring down a United Airlines plane, in Pennsylvania, that was speeding toward either the White House or the Capitol. There are no words for real, impromptu bravery like that, which helped save our republic from worse than actually befell." ["Unfairenheit 9/11," *Slate*, 6/21/04]

"The nineteen suicide murderers of New York and Washington and Pennsylvania were beyond any doubt the most sincere believers on those planes. Perhaps we can hear a little less about how 'people of faith' possess moral advantages that others can only envy." [*God Is Not Great* (New York: Twelve, 2007), 32]

"Faith-based fanatics could not design anything as useful or beautiful as a sky-scraper or a passenger aircraft. But, continuing their long history of plagiarism, they could borrow and steal these things and use them as a negation." [*God Is Not Great* (New York: Twelve, 2007), 280]

"The supposed 'feelings' of the 9/11 relatives have already deprived us all of the opportunity to see the real-time footage of the attacks—a huge concession to the general dulling of what ought to be a sober and continuous memory of genuine outrage." ["Mau-Mauing the Mosque," *Slate*, 8/09/10]

Servility
"Regular obedience to orders by people who are just doing their job and don't make the rules is one of those chilling banalities that keeps on coming up. . . . Given the 'right' circumstances, average humans are capable of doing pretty much anything." ["A Monster Inside the Average Man," *Newsday*, 3/25/92]

"The old slogan of the anarchist left used to be that the problem is not those who have the will to command. They will always be there, and we feel we understand where the authoritarians come from. The problem is the will to obey. The prob-lem is the people who want to be pushed around, the people who want to be taken care of, the people who want to be a part of it all, the people who want to be work-ing for a big protective brother." ["Tobacco, Smoking, and Insider Trading," *Cato Policy Report*, March/April 2005]

Sewage
"... Sewage knows no boundaries." [*Letters to a Young Contrarian* (New York: Basic Books, 2001), 108]

Sex
"Here we are in America in 1997. Has there ever been a culture in which so much needless misery and superstition was generated by the question of where babies come from? The lazy term for societies dominated by sexual hypocrisy (always think of it, never speak of it) is 'Victorian.' But the English of those decades were robust and candid compared with the Americans of a century later." ["Dirty Sto-ries," *Nation*, 7/07/97]

"... When sex is difficult and strenuous for chaps, it's also rather hard on girls. . . ." ["It's Magic Darling," *Evening Standard*, 4/28/98]

"Sex has been divorced from procreation to a degree hard to imagine even in 1963. . . ." [Foreword to *Brave New World*, by Aldous Huxley (New York: Harper-Collins, 2004), vii]

"Sexual innocence, which can be charming in the young if it is not needlessly pro-tracted, is positively corrosive and repulsive in the mature adult." [*God Is Not Great* (New York: Twelve, 2007), 227]

Sexual Organs
". . . A distressing human fact—the proximity of the sexual and the excretory or-gans." ["Minority Report," *Nation*, 7/30/90–8/06/90]

"Some feminist theorists who compare the penis to a species of heat-seeking mis-sile are being too flattering as well as too harsh." ["Call of the Wilding," *Vanity Fair*, July 1993]

"'Mother' Nature has so arranged matters that the most crucial [male] organ is the most capricious, and often puts on gravity-defying performances when least required as well as, so to speak, vice versa. Wrestling the thing into some form of predictability is a plus, no error." ["It's Magic Darling," *Evening Standard*, 4/28/98]

"Erections could be like cops: often there when you emphatically didn't require them and sometimes absent when you did. Or so I have been told by friends who thought they could trust me." ["Viagra Falls," *Nation*, 5/25/98]

Shakespeare, William
". . . The greatest plumber of human nature. . . ." ["Viagra Falls," *Nation*, 5/25/98]

"In the foolishness of today, those who say that Shakespeare is for elitists are themselves a somewhat emaciated elite. But there was a time, not long past, when he was the people's poet and playwright, as he had been in his own day." ["Signa-ture Sontag," *Vanity Fair*, March 2000]

Shame
"There is a good reason the words 'shameful' and 'shameless' define the same conduct. You know you've behaved shamefully if you have exposed other people to needless annoyance or embarrassment. You don't know you've behaved shamelessly if you don't get this point." ["The Death of Shame," *Vanity Fair*, March 1996]

"Just as people with blowtorch breath are the ones who are keenest on thrusting their face right into yours as they, so to speak, ram home their point, so people without shame are those with the least gift of reticence." ["The Death of Shame," *Vanity Fair*, March 1996]

Sharpton, Al
". . . Al Sharpton: another person who can get away with anything under the rubric of *Reverend*." ["Faith-Based Fraud," *Slate*, 5/16/07]

Sheehan, Cindy
"Sheehan has obviously taken a short course in the Michael Moore/Ramsey Clark school of Iraq analysis and has not succeeded in making it one atom more elegant or persuasive. I dare say that her 'moral authority' to do this is indeed absolute, if we agree for a moment on the weird idea that moral authority is required to adopt overtly political positions, but then so is my 'moral' right to say that she is spouting sinister piffle." ["Cindy Sheehan's Sinister Piffle," *Slate*, 8/15/05]

"Any citizen has the right to petition the president for redress of grievance, or for that matter to insult him to his face. But the potential number of such people is very large, and you don't have the right to cut in line by having so much free time that you can set up camp near his drive." ["Cindy Sheehan's Sinister Piffle," *Slate*, 8/15/05]

Shopping
"Not only do most men not see the joy in shopping. . . but they don't want to be caught helping out. The image of the man carrying parcels while the wife strips the shelves is right up there with mother-in-law jokes." ["The Men Who Go Shopping with Their Women," *Evening Standard*, 7/24/97]

Shultz, George
"Consider, if you will, the figure of George Shultz. Because he is not, on the face of it, either an ideological fanatic or a pathological liar, he does duty as the official moderate of the Reagan administration. His chief talent is that of being absent when hair-raising and illegal decisions are taken and of remaining adequately uninformed about the nature of such decisions until it is far too late." ["Minority Report," *Nation*, 10/10/87]

Silent Majority
"Silent majorities do not make history. . . ." ["King Billy's Scattered Legions," *New Statesman*, 10/27/72]

Simpson, O. J.
"The title [of his book] is, of course, illiterate to start with ('If I Did It, Here's How It Happened' rather than 'If I Had Done It, Here's How I Would Have') as well as an admission. . . . The only thing that definitely didn't happen, rather like his ongoing search for the real killer, was Simpson bringing in a manuscript and submitting it for publication. He didn't write it, in other words, and wouldn't be able to read it, either." ["Chronicle of a Death Retold," *Wall Street Journal*, 11/20/06]

Sin
". . . The old distinction, between hating the sin and loving the sinner, is in reality a false antithesis." ["Getting Used to It," *Times Literary Supplement*, 11/24/95]

"In Catholic doctrine one is supposed to hate the sin and love the sinner. This can be a distinction without a difference if the 'sin' is to be something (a Jew, a homosexual, even a divorcée) rather than to do something." ["The Permanent Adolescent," *Atlantic Monthly*, May 2003]

Sincerity

". . . It can be exhausting when people assume you are merely being outrageous when in fact your intention is serious and sincere." [Introduction to *Ancient Gonzo Wisdom: Interviews with Hunter S. Thompson*, ed. Anita Thompson (New York: Da Capo Press, 2009), xvi]

The Sixties

"Mention of the 1960s need not and should not be an occasion for sneering, embarrassment, or amnesia. Those who took part, however slightly, helped to break the back of segregation. They helped terminate a criminal colonial war, to hold Congress to account, and to instill a sense of outrage against official corruption and mendacity." ["Minority Report," *Nation*, 10/20/84]

"Who believes everything that he or she believed in 1968?" ["Minority Report," *Nation*, 11/07/87]

"It didn't seem at all abnormal to be involved in about three dramas a day. One had become accustomed to registering the extraordinary." ["The Children of '68," *Vanity Fair*, June 1998]

"Just to blink in 1968, a year in which I always kept a transistor radio by my bed, was to risk missing something that would have kept a 'normal' news cycle going for a month." ["The Children of '68," *Vanity Fair*, June 1998]

"We weren't just serious. We could be solemn. (Excuse me, but this is a *revolution* we are having here.)" ["The Children of '68," *Vanity Fair*, June 1998]

"A country that could convulse over an unjust war, engage in the most profound election of the century, become embattled over civil rights, *and* give birth to a women's movement all at the same time was, I decided there and then, for me." ["The Children of '68," *Vanity Fair*, June 1998]

"Anyone raising his own voice against the nexus and system of deception in 1968 had to count on being defamed and misrepresented in his turn." [Foreword to *1968: War & Democracy*, by Eugene J. McCarthy (Petersham, MA: Lone Oak Press, 2000), 6]

". . . Nothing is more tedious than the front-line recollections of a sixties radical." [*Letters to a Young Contrarian* (New York: Basic Books, 2001), 36]

". . . If you claim to recall the decade you were not really there. (Also, if you lay any claim to have been commemorating the high points of the 60's after a lapse of two further decades there is no proof that you were there, either.)" ["Where Aquarius Went," *New York Times*, 12/19/04]

"To the extent that the decade had a moral seriousness that could be transmitted forward, this inhered in the partly spontaneous opposition to an unjust war in Indochina, and to the coincidence of this movement with the battle for civil rights. To this day, there are people who are convinced that they took part in these struggles just by being young and alive at the time, and who have the beads and the Dylan albums to prove it." ["Where Aquarius Went," *New York Times*, 12/19/04]

"Every now and then, one would hear people talk in mysterious tones about log cabins or geodesic domes on virgin land in Vermont or Montana, and the growing of organic vegetables. . . . There was always a slight embarrassment to be experienced when these would-be Amish came sidling back to town, to resume work in brokerages and banks and universities. To this day, that especially vile reminder of the epoch—the graying and greasy ponytail trailing off the balding pate—is their living memorial." ["Where Aquarius Went," *New York Times*, 12/19/04]

"We didn't grow our hair too long, because we wanted to mingle with the workers at the factory gate and on the housing estates. We didn't 'do' drugs, which we regarded as a pathetic, weak-minded escapism almost as contemptible as religion (as well as a bad habit that could expose us to a 'plant' from the police). Rock and roll and sex were OK. Looking back, I still think we picked the right options." [*Hitch-22* (New York: Twelve, 2010), 89]

Skepticism

"The high ambition. . . seems to me to be this: That one should strive to combine the maximum of impatience with the maximum of skepticism, the maximum of hatred of injustice and irrationality with the maximum of ironic self-criticism. This would mean really deciding to learn from history rather than invoking or sloganizing it." [*Letters to a Young Contrarian* (New York: Basic Books, 2001), 138]

"Membership in the skeptical faction or tendency is not at all a soft option. . . . To be an unbeliever is not to be merely 'open-minded.' It is, rather, a decisive admission of uncertainty that is dialectically connected to the repudiation of the totalitarian principle, in the mind as well as in politics." [*Hitch-22* (New York: Twelve, 2010), 422]

Slogans

". . . 'The New Covenant' (a slogan so treacly in its unction that it died a-borning and is never, ever mentioned even for satirical purposes. Its companion exhortation, 'Putting People First,' is so vacuous that one imagines a careful caucus being convened to design it—presumably when the Animal Rights absolutists were out of the room)." ["Washington Diary," *London Review of Books*, 8/20/92]

"I don't wish to furnish the sort of slogan that might appear on some cheery poster or be used as some uplifting motto." [*Letters to a Young Contrarian* (New York: Basic Books, 2001), 28]

"The old slogans still sometimes strike me as the best ones, and 'Death to Fascism' requires no improvement." [*Hitch-22* (New York: Twelve, 2010), 412]

Smart Weapons

"I don't think that the smartness of the weapon means that it's in any sense any more humane." ["Persian Gulf War," C-SPAN, 2/04/91]

Smith, Joseph

"Like Muhammad, Smith could produce divine revelations at short notice and often simply to suit himself (especially, and like Muhammad, when he wanted a new girl and wished to take her as another wife)." [*God Is Not Great* (New York: Twelve, 2007), 164–165]

"Smith obviously seems like a mere cynic, in that he was never happier than when using his 'revelation' to claim supreme authority, or to justify the idea that the flock should make over their property to him, or to sleep with every available woman." [*God Is Not Great* (New York: Twelve, 2007), 165–166]

". . . Joseph Smith, a convicted fraud and serial practitioner of statutory rape. . . ." ["Holy Nonsense," *Slate*, 12/06/07]

Smoking

"'A smoker' is something you are, not something you do. The idea of a smoking jacket is faintly absurd, but not as absurd as a drinking jacket (though, come to think of it. . .)." ["Smoke Signals," *Independent*, 1/16/94]

"Every smoker knows that he is a dead man on leave (or on leaf, if you'll allow me) and this sits better with the Stoic temperament than it does with the Saturnalian. People have smoked to stay cool, to remain detached, to achieve the contemplative or at worst the world-weary mode. A smoking debauch, though theoretically feasible, is antithetical to the main scheme. Wreathed in faint blue-grey rings, one can idly and even pleasurably reflect upon one's own insignificance." ["Smoke Signals," *Independent*, 1/16/94]

"Since the title of 'smoker' denotes something you are as well as something you do (like 'poet,' for example, or 'dreamer'), I wasn't too surprised to discover a few years ago that it was one of the few pursuits that allowed me to play the active and the passive role simultaneously." ["Smoke and Mirrors," *Vanity Fair*, October 1994]

"Ever since I began lighting up, I have known two things perfectly well. First, it is bad for me as well as good (I'll complete that sentence later on, if I may, which will be about half a pack from now). Second, it is not liked by many people." ["Smoke and Mirrors," *Vanity Fair*, October 1994]

"There are no statistics to prove it, and I wouldn't bore you with them if there were, but cigarettes improve my short-term concentration, aid my digestion, make me a finer writer and a better dinner companion, and, in several other ways, prolong my life." ["Smoke and Mirrors," *Vanity Fair*, October 1994]

". . . The world of smoke is a world of fatalism and irony, while the world of the anti-smoker is a world of certainty, purity, and the literal mind." ["Smoke and Mirrors," *Vanity Fair*, October 1994]

"You want to drink less when you're not smoking. It's one of the many disadvantages about trying to give it up." ["Newspaper Roundtable," C-SPAN, 1/30/98]

"Smoking is a vice, I will admit, but one has to have a hobby." ["On the Limits of Self-Improvement, Part I," *Vanity Fair*, October 2007]

"My keystone addiction is to cigarettes, without which cocktails and caffeine (and food) are meaningless." ["On the Limits of Self-Improvement, Part II," *Vanity Fair*, December 2007]

". . . There are things about quitting the smoking habit for which nobody prepares you. Did I have any idea that I would indulge in long, drooling—nay, dribbling—lascivious dreams in which I was still wreathed in fragrant blue fumes? I'm embarrassed to say that almost no nocturnal reverie has ever been so vivid or so actual: had the damn ciggies come to mean that much to me? I would wake with the complete and guilty conviction that I had sinned in word and deed while I was asleep. (In bold contrast, the morning mouth felt much better.)" ["On the Limits of Self-Improvement, Part III," *Vanity Fair*, September 2008]

"Is there anything apart from global warming that American liberals despise more than a smoker?" ["Across the Great Divide," *Guardian*, 5/01/10]

Smoking Bans

"Sure, I'll hold it down if other people in the room or the restaurant really care. But under a host of new ordinances, I would not be able to light up in a bar where everyone else present was a chain smoker. . . . This is not a health matter, in other words. It is a frenzy of moralism." ["Why I Blow Smoke at This Moral Frenzy," *Evening Standard*, 4/15/94]

". . . Why follow me into my favorite hangout and deny me at least two constitutional rights? These are, to recapitulate, the right to assemble peacefully and the right to pursue happiness. Yes, I know they are vague and implied, but that's what I like about them." ["Smoke and Mirrors," *Vanity Fair*, October 1994]

"Much of this militant prohibitionism is fueled by a stern sense that those who practice it are standing up to the big, ruthless corporations. . . . I am, of course, as shocked as anyone else to find out that big corporations can behave unethically when it comes to research and marketing. But I have never met a smoker who began the habit under the impression it was good for the pipes, and neither have you. Anyway, try a simple thought experiment. Would great and courageous social reformers. . . relax their attitude one bit if I grew my own tobacco and rolled my own, handmade cigarettes? The question answers itself." ["Smoke and Mirrors," *Vanity Fair*, October 1994]

"More is at stake here than the mere rights of smokers. You could call it ambience. You could call it attitude. You could even call it culture." ["We Know Best," *Vanity Fair*, May 2001]

"The person who smells cigarette smoke and wrinkles his nose before batting the air like a loon is now in the same position as the Peeping Tom neighbor who climbs precariously atop the fridge, binoculars clutched in leprous palm, in order to report the vile bedroom antics of the couple next door. You have to go out of your way to be offended. Never doubt that there are such people; never give them an inch, either, if you value privacy or diversity." ["We Know Best," *Vanity Fair*, May 2001]

"Nobody has to endure any real risk of involuntary smoke inhalation, and no further laws are necessary to secure this existing immunity from harm. . . . Don't pursue me to the park bench if you prevent me from smoking indoors; I will of course ask permission of anyone else sitting there. I will even ask permission to smoke from people who visit me in my own home. But I won't let them visit me and then tell me to put my cigarette out. Anyone failing to see this distinction is a moral cretin, and several other kinds of idiot as well, the sort of person who thinks that a fine bar can be reduced to the utilitarian definition of a 'workplace.'" ["We Know Best," *Vanity Fair*, May 2001]

"There's something essentially un-American in the idea that I could not now open a bar in San Francisco that says, 'Smokers Welcome.'" [Quoted in "Free Radical," *Reason* magazine, November 2001]

"So everyone is made into a snitch. Everyone is made into an enforcer. And everyone is working for the government. And all of this in the name of our health." ["Tobacco, Smoking, and Insider Trading," *Cato Policy Report*, March/April 2005]

"As long as it [smoking] remains a legal—and if you insist, a revenue-raising—activity, a bar owner who doesn't mind it should be able to tell his customers that they are free to do as they wish, or to go elsewhere." ["Let Them Smoke," *Washington Examiner*, 6/23/05]

"For the rest of the time, 'diversity' is a near-magic term for these people: It vanishes, though, when it clashes with their own prejudice." ["Let Them Smoke," *Washington Examiner*, 6/23/05]

"I know that any government that considers itself qualified to decide on what people can ingest will either fail to enforce its will or will have to adopt tyrannical and arbitrary measures in the attempt. Or both." ["Is the Smoking Ban a Good Idea?," *Guardian*, 5/14/07]

Snitching
"As it is, the state now has a new weapon against the press. Don't be calling the president a liar. You'll be accused of snitching on his juniors." ["I'll Never Eat Lunch in This Town Again," *Vanity Fair*, May 1999]

Snoring
"Snoring is a funny thing. It can arouse a sort of grudging admiration as well as a passionate hatred." ["A Little Night Music," *Men's Vogue*, May 2008]

Soccer
"Nine times out of ten, soccer matches are numbingly boring. Without pathetic local patriotism and the chance of a punch-up, there would be no relish in attending." ["Sport Is Guaranteed to Stir Up Foul Play," *Guardian*, 2/20/02]

Social Democrats

"Your typical Social Democrat has a wised-up, pitying manner. You are looking at someone, he seems to say, who has left illusions behind him. No flies can settle on this smirking countenance. Don't you know, the face seems to ask, that the world is a dangerous place? Haven't you read *The Gulag Archipelago*? Ever heard of the boat people? Don't you want America to be strong? Aren't you aware that you can't demonstrate for nuclear disarmament in the Soviet Union? At about this point, and to distract myself from the overmastering desire to slap the face, I imagine myself demonstrating for nuclear disarmament in the Soviet Union and being locked up by someone with precisely those features and that tone of voice." ["Minority Report," *Nation*, 7/06/85–7/13/85]

". . . For all their worldly wisdom, the SDs are extremely naïve. They are the useful idiots of the Reagan revolution." ["Minority Report," *Nation*, 7/06/85–7/13/85]

"As with Guatemala or Vietnam, the SDs will be somewhere else while the actual slaughtering is done—probably accusing the journalists who report it of 'blaming America first.'" ["Minority Report," *Nation*, 7/06/85–7/13/85]

Socialism

". . . Most people are not socialists because most people are suspicious of, or hostile to, the extent of bureaucracy, conformity, and mediocrity that socialism seems to necessitate." ["Choosing Between Clichés," *Times Literary Supplement*, 6/25/82]

"The socialist movement enabled universal suffrage, the imposition of limits upon exploitation, and the independence of colonial and subject populations. Where it succeeded, one can be proud of it. Where it failed—as in the attempt to stop the First World War and later to arrest the growth of fascism—one can honorably regret its failure." [*Letters to a Young Contrarian* (New York: Basic Books, 2001), 97]

Socialist International

"Membership in the Socialist International is rather like the Labor Party or the Church of England. It commits you to nothing." ["Socialism from St. John's Wood," *New Statesman*, 7/21/72]

Socialist Workers Party

"Together with the decision to declare as a 'party' rather than a 'group' or 'tendency'—much Talmudic weight attached to such distinctions—came a certain opportunism and even occasional thuggishness. . . . [N]ot only had the comrades moved from Luxemburg to the worst of Lenin, but in making this shift of principle they had also changed ships on a falling tide. Time to go." ["In the Bright Autumn of My Senescence," *London Review of Books*, 1/06/94]

Society

"Society, thank heaven, is not a family and does not need tribal or feudal cement." ["Our Martyred Monarchy," *Guardian*, 10/17/94]

"Society and government may be quite distinct concepts, but the study of history makes it very difficult to determine that there ever was a society without a government, let alone vice versa." [*Thomas Paine's Rights of Man: A Biography* (New York: Atlantic Monthly Press, 2006), 95]

Socrates
"All he really 'knew,' he said, was the extent of his own ignorance. (This to me is still the definition of an educated person.)" [*God Is Not Great* (New York: Twelve, 2007), 256]

Solidarity
"The pressure of 'solidarity,' with its quasi-moral claim on the loyalty of the embattled remnant, is one that must be felt to be appreciated." ["Missionary Positions," *Wilson Quarterly*, Winter 1991]

"Solidarity with others is mandated by self-interest." [Quoted in "Christopher Hitchens," *Prospect Magazine*, May 2008]

Solipsism
"Obviously, when people are so sure that everything is all about *themselves*, and that a Creator maintains a personal, ongoing, and above all *friendly* interest in their doings, it will take more than a bit of radical cosmology to shake them. Solipsism survived the discovery that the earth was not the center of the solar system; it survived the discovery that the sun was not the center of the universe; it will blithely survive the discovery that the universe is not the *center* of anything." ["Mr. Universe," *Vanity Fair*, December 1992]

Solitude
"I'm very happy by myself—I'm lucky in that way—if I've got enough to read and something to write about and a bit of alcohol for me to add an edge, not to dull it." ["Q&A with Christopher Hitchens," C-SPAN, 1/14/11 (first aired: 1/23/11)]

Solutions
". . . Temporary expedients become dogma very quickly—especially if they seem to work." [Quoted in "Free Radical," *Reason* magazine, November 2001]

"Conflict may be painful, but the painless solution does not exist in any case and the pursuit of it leads to the painful outcome of mindlessness and pointlessness; the apotheosis of the ostrich." [*Letters to a Young Contrarian* (New York: Basic Books, 2001), 31]

". . . The very concept of a total solution had led to the most appalling human sacrifices, and to the invention of excuses for them." [*God Is Not Great* (New York: Twelve, 2007), 153]

"I'm happy to say some problems don't have solutions." [Quoted in Lisa Miller, "No God—And No Abortions," *Newsweek*, 12/08/08]

Somalia
"Somalia is, geopolitically, a Gulf state. Military occupations there are undertaken for imperial reasons." ["Minority Report," *Nation*, 1/03/94–1/10/94]

Sontag, Susan

"She brings out the beast in people." ["American Notes," *Times Literary Supplement*, 3/04/83]

". . . To be thought too vulgar by the Old Guard and too pretentious by·the mob idols is to have brushed against the national cortex in a noticeable way. Who else could say that if you understood Nietzsche you could appreciate a Patti Smith concert?" ["Signature Sontag," *Vanity Fair*, March 2000]

"I suppose I have my tiny criticisms, too. I admire, in theory, her refusal to own a television set. But is this advisable in a monitor of popular culture? And I can never *quite* believe anyone who says that they don't read the reviews of their work. Yet anchoring all her enthusiasms and gaieties and eccentricities is a very strong moral sense, which is expressed in that most admirable and rare quality—physical and intellectual courage. She's brave." ["Signature Sontag," *Vanity Fair*, March 2000]

"For her, the act of literary consumption was the generous parent of the act of literary production. She was so much impressed by the marvelous people she had read. . . that she was almost shy about offering her own prose to the reader. Look at her output and you will see that she was not at all prolific." ["Susan Sontag," *Slate*, 12/29/04]

South Africa

"South Africa is a totalitarian state in the strict definition of the term. That is, the private life of the citizen is determined by the state on the basis of color, with even matters such as sexual relations mandated by law, and the citizen, in large measure, is the property of the state. I think that is what a totalitarian state is. South Africa passes the test with flying colors. If most black South Africans moved to Cuba, they would think they had died and gone to heaven. Cuba is not, for example, a totalitarian state in that way. Cuba belongs to no totalitarian camp." [Quoted in "Promoting Democracy: A Panel Discussion," *Temple Law Quarterly*, Winter 1987)]

"At long last, the rulers of South Africa conceded what the ANC had been trying to teach them: You cannot run a modern society on the scientifically and morally false basis of racial classification." ["An Informed View of the Post-Apartheid Era," *Newsday*, 4/01/92]

"The connection between religion, racism, and totalitarianism is also to be found in the other most hateful dictatorship of the twentieth century: the vile system of apartheid in South Africa. This was not just the ideology of a Dutch-speaking tribe bent on extorting forced labor from peoples of a different shade of pigmentation, it was also a form of Calvinism in practice." [*God Is Not Great* (New York: Twelve, 2007), 251]

South Korea

"In the case of South Korea, the conservatives and their sidekicks have proved once again that they prefer not authoritarianism to totalitarianism but authoritarianism to democracy." ["Minority Report," *Nation*, 1/19/85]

"My guide. . . pointed to the famous tree where American officers were slain by North Koreans wielding axes in an 'incident' in 1976, as they were supervising an attempt to lop off the branches and clear a view of a nearby American outpost. . . . Reassuring for the tree-trimmers, I suppose, but the idea of going on full alert for a disputed poplar is one to give anybody, however anticommunist, pause for thought." ["Going Home With Kim Dae Jung," *Mother Jones*, May 1985]

The South (U.S.)

"You often notice, in the South, that people don't at all mind if they live up to their own clichés and stereotypes." ["My Red-State Odyssey," *Vanity Fair*, September 2005]

"Never quite able to get over a lost past, never quite at ease with the federal government (though very much at ease with the armed forces), and just not quite large enough to impose itself on the rest of the country, the South keeps on 'reviving' and redefining itself, always pushing at its limits and limitations—and always finding them." ["My Red-State Odyssey," *Vanity Fair*, September 2005]

Soviet Union

"The Russians have no desire to see a successful experiment [in Communism] carried out by people who reject their leadership." ["The Politics of Terror Tearing Italy in Two," *Daily Express*, 6/10/77]

"In one deft illustration we see how a system that fails the consumer also fails the producer." ["Christopher Hitchens on the Great Question of the Day," *London Review of Books*, 3/08/90]

"What possible reason can there be for nostalgia at the closure of this abysmal system?" ["Minority Report," *Nation*, 10/07/91]

"By any knowable definition, which must include the socialist one, the Soviet system was the perfect failure. In the lives of its own citizens and subjects, and in its contact with any real movement outside its own borders, it killed everything it touched." ["Minority Report," *Nation*, 10/07/91]

"In 1988, four years after 1984, the Soviet Union scrapped its official history curriculum and announced that a newly authorized version was somewhere in the works. That was the precise moment at which the regime conceded its own extinction." ["Goodbye to All That," *Harper's*, November 1998]

"Dissidents used to be locked up in Soviet lunatic asylums for 'reformist delusions,' it being quite naturally and reasonably assumed that anybody mad enough to propose reforms had lost all sense of self-preservation." [*God Is Not Great* (New York: Twelve, 2007), 254]

Spain

"Some defeats are exemplary as well as moving, and the murder of the Spanish Republic is indubitably preeminent among them." ["Who Lost Spain?," *Wilson Quarterly*, Summer 2001]

"The Special Relationship"
"The Germans and the Saudis may be able to do many things for their American guests, but one thing they cannot do is take them to Buckingham Palace and lay a ceremonial sword on their shoulders." ["Windsor Knot," *New York Times Magazine*, 5/12/91]

Spinoza, Baruch
"This derided heretic is now credited with the most original philosophical work ever done on the mind/body distinction, and his meditations on the human condition have provided more real consolation to thoughtful people than has any religion." [*God Is Not Great* (New York: Twelve, 2007), 262]

Spokesmen
"One of the advantages held by the rich and powerful is that they very seldom tolerate self-appointed spokesmen, preferring like most élites to appoint their own. The wretched of the earth, by contrast, have to put up with all kinds of poseurs and windbags speaking and writing on their behalf." ["Last Swing of the Crane," *New Statesman*, 10/06/72]

Sports
"Put the sporting atmosphere together with the cult of celebrity and you can always see the critical faculties of the culture collapse." ["This Forlorn Chase for the Wrong Role Model," *Evening Standard*, 6/20/94]

". . . The essence of fandom is to be an uncritical applauder. . . ." ["This Forlorn Chase for the Wrong Role Model," *Evening Standard*, 6/20/94]

"If I am stuck next to a fellow-male on United Airlines and he asks me an opening question about 'the play-offs,' I say that we'll have to cut straight to sex or politics because I can't and won't have an opinion about games. As often as not, he is relieved." ["Sport Is Guaranteed to Stir Up Foul Play," *Guardian*, 2/20/02]

"Incidentally, isn't there something simultaneously grandiose and pathetic about the words 'World Cup'? Not unlike the micro-megalomaniac expression 'World Series' for a game that only a handful of countries bother to play." ["Fool's Gold," *Newsweek*, 2/15/10]

"Whether it's the exacerbation of national rivalries that you want. . . or the exhibition of the most depressing traits of the human personality (guns in locker rooms, golf clubs wielded in the home, dogs maimed and tortured at stars' homes to make them fight, dope and steroids everywhere), you need only look to the wide world of sports for the most rank and vivid examples." ["Fool's Gold," *Newsweek*, 2/15/10]

"I can't count the number of times that I have picked up the newspaper at a time of crisis and found whole swaths of the front page given over either to the *already known* result of some other dull game or to the moral or criminal depredations of some overpaid steroid swallower. Listen: the paper has a whole separate section devoted to people who want to degrade the act of reading by staring enthusiastically at the outcomes of sporting events that occurred the previous day. These avid consumers also have tons of dedicated channels and publications that are lovingly contoured to their special needs. All I ask is that they keep out of the grown-up parts of the paper." ["Fool's Gold," *Newsweek*, 2/15/10]

"Or picture this: I take a seat in a bar or restaurant and suddenly leap to my feet, face contorted with delight or woe, yelling and gesticulating and looking as if I am fighting bees. I would expect the maitre d' to say a quietening word at the least, mentioning the presence of other people. But then all I need do is utter some dumb incantation—'Steelers,' say, or even 'Cubs,' for crumb's sake—and everybody decides I am a special case who deserves to be treated in a soothing manner." ["Fool's Gold," *Newsweek*, 2/15/10]

Sports Metaphors

"If you hear someone using sporting metaphors to describe the political scene, you can usually count on being patronized, bored and misled (c.f. George Will's 'The New Season' for a thunderous classic in this genre)." ["Political Curve Balls Thrown from the Hill," *Newsday*, 8/31/88]

". . . Any use of sporting metaphors to describe politics is an infallible sign of an exhausted hack." ["Washington Notebook," *Spectator*, 2/06/10]

"Our own political discourse, already emaciated enough, has been further degraded by the continuous importation of sports 'metaphors': lame and vapid and cheery expressions like 'bottom of the ninth,' 'goal line,' and who knows what other tripe. Hard enough on the eyes and ears as this is—and there are some cartoonists who can't seem to draw without it—it also increases the deplorable tendency to look at the party system as a matter of team loyalty, which is the most trivial and parochial form that attachment can take." ["Fool's Gold," *Newsweek*, 2/15/10]

Stalinism

"Professedly godless men have shown themselves capable of great crimes. But they have not invented any that they did not learn from the religious, and so they find themselves heaping up new 'infallible' icons and idols. Stalinism, which was actually Stalin worship, could not have occurred in a country that had not endured several centuries of the divine right of kings." ["The Lord and the Intellectuals," *Harper's*, July 1982]

"Stalinism replaced all debate about the merit of an argument, or a position, or even a person, with an inquiry about motive." [*No One Left to Lie To* (New York: Verso, 2000), 148]

"Stalinism was, among other things, a triumph of the torturing of language. And, unlike Nazism or fascism or nuclear warfare, it secured at least the respect, and sometimes the admiration, of liberal intellectuals." ["Lightness at Midnight," *Atlantic Monthly*, September 2002]

The State

". . . The state. . . is never as reluctant as liberals suppose to resort to indiscriminate terror on its own account." ["Minority Report," *Nation*, 8/03/85–8/10/85]

"A regime that treats the citizen as property will sooner or later let that property decay, just as feudalism did. Not even the self-interest of the government monopoly will prevent it. Some of our best friends in the Third World prove this point by mounting literacy campaigns and censorship drives at the same time." ["Minority Report," *Nation*, 1/25/86]

"The state is a control freak." ["Smoke and Mirrors," *Vanity Fair*, October 1994]

"In fact, it can be at its most sinister when it decides that what it's doing is for your own good." [Quoted in "Free Radical," *Reason* magazine, November 2001]

"Some regimes have been popular not in spite of their irrationality and cruelty, but because of it." [*Why Orwell Matters* (New York: Basic Books, 2002), 191]

Stem Cells
". . . [Already existing] embryos are going nowhere as it is. But now religious maniacs strive to forbid even their use, which would help what the same maniacs regard as the unformed embryo's fellow humans! The politicized sponsors of this pseudo-scientific nonsense should be ashamed to live, let alone die." ["Tumortown," *Vanity Fair*, November 2010]

Stereotypes
"Cartoons of Arabs in the American press represent them as both plutocrats and subversives—the very same double jeopardy that was visited upon the Jews of Europe." ["Hispanics and Arabs in a Changing America," *Newsday*, 7/06/88]

Stewart, Martha
"This is emphatically not Betty Crocker about whom we are talking here." ["Martha Inc.," *Vanity Fair*, October 1993]

"'This is something that everyone in the country can enjoy,' she averred breathily, before gliding straight to an everyday discussion on the finer points of the serving of champagne, the care of crystal, and the maintenance of silver." ["Martha Inc.," *Vanity Fair*, October 1993]

"It occurred to me, as I read this alarming taxonomy, that Martha Stewart might think people were stupid. How dumb do you have to be in order to be reminded to 'buy or borrow any luggage you need'?" ["Martha Inc.," *Vanity Fair*, October 1993]

Stimson, Henry
"Stimson always sought the lofty motive, and would probably have preferred the motive to be lofty. But in every instance in his career, the absence of a lofty motive did not disable him with futile attacks of conscience." ["An Unlikely Gentleman Among the Buccaneers," *Newsday*, 10/24/90]

"Stimson, who very often was involved in very difficult and nerve-racking and risky decisions, never sought to conceal or soften his role in them. He believed in accepting responsibility—a form of manners that virtually has died out in today's practice of deniable diplomacy." ["An Unlikely Gentleman Among the Buccaneers," *Newsday*, 10/24/90]

Stockman, David

"Stockman, we always knew, was fantasizing—we hardly needed his self-important confirmation of the fact. . . ." ["Minority Report," *Nation*, 5/17/86]

Stoicism

"What one needs in this society is less sentimentality and more stoicism." [Quoted in Boris Kachka, "Are You There, God? It's Me, Hitchens," *New York*, 5/07/07]

"Now, those who fail to register emotion under pressure are often apparently good officer material, but that very stoicism can also conceal—as with officers who don't suffer from battle fatigue or post-traumatic stress—a psychopathic calm that sends the whole platoon into a ditch full of barbed wire and sheds no tears." ["The Blair-Hitch Project," *Vanity Fair*, February 2011]

Stomach

"A bit of a stomach gives a chap a position in society." ["On the Limits of Self-Improvement, Part I," *Vanity Fair*, October 2007]

Strauss, Leo

"Of those who conversely believe in religion but not in God, the most important was probably Leo Strauss, semi-official philosopher of American conservatism and the man who shaped the minds of Allan Bloom, Francis Fukuyama, and (admittedly through intermediaries such as Carnes Lord and William Kristol) J. Danforth Quayle. Strauss believed that Athens was the superior of Jerusalem and that pure philosophy was the key to human understanding, but he also believed that this insight was too exciting and too difficult for the rabble, and proposed that they be given religion as a substitute." ["Mr. Universe," *Vanity Fair*, December 1992]

"Say what you will about the Straussians, they aren't hypocrites or weaklings, and they don't burble about heavenly rewards to make up for when the mind has gone." ["The Egg-Head's Egger-On," *London Review of Books*, 4/27/00]

Stress

". . . I positively *like* stress, arrange to inflict it on myself, and sheer awkwardly away from anybody who tries to promise me a more soothed or relaxed existence." ["On the Limits of Self-Improvement, Part I," *Vanity Fair*, October 2007]

Stupidity

". . . There *is* something frightening about stupidity; more especially, about stupidity in its mass, organized form." ["Minority Report," *Nation*, 10/04/86]

"Stupid answers traditionally come from stupid questions. Stupid questions, however, need not come from stupid people." ["Voting in the Passive Voice," *Harper's*, April 1992]

"The connection between stupidity and cruelty is a close one." ["Political Animals," *Atlantic Monthly*, November 2002]

"The problem is people who are dumb but think they are bright, like [Jimmy] Carter or [Bill] Clinton." [Quoted in "Christopher Hitchens: Off the Cuff, in His Own Words," *Georgetowner*, 5/27/04]

Sub Judice

"When used by a panicky public official, the sub judice defense is a bit like the date stamped on foods by bent wholesalers trying to conceal the putrefying state of their perishable goods. In other words, it expires." ["Minority Report," *Nation*, 5/08/89]

Subordinates

"If you are fated to be Osric, then count yourself lucky to toil for a weak and vain king." ["Bill and Dick's Excellent Adventure," *London Review of Books*, 2/20/97]

Subprime Mortgage Crisis

"There are many causes of the subprime and derivative horror show that has destroyed our trust in the idea of credit, but one way of defining it would be to say that everybody was promised everything, and almost everybody fell for the populist bait." ["Barack to Reality," *Slate*, 11/10/08]

Suburbia

"More Americans now live in the suburbs than anywhere else, and more do so by choice. Anachronisms of two kinds persist in respect of this phenomenon. The first is the apparently unshakable belief of political candidates that they will sound better, and appear more authentic, if they can claim to come from a small town (something we were almost spared this year, until the chiller from Wasilla). The second is the continued stern disapproval of anything 'suburban' by the strategic majority of our country's intellectuals. The idiocy of rural life? If you must. The big city? All very well. Bohemia, or perhaps Paris or Prague? Yes indeed. The suburbs? No thank you." ["Suburbs of Our Discontent," *Atlantic Monthly*, December 2008]

Sudan

"Meanwhile, the State Department has upgraded Sudan's status on the chart that shows 'cooperation' in the matter of slave-trafficking. Apparently, you can be on this list and still be awarded points for good behavior." ["Realism in Darfur," *Slate*, 11/07/05]

"Our policy in Darfur has not just failed to rescue a stricken black African population: It has actually assisted the Sudanese Islamists in completing their policy of racist murder. Thank heaven that we are tough enough to bear the shame of this, and strong enough to forgive ourselves." ["Realism in Darfur," *Slate*, 11/07/05]

Suez Crisis

"The fall of 1956 was one of the few occasions on which Washington could not be accused of colonialism, of vulgar self-interest or of hasty if altruistic interference in the affairs of others." ["Mad Dogs and Others: Suez 1956," *Grand Street*, Autumn 1986]

"By forever disabling European colonialism in the Middle East, it [the United States] had also subconsciously prepared to supplant it." ["Mad Dogs and Others: Suez 1956," *Grand Street*, Autumn 1986]

"The Suez War enabled Eisenhower to make the idea of receivership popular not just in the United States but also in Britain, where it came to all but a diehard minority as a welcome if shamefaced relief." [*Blood, Class and Empire* (New York: Nation Books, 2004), 284]

Superpower Self-Pity
"What is unpardonable is the superpower self-pity, so deftly evoked by the Reaganites. Since Reagan came to power, the United States has bombed or shelled, or armed and supported the bombing and shelling of, Lebanon, Syria, Iraq, Tunisia, and Libya.... Looking back, or rather not looking back, on this record, Americans dolefully ask why the Arab world is so ungrateful, and Europe so lacking in will. We are asked to applaud a demonstration of American willingness to use force. Who in the Middle East is supposed to have doubted that willingness?" ["Minority Report," *Nation*, 5/03/86]

Superstition
"Superstitions die hard, if they die at all. The belief that capital punishment deters homicide is a perennial. Less common but also hardy is the idea that gold represents a real store of value. (It's always gold for some reason, never any other equally rare and useless metal.)" ["Minority Report," *Nation*, 11/27/82]

"Good times often make people more, not less, superstitious." ["Greenspan Shrugged," *Vanity Fair*, December 2000]

"Since human beings are naturally solipsistic, all forms of superstition enjoy what might be called a natural advantage." [*God Is Not Great* (New York: Twelve, 2007), 74]

"To regret that we cannot be done with superstition is no more than to regret that we have a common ancestry with apes and plants and fish." ["God's Still Dead," *Slate*, 8/20/07]

Supply-Side Economics
"As an idea its chief recommendation is that it is so old, and so long discredited, that it can now be packaged as new. Remove crippling tax burdens and let free enterprise rip! A rising tide lifts all boats! One expects hourly to read of an 'invisible hand' school, which will burst on conventional economists with all the force of revelation employed by that ancient 'neo' Adam Smith." ["Minority Report," *Nation*, 5/17/86]

Taliban
"I must say that I thought the questioner's supposition—that if we had made a nice offer of creating a modern and developed society the Taliban may have been nice enough to accept it—has a long way to go before it's even naïve." [*Sunday Live with Adam Boulton*, Sky News, 5/30/10]

Talking
"I came here to talk, not to listen to you. You invited me on for my opinions, not to listen to yours." [*Scarborough Country*, MSNBC, 12/01/05]

Taxes

"Very few nations or individuals regard themselves as liable to pay too little tax." ["Taxing the Hilt, Too," *New York Times*, 5/06/79]

"History shows that even one unjust or anomalous tax can create immense political unrest and ill-feeling." ["Taxing the Hilt, Too," *New York Times*, 5/06/79]

"... We have a paradoxical situation where the least heavily taxed are the most resentful. But perhaps this is less of a paradox than it seems. People who are accustomed to a large disposable income will be inclined to think that they can find better uses for the money than the government can." ["Taxing the Hilt, Too," *New York Times*, 5/06/79]

Tea Party Movement

"They come from a long and frankly somewhat boring tradition of anti-incumbency and anti-Washington rhetoric, and they are rather an insult to anyone with anything of a political memory. Since when is it truly insurgent to rail against the state of affairs in the nation's capital?" ["The Politicians We Deserve," *Slate*, 10/11/10]

"I don't remember ever seeing grown-ups behave less seriously, at least in an election season." ["Tea'd Off," *Vanity Fair*, January 2011]

Teeth

"... Gallows humor is inseparable from dentistry: at one point I heard the good doctor say, as he plowed through the layers of plaque and tartar, 'Good news. I've found some of your teeth.'" ["On the Limits of Self-Improvement, Part II," *Vanity Fair*, December 2007]

Television

"Television is a megaphone for the transmission of official wisdom." ["Minority Report," *Nation*, 6/17/91]

Ten Commandments

"The next instruction [the fifth commandment] is to honor one's parents: a harmless enough idea, but again unenforceable in law and inapplicable to the many orphans that nature or god sees fit to create." ["Moore's Law," *Slate*, 8/27/03]

"To insist that people not annex their neighbor's cattle or wife 'or anything that is his' might be reasonable, even if it does place the wife in the same category as the cattle, and presumably to that extent diminishes the offense of adultery. But to demand 'don't even *think* about it' is absurd and totalitarian, and furthermore inhibiting to the Protestant spirit of entrepreneurship and competition." ["Moore's Law," *Slate*, 8/27/03]

"It's obviously too much to expect that a Bronze Age demagogue should have remembered to condemn drug abuse, drunken driving, or offenses against gender equality, or to demand prayer in the schools. Still, to have left rape and child abuse and genocide and slavery out of the account is to have been negligent to some degree, even by the lax standards of the time." ["Moore's Law," *Slate*, 8/27/03]

"There are many more than ten commandments in the Old Testament, and I live for the day when Americans are obliged to observe all of them, including the ox-goring and witch-burning ones." ["Moore's Law," *Slate*, 8/27/03]

"But however little one thinks of the Jewish tradition, it is surely insulting to the people of Moses to imagine that they had come this far under the impression that murder, adultery, theft, and perjury were permissible." [*God Is Not Great* (New York: Twelve, 2007), 99]

"No society ever discovered has failed to protect itself from self-evident crimes like those supposedly stipulated at Mount Sinai." [*God Is Not Great* (New York: Twelve, 2007), 100]

"Finally, instead of the condemnation of evil actions, there is an oddly phrased condemnation of impure thoughts. . . . One may be forcibly restrained from wicked actions, or barred from committing them, but to forbid people from *contemplating* them is too much. . . . If god really wanted people to be free of such thoughts, he should have taken more care to invent a different species." [*God Is Not Great* (New York: Twelve, 2007), 100]

"Then there is the very salient question of what the commandments do *not* say. Is it too modern to notice that there is nothing about the protection of children from cruelty, nothing about rape, nothing about slavery, and nothing about genocide? Or is it too exactly 'in context' to notice that some of these very offenses are about to be positively recommended?" [*God Is Not Great* (New York: Twelve, 2007), 100]

"The order to 'love thy neighbor *as thyself*' is too extreme and too strenuous to be obeyed, as is the hard-to-interpret instruction to love others 'as I have loved you.' Humans are not so constituted as to care for others as much as themselves: the thing simply cannot be done (as any intelligent 'creator' would well understand from studying his own design). Urging humans to be superhumans, on pain of death and torture, is the urging of terrible self-abasement at their repeated and inevitable failure to keep the rules." [*God Is Not Great* (New York: Twelve, 2007), 213]

". . . The giving of the divine Law by Moses appears in three or four wildly different scriptural versions. (When you hear people demanding that the Ten Commandments be displayed in courtrooms and schoolrooms, always be sure to ask which set. It works every time.)" ["The New Commandments," *Vanity Fair*, April 2010]

"*Thou shalt not covet thy neighbor's house, thou shalt not covet thy neighbor's wife, nor his manservant, nor his maidservant, nor his ox, nor his ass, nor any thing that is thy neighbor's.* There are several details that make this perhaps the most questionable of the commandments. Leaving aside the many jokes about whether or not it's O.K. or kosher to covet thy neighbor's wife's ass, you are bound to notice once again that, like the

Sabbath order, it's addressed to the servant-owning and property-owning class. . . . Notice also that no specific act is being pronounced as either compulsory (the Sabbath) or forbidden (perjury). Instead, this is the first but not the last introduction in the Bible of the totalitarian concept of *'thought crime.'* You are being told, in effect, not even to think about it. . . . Wise lawmakers know that it is a mistake to promulgate legislation that is impossible to obey." ["The New Commandments," *Vanity Fair*, April 2010]

". . . The Ten Commandments were derived from situational ethics. They show every symptom of having been man-made and improvised under pressure. They are addressed to a nomadic tribe whose main economy is primitive agriculture and whose wealth is sometimes counted in people as well as animals. They are also addressed to a group that has been promised the land and flocks of other people: the Amalekites and Midianites and others whom God orders them to kill, rape, enslave, or exterminate. And this, too, is important because at every step of their arduous journey the Israelites are reminded to keep to the laws, not because they are right but just because they will lead them to become conquerors (of, as it happens, almost the only part of the Middle East that has no oil)." ["The New Commandments," *Vanity Fair*, April 2010]

"Numbers One through Three can simply go, since they have nothing to do with morality and are no more than a long, rasping throat clearing by an admittedly touchy dictator." ["The New Commandments," *Vanity Fair*, April 2010]

"Number Seven: Fair enough if you must, but is polygamy adultery? Also, could not permanent monogamy have been made slightly more consonant with human nature? Why create people with lust in their hearts? Then again, what about rape? It seems to be very strongly recommended, along with genocide, slavery, and infanticide, in Numbers 31:1–18, and surely constitutes a rather extreme version of sex outside marriage." ["The New Commandments," *Vanity Fair*, April 2010]

"It's difficult to take oneself with sufficient seriousness to begin any sentence with the words 'Thou shalt not.' But who cannot summon the confidence to say: *Do not* condemn people on the basis of their ethnicity or color. *Do not* ever use people as private property. Despise those who use violence or the threat of it in sexual relations. Hide your face and weep if you dare to harm a child. *Do not* condemn people for their inborn *nature*—why would God create so many homosexuals only in order to torture and destroy them? Be aware that you too are an animal and dependent on the web of nature, and think and act accordingly. *Do not* imagine that you can escape judgment if you rob people with a false prospectus rather than with a knife. Turn off that fucking cell phone—you have no idea how *unimportant* your call is to us." ["The New Commandments," *Vanity Fair*, April 2010]

Tenet, George

"George Tenet's reaction to hearing of the Twin Towers in conflagration was to say that he wondered if it had anything to do with that guy in the flight-training school in Minnesota. For this, Bush gave him a Presidential Medal of Freedom." ["Power Suits," *Vanity Fair*, April 2006]

Tennis

"In countless British middlebrow plays and television drawing-room dramas, the cry of 'Anyone for tennis?' is the one that evokes contented country weekends. The idea, of course, is not actually to win, or anything as vulgar as that. British amateurism is the style required—it is thought to be quite bad manners to care about the result." ["Wimbledon: Recapturing a Fine and Careless Rapture," *Los Angeles Times*, 6/29/80]

Terkel, Studs

"Terkel's mode (unvarying on the few occasions I've run into him) is one of affirmative over-praise. He won't let you defend yourself from the charge of being a great guy." ["Open Letter to Readers and Letter Exchange with Victor Navasky," Christopher Hitchens Web, 2003]

Term Limits

"Since the only way of testing the will of the electorate is, or should be, at an election, there is no way to be sure if people really desire term limits. In local referenda and ballot initiatives they sometimes seem to say that they do, at least until they reckon the consequences, or until they find someone they'd like to re-elect." ["The Limits of Democracy," *Vanity Fair*, September 2001]

"If an American wants to run for elected office, that is his or her right. And those who desire to vote for any candidate should be permitted to make up their own minds on the point." ["The Limits of Democracy," *Vanity Fair*, September 2001]

"The essential absurdity of term limits is that they disqualify from the democratic process persons who are too successful at it." ["The Limits of Democracy," *Vanity Fair*, September 2001]

"Banana republics we know about. Term limits are a lunge toward bananas democracy." ["The Limits of Democracy," *Vanity Fair*, September 2001]

Terrorism

"Terrorism threatens to emerge as one of the great junk subjects of our era." ["Minority Report," *Nation*, 8/03/85–8/10/85]

"One can define a terrorist as someone who possesses the following qualities: His chief targets must be civilians and noncombatants (not always the same thing), and there must be a political reason why they are his prey. His cause must be a hopeless one. He must be without a realizable manifesto, program, or objective. In other words, violence must be his end as well as his means." ["Minority Report," *Nation*, 8/03/85–8/10/85]

"All states and all armies employ terror, but they do not, except in rare cases, depend solely on its use." ["Minority Report," *Nation*, 8/03/85–8/10/85]

"No interviewer, spokesperson, or interviewee should henceforth be allowed to utter the word 'terrorism' unless he or she can supply a definition that does not outrage decency and/or common sense." ["Minority Report," *Nation*, 5/03/86]

". . . The word ['terrorism'] carries a conservative freight. It is almost always used to describe revolutionary or subversive action. . . . And I think one could also add that it's taken on a faint but unmistakable racist undertone (or overtone), in much the same way as the word 'mugger' once did." ["Wanton Acts of Usage," *Harper's*, September 1986]

"The word 'terrorist' is not—like 'communist' and 'fascist'—being abused; it is itself an abuse. It disguises reality and impoverishes language and makes a banality out of the discussion of war and revolution and politics. It's the perfect instrument for the cheapening of public opinion and for the intimidation of dissent." ["Wanton Acts of Usage," *Harper's*, September 1986]

"'Terrorist'. . . is a convenience word, a junk word, designed to obliterate distinctions. It must be this that recommends it so much to governments with something to hide, to the practitioners of instant journalism, and to shady 'consultants.'" ["Wanton Acts of Usage," *Harper's*, September 1986]

"The terrorist is always, and by definition, the Other. Call your enemy communist or fascist and, whatever your intentions, you will one day meet someone who proudly claims to be a communist or fascist. Define your foe as authoritarian or totalitarian and, however ill-crafted your analysis, you are bound to find a target that amplifies the definition. But 'terrorist' is hardly more useful than a term of abuse, and probably less so." ["Wanton Acts of Usage," *Harper's*, September 1986]

"Random violence is one thing, say the well-funded experts, but it gets really serious when it's 'state-sponsored' terrorism. The two words that are supposed to intensify the effect of the third actually have the effect, if we pause for thought, of diminishing it. It is terrifying to be held at gunpoint by a person who has *no demands*. A moment of *terror* is the moment when the irrational intrudes—when the man with the gun is hearing voices or wants his girlfriend back or has a theory about the Middle Pyramid. But if the gunman is a proxy for Syria or Iran or Bangladesh or Chile (the fourth being the only government mentioned here that has ever detonated a lethal bomb on American soil), then it isn't, strictly speaking, the irrational that we face. It may be an apparently irreconcilable quarrel or an apparently unappeasable grievance, but it is, finally, political. And propaganda terms, whether vulgar or ingenious, have always aimed at making political problems seem one-sided." ["Wanton Acts of Usage," *Harper's*, September 1986]

"The cause of Islamist terrorism. . . is the ideology of Islamic terror. That's what its root cause is." ["In Depth with Christopher Hitchens," C-SPAN, 9/02/07]

". . . I do not say that all Muslims are terrorists, but I have noticed that an alarmingly high proportion of terrorists are Muslim. A paranoid or depressive person—of whom we have many millions in our midst—does not *have* to end up screaming religious slogans while butchering his fellow creatures. But a paranoid or depressive person who is in regular touch with a jihadist 'spiritual leader' is presented with a ready-made script that offers him paradise in exchange for homicide." ["Hard Evidence," *Slate*, 11/16/09]

Texas

"One always strives to avoid 'land of contrast' clichés, but in Texas the more people live up to their reputation, the more they don't. And the more it stays the same, the more it changes." ["My Red-State Odyssey," *Vanity Fair*, September 2005]

Thatcher, Margaret

"The middle-class crusade, in fact, is what Mrs. Thatcher was born and cut out to lead. It is probably the reason why she did not shine in the fat, prosperous, and *petit-bourgeois* fifties and early sixties. But face a suburban mother in hard times with the prospect of sending her children to state schools and 'hark, what discord follows.' The possibility of this happening as a general social fact has brought out the feline in her and her class." ["Downstairs Upstairs," *New York Times Magazine*, 6/01/75]

"When it comes to visions, Thatcher has established a virtual monopoly, demonstrating that there is a place for Conservative Utopianism." ["Haven for British Dissent Is in Full Eclipse," *Los Angeles Times*, 6/19/83]

"How odd it is that a decade of Thatcher has not taught Laborites the essential distinction between being liked and being respected. The Prime Minister has demonstrated a willingness to take life and to risk her own in the forwarding of certain convictions, and by doing so has won the grudging admiration that is the sincerest compliment the British electorate can bestow." ["Credibility Brown," *London Review of Books*, 8/31/89]

"There is usually something absurd and contrived in the idea of a person—especially a politician—being 'a legend in their own lifetime.' But Margaret Hilda Thatcher has genuinely attained this apotheosis." ["Thatcher: An 'Ism' in Her Own Time," *Newsday*, 10/12/89]

". . . She has name recognition and personal impact on a scale that is reliably said to have disconcerted Her Majesty the Queen, who has been on the throne for nearly forty years and could stand a little competition." ["Thatcher: An 'Ism' in Her Own Time," *Newsday*, 10/12/89]

"Foreigners, as the English call them, know who she is. The Brits, as foreigners call them, don't much like her but do have a great respect for her. This is political success on a scale that no London politician could have expected a decade ago, when she was first elected." ["Thatcher: An 'Ism' in Her Own Time," *Newsday*, 10/12/89]

"Put it this way: She thinks she is Churchill, and she isn't." ["Thatcher: An 'Ism' in Her Own Time," *Newsday*, 10/12/89]

"She does not care if she is liked so long as she is feared and respected." ["Minority Report," *Nation*, 4/30/90]

"'I make up my mind about people in the first ten seconds, and I very rarely change it.' So the *New York Times* quoted Margaret Thatcher as saying on the day of her resignation. I would be happy to think that the statement was truthful, since within minutes of first being introduced to me, Thatcher lashed me across the buttocks with a rolled-up parliamentary order paper." ["Lessons Maggie Taught Me," *Nation*, 12/17/90]

"It is easy to summarize the foulness of the Thatcher years: the combination of Malthus and Ayn Rand that went to make up her social philosophy; the police mentality that she evinced when faced with dissent; the awful toadying to Reagan and now Bush; the indulgence shown to apartheid; the coarse, racist betrayal of Hong Kong; the destruction of local democracy and autonomous popular institutions." ["Lessons Maggie Taught Me," *Nation*, 12/17/90]

"Detestable though she was, she was a radical and not a reactionary." ["Lessons Maggie Taught Me," *Nation*, 12/17/90]

"'Thatcherism' has made possible a movement for a serious, law-based constitutional republic in Britain and has hacked away at the encrusted institutions and attitudes that stood in its path. Thatcher has herself shown that there is power and dignity to be won by defying the status quo and the majority rather than by adapting to them. If the British left, which she froze into immobility like Medusa, could bring itself to learn from this, then we might not have to look upon her like again." ["Lessons Maggie Taught Me," *Nation*, 12/17/90]

"At once we were in an argument. . . . On one point of fact, too abstruse to detail here, I was right (as it happens) and she was wrong. But she *would not* concede this and so, rather than be a bore, I gave her the point and made a slight bow of acknowledgment. She pierced me with a glance. 'Bow lower,' she commanded. With what I thought was an insouciant look, I bowed a little lower. 'No, no—*much* lower!' A silence had fallen over our group. I stooped lower, with an odd sense of having lost all independent volition. Having arranged matters to her entire satisfaction, she produced from behind her back a rolled-up Parliamentary order-paper and struck—no, she thwacked—me on the behind. I reattained the perpendicular with some difficulty. 'Naughty boy,' she sang out over her shoulder as she flounced away. Nothing that happened to the country in the next dozen years surprised me in the least." ["On Spanking," *London Review of Books*, 10/20/94]

"And the worst of 'Thatcherism,' as I was beginning by degrees to discover, was the rodent slowly stirring in my viscera: the uneasy but unbanishable feeling that on some essential matters she might be right." [*Hitch-22* (New York: Twelve, 2010), 178]

"I didn't really like anything about her, except, that is, for the most important thing about her, which was that she was 'a conviction politician.' In the Labor Party, this sort of principled character had effectively ceased to exist." [*Hitch-22* (New York: Twelve, 2010), 202]

Theocracy

"Try and run a society out of the teachings of one holy book, and you will end with every kind of ignominy and collapse." ["God's Still Dead," *Slate*, 8/20/07]

". . . Could we hear a little less from the apologists of religion about how 'secular' regimes can be just as bad as theocratic ones? Of course, they can—if they indulge in acts of faith and see themselves as possessing supernatural authority." ["God's Still Dead," *Slate*, 8/20/07]

". . . The original form of tyranny of man over man, and of man over the mind of man (sometimes called totalitarianism) was certainly theocratic, and no overcoming of the absolutist or of the arbitrary is complete unless it includes a clear-eyed rejection of any dictator whose rule is founded on the supernatural." [Introduction to *The Portable Atheist* (New York: Da Capo Press, 2007), xxii]

". . . Any government that imagines it has a divine warrant will perforce deal with its critics as if they were profane and thus illegitimate by definition." ["The Death of Theocracy," *Newsweek*, 1/11/10]

"A country that attempts to govern itself from a holy book will immediately find itself in decline: the talents of its females repressed and squandered, its children stultified by rote learning in madrassas, and its qualified and educated people in exile or in prison. There are no exceptions to this rule: Afghanistan under the Taliban was the worst single example of beggary-cum-terrorism, and even the Iranians were forced to denounce it—because of its massacre of the Shia—without seeing the irony." ["The Death of Theocracy," *Newsweek*, 1/11/10]

"A failed state that cannot allow any grown-up, internal debate, or any appeal against the divine edict, will swiftly become an even more failed state and then a rogue one because its limitless paranoia and self-pity must be projected outward." ["The Death of Theocracy," *Newsweek*, 1/11/10]

Theodoracopulos, Taki
". . . Taki Theodoracopulos, a reactionary and a bilious little snob perhaps most notorious for his articles about 'ugly women' in the *American Spectator*. . . . He is a karate fan and likes to mention that fact in arguments. . . . He's not stylish. He's *vulgar*. I know him. I can't stand him. *Nobody* can." ["A Wolfe in Chic Clothing," *Mother Jones*, January 1983]

Theory
". . . A theory that fits all the known facts usually has some merit, but it does need to be tested." ["Minority Report," *Nation*, 7/17/89]

Thinking
". . . It is a mistake to let a regime of any stripe dictate one's thinking." ["Minority Report," *Nation*, 1/25/86]

"When what 'we' think jibes with the official and commissioning temperature-takers, we hear about it. Otherwise we don't get to know our own minds." ["Voting in the Passive Voice," *Harper's*, April 1992]

"The essence of the independent mind lies not in *what* it thinks, but in *how* it thinks." [*Letters to a Young Contrarian* (New York: Basic Books, 2001), 3]

"... Even uneducated people... have an innate capacity to resist and, if not even to think for themselves, to have thoughts occur to them." [*Letters to a Young Contrarian* (New York: Basic Books, 2001), 24]

"If you want to know what, and how, people really think, then catch them talking in private during wartime." [*Blood, Class and Empire* (New York: Nation Books, 2004), 5]

"... An extraordinary number of people appear to believe that the mind, and the reasoning faculty—the only thing that divides us from our animal relatives—is something to be distrusted and even, as far as possible, dulled. The search for nirvana, and the dissolution of the intellect, goes on. And whenever it is tried, it produces a Kool-Aid effect in the real world." [*God Is Not Great* (New York: Twelve, 2007), 198]

"... Contempt for the intellect has a strange way of *not* being passive." [*God Is Not Great* (New York: Twelve, 2007), 204]

Thomas, Clarence

"Clarence ('Bitch set me up') Thomas, naturally a bit stunned to have his theoretical dong handled in public by Joe Biden and Strom Thurmond, called it worse than a Klan raid and the toughest experience of his life as a black man.... On the first day of the hearings, he fatuously said that allegations like Professor [Anita] Hill's were part of 'a high-tech lynching for uppity blacks who in any way deign to think for themselves.'... This will be the first lynching in American history to have ended with the victim holding a lifetime tenure in black robes on the highest court in the land." ["Minority Report," *Nation*, 11/04/91]

"The nomination of poor, stupid Clarence to the Court came from the same mind as conjured Willie Horton." ["Minority Report," *Nation*, 11/04/91]

"It became... a bear-pit, where the cynics of the Bush White House could do brinkmanship with the pseudo-liberals and say, in effect, we back our lynched black man against your abused woman. Wanna play?" ["The Wrong Questions," *Washington Post*, 11/09/97]

"There are not enough lifetimes to excuse the pseudo-liberal sneaks who tried to arraign Thomas not for his ideas or his uncertain jurisprudence but for his vulnerability to gossip." ["The Wrong Questions," *Washington Post*, 11/09/97]

Thompson, Hunter S.

"The career of Hunter Thompson (1937–2005) is probably the one that the largest number of American scribblers wish they could emulate, or even (in their more uncritical moments) wish they could themselves have lived. From lofty Tory eminences such as Tom Wolfe to committed liberal historians like Douglas Brinkley, there comes a consensus that this was a man like no other since... Mark Twain or H. L. Mencken." ["King of the Lost Frontier," *Sunday Times* (London), 10/12/08]

Time

"Time has a way of assigning value." ["Where's the Aura?," *Wall Street Journal*, 11/21/03]

Tobacco [See: Smoking]

Tobacco Industry

"The naïve indignation about the tobacco industry is no more than a populist decoration for a campaign that actually targets the consumers rather than the producers." ["Smoke and Mirrors," *Vanity Fair*, October 1994]

Tolerance

"The enemies of intolerance cannot be tolerant, or neutral, without inviting their own suicide." ["God-Fearing People," *Slate*, 7/30/07]

Tories

"In normal times, British Tories are nothing if not empiricist (and for that matter, nothing if not suspicious of foreign theories)." ["Downstairs Upstairs," *New York Times Magazine*, 6/01/75]

"Tory conferences are rather like the Tory Party—eccentric, fascinating, occasionally even quite touching, but with a mean streak a mile wide." ["Blackpool Diary," *New Statesman*, 10/10/75]

"If there is one thing nastier than the sight of Tories flushed with success it is Tories when they are rattled. You might think a government that waved the flag with one hand and mortgaged the country to cruise missiles with the other could sink no lower. But if you thought that, you would be wrong." ["Minority Report," *Nation*, 2/22/86]

"Having announced a 'back to basics' campaign at his last party conference, and having taken the stage in the guise of a moral guardian, the contemptible John Major placed an impossible strain on his cohorts. The number of adulterers, out-of-wedlock fathers, washroom-haunters and lingerie-artists on his back benches must be roughly constant over time. It's only when they have to go on TV as Puritans that the cover story falters, the cruising becomes a strain and the noose, annoyingly, develops that nagging tendency to slip. As I write, five Tory lawmakers have been unmasked in as many weeks. . . . Now, as I look upon the Major front bench in Parliament, the only alleviation of this rank of stuffed shirts and padded suits is supplied by the guessing game: Which of them has a nurse's uniform demurely concealed beneath?" ["Minority Report," *Nation*, 3/07/94]

Torture

". . . We have no right to consider torture medieval while it is still legally practiced in the New World." ["Minority Report," *Nation*, 8/29/87]

". . . Torture and coercion: history's most tried-and-tested weapons of failure and disgrace." ["American Conservatism: A View from the Left," *Wall Street Journal*, 1/13/03]

"Skill, in these matters [interrogations], depends on taking pains and not on inflicting them. . . . If you have got the wrong guy—and it does happen—you let him go and offer him a ride home and an apology. And you know what? It often works. Only a lazy and incompetent dirtbag looks for brutal shortcuts so that he can get off his shift early." ["A Moral Chernobyl," *Slate*, 6/14/04]

"You don't have to tell them what time of day it is, or where they are, or when the next meal will be served. (Though it must be served.) But you must not bring in that pig or that electrode. That way lies madness and corruption and the extraction of junk confessions." ["A Moral Chernobyl," *Slate*, 6/14/04]

"If it gives anyone pleasure, then you are doing it wrong and doing wrong into the bargain." ["A Moral Chernobyl," *Slate*, 6/14/04]

Totalitarianism

"The revolutions of 1989 negated every *single* one of the assumptions upon which the 'totalitarian' hypothesis rested. The Soviet Union did not intend to move its massed armor across the north German plain into Western Europe. The massed armor, which was always actually for the control of Eastern Europe, was even to be withdrawn from there. This was not done to impress the West, which had neither asked for nor expected the dissolution of the Warsaw Pact. And the population—ah, what can one say of the population? Cheerful, orderly, well informed, happily familiar with all the values and procedures of democracy, antimilitarist, conscious of history—much more laughter than forgetting. Where had they all come from? How could such a people have been incubated under a 'totalitarian' system, where obedience and thought control were the norms?" ["How Neoconservatives Perish," *Harper's*, July 1990]

"A classic definition of a totalitarian society is one where it's impossible to obey the law because you can always be found guilty of something." [Quoted in "The Year in Review," *American Enterprise*, January/February 1998]

"If there turns out to be a connection between the utilitarian and the totalitarian, then we wretched mammals are in even worse straits than we suspect." ["Lightness at Midnight," *Atlantic Monthly*, September 2002]

"In order to be a part of the totalitarian mindset, it is not necessary to wear a uniform or carry a club or a whip. It is only necessary to *wish* for your own subjection, and to delight in the subjection of others. What is a totalitarian system if not one where the abject glorification of the perfect leader is matched by the surrender of all privacy and individuality, especially in matters sexual, and in denunciation and punishment—'for their own good'—of those who transgress?" [*God Is Not Great* (New York: Twelve, 2007), 232]

"The urge to ban and censor books, silence dissenters, condemn outsiders, invade the private sphere, and invoke an exclusive salvation is the very essence of the totalitarian." [*God Is Not Great* (New York: Twelve, 2007), 234]

"All that the totalitarians have demonstrated is that the religious impulse—the need to worship—can take even more monstrous forms if it is repressed. This might not necessarily be a compliment to our worshipping tendency." [*God Is Not Great* (New York: Twelve, 2007), 247]

"Totalitarian systems, whatever outward form they may take, are fundamentalist and, as we would now say, 'faith-based.'" [*God Is Not Great* (New York: Twelve, 2007), 250]

"Totalitarianism is itself a cliché (as well as a tundra of pulverizing boredom). . . ." [*Hitch-22* (New York: Twelve, 2010), 338]

Tragedy

". . . 'Tragedy' is a term that ought not to be cheapened; especially in its original sense of the awful unintended consequences of human action. The pity and terror are enhanced, of course, if the consequences are the result of human action that is idealistic." ["A Briton's Illusions Shattered in Prague," *Newsday*, 9/14/88]

". . . Without tragedy there could be no comedy." ["Why Women Aren't Funny," *Vanity Fair*, January 2007]

Travel

"I've been in Kurdistan and Bosnia and Zaire and Ethiopia—I've done my share of the toilet bowls of the world." [Quoted in Bill Steigerwald and Bob Hoover, "Objectivity and Other Lies," *Pittsburgh Post-Gazette*, 4/27/97]

"In one way, travelling has narrowed my mind. What I have discovered is something very ordinary and unexciting, which is that humans are the same everywhere and that the degree of variation between members of our species is very slight. This is of course an encouraging finding; it helps arm you against news programs back home that show seething or abject masses of either fanatical or torpid people. In another way it is a depressing finding; the sorts of things that make people quarrel and make them stupid are the same everywhere. The two worst things, as one can work out without leaving home, are racism and religion." [*Letters to a Young Contrarian* (New York: Basic Books, 2001), 107]

"The meanness of everyday existence is found at the bottom of every suitcase, and has in fact been packed along with everything else. Nonetheless, it is sometimes when they are far from home and routine that people will stir to make an unwonted exertion of the spirit or of the will." [Introduction to *Orient Express*, by Graham Greene (New York: Penguin Books, 2004), ix]

"Once you have been told that you can't leave a place, its attractions may be many, but its charm will instantly be void." [*Hitch-22* (New York: Twelve, 2010), 113]

Triangulation

"This is a small-minded, not to say simple-minded concept, with sinister implications. The essence of it is a kind of gutless ju-jitsu, where you borrow the strength of your opponent to use against him, before unctuously handing it back again." ["Bill and Dick's Excellent Adventure," *London Review of Books*, 2/20/97]

"The campaign strategy of 'triangulation' was a very simple one: adopt the Republican slogans, and harvest the usual Republican donors before they can." ["It's Not the Sin. It's the Cynicism," *Vanity Fair*, December 1998]

"In the Clinton administration's relationship with the international community, the policy of triangulation almost satirizes itself." [*No One Left to Lie To* (New York: Verso, 2000), 71]

". . . It's important for the maintenance of consensus that some people keep on being scared of what might happen and probably won't; otherwise, they would not be such easy prey for what can happen and actually has. There is even a name for this tactic—it's called 'triangulation'—and eight years of it have been much more than enough." ["Bill of Goods?," *Mother Jones*, September/October 2000]

Triviality

"Pointlessness is the point. Missing the point is the point." ["Bourgeois Blues," *Vanity Fair*, November 1992]

"Pettiness often leads both to error and to the digging of a trap for oneself." [Rebuttal to Sidney Blumenthal's charges in *The Clinton Wars*, Christopher Hitchens Web, 5/13/03]

"Is not the focus on the trivial a product, at least in part, of the repression of the serious?" ["Bring on the Mud," *Wilson Quarterly*, Fall 2004]

Trotsky, Leon

"Trotsky was so much an intellectual that in the final analysis, Marxism was not quite enough for him." ["The Old Man," *Atlantic Monthly*, July/August 2004]

"In spite of the most appalling discouragements and reverses and persecution, Trotsky did continue almost to the end in a belief that the workers would rise again, and that Hitlerism and Stalinism and imperialism would be overthrown by a self-aware and emancipated class. It was this that led him to his only truly banal or farcical initiative: the proclamation of a Fourth International to succeed the Social-Democratic and Communist ones." ["The Old Man," *Atlantic Monthly*, July/August 2004]

". . . The epigones of the Old Man had, partly inadvertently, carried out his final wish by taking part at last in a successful revolution—against communism." ["The Old Man," *Atlantic Monthly*, July/August 2004]

"Even today a faint, saintly penumbra still emanates from the Old Man. Where once the Stalinist press and propaganda machine employed the curse of Trotskyism to criminalize and defame the 'rotten elements' and 'rootless cosmopolitans,' now the tribunes of the isolationist right level the same charge at neoconservatives and the supporters of regime change." ["The Old Man," *Atlantic Monthly*, July/August 2004]

Trump, Donald

"Donald Trump—a ludicrous figure, but at least he's lived it up a bit in the real world, and at least he's worked out how to cover 90 percent of his skull with 30 percent of his hair." ["Diary," *London Review of Books*, 1/06/00]

Truth

"The truth seldom lies, but when it does lie it lies somewhere in between." [Introduction to *For the Sake of Argument* (New York: Verso, 1993), 3]

". . . It can be better to start with the truth and then look for clarification than to start with a falsehood and then search for wiggle room." ["Another Clinton Human Sacrifice?," *Washington Post*, 2/09/99]

"Objective truth. . . is another term that has lost some of its shapeliness lately. There is a tendency, in our 'postmodern' discourse, to inquire first about *whose* truth and *which* power stands to gain, and only then to take an interest in things like verification." ["'It's Our Turn,'" *American Enterprise*, May/June 1999]

"Parties and churches and states cannot be honest, but individuals can." ["Prophet with a Typewriter," *Wilson Quarterly*, Autumn 2000]

"Unearthing the truth is no mere antiquarian task." ["Who Lost Spain?," *Wilson Quarterly*, Summer 2001]

"It may one day seem strange that, in our own time of extraordinary and revolutionary innovation in the physical sciences, from the human genome to the Hubble telescope, so many 'radicals' spent so much time casting casuistic doubt on the concept of verifiable truth." [*Why Orwell Matters* (New York: Basic Books, 2002), 199]

"Many truths or useful remarks go unspoken for fear of rupturing intimacy [between friends]. . . ." [*Hitch-22* (New York: Twelve, 2010), 417]

Turkey

"Turkey cannot be thought of as European until it stops lying about Armenia, gets its invading troops out of Cyprus, and grants full rights to its huge Kurdish population." ["Israel and Turkey: It's Complicated," *Slate*, 6/07/10]

Twain, Mark

"The only objectors to his presence in the schoolroom are mediocre or fanatical racial nationalists or 'inclusivists'. . . who object to Twain's use—in or out of 'context'—of the expression 'nigger.' An empty and formal 'debate' on this has dragged on for decades and flares up every now and again to bore us." ["Goodbye to All That," *Harper's*, November 1998]

Twentieth Century

"The three great subjects of the twentieth century were imperialism, fascism, and Stalinism. It would be trite to say that these 'issues' are only of historical interest to ourselves; they have bequeathed the whole shape and tone of our era. Most of the intellectual class were fatally compromised by accommodation with one or other of these man-made structures of inhumanity, and some by more than one." [*Why Orwell Matters* (New York: Basic Books, 2002), 5]

Tyranny

"*Caudillismo* is never radical, even when it comes decked out as populism." ["Minority Report," *Nation*, 5/25/85]

"... The opponents of dictatorships in their own country have no business euphemizing dictators elsewhere." ["Minority Report," *Nation*, 5/25/85]

"Tyrants, after all, are in power in order to be in power. Like other human beings, they may desire to invest their actions with something of the noble and the grandiose. They may wish for commemorative poems and statues—the Ozymandias complex. But they are hopelessly old-fashioned. . . ." ["Tio Sam," *London Review of Books*, 12/20/90]

"You're a despot if you can make your subjects feel sorry for you." [Quoted in "The Year in Review," *American Enterprise*, January/February 1998]

"The essence of tyranny is not iron law. It is capricious law." ["I Fought the Law," *Vanity Fair*, February 2004]

"... History has taught us that tyranny often looks stronger than it really is, that it has unexpected vulnerabilities (very often to do with the blunt fact that tyranny, as such, is incapable of self-analysis), and that taking a stand on principle, even if not immediately rewarded with pragmatic results, can be an excellent dress rehearsal for the real thing." ["Just Causes," *Foreign Affairs*, September/October 2008]

"... Those who make the presumption of innocence in the case of homicidal dictators take a lot of persuading." [*Hitch-22* (New York: Twelve, 2010), 301]

Unification Church
"Moon's cult is one of those that is easy to join and very difficult to leave." ["American Notes," *Times Literary Supplement*, 4/13/84]

Unilateralism
"... The Iraqi delegation, for some reason, has been flagrantly in breach of a number of overwhelmingly passed [U.N.] resolutions for more than a decade. And yet one never seems to read any well-reasoned denunciation of this 'unilateralist' attitude on the part of Baghdad. Add another clause to the regime-change manifesto: Intervention will put an end to Saddam Hussein's unilateralism." ["Multilateralism and Unilateralism," *Slate*, 12/18/02]

Unity
"'Unity' is one of those objectives that, once desired, are very easily attained. That is how it may be distinguished from 'clarity,' say, or 'principle.'" ["Fashion Parade in Philadelphia," *Nation*, 7/10/82–7/17/82]

Universe
"It is, indeed, only because of the frightening emptiness elsewhere that we are bound to be impressed by the apparently unique and beautiful conditions that have allowed intelligent life to occur on earth." [*God Is Not Great* (New York: Twelve, 2007), 80]

"The natural order does not respond to prayer or propitiation: it maintains its extraordinary regularity. This may not rule out a certain nonspecific deism or pantheism, but it does make nonsense of the idea of a god to which human beings can address themselves." [Debate with Kenneth R. Miller ("Does science make belief in God obsolete?"), A Templeton Conversation]

Utopianism

"Man cannot live on Utopias alone." ["The Children of '68," *Vanity Fair*, June 1998]

". . . Utopianism tends to become the subconscious enabler of cynicism." ["Thinking Like an Apparatchik," *Atlantic Monthly*, July/August 2003]

"The search for Nirvana, like the search for Utopia or the end of history or the classless society, is ultimately a futile and dangerous one. It involves, if it does not necessitate, the sleep of reason. There is no escape from anxiety and struggle. . . ." [Foreword to *Brave New World*, by Aldous Huxley (New York: HarperCollins, 2004), xxi]

"The human desire to imagine a better world may be the root of much idiocy and crime, but it does seem to be innate and it might, like religion, be ineradicable." ["Bang to Rights," *Times Literary Supplement*, 2/17/06]

"The idea of a utopian state on earth, perhaps modeled on some heavenly ideal, is very hard to efface and has led people to commit terrible crimes in the name of the ideal. One of the very first attempts to create such an ideal Edenic society, patterned on the scheme of human equality, was the totalitarian socialist state established by the Jesuit missionaries in Paraguay. It managed to combine the maximum of egalitarianism with the maximum of unfreedom, and could only be kept going by the maximum of fear. This ought to have been a warning to those who sought to perfect the human species. Yet the object of perfecting the species—which is the very root and source of the totalitarian impulse—is in essence a religious one." [*God Is Not Great* (New York: Twelve, 2007), 231–232]

Vanity Fair

"Mr. [Robert] Benchley once observed that the joy of being a *Vanity Fair* contributor was this: You could write about any subject you liked, no matter how outrageous, as long as you said it in evening clothes. I have devoted my professional life to the emulation of this fine line." ["Rebel in Evening Clothes," *Vanity Fair*, October 1999]

Versailles Treaty

"If a population is told that it can never apologize enough, or atone enough, then it may be tempted to lose interest, if it has any self-respect, in apologizing or atoning. This was the original problem of the Versailles treaty, when the arrogance of the British and French empires made the task of German democrats even harder than it already was." ["Minority Report," *Nation*, 4/26/93]

Viagra

"If you call quite a number of physicians in the United States today, and get their answering systems, you will be told to press one for emergency, two for appointments, and three for Viagra. It used to be said that the glory of American democracy was that anyone could be president. Now, anyone—any male at least—can behave like the president." ["It's Magic Darling," *Evening Standard*, 4/28/98]

"Will this lead to more caring and sharing and sensitive blokes, with more time to spare for their partners' needs? The mature, reflective answer to that is, as ever: 'Who cares?'" ["It's Magic Darling," *Evening Standard*, 4/28/98]

Vicarious Redemption

"Ask yourself the question: how moral is the following? I am told of a human sacrifice that took place two thousand years ago, without my wishing it and in circumstances so ghastly that, had I been present and in possession of any influence, I would have been duty-bound to try and stop it. In consequence of this murder, my own manifold sins are forgiven me, and I may hope to enjoy everlasting life. . . . For a start, and in order to gain the benefit of this wondrous offer, I have to accept that I am *responsible* for the flogging and mocking and crucifixion, in which I had no say and no part, and agree that every time I decline this responsibility, or that I sin in word or deed, I am intensifying the agony of it. . . . However, I am still granted free will with which to reject the offer of vicarious redemption. Should I exercise this choice, however, I face an eternity of torture much more awful than anything endured at Calvary, or anything threatened to those who first heard the Ten Commandments." [*God Is Not Great* (New York: Twelve, 2007), 209–210]

"Jesus asks, in effect, 'Do I have to go through with this?' It is an impressive and unforgettable question, and I long ago decided that I would cheerfully wager my own soul on the belief that the only right answer to it is 'no.' We cannot, like fear-ridden peasants of antiquity, hope to load all our crimes onto a goat, and then drive the hapless animal into the desert. Our everyday idiom is quite sound in regarding 'scapegoating' with contempt. And religion is scapegoating writ large." [*God Is Not Great* (New York: Twelve, 2007), 211]

Vidal, Gore

"He is a man to make excellent use of his acquaintance, both as raconteur of the celebrated and as promoter of the unfairly scorned." ["Subversive Dispatches from the Outside In," *Independent*, 11/10/91]

". . . If it's true, even to any degree that we were all changed by September 11, 2001, it's probably truer of Vidal that it made him more the way he already was, and accentuated a crackpot strain that gradually asserted itself as dominant." ["Vidal Loco," *Vanity Fair*, February 2010]

". . . Vidal in his decline has fans like David Letterman's, who laugh in all the wrong places lest they suspect themselves of not having a good time." ["Vidal Loco," *Vanity Fair*, February 2010]

Vietnam Syndrome

"According to those who employ this smooth and evasive construction, the lesson of the Vietnam War is that the United States suffered greatly from being 'entangled' in a 'quagmire' in Indo-China, and should henceforth be extremely prudent about overseas military commitments. . . . This connects perfectly to the sickly fashion for therapy and esteem which it partially prefigures, and to the essentially Stalinist reading of history which allows that 'mistakes were made' but maintains that it was either everybody's fault or nobody's. I can only say, for myself, that I don't remember Vietnam in this way *at all*." ["In the Bright Autumn of My Senescence," *London Review of Books*, 1/06/94]

Vietnam Veterans Memorial

"Almost half the names on that wall in Washington are inscribed with a date after Nixon and Kissinger took office. We still cringe from counting the number of Vietnamese, Laotians, and Cambodians." ["Let Me Say This About That," *New York Times*, 10/08/00]

Vietnam War

"There you have it. America was stabbed in the back—the same back it was fighting with one hand tied behind." ["A Wolfe in Chic Clothing," *Mother Jones*, January 1983]

"It's pretty clear that there can be no healing while there are those who believe that the war could or should have been won and those who believe it should never have been fought, or even that it deserved to be 'lost.'" ["Minority Report," *Nation*, 12/01/84]

"The Vietnam War was *founded* on lies. . . . No truthful statement was, or could have been, made by any defender of the war policy." ["Minority Report," *Nation*, 12/01/84]

". . . The effort of certain forces in the United States to persuade the Vietnamese that they knew what was good for them was a stupid effort, doomed to fail but also doomed to fail absolutely disastrously." ["How We Lost Hearts, Minds and the War," *Newsday*, 1/16/91]

"In case people have forgotten, the United States played the role of Milosevic in Vietnam, and the job of the 'peace' movement, then as now, was to demand an end to the aggression and to take the side of the victim. Anyone who thinks that the 'lesson' of Vietnam is the avoidance of awkward overseas commitments has accepted a gross rewriting of history and is cloaking right-wing isolationism in a white flag." ["Minority Report," *Nation*, 5/30/94]

"Vietnam was a 'quagmire' precisely because it was a war against a popular insurgency." ["Minority Report," *Nation*, 5/30/94]

"The disgraceful thuggery of the authorities. . . makes it plain without further emphasis that the battle against the war in Vietnam was, necessarily and inextricably, a battle not just to extend popular democracy at home but to preserve it from its enemies." [Foreword to *1968: War & Democracy*, by Eugene J. McCarthy (Petersham, MA: Lone Oak Press, 2000), 9]

"If one question is rightly settled in the American and, indeed, the international memory, it is that the Vietnam War was at best a titanic blunder and at worst a campaign of atrocity and aggression." ["To Invoke Vietnam Was a Blunder Too Far for Bush," *Observer*, 8/26/07]

Violence

". . . No state or party has the moral right to condemn the use of violence. . . ." ["Minority Report," *Nation*, 8/03/85–8/10/85]

"Those who oppose violence on principle are called pacifists. Those who oppose it until its use is too little and too late, or too *much* and too late, should be called casuists." ["Scorched Earth," *Weekly Standard*, 7/31/06]

Virgin Mary

"Polish devotees of Our Lady believe their country to be under her special protection—in which case the woman has a lot to answer for." ["Holy Men," *Nation*, 1/15/83]

". . . The case of the Virgin Birth is the easiest possible proof that humans were involved in the manufacture of a legend. Jesus makes large claims for his heavenly father but never mentions that his mother is or was a virgin, and is repeatedly very rude and coarse to her when she makes an appearance, as Jewish mothers will, to ask or to see how he is getting on. . . . In all accounts, everything that her son does comes to her as a complete surprise, if not a shock. . . . One might have expected a stronger maternal memory, especially from someone who had undergone the experience, alone among all women, of discovering herself pregnant without having undergone the notorious preconditions for that happy state." [*God Is Not Great* (New York: Twelve, 2007), 116]

Virginity

"If asked my opinion about virginity, I would say, 'I'm opposed to it.'" [Quoted in Gregg LaGambina, "Christmas with Christopher Hitchens," *A. V. Club*, 12/20/07]

"At the point you know that you are a virgin, I think you decide, 'Well, this is not a condition in which I want to persist very much longer.' I think erring always on the side of the ambition to transcend virginity would be good." [Quoted in Gregg LaGambina, "Christmas with Christopher Hitchens," *A. V. Club*, 12/20/07]

Virtue

"In any time of sniggering relativism and overbred despair, such as we have known and may know again, it is good to know that some enduring virtues can be affirmed, even if the wrong people sometimes take the right line, and even if people of education and refinement are often a little reluctant to trust their guts." [Introduction to *Black Lamb and Grey Falcon*, by Rebecca West (New York: Penguin Classics, 2007), xli]

Visibility

"There is a concept, not peculiar to America but somehow special to it, which defines whether a topic or a person is chic or controversial or otherwise worthy of note. The media vernacular for this concept is 'visibility.' Visibility is, naturally, variable to the point of fickleness. . . . To be 'visible,' a figure or an issue need not be popular or in vogue. It is possible to be quite *démodé* (like Elizabeth Taylor) but still to be instantly recognizable even after prolonged absence from the centre stage. Those without visibility are said to wish that they possessed it. Some who have it wonder how they acquired it. A few wish they could lose it." ["American Notes," *Times Literary Supplement*, 3/04/83]

Vision
"It can be more satisfying to look back than to look forward." ["It Happened on Sunset," *Vanity Fair*, April 1995]

"One problem with keyhole vision, then, is the want of perspective. Where the perspective is not too constricted, it is too broad." ["Performing Seals," *London Review of Books*, 8/10/00]

Wages
". . . One man's wage increase is *not* another's price increase, for the simple reason that large firms are inhibited by international competition from passing on the gains of wage earners in this way. Instead, big business and its political leaders have embarked upon a concerted campaign to reduce labor's share by means of unemployment, mergers, and anti-union legislation." ["Monkey's Paw," *New Statesman*, 8/18/72]

Walking
"This walking business is overrated: I mastered the art of doing it when I was quite small, and in any case, what are taxis for?" ["On the Limits of Self-Improvement, Part I," *Vanity Fair*, October 2007]

Walters, Barbara
". . . Doyenne of drool and sultana of shlock." ["Diary," *London Review of Books*, 12/14/95]

War
"There are war crimes, and there is the crime of war." ["Minority Report," *Nation*, 12/01/84]

"And there's nothing wrong in wishing that you had had a good war, but something, well, *rum* about pretending that you did. Something rummer still about defaming those who opposed the last war or who are unenthusiastic about the next." ["The Hawks with White Feathers," *Spectator*, 8/10/85]

". . . If you happen to want a war, preparing for it is a very good way to get it." ["Washington Diary," *London Review of Books*, 2/07/91]

"Before you support bombing a country off the map, perhaps you should pay it the compliment of finding out where it is." [CNN, 2/05/91]

"There is an obligation, if your 'own' government is engaged in an unjust and deceitful war, to oppose it and to obstruct it and to take the side of the victims." [*Letters to a Young Contrarian* (New York: Basic Books, 2001), 101]

"The war gene is part of our common mammalian makeup, proof of our animal and partly evolved status as well as a potent spur to innovation. With such large adrenal glands, we may one day exterminate each other completely; without them, we might have died out already." ["Preview of Coming Attractions: Sontag Looks at Images of War," *New York Observer*, 3/17/03]

"Those who are most genuinely repelled by war and violence are also those who are most likely to decide that some things, after all, are worth fighting for." ["Preview of Coming Attractions: Sontag Looks at Images of War," *New York Observer*, 3/17/03]

"If you want to avoid a very big and very bad war later, be prepared to fight a small and principled war now." ["Just Give Peace a Chance?," *New Statesman*, 5/19/08]

War on Drugs

". . . Every known civil liberty is mortgaged to a 'war on drugs' that, in city after city, has meant police collusion with the drug dealers." ["Minority Report," *Nation*, 1/24/94]

"The terrifying results of the 'war on drugs'—the incarceration of the harmless, the corruption of the forces of law and order, the misappropriation of resources, the militarization of civil society, and the handing of a profit margin to the forces of organized crime—have taught the control freaks nothing." ["Smoke and Mirrors," *Vanity Fair*, October 1994]

"Maybe I choose my friends with insufficient care, but I have never even met anyone who has ever met anyone who thinks that this 'war' makes a particle of sense." ["Hollywood Tells the Truth," *Evening Standard*, 1/11/01]

". . . Official anti-drug policy is futile at best, and corrupt at worst, resulting in contempt for unenforceable laws and in the manipulation of policemen by incredibly rich criminals." ["Hollywood Tells the Truth," *Evening Standard*, 1/11/01]

"The War on Drugs is an attempt by force, by the state, at mass behavior modification." [Quoted in "Free Radical," *Reason* magazine, November 2001]

"The 'war on drugs' is now being extended to a state-sponsored campaign against tobacco and alcohol and painkillers: If the ruling class wants people to be blissed-out, it has a strange way of pursuing this elementary goal." [Foreword to *Brave New World*, by Aldous Huxley (New York: HarperCollins, 2004), xx]

"In our time, the symbol of state intrusion into the private life is the mandatory urine test." [Foreword to *Brave New World*, by Aldous Huxley (New York: HarperCollins, 2004), xx]

"The largest single change for the better in U.S. foreign policy, and one that could be accomplished simply by an act of political will, would be the abandonment of the so-called War on Drugs." ["Legalize It," *Foreign Policy*, May/June 2007]

War on Poverty

". . . The presidential 'war on poverty,' which, under its sponsor Kennedy and its inheritor Johnson, soon became a war on the poor." ["Minority Report," *Nation*, 8/09/93–8/16/93]

War on Terrorism

"The Taliban will soon be history. Al-Qaeda will take longer. There will be other mutants to fight. But if, as the peaceniks like to moan, more bin Ladens will spring up to take his place, I can offer this assurance: Should that be the case, there are many many more who will also spring up to kill him all over again." ["Ha Ha Ha to the Pacifists," *Guardian*, 11/14/01]

"War is hell, as some people are fond of saying. And so it is. But religious fascism is hell as well. Not only is it hell, but it also demands and guarantees war. Thus a victory over it is something that peace-lovers should actively welcome. How strange and how sad that so few of them do." ["Christopher Hitchens on Why Peace-Lovers Must Welcome This War," *Mirror*, 11/15/01]

"This time around, the analysis of the enemy is basically sound. The tactics of the foe are fascistic, as is its demented rhetoric and the aim for an outcome of Stone Age barbarism. Bush 'gets' this, in a way that many liberal intellectuals have failed to." ["My Dimmest Student Is Better Qualified to Be the President of the United States," *Mirror*, 9/11/02]

"The United States is now at war with the forces of reaction, and nobody is entitled to view this battle as a spectator." ["Chew on This," *Stranger*, 1/16/03–1/22/03]

". . . We don't have the right to forget why we are in Afghanistan and Iraq in the first place: to make up for past crimes of both omission and commission and to help safeguard emergent systems of self-government who have the same deadly enemies as we do, and to whom, not quite incidentally, we gave our word." ["Don't Forget Why We're in Afghanistan and Iraq," *Slate*, 9/07/09]

"The battle will go on for the rest of our lives. Those who plan our destruction know what they want, and they are prepared to kill and die for it. Those who don't get the point prefer to whine about 'endless war,' accidentally speaking the truth. . . ." ["Flying High," *Slate*, 12/28/09]

Warhol, Andy

"Having been pronounced clinically dead twenty years too soon, Warhol was pronounced actually dead several years too early. He survives in our references, in our imagination, and in the relationship of his own sense of timing to ours. Just because he knew the price of everything doesn't mean he didn't know the value of some things." ["The Importance of Being Andy," *Critical Quarterly*, Spring 1996]

Warren, Rick

". . . [Rick Warren] is a relentless, clerical businessman who raises money on the proposition that certain Americans—non-Christians, the wrong kind of Christians, homosexuals, nonbelievers—are of less worth and littler virtue than his own lovely flock of redeemed and salvaged and paid-up donors." ["Three Questions About Rick Warren's Role in the Inauguration," *Slate*, 12/19/08]

"... A tree-shaking huckster and publicity seeker who believes that millions of his fellow citizens are hellbound because they do not meet his own low and vulgar standards." ["Three Questions About Rick Warren's Role in the Inauguration," *Slate*, 12/19/08]

Washington, George

"George Washington never owned up to cutting down that cherry tree because there was no tree, and he didn't cut it down anyway." ["Whose History Is It?," *Vanity Fair*, December 1993]

"Perhaps never before in history had a man of such political power agreed to surrender it: Certainly nobody has ever provided a better illustration of the maxim that one does best to quit when one is ahead." [Foreword to *First in Peace: How George Washington Set the Course for America*, by Conor Cruise O'Brien (New York: Da Capo Press, 2009), 14–15]

"Washington's achievement was so large, and his execution of it so impeccably and magnanimously timed, that the attacks on him, even by men of the stature of Thomas Paine, appear in retrospect to be petty and irrelevant." [Foreword to *First in Peace: How George Washington Set the Course for America*, by Conor Cruise O'Brien (New York: Da Capo Press, 2009), 15]

Washington, DC

"There are two ways in which the city of Washington discloses its contempt for the life of the mind. The first is in its general bovine indifference to ideas and theories and to anything else that doesn't assimilate to 'the bottom line.' The second is in its occasional, febrile enthusiasm for a crackpot hypothesis." ["Minority Report," *Nation*, 9/25/89]

"Welcome to Washington, where the unploughed snow at least helps to cover up the uncollected garbage. Where the official advice is that children, old people, and sick people should not drink the tap water unless they boil it." ["Washington Decay," *Evening Standard*, 2/13/97]

"There is no pollution, because government is practically the only industry." ["District of Contempt," *Vanity Fair*, March 1998]

"You may feel patriotic about the United States, but you can't quite feel patriotic about Washington, DC." ["For Patriotic Dreams," *Vanity Fair*, December 2001]

"... For the Right, the Federal City is both the belly of the beast and a place of opportunity. (By something more than chance, that duality could fairly describe the long-standing attitude of many leftists to America itself.)" [Introduction to *Left Hooks, Right Crosses: A Decade of Political Writing*, ed. Christopher Caldwell and Christopher Hitchens (New York: Nation Books, 2002), 211]

"The verbiage of Washington is what makes it hardest for me to live there. Your ears hurt at the way people talk." [Quoted in Neil Munro, "Leaving the Left," *National Journal*, 4/05/03]

"I had lived in the nation's capital for many years and never particularly liked it. But when it was exposed to attack, and looked and felt so goddamn vulnerable, I fused myself with it. I know now that no solvent can ever unglue that bond." ["On Becoming American," *Atlantic Monthly*, May 2005]

"Aspects of the District of Columbia are Dixie-ish enough: it gets very hot and muggy in the summer; and its neighborhoods are very segregated." ["My Red-State Odyssey," *Vanity Fair*, September 2005]

"To become a Washingtonian is to choose a very odd way of becoming an American. It felt at first like moving to a company town where nothing ever actually got itself made." [*Hitch-22* (New York: Twelve, 2010), 235]

WASP
"A small suggestion. Can we not eliminate the redundancy from the acronym WASP? It's not as if there were any BASPs. Doesn't ASP convey precisely the same connotation with even more economy?" ["American Notes," *Times Literary Supplement*, 11/14/86]

"The WASP élite makes sacrifices that we know not of." ["Washington Diary," *London Review of Books*, 8/20/92]

"'Redneck' is only a rude word for Wasp. In any case, I have long believed that the acronym certainly doesn't need its *W* and barely needs its *p*. (William F. Buckley Jr. is Waspy despite being Irish and Catholic; George Wallace could never have achieved Waspdom in spite of being aggressively white, Anglo-Saxon, and Protestant. That's because Wasp is a term of class, not ethnicity. . . ." ["My Red-State Odyssey," *Vanity Fair*, September 2005]

Waterboarding
"Waterboarding is for Green Berets in training, or wiry young jihadists whose teeth can bite through the gristle of an old goat. It's not for wheezing, paunchy scribblers. For my current 'handlers' I had had to produce a doctor's certificate assuring them that I did not have asthma, but I wondered whether I should tell them about the 15,000 cigarettes I had inhaled every year for the last several decades." ["Believe Me, It's Torture," *Vanity Fair*, August 2008]

". . . If waterboarding does not constitute torture, then there is no such thing as torture." ["Believe Me, It's Torture," *Vanity Fair*, August 2008]

Watergate
"Analogies with Watergate are too easily made, but they may turn out to be more profound than they first appear." ["Reality Time," *Spectator*, 11/29/86]

"Watergate was a raising of the curtain on the world of illicit campaign finance, of covert action as a political principle, of the power of organized crime, of the consequences of imperial brutality and of the annexation of national police and bureaucratic agencies to the ends of domestic power. The sight was so alarming that many in the *polis* successfully demanded that the curtain be rung down again." ["Strait Is the Gate," *London Review of Books*, 7/21/94]

"You may choose, if you wish, to parrot the line that Watergate was a 'long national nightmare,' but some of us found it rather exhilarating to see a criminal president successfully investigated and exposed and discredited. And we do not think it in the least bit nightmarish that the Constitution says that such a man is not above the law." ["Our Short National Nightmare," *Slate*, 12/29/06]

Waugh, Evelyn

". . . If Evelyn Waugh later became a byword for port-sodden Blimpery it was because his face shaped itself to fit a mask." [Introduction to *Scoop*, by Evelyn Waugh (New York: Penguin Classics, 2000), v]

"Evelyn Waugh was a reactionary and that's that. But he combined in the same person an attachment to modernism." [Introduction to *Scoop*, by Evelyn Waugh (New York: Penguin Classics, 2000), x]

". . . Any examination of Waugh's actual life shows that its most wicked elements arose precisely from his faith." [*God Is Not Great* (New York: Twelve, 2007), 187]

". . . One cannot have the novels without the torments and evils of its author." [*God Is Not Great* (New York: Twelve, 2007), 188]

Weapons

". . . Missiles are almost as common as steeples on American soil. . . ." ["Minority Report," *Nation*, 10/20/84]

"The cluster bombs are being used [in Kosovo] to save money—because costly smart missiles aren't to be hurled around like confetti to help people little better than Gypsies—and the civilian casualties occur because the military is too nervous about fighting, not because it is too gung-ho. Once you decide to bomb from above a ceiling of 15,000 feet, in order to bring the expensive planes and popular pilots home in safety, then indeed you do accept that civilian losses are more likely." ["Port Huron Piffle," *Nation*, 6/14/99]

Weapons of Mass Destruction

"There are many scary things about WMDs. One of them—given that a 'rogue state' would be committing suicide if it even fired a single missile in the general direction of the United States—is that they can be smuggled across frontiers or even constructed inside them, quite immune to any missile system, however accurate." ["Political Defense System," *Nation*, 2/01/99]

Weinberger, Caspar

"Caspar Weinberger is a man with a long record as a liar and an opportunist. He is also the man who tries to sucker Congress into supporting first-strike weaponry that will enrich the businesses he really represents. Such a man stinks of his European predecessors—the morally neutral oven contractor and the crematorium concessionaire." ["Minority Report," *Nation*, 4/13/85]

Welfare

"Welfare costs absorb a whole 1 percent of the federal budget, but the welfare underclass supplies perhaps 50 percent of America's political anecdotes—a productivity factor that is a story in itself." ["Newtopia," *London Review of Books*, 8/24/95]

West, Rebecca

". . . West deploys a rhetorical skill that is perhaps too little associated with feminism: the ability to detect a pure bitch at twenty paces." [Introduction to *Black Lamb and Grey Falcon*, by Rebecca West (New York: Penguin Classics, 2007), xvii]

The White House

". . . My minority view [is] that the White House and the Rose Garden have long been used, by a superior civilization on another planet, as a combination of prison farm and lunatic asylum. Who will be the first to have the courage to break that story?" ["Muddy Insights from an Ex-Grand Vizier," *Newsday*, 5/25/88]

Wilde, Oscar

"Oscar Wilde's weapon was paradox, and his secret was his seriousness. He was flippant about serious things, and serious about apparently trivial ones." ["The Wilde Side," *Vanity Fair*, May 1995]

"Wilde could never hope to escape the judgment of the pompous and the hypocritical, because he could not help teasing them." ["The Wilde Side," *Vanity Fair*, May 1995]

"Wilde, who did not outlive the nineteenth century (he died in 1900), is nonetheless a uniquely modern figure. If it is safe to say that the work of writers such as P. G. Wodehouse and Evelyn Waugh and Ronald Firbank and Noël Coward is inconceivable without him, then it is safe to say that he is immortal." ["The Wilde Side," *Vanity Fair*, May 1995]

"So, rather like Gore Vidal in our time, Wilde was able to be mordant and witty because he was, deep down and on the surface, *un homme sérieux*." ["The Wilde Side," *Vanity Fair*, May 1995]

Will, George F.

"As a stylist, Will is the idol of the half-educated. His blizzard of literary tags and historical allusions is a mere show of learning." ["A Political Pundit Who Need Never Dine Alone," *Newsday*, 11/07/90]

"Increasingly he has turned to baseball, where for all I know he can keep a better score, or to episodes in his private and family life, which he depicts with excruciating archness. 'Let me tell you about our cat' is a one-line introductory paragraph that summons the instant response of 'Hold it right there!'" ["A Political Pundit Who Need Never Dine Alone," *Newsday*, 11/07/90]

Prince William

"Prince William has had himself photographed as he charmingly and democratically scrubs a lavatory in Chile, of all places; the shot redefines the concept of his relationship to the 'throne.'" ["Throne of Contention," *Vanity Fair*, March 2001]

Wilson, Joseph

"Joseph Wilson comes before us as a man whose word is effectively worthless." ["Rove Rage," *Slate*, 7/18/05]

House of Windsor

". . . The House of Windsor, apex of a crumbling and rancorous British class system and occasional decorative camouflage at white trash binges in Reagan's Washington." ["Minority Report," *Nation*, 11/23/85]

". . . The Windsors are a burden on us, not the other way about. . . ." ["How's the Vampire?," *London Review of Books*, 11/08/90]

"The essential strength of the House of Windsor reposes in its image as a family: the pattern of order in society and the microcosm of the domestic ideal. Yet it is precisely as a family that the Windsors are beginning to fray. Without even looking for skeletons in the closet, it is possible to find them thrust in one's face in the most alarming way." ["Windsor Knot," *New York Times Magazine*, 5/12/91]

"The House of Windsor has achieved the near-impossible by way of its own negation. Its misery and frustration, which are inseparable from the hereditary principle of random selection—the same principle that undid the Cromwells and will undo Kim Il-sung—are such as to make Britain look more like a banana republic, not less." ["Away with Them and Their Overweening Power," *Independent*, 6/02/93]

"The British people are now in the absurd—no, indecent—position of insisting upon the public immolation of a whole family, in order that the values of family be upheld." ["Our Martyred Monarchy," *Guardian*, 10/17/94]

"It used to be said that the royal family's role and job in our national life was to be a model British family. And in a sense, they are a model British family now. They've got—let's see—anorexia, bulimia, mass infidelity, divorce, frightened, worried children, painful separations, property disputes, the lot. They are the perfect symbol of family life and family values." [*Eye to Eye with Connie Chung*, CBS, 11/10/94]

"It is no longer defensible that we demand the human sacrifice of an entire family as a burnt offering to an illusory national unity. The sacrifice demeans and degrades both those who watch it and those who undergo it." [Quoted in "Should We Scrap Our Royals?," *Daily Express*, 3/12/96]

House of Windsor and World War II

"Almost the entire moral capital of this rather odd little German dynasty is invested in the post-fabricated myth of its participation in 'Britain's finest hour.' In fact, had it been up to them, the finest hour would never have taken place." ["Churchill Didn't Say That," *Slate*, 1/24/11]

Wit

"There is a revenge that the bores and the bullies and the bigots exact on those who are too witty." ["The Wilde Side," *Vanity Fair*, May 1995]

"Wit, after all, is the unfailing symptom of intelligence." ["Why Women Aren't Funny," *Vanity Fair*, January 2007]

Witness

"With its ostentatious religiosity and its relentless emphasis on redemption and conversion—and its subplot concerning the triumph of the plain man over the devious intellectuals and sinister pointy-heads—it was one of the building blocks for McCarthyism, for the Goldwater campaign, and for what eventually became the 'Reagan revolution.'" ["A Regular Bull," *London Review of Books*, 9/18/97]

Wodehouse, P. G.

"You get into terrifically bad company some of the time if you're a fan of Wodehouse." ["Booknotes," C-SPAN, 9/01/93 (first aired: 10/17/93)]

"Too often, a certain type of Wodehouse addict possesses—in addition to the irritating habit of calling him 'The Master'—a prejudice against neologisms and Americanisms. It deserves to be said, then, that one of the ways in which Wodehouse replenished the well of English was by stirring, into the bland orange juice, the gin of transatlantic vim and pith." [Introduction to *The Mating Season*, by P. G. Wodehouse (New York: Penguin Classics, 1999), vi–vii]

"The new Penguin edition of *The Mating Season* contains my introduction. Now that my name appears on the flyleaf on the same page as P. G. Wodehouse, I have no other literary ambitions." [Quoted in Michael Rust, "Clinton's Lies Stopped at Hitchens' Door," *Insight on the News*, 6/28/99]

Wolfe, Tom

". . . Typical Wolfe: apparently poised and polished, with a certain assurance and some show of learning, but finally shallow and affected. (Have you ever, really, read anything of his twice?)" ["A Wolfe in Chic Clothing," *Mother Jones*, January 1983]

". . . He has lampooned wealth only in the form of conscience money—what used to be called 'limousine liberalism.' The Super Rich, those who just *have* great wealth and consider it their right, are safe from Wolfe's waspish pen. Crass Republican money, 'new' or 'old,' is O.K. by him. As long as you don't try to pose as a friend of the masses, he'll leave you in peace to enjoy your dough." ["A Wolfe in Chic Clothing," *Mother Jones*, January 1983]

"Amid the dash and glitter of Ronnie's new America, Wolfe looks less like a performing flea than a rather moth-eaten court jester." ["A Wolfe in Chic Clothing," *Mother Jones*, January 1983]

". . . The three things that go to make up the Tom Wolfe effect. One, a glibness that is designed for speed-reading. Two, a facility with rapidly cross-cut images and references: a show of learning. Three, a strongly marked conservatism." ["The Wrong Stuff," *London Review of Books*, 4/01/83]

"He is simply, as was once said of the old German ruling establishment, blind in the right eye." ["The Wrong Stuff," *London Review of Books*, 4/01/83]

"Reading Wolfe, you could suppose that New York City over the past decade had seen the victimization of the rich by the poor, the white by the black." ["Mugged by Reality," *Times Literary Supplement*, 3/18/88–3/24/88]

Wolfowitz, Paul

"It's easy to look up the official papers and public essays in which Paul Wolfowitz, for example, has stressed the menace of Saddam Hussein since as far back as 1978. He has never deviated from this conviction. What could possibly be more sinister? The consistency with which a view is held is of course no guarantee of that view's integrity. But it seems odd to blame Wolfowitz for having in effect been right all along." ["(Un)Intended Consequences," *Slate*, 3/17/03]

Women

". . . The chief cultural difference between English and American girls is that English girls lose their virginity before administering BJ, and American girls preserve their virginity by the selfsame method." ["Dear Bridget," *Evening Standard*, 3/31/98]

"Conversations among the male trade union will turn up as many yearning or enviable observations about merry widows and mature divorcees as it will boastful remarks about cradle-snatching or jailbait (well, almost as many). And yet huge numbers of women refuse to believe this, and can't credit the fact that men often like someone with a bit of mileage on her. Better company, for one thing. And it can help to have been round the block a few times. Stop me before I say that there's no substitute for experience." ["She's the Real Thing," *Evening Standard*, 8/24/99]

Women and Humor

". . . There is something that you absolutely never hear from a male friend who is hymning his latest (female) love interest: 'She's a real honey, has a life of her own. . . [interlude for attributes that are none of your business]. . . and, man, does she ever make 'em laugh.'" ["Why Women Aren't Funny," *Vanity Fair*, January 2007]

"Why are women, who have the whole male world at their mercy, not funny? Please do not pretend not to know what I am talking about." ["Why Women Aren't Funny," *Vanity Fair*, January 2007]

"There are more terrible female comedians than there are terrible male comedians, but there are some impressive ladies out there. Most of them, though, when you come to review the situation, are hefty or dykey or Jewish, or some combo of the three. When Roseanne stands up and tells biker jokes and invites people who don't dig her shtick to suck her dick—know what I am saying?" ["Why Women Aren't Funny," *Vanity Fair*, January 2007]

"Precisely because humor is a sign of intelligence (and many women believe, or were taught by their mothers, that they become threatening to men if they appear too bright), it could be that in some way men do not *want* women to be funny. They want them as an audience, not as rivals." ["Why Women Aren't Funny," *Vanity Fair*, January 2007]

"If I am correct about this, which I am, then the explanation for the superior funniness of men is much the same as for the inferior funniness of women. Men have to pretend, to themselves as well as to women, that they are not the servants and supplicants. Women, cunning minxes that they are, have to affect not to be the potentates. This is the unspoken compromise." ["Why Women Aren't Funny," *Vanity Fair*, January 2007]

Word Games
". . . Word games, like limericks and acrostics and acronyms and crosswords, are good training in and of themselves." [*Hitch-22* (New York: Twelve, 2010), 130]

Words
"One word, in intelligent journalism, is and always has been worth a thousand pictures." [Introduction to *Lines of Dissent: Writing from the New Statesman 1913 to 1988*, ed. Stephen Howe (New York: Verso, 1988), 11]

"A key weasel word. . . is 'reportedly.' An innocuous word on the face of it, but one that always makes me put my hand on my wallet." ["Minority Report," *Nation*, 7/17/89]

"You need an exquisite handling of words to avoid the mawkish, and to get the best out of the semi-articulate." ["Potter's Field," *Vanity Fair*, August 1994]

"By the way, hasn't the word 'offensive' become really offensive lately?" ["Cartoon Debate," *Slate*, 2/04/06]

"When will we learn that there is more to political and social emancipation than the simple addition of the 'ism' suffix to any commonplace word?" ["The First Excuse," *Slate*, 6/16/08]

"When mindlessly and endlessly reiterated, ordinary words begin to lose their anchorage in original meaning. *Dream* is now so vague as to be strictly without content, and, with strong assistance from Barack Obama, *hope* is rapidly going the same way. (Twice on Saturday I heard the closing words of the Roman Catholic funeral liturgy, which sonorously intone 'the sure and certain hope of the resurrection.' If this means anything, it means not that there is anything certain about the prospect of the resurrection but that people sure think that there is something certain about hoping for it.)" ["Redemption Song," *Slate*, 8/31/09]

World War I
"The years immediately preceding World War I . . . are an unceasing source of interest to many readers and historians. I suspect that this is because we read about the polished statesmen, the crowned heads, the sophisticated diplomats, and the confident generals and think: They have no idea what is about to happen." ["Ships of Fools," *Newsday*, 11/17/91]

"World War I was the outcome of imperialist rivalry and human folly." ["Ships of Fools," *Newsday*, 11/17/91]

"The First World War was, like the abattoir in Vietnam, quite describable as a liberals' war. Any medium-run view of history will show that it did more damage to 'Western civilization' than any form of ideology, not least in clearing the very path, through the ruins and cadavers, along which totalitarians could later instate and militarize themselves." ["Moderation or Death," *London Review of Books*, 11/26/98]

"Ninety-two years on, and liberals, conservatives, and Marxists can all reckon August of 1914 as the month from which everything measurable is—to annex the title of Leonard Woolf's autobiography—downhill all the way. . . . The mechanization of warfare, the glorification of the state, the mass mobilization of peoples, the advantage given to demagogues, and the permission to engage in genocide under the color of warfare: All this would have raised the eyebrows of the most self-confident Victorian imperialist." ["Downhill All the Way," *Atlantic Monthly*, January/February 2006]

World War II
"America. . . entered the greatest conflict in world history having had an advantage possessed by no other country—time to weigh and consider its options." ["FDR as the Premier Leader of World War II," *Newsday*, 10/26/88]

". . . An imperialist war that was nonetheless fought for freedom." ["The Cosmopolitan Man," *New York Review of Books*, 4/22/99]

"There is something unbearable in the idea of a British regime, that would not fire or risk a shot against Hitler in 1938, later deploying horrific violence against German civilians instead. . . . I will never be one of those Englishmen who can complacently regard the years between 1940 and 1945 as a 'finest hour.'" ["Scorched Earth," *Weekly Standard*, 7/31/06]

Worship
"The desire to worship and obey is the problem—the object of adoration is a secondary issue." ["The Lord and the Intellectuals," *Harper's*, July 1982]

Writers
"The twentieth century is kinder than it looks to us, the minor scribes. We do not often risk persecution, exile, or torture—though we feel keenly for those writers who do. We register shocks, as far-off seismographs record earthquakes or thermo-nuclear detonations; which is to say that we have no choice in the matter and need feel none of the pain. The only risk that is ever-present is the risk of being boring; the danger of missing a point through excess of solemnity." ["American Notes," *Times Literary Supplement*, 1/06/84]

". . . Of course, great, brave, original writers don't need their 'immortality' to be 'validated.' So maybe it's just as well that they hardly ever get visited by the validators." ["These Glittering Prizes," *Vanity Fair*, January 1993]

". . . The one question that authors usually and rightly most resent—any version of 'Where Do You Get Your Ideas?'" ["Signature Sontag," *Vanity Fair*, March 2000]

"The openly, directly politicized writer is something we have learned to distrust—who now remembers Mikhail Sholokhov?—and the surreptitiously politicized one (I give here the instance of Tom Wolfe) is no great improvement." [Foreword to *Unacknowledged Legislation* (New York: Verso, 2000), xii]

". . . It ought to be an axiom that an author is not *ipso facto* responsible for the thoughts of his characters." ["The Stupidest Religion," *Free Inquiry*, Fall 2002]

Writers (Conservative)

". . . Many a conservative, and even conservative radical, writer has had to answer the question, from parents or professors, about when he or she is going to get a proper or serious job." [Introduction to *Left Hooks, Right Crosses: A Decade of Political Writing*, ed. Christopher Caldwell and Christopher Hitchens (New York: Nation Books, 2002), 207]

Writers (Liberal)

"I don't think liberals make very good writers. I think liberals are always trying to have it both ways. They want to share in the idea that capitalism is basically the best humanity can do, but they want to be able to be compassionate about it. I think that leads to a lot of sickly writing. I find it very hard to read, and I think it is harder to read than it is to write." ["Booknotes," C-SPAN, 9/01/93 (first aired: 10/17/93)]

Writing

"Good writing is in some degree dependent on good conversation, and solitary stupefaction isn't any good for that purpose." ["Why Genius Cries Out for a Drink," *Evening Standard*, 4/02/92]

"I don't really know if I enjoy writing or not. I'd hate not writing, I know that. I sort of do it because I feel I have to. Sometimes it's a real pleasure doing it. Usually the pleasure comes, though, when you see it in print—not until then, and usually not until some time after." ["Booknotes," C-SPAN, 9/01/93 (first aired: 10/17/93)]

"I devoutly believe that words ought to be weapons. That is why I got into this business in the first place. I don't seek the title of 'inoffensive,' which I think is one of the nastiest things that could be said about an individual writer." [Quoted in "Forbidden Thoughts: A Roundtable on Taboo Research," *American Enterprise*, January/February 1995]

"There's nothing like not writing for making you unhappy." ["Political Books," C-SPAN2, 10/26/97]

"It gets harder the more you do it. Now that seems a shame. It should get easier. It should become more like a facility, for example. But it becomes more difficult, and it becomes more difficult because you are reading more and more work by better and better people." ["Political Books," C-SPAN2, 10/26/97]

"The sword, as we have reason to know, is often much mightier than the pen. However, there are things that pens can do, and swords cannot." [Foreword to *Unacknowledged Legislation* (New York: Verso, 2000), x]

"If you're a self-employed writer, there's a tendency always to feel guilty any time you're not working." ["In Depth with Christopher Hitchens," C-SPAN, 9/02/07]

"If you can talk, you can write." [Interview with Peter Fitzsimons, Sydney Writers' Festival, Sydney, Australia, 5/24/10]

"It would be useful to keep a diary, but I don't like writing unpaid. I don't like writing checks without getting paid." [Quoted in Deborah Solomon, "The Contrarian," *New York Times Magazine*, 6/02/10]

". . . Leaden prose always tends to be a symptom of other problems. . . ." [*Hitch-22* (New York: Twelve, 2010), 282]

X, Malcolm
". . . He was in transition from racial nationalism to radicalism and was a man who could sicken of his own bile." ["The Charmer," *Grand Street*, Winter 1986]

Yeltsin, Boris
"Once secure in his position as a 'lesser' evil, Yeltsin is free to be more and more 'great' an evil, if not indeed greater." ["Against Lesser Evilism," *Dissent*, Fall 1996]

Yeltsin, Boris: Autobiography
"'No doubt it will sound banal, but what surprised me most were precisely those ordinary people in America, who radiated optimism, faith in themselves and in their country.' Well, yes, as a matter of fact it *does* sound banal. This could also be said of Yeltsin's roguish admission that while at school he was a hard worker but a bit of a rebel; his incessant resort to stories and metaphors drawn from sport, particularly his beloved volleyball, and his claim at one point to have 'reacted calmly enough to what sociologists would call a drop in my rating.' Actually it's psephologists. . . ." ["Thousands of Cans and Cartons," *London Review of Books*, 5/24/90]

Yorkshire
"I can rub along with pretty much anyone of any, as it were, origin or sexual orientation or language group—except people from Yorkshire, of course." [Debate ("Be It Resolved: Freedom of Speech Includes the Freedom to Hate"), University of Toronto, Toronto, Canada, 11/15/06]

Youth
"One's attachment to a lost youth is something that never quite dies. . . ." ["*New Statesman* Downed by Law," *Nation*, 2/21/87]

"Youth is gone; there may be some comfort to be found in sex and alcohol, but. . . youth is gone all the same, and is irretrievable. Needless to add, innocence departed before youth did." ["The Road to West Egg," *Vanity Fair*, May 2000]

"As far as one can tell, most youth culture is as inarticulate and illiterate and mannerless as Sacha Baron Cohen made it out to be [in *Da Ali G Show*]: The elderly dupes who did their best to respond (Gen. Brent Scowcroft on the anthrax/Tampax distinction being the most notable) were evidently resigned in advance to quite a low standard of questioning." ["Kazakh Like Me," *Slate*, 11/13/06]

YouTube

"I have just been sent a link to an Internet site that shows me delivering a speech some years ago. This is my quite unsolicited introduction to the now-inescapable phenomenon of YouTube. It comes with another link, enabling me to see other movies of myself all over the place. What's 'You' about this? It's a MeTube, for me. And I can only suppose that, for my friends and foes alike, it's a HimTube." ["The You Decade," *Slate*, 4/09/07]

Al-Zarqawi, Abu Musab

"Faced with a complete beast like the late Abu-Musab al-Zarqawi, who has been trying to kill us for several years, millions of Americans appear to believe that he only appeared in Iraq because in some way we made him upset. Well, even if this was true—which it is not—it wouldn't be such a bad thing. (What would you say to a policy that made him contented, instead?)." ["This July Fourth, Ignore Polls on America's Image," *Washington Examiner*, 7/04/06]

Zero Tolerance

"'Zero tolerance,' they call it—one of those terms (like 'Drug Czar') that are unintentionally and usefully revealing. 'Zero tolerance' literally means, and literally intends, complete intolerance. Yet it is proclaimed by prissy liberals for whom the word 'tolerance' is a mantra, one of the fuzz-words of the room-temperature America that they have in mind." ["We Know Best," *Vanity Fair*, May 2001]

Zimbabwe

"There were many sighs of relief when Rhodesia belatedly became Zimbabwe, and many of these sighs came from the white establishment. I've often thought that they must have rejoiced to be rid of the strain of calling all Africans 'terrorists' or 'terrorist sympathizers.'" ["Wanton Acts of Usage," *Harper's*, September 1986]

Zionism

"Where once the ultra-Orthodox were mainly anti-Zionist—fearing as ever the secular above all else—and the fervent nationalists tended to be irreligious, there is now a tendency among fanatics of both camps to make common cause. This is 'fundamentalism' with a vengeance, though our press almost never employs the term in this context." ["Minority Report," *Nation*, 7/25/94–8/01/94]

"Many people's attitude to Zionism is conditioned by their exposure to anti-Semitism. . . ." ["Moderation or Death," *London Review of Books*, 11/26/98]

"Zionism must constitute one of the greatest potential non sequiturs in human history." [*Hitch-22* (New York: Twelve, 2010), 383]

"One of my first reservations about Zionism was and is that, semiconsciously at least, it grants the anti-Semite's first premise about the abnormality of the Jew." [*Hitch-22* (New York: Twelve, 2010), 383]

Index

Credits

Unless otherwise noted, all quotations are © Christopher Hitchens. Reprinted by arrangement with the author.

American Enterprise

"Forbidden Thoughts," *The American Enterprise*, January 1995. "The Year in Review," *The American Enterprise*, January/February 1998. "'It's Our Turn,'" *The American Enterprise*, May/June 1999. "Is Hillary Clinton Eleanor Roosevelt?" *The American Enterprise*, July/August 2000. Reprinted by permission.

A. V. Club

Gregg LaGambina, "Christmas with Christopher Hitchens," *A.V. Club*, 12/20/07. Reprinted by permission.

Basic Books

Letters to a Young Contrarian by Christopher Hitchens. Copyright © 2001. Reprinted by permission of Perseus Books.

Berkeley Monthly

Interview with Paul Kilduff, *The Berkeley Monthly*, May 1998. Reprinted by permission of *The East Bay Monthly*, formerly *The Berkeley Monthly*.

Canon Press

Excerpts from *Is Christianity Good for the World?* © 2008 by Christopher Hitchens and Douglas J. Wilson. Published by Canon Press, P.O. Box 8729, Moscow, ID 83843. (800) 488-2034. www.canonpress.com

Cato Policy Report

© Cato Institute. 2005. Excerpted from *Cato Policy Report*, Vol. XXVII, No. 2 (March/April 2005). Used by permission.

Claremont Review of Books

"Theater of War," *Claremont Review of Books*, Winter 2006. Reprinted by permission.

Common Review

"Don't Cross Over If You Have Any Intention of Going Back," Summer 2005. Reprinted by permission of *The Common Review*.

Critical Quarterly

"The Importance of Being Andy," *Critical Quarterly*, Spring 1996. Reprinted by permission of *Critical Quarterly*. "Ireland," *Critical Quarterly*, Spring 1998. Reprinted by permission of *Critical Quarterly*.

Daedalus

Reprinted by permission of *Daedalus*.

Daily Express

Reprinted by permission.

Daily Mail

"Last orders catch for Catch-22," *Daily Mail*, 9/24/94.

Dissent
Reprinted by permission.

Evening Standard
Various articles, reprinted by permission of
Evening Standard.

Foreign Affairs
"Just Causes," September/October 2008.
Reprinted by permission of *Foreign
Affairs*.

Foreign Policy
"Farewell to the Helmsman,"
September/October 2001. Reprinted by
permission of *Foreign Policy*.
"Powell Valediction," November/December
2004. Reprinted by permission of
Foreign Policy.
"Legalize It," May/June 2007. Reprinted by
permission of *Foreign Policy*.
"The Plight of the Public Intellectual,"
May/June 2008. Reprinted by
permission of *Foreign Policy*.

Free Inquiry
Various articles, reprinted by permission of
Free Inquiry.

Grand Street
"The Chorus and Cassandra," *Grand Street*,
Autumn 1985.

Harper's
Various articles, reprinted by permission of
Harper's.

Hatchette Books
God Is Not Great by Christopher Hitchens.
Copyright © 2007. Reprinted by
permission of Hatchette Books.
Hitch-22 by Christopher Hitchens.
Copyright © 2010. Reprinted by
permission of Hatchette Books.

In These Times
Various articles, reprinted by permission of
In These Times.

Independent
Various articles, reprinted by permission of
The Independent.

Insight on the News
Michael Rust, "Clinton's Lies Stopped at
Hitchens' Door," *Insight on the News*,
6/28/99. Reprinted by permission.

La Regle Du Jeu
"How I Became a Neoconservative,"
9/15/05. Reprinted by permission of *La
Regle Du Jeu*.

London Review of Books
Various articles, reprinted by permission of
London Review of Books.

Mother Jones
"Britain's Punks Go Fascist," August 1978.
Reprinted by permission of *Mother Jones*.
"A Wolfe in Chic Clothing," January 1983.
Reprinted by permission of *Mother Jones*.
"Going Home with Kim Dae Jung," May
1985. Reprinted by permission of *Mother
Jones*.
"Bill of Goods?" September/October 2000.
Reprinted by permission of *Mother Jones*.

Nation
Various articles, reprinted by permission of
The Nation.

National Journal
Neil Munro, "Leaving the Left," 4/05/03.
Reprinted by permission of *National
Journal*.

National Post
Reprinted by permission of the *National
Post*.

New Left Review
Reprinted by permission of *New Left
Review*.

New Statesman
Various articles, reprinted by permission of
New Statesman.

New York Observer
Reprinted by permission of *New York Observer.*

New York Review of Books
Reprinted by permission of *New York Review of Books.*

New York Times
Various articles, reprinted by permission of *New York Times.*

New York University Press
Afterword to *Christopher Hitchens and His Critics: Terror, Iraq, and the Left*, edited by Simon Cottee and Thomas Cushman. Copyright © 2008. Reprinted by permission of New York University Press.

New Yorker
Ian Parker, "He Knew He Was Right," 10/16/06. Copyright © 2006. Reprinted by permission of *The New Yorker.*

New Zealand Herald
Christopher Garland, "Incendiary Author Spares No Targets," 5/24/08. Copyright © 2008. Reprinted by permission of *New Zealand Herald.*

Newsday
Various articles, reprinted by permission of *Newsday.*

Newsweek
Various articles, reprinted by permission of *Newsweek.*

Observer
Various articles, reprinted by permission of *The Observer.*

Pittsburgh Post-Gazette
Bill Steigerwald and Bob Hoover, "Objectivity and Other Lies," 4/27/97. Copyright © 1997. Reprinted by permission of *Pittsburgh Post-Gazette.*

Prospect Magazine
"Christopher Hitchens," May 2008. Copyright © 2008. Reprinted by permission of *Prospect Magazine.* www.prospect-magazine.co.uk.

Quartet Books
Cyprus. Copyright © 1984. Reprinted by permission of Quartet Books.

Random House
The Monarchy: A Critique of Britain's Favourite Fetish by Christopher Hitchens, published by Chatto & Windus. Reprinted by permission of The Random House Group Ltd.

Reason
"Free Radical," November 2001. Reprinted by permission of *Reason* magazine.
"Forcing Freedom," August 2003. Reprinted by permission of *Reason* magazine.

Salmagundi
"Pre-Millennial Syndrome," Summer 1996. Reprinted by permission of *Salmagundi.*
"Secular Values and Republican Virtues," Spring/Summer 1998. Reprinted by permission of *Salmagundi.*

Salon
"A Good Man, Very Fair, Very Witty, Very Loyal," Salon, 7/17/99. Copyright © 1999. Reprinted by permission of Salon.

Science & Spirit
"Finding Morals Under Empty Heavens," *Science & Spirit*, July/August 2007. Reprinted by permission.

Slate
Various articles, reprinted by permission of Slate.

Temple Law Quarterly
Reprinted by permission of *Temple Law Quarterly.*